DEVELOPING CONTEMPORARY MARXISM

DEVELOPING CONTEMPORARY MARXISM

Edited by Zygmunt G. Barański
and John R. Short

© Zygmunt G. Barański and John R. Short 1985
Softcover reprint of the hardcover 1st edition 1985

All rights reserved. No part of this publication
may be reproduced or transmitted, in any form
or by any means, without permission

First published 1985 by
THE MACMILLAN PRESS LTD
London and Basingstoke
Companies and representatives
throughout the world

Typeset by
Wessex Typesetters Ltd
Frome, Somerset

British Library Cataloguing in Publication Data
Developing contemporary Marxism.
1. Communism
I. Barański, Zygmunt G. II. Short, John R.
335.4'01 HX73
ISBN 978-0-333-38260-8 ISBN 978-1-349-17761-5 (eBook)
DOI 10.1007/978-1-349-17761-5

Contents

Acknowledgements vii
Notes on the Contributors viii

Introduction: Developing Contemporary Marxism 1
    Zygmunt G. Barański and John R. Short

PART I ECONOMIC THEORY

1 Crisis Theory 11
   Ron Smith

2 Value Theory 30
   Simon Mohun

3 The Agrarian Question 58
   Richard Pearce

PART II THEORIES OF SOCIETY

4 Marxism and the British Historiographical Tradition 89
   Paul Corner

5 Social Theory 112
   John Urry

6 Political Theory 141
   Patrick Dunleavy

7 Human Geography and Marxism 165
   John R. Short

PART III CULTURAL THEORY

8 Linguistics 199
   Giulio Lepschy

9	Literary Theory *Zygmunt G. Barański*	229
10	Media and Cultural Studies *Bob Lumley and Michael O'Shaughnessey*	268

Index 293

Acknowledgements

We should like to thank Anne-Lucie Norton of Macmillan for her help, advice and patience, all our contributors for making this project possible, and Maggie Barański and Chris Holland for their help with some of the typing. We also owe a different kind of debt to Reading University Staff Academic Football Club which permitted us to meet and which, regardless of its other merits, is an excellent forum for enlightened interdisciplinary discussion. We are grateful to Richard Pearce for his helpful comments and suggestions concerning the contributions to Part 1.

Notes on the Contributors

Zygmunt G. Barański is Lecturer in the Department of Italian Studies at the University of Reading.

Paul Corner is Reader in the Department of Italian Studies and Director of the Centre for the Advanced Study of Italian Society at the University of Reading.

Patrick Dunleavy is Lecturer in Government at the London School of Economics.

Giulio Lepschy is Professor in the Department of Italian Studies at the University of Reading.

Bob Lumley teaches media studies.

Simon Mohun is Lecturer in Economics at Queen Mary College, London.

Michael O'Shaughnessey teaches film and media studies.

Richard Pearce was Lecturer in the Department of Agricultural Economics and Management at the University of Reading.

John R. Short is Lecturer in the Department of Geography at the University of Reading.

Ron Smith is Reader in Applied Economics at Birkbeck College.

John Urry is Senior Lecturer in Sociology at the University of Lancaster.

Introduction: Developing Contemporary Marxism

ZYGMUNT G. BARAŃSKI AND JOHN R. SHORT

In the West today, Marxism has become a major intellectual language. But it is a language made up of many dialects, whose common root is not always easily discernible. This divergence and diversity has been occasioned both by specific historical conditions and by different utilisations of Marxism. Traditionally, and possibly also popularly, it has been seen primarily as an adjunct, guide and stimulant to political action. However, at least since the contributions of the Frankfurt School in the 1920s, it has been used with efficacy as an academic approach, an independent method whose direct connection with immediate political activity has been tangential or unclear. In post-war Western Europe, as Perry Anderson has shown (1976; and see also 1983), Marxism has been heard much more loudly in academia than in political debating chambers, more in the lecture room than on the factory floor, and the most interesting developments of Marxist thought have occurred almost exclusively in this intellectual forum. The historical and social reasons for the use of Marxist categories as epistemological tools rather than as political weapons, a use which negates the well-known Marxist insistence on the necessary relationship between theory and practice, are complex and beyond the scope of our brief introduction – Anderson traces some of these causes with great clarity. However, it is obvious that such a division does exist. This book is a recognition of this fact, and its main aim is to offer a guide to some of the principal developments, especially contemporary ones, of Marxism as an academic methodology and of the ways in which it has influenced and, in its own turn, has been influenced by the various disciplines with which it has come into contact.

A striking feature of this meeting has been the assimilation of Marxism in a fractured and fragmentary manner so that it could fit into the confines of already established academic disciplines. This has ensured that Marxism's ambition to be able to offer a comprehensive insight into the functioning of life under capitalism has been left behind or conveniently ignored. This may not be a bad thing, since there are obvious dangers to any totalising position; however it has resulted in a diffusion of Marxist writing much of which ignores the suggestions made by fellow Marxists in contiguous areas of enquiry. This book should like to restate and remind about the common bonds which unite such work. Each chapter is to be read as a summary of Marxism's presence in a particular field of knowledge, and also as part of a wider whole – an assessment of the development and efficacy of Marxism as a distinct intellectual method. By providing a discussion of a variety of applications of Marxism and by pointing out some of the possible interconnections between these (the index and the cross-references between chapters are meant to be of use here), this book may help to question and overcome intellectual parochialisms which not only mark discipline divisions, but are also apparent in and bolstered by the writings of Marxists. The book would like to encourage readers to go beyond their immediate specialist interests and to examine for themselves the fortunes of Marxism. We do not intend to offer in this introduction, as is often the case in volumes of this kind, a summary of the book's content together with our personal opinions and prognostications on problems raised. The former would seem to be tautologous; the latter would suggest an 'authority' for our statements which we would be loathe to claim, and which would relegate the expert comments of our contributors to a subsidiary position, when we believe that precisely the opposite hierarchy ought to be maintained and made evident. Instead, aware of some of the possible questions and objections which a book such as ours might engender, with its inevitable selectivity and purporting to deal with as vague and problematic a notion as 'contemporary Marxism', we have decided to concentrate, albeit briefly, upon clarifying our guiding principles and to explain the rationale behind this book and its structure. While encouraging critiques of our positions and

Introduction

choices, we hope that by not trying to conceal the reasons for our decisions we can forestall that kind of partisan criticism, which might end up by distorting the intentions and modest aims of this book, and which often reveals little more than the critic's own ideological presuppositions.

The title of our book contains an intentional semantic ambiguity, which we believe can offer a first clue to the overall directions of this collection. Firstly, it suggests that 'contemporary Marxism' belongs to and has its origins in a tradition of which it is the most recent manifestation; and secondly, it points to the fact that this 'contemporary Marxism' is an active rather than a static force. This historical emphasis and the one on the present neatly combine to produce that synthesis of focus which we see as the basis of this book. Similarly, a flexible attitude to what can be included under the term 'contemporary' implicitly supports this dual perspective. Authors from the past are still read and interpreted today, and their influences persist – they continue to be our 'contemporaries' as much as the author of the most recent book or learned paper. As regards the last term of our title, it is obviously the most important, and the one most in need of some definition. It is almost a commonplace of Marxist literature to challenge the 'Marxist' credentials of other positions which announce themselves with this same label. This in-fighting has been the stimulus to much important work, but it has rarely managed to define with precision the specific values of the term 'Marxist'. This is almost certainly impossible, as new concerns reach the attention of Marxists or new critiques of old positions evolve. We do not intend to try to disentangle this knot here, although all our contributions manage to offer some advice and ideas on this problem. In this book, we accept as 'Marxist' those positions which make an explicit recourse, regardless of their own subsequent directions, to the work of Marx and Engels or to some other major thinker whose writings are deeply marked by their presence. We also accept under this umbrella those authors who declare themselves to be Marxists. Such catholicism ensures that the breadth of this tradition is respected. At the same time the extent to which different 'Marxist' positions manage to maintain a continuity between themselves and their sources is underlined at various points in the book.

Perhaps the clearest signpost to the directions of this book is to give a brief summary of the notes we gave to our contributors, although these were then adapted to the peculiarities of specific topics, thus introducing a healthy variety of tone and approach between the different chapters. Each author was asked to provide a *résumé* of Marx and Engel's statements, of subsequent work and of contemporary debates in a particular field. The aim was not to present Marxism as an all-embracing truth able to offer solutions to every problem of existence under capitalism. Instead, we hoped to arrive at an evaluation of the importance of the Marxist contribution to particular areas of enquiry where it is evident that it has attempted to make a direct intervention. Furthermore, we wished to establish the ways in which these disciplines and the other epistemological systems employed within them have in their turn modified and affected Marxism. In order to achieve this broad-based assessment in each chapter, we sought scholars who were prepared to examine equitably and critically basic Marxist positions. The majority of the authors are not Marxists, and some rarely use Marxist notions in their research. However, all would admit, naturally in differing ways, to the important intellectual contributions which Marxism has made to Western thought since the middle of the 19th century.

We have organised the chapters around three major themes: the economic, the social and the cultural. These correspond to major concerns in both traditional and contemporary Marxism but some vindication of the specific choices within these broad categories is necessary.

The major legacy of Marxism is within economics, and no study of contemporary Marxism can afford to ignore this. We have decided, therefore, to look in some detail at what have emerged as the central concerns of Marxist economic theory, rather than merely giving an overview of the whole field (although see the valuable and useful survey by Mandel, 1983). The three chapters in Part I address themselves to theory of crisis, value theory and the agricultural question. Chapters 1 and 2 need little justification, comprising the very essence of Marx's contribution and those of subsequent Marxist scholars to the functioning of the economic within society. As is well known, these theories focus almost exclusively on advanced industrial capitalism. However, Marxism has made a more direct and practical contribution in predominantly peasant societies, for example, Tsarist Russia, China, Cuba, Vietnam and the Third World in general. We have, therefore, thought fit to include a survey which concentrates on the development of the 'agrarian question' within the Marxist tradition (Chapter 3): a topic cursorily and idiosyncratically treated by Marx, but which has increasingly interested contemporary Marxists, in particular those studying the Third World.

For many students of Marx and his heritage, Marxism is not so much a specific economic doctrine, but a more general theory of society and the movement of history. Under the heading of 'Theories of Society', we have placed four chapters in Part II which investigate these positions. Chapter 4 considers the Marxist contribution to historiography, with particular reference to contemporary debates in the United Kingdom, where the most noteworthy advances have been made, and discusses Marxism's claim to being a science of history. It is followed by Chapter 5 on social theory which examines Marxist ideas on the structure and functioning of societies. Chapters 6 and 7 concentrate on more specific themes. Chapter 6 attempts to identify and assess the political theory implicit and explicit in Marxist social thought, while Chapter 7 seeks to discuss the Marxist contribution to debates on the environmental context of social relations. This is a topic which has increasingly become a central concern of the European and North American left as a whole.

Interesting connections unite this last trend with that range of questions which can be subsumed under the category of the 'cultural' (for a fundamental survey of the limits of this term, see Williams, 1976), in particular, the humanist bias of both these perspectives and their common interest in the ways in which human beings perceive and modify their relationships to each other and to their environment. Discussions of these matters have increasingly grown more sophisticated and wide-ranging since Marx and Engels' scattered comments. In fact, certain Marxist thinkers, moving from an acknowledgement that all cultural phenomena function like languages, have argued that our appropriation of the world is achieved predominantly in linguistic terms. Therefore, we thought it might be useful to include Chapter 8 which offers some explanation of this position and which examines the linguistic views of Marxists. This emphasis on language is recent, although an interest in its workings is not. In the past, Marxists tended to confront questions of 'culture' in terms of established aesthetic categories, in which the study of literature held the place of honour. Such discussions are synthesised in Chapter 9 on literary theory. Chapter 10 goes beyond an examination of these essentially élitist and reductionist positions. It assesses the impact of Marxism on contemporary debates around much more flexible conceptions of culture, an area of study in which its perspectives dominate and structure the field.

It is obvious that certain notable topics have been omitted from this book. Perhaps the most glaring is a discussion of Marxism's claim to being a distinctive theory of knowledge, a philosophical system. We feel, however, that in their different ways each chapter contributes towards such an assessment. Similarly, all the chapters, and especially those in Parts II and III, touch on another theme which has not been addressed directly, namely, the study of interpersonal relations. These have, however, tended to occupy a subsidiary position within Marxism, which has preferred to concentrate on broader categories of economic-based class relations. And this brings us to the most delicate decision we made: the omission of specific chapters on questions of gender and race. These are problems of enormous significance and relevance, and they occupy much intellectual space in the present-day, but their connections with Marxism are controversial. Both, and especially feminism, represent distinct traditions which have developed independently of Marxism. In fact, until recently they have frequently been attacked or marginalised by Marxists. When efforts at *rapprochement* have been made, their differences have merely been brought into sharper relief. Marxism's analysis of oppression in terms of class and production jars with theories of exploitation centring on gender and race. It is unhelpful to amalgamate the left's different voices. For debate and action to develop healthily, a plurality of suggestions is the best prerequisite. Thus, it seems unnecessary at present to invent new categories such as, for example, 'feminist–Marxism', especially as it would be far from clear what could be contained within it (see Michèle Barrett's important work in this direction (1980), particularly her suggestions where co-operation might be possible). This is not to exclude the possibilities of more successful integrations in the future. Already, within Marxism, long-established notions of class are being undermined by contact with studies on gender and race, whose categories, as several of our chapters show, are being gingerly recognised by Marxists. These alliances, if they can be called this, are very much in their initial stages. Clearcut positions in these new areas have not been delineated by Marxism, as it has done, for example, in relation to language and cultural studies, which, until recently, tended also, albeit less problematically, to occupy the peripheries of Marxist thought. We, therefore, do not think that independent studies of theories of gender and race from a Marxist standpoint could comfortably be justified or accommodated in a book which attempts both to examine the progress Marxism has made since the fundamental contributions of its founders and to highlight its most characteristic contemporary features. That Marxism finds it very difficult to accommodate into its structures questions of race and gender is not through any fault of these, rather it is a telling clue to its own epistemological limits and restrictions and to the ingenuousness of any theory which would present itself as comprehensive.

We hope that even with these omissions, and given the constraints of space, our book can represent a broad survey of contemporary Marxism, which both delineates its origins and its present-day relevance and applications, and which does not try to conceal its deficiencies or *lacunae*.

REFERENCES

Anderson, P. (1976), *Considerations on Western Marxism* (London: New Left Books).
—— (1983), *In the Tracks of Historical Materialism* (London: Verso).
Barrett, M. (1980), *Women's Oppression Today: Problems in Marxist Feminist Analysis* (London: Verso).
Mandel, E. (1983), 'Economics', in D. McLellan (ed.), *Marx: the First Hundred Years* (London: Fontana) pp. 189–238.
Williams, R. (1976), *Keywords* (Glasgow: Fontana/Croom Helm).

Part I
Economic Theory

1 Crisis Theory*

RON SMITH

1.1 INTRODUCTION

The history of capitalism is marked by repeated industrial revolutions; by continuous transformation of technology and institutions; by alternating boom and slump; by ceaseless innovation and expansion; and by the uneven growth and decay of firms, regions, countries. Orthodox neoclassical economics explains this eventful history within an equilibrium framework, in terms of a system converging to a steady state where there are no forces or pressures for change. Such a description does no justice to the dynamic and turbulent process of capitalist development. In contrast, Marxist theory emphasises the conflicts, hidden tensions and inner contradictions within seemingly well-established institutions and circumstances which lead to the evolution of the latter into something quite different. This evolution is rarely through smooth steady advance, but rather through abrupt, conflict-laden transformations: through crises.

The term crisis has medical origins, originally denoting the turning point in a disease, after which the patient either dies or recovers. It denotes an acute phenomenon, and, strictly speaking, should not be applied to chronic conditions, like the structural failure of the British economy which has persisted for a century. Marx himself does not provide a systematic treatment of crises. In an early plan, they were to be dealt with in volume 6 of his projected work on economics together with world trade. Nonetheless Volumes 2 and 3 of *Capital* and *Theories of Surplus Value* discuss them extensively. There is also a succinct statement of the process

---

* I am grateful to Bob Rowthorn and Ben Fine for helpful discussions, and to the SSRC for financial support. An earlier version of this paper benefited from the comments of the Department of Economics Seminar at Essex Unversity.

11

in the *Communist Manifesto*. Here Marx and Engels compare the bourgeois society which has conjured up such gigantic means of production to a sorcerer no longer able to control the dark powers summoned up by his spells. The productive forces, labour and capital, revolt against the conditions of production. Bourgeois property relations and the conditions of bourgeois society become too narrow to contain the wealth it has created. The methods the bourgeoisie use to resolve these crises – the enforced destruction of a mass of productive forces, the conquest of new markets, and the more thorough exploitation of the workers – pave the way for more extensive and destructive crises and diminish the means whereby crises are prevented. Crises are thus a violent but temporary resolution of the internal contradictions of capitalist accumulation.

In structure all the various Marxist crisis theories follow the outline given in the *Communist Manifesto*. It contains three elements. First, accumulation, the process by which capital expands, contains contradictions. Because of the nature of capitalism, the growth in the forces of production, labour, machines, technology, creates barriers or obstacles to the continuation of that expansion process. Second, at some point these barriers will bring accumulation to a halt, break the circuits of capital, and throw the system into crisis. Third, the crisis temporarily removes these barriers through the restructuring of capital associated with it. Accumulation thus can recommence, heralding future crises. It should be noted that capitalist growth and crisis are not different opposing features of the system, they are part of the same phenomenon. Growth causes crisis, and crises are a necessary condition for growth. They are an integral part of the accumulation process, not merely an accidental aberration.

Capitalism is a rational system in the sense that its operation contributes to its purpose – the expansion of production for private profit. It is irrational in that the purpose, production for profit, does not contribute to the general goal of production for social need. Crises provide an example of the tension between goals; they reconstitute the conditions for profitable accumulation, but only at vast social cost, through redundancy, disruption and waste.

At this level of generality there would be little dispute among Marxist economists. But with respect to the more specific questions raised by this account there are considerable divisions. The discussion below will be organised around three questions. First, what is the form of the crisis? This involves examining their historical manifestation. Second, what are the mechanisms involved? This involves analysing how accumulation creates obstacles to itself, specifying the nature of these obstacles, showing how they generate crisis, and considering how crisis temporarily removes them. Third, what is it in the nature of capitalism that makes crisis inevitable? In many cases the discussion will be rather brief, but more historical and theoretical background to these issues can be found in Wright (1978); Fine and Harris (1979); Rowthorn (1980); Aaronovitch and Smith (1981); and Harvey (1982).

1.2 FORMS OF CRISIS

1.2.1 The Circuit of Capital

Crises appear as sharp breaks in the circuit of capital, when firms go bankrupt, cannot sell all their goods, or cease employing workers. Therefore, it is the nature of the circuit of capital that determines the form of crisis, so to begin let us consider this circuit. A capitalist starts with an amount of money M. This may have been acquired from previous production or it may have been borrowed from the financial system. This money is exchanged for productive capital, made up of labour power (variable capital) with value v, and means of production (constant capital) of value c. These are then used by the capitalist to produce commodities for sale. The value of these include the surplus generated by labour in production s, and thus they have total value $c + v + s$. To turn this surplus into profit, the commodities have to be sold, realising an amount of money M', greater than the initial stake. Chapter 2 discusses this process in more detail.

The money obtained may be used to buy more productive capital or it may be lent to financial institutions who may pass it on to other capitalists. If the circuit proceeds it can be represented by a continuous chain:

$$M-(c+v) \rightarrow (c+v+s)-M'-(c+v)' \rightarrow (c+v+s)' \rightarrow M''$$

(The arrow denotes production in which surplus is generated.)

This chain, which links the spheres of exchange, production and distribution, is often abbreviated as $M-C-M'$, with C representing commodities. Crisis breaks this chain, interrupts the circuits of capital. The chain can be thought of as being made up of particular forms of capital, corresponding to the form in which they start and finish the circuit, i.e. as money, commodity or productive capital. In any particular crisis there will be breaks at a variety of stages, but one can roughly classify them in terms of the dominant break. The break may be either in the circuit of money capital giving a financial crisis, or in that of productive capital, producing a 'Kondratieff' long wave slump, pervading the whole structure of production, or in that of commodity capital leading to a regular trade-cycle downturn.

This distinction between forms of crisis, in terms of the dominant break in the circuit of capital, can only be very broad because all the links in the chain are connected. Nonetheless it is useful in allowing us to distinguish between different forms of crisis. A certain amount of confusion is created in some Marxist literature, because it is not always made clear which form of crisis is being referred to, and over what time period the processes discussed are supposed to operate. The three forms examined here, financial collapse, long wave slump, and trade cycle downturn, possess distinct features and involve forces which operate at different speeds. There is a fourth form of crisis, the ultimate collapse of capitalism, to which we shall return in the conclusion. It should also be remembered that these forms are not mutually exclusive. The last decade has seen two trade cycle recessions and two financial crises superimposed on a long wave slump.

The fact that forms of crisis are inevitably mixed in any particular historical episode, indicates another feature of this kind of analysis. The discussions of circuits of capital above and of the mechanisms involved in crisis in section 1.3 below are conducted at a high level of abstraction. They focus on the essential processes abstracting from a range of particular features. The historical descriptions in the rest of this section are much more concrete, illustrating the breaks in the circuits of capital by particular instances. But specific cases (in which the articulation of all the various forms at work is taken into account), have to be analysed at a much lower level of abstraction. For instance, in the case of Britain in the last decade, the effects of the general crisis in capitalism have been conditioned by specific features produced

Crisis Theory 15

by Britain's long decline from its 19th-century hegemonic role. These include such factors as the dominance of international rather than domestic industry and finance, the particular structure of working class organisation, high military expenditure, etc.

1.2.2 Financial Collapse

Early capitalism was characterised by regular national credit crises. From the South Sea Bubble in London and the Mississippi Bubble in Paris in 1719–20 to the Wall Street Crash in 1929, depression tended to be preceded by financial collapse. Towards the end of a speculative boom some incident led to a sharp switch in expectations of profit. Capitalists then tried to switch from holding commodity or productive capital to money capital. Interest rates shot up as everyone tried to get out of illiquid assets and into cash, and credit and confidence dried up. Some banks or firms failed and started a domino effect with bankruptcies and liquidations following on each other. Kindleberger (1978) provides a lively analysis of these manias, panics and crashes with copious historical illustrations.

The fragility of the financial system, its tendency towards destabilising speculation, and its propensity to collapse regularly were for a long time a focus of concern for monetary theorists. But with the disappearance of large scale national financial collapses, since 1890 in the UK, since 1930 in the US, and since World War II generally, interest waned. However, after 1973, the threat of an international financial collapse rearoused concern.

To understand the current potential for international financial collapse, it is worth starting with the disappearance of national financial crises. These were largely prevented through systematic intervention by central banks or other state monetary authorities. This intervention took two forms. First, there was extensive prudential regulation. This imposed on banks and other financial institutions various types of requirements that increased the safety of their investments and ensured that they stayed solvent. Regulations on reserve–asset ratios, margin-trading, and the organisation of financial markets limited speculative overtrading. Second, central banks provided lender of last resort facilities to financial institutions in order to maintain liquidity and confidence in the face of unexpected shocks or demands. This also meant that depositors felt more secure that they would be able to get their money back, thus discouraging precipitate withdrawals which could trigger a collapse. Both aspects of intervention are necessary. Lender of last resort facilities without regulation would be destabilising, since they give banks incentives to take imprudent risks, knowing that should speculative investments fail the central bank will bail them out. Regulation alone is inadequate, because risk is unavoidable, however prudent the practice. Therefore, some safety net is needed to protect banks and firms which are fundamentally sound, in that they have profitable investments, but are temporarily short of cash.

The regulation and guarantees that ensured the stability of national financial systems could not extend to international transactions, because there is no world monetary authority or world central bank. This problem grew during the post-war period as the international financial system mushroomed. Not only did it grow, but it grew most rapidly in forms like the Eurocurrency markets, which were 'offshore' to every regulatory authority. A Bermuda subsidiary of an Italian bank located in London, borrowing dollars from OPEC countries to lend to Argentina is neither regulated by nor the responsibility of any particular central bank. The lack of regulation, such as required reserve-asset ratios, make Eurocurrency lending more profitable, but at the same time more risky. The risks are also increased by the low quality of the assets in which the money is eventually invested. For banks, loans to other people are their assets, and the ability of the borrower to pay interest and repay the debt determines their profits. Much of the lending and borrowing is between banks, but eventually the money reaches a final borrower, who wishes to use it. A large group of final borrowers, particularly in the Third World and Eastern Europe, have faced great difficulty in meeting their debts. This large debt has now become a major source of potential crisis.

The fragility of the system became clear in 1974–75, when concerted action by a group of central banks only just managed to stave off a general panic in the wake of a series of bank failures. The collapse of the Herstadt bank in Germany, of a series of secondary banks heavily invested in property in the UK, of the Franklin National in the US, and of others in Israel, Italy and elsewhere, together with the financial difficulties of several heavily indebted Third World countries, all put great strain on the system. In many ways the position at the beginning of 1983 was worse. The quality of the investments was lower, with greater danger of default on debts by various countries. The balance sheets of major banks particularly in the US was weaker. The difficulty of coordinating between central banks to ensure the supply of liquidity and the protection of depositors was greater. The size of the outstanding debt was by the early 1980s so large that it was not obvious that central bankers, even acting in concert, would have adequate reserves to stop a collapse. Therefore, although hectic efforts are being made to patch the system together, as with the Polish, Mexican and Brazilian debts, the risk of a major financial collapse remains. The danger is that the failure of one large bank tends to cause another to fail, and so a chain reaction can lead to mass bankruptcies and redundancies on top of those which already exist.

1.2.3 Long Waves

Historians tend to break the economic history of capitalism into broad phases of boom and slump, each phase lasting about fifty years. There are disagreements on the exact dating of these, but the following periods are usually seen as periods of economic trouble: (a) from the end of the Napoleonic Wars to 1848; (b) the 'Great Depression' from 1870 to 1896; (c) the inter-war slump from 1920 to 1939; (d) the present troubles from 1970 onwards. In the 1920s Kondratieff, a Russian economist, identified the first two and the beginning of the third, and hypothesised a fifty-year cycle in capitalism. During the 1930s his work was followed up by Western economists, particularly Schumpeter, but with the coming of the long post-war boom, the approach was largely ignored. However, the return of generalised recession revived interest in his work. In booms there is a tendency to believe the process will continue indefinitely, in slumps, that things must turn up again. The best general, though hostile, introduction to long waves is Maddison (1982).

Although there is support for the qualitative historical periodisation of long waves, the evidence for a quantitative cycle is ambiguous. Kondratieff relied mainly on price data, but whereas the latest slump was a period of inflation, previous slumps saw falling prices. Output data do not show any marked fifty-year cycle. Both the 'Great Depression' and the 1930s were periods of normal growth in national output in the UK, despite their turbulence and hardship. Major wars also complicate the quantitative analysis.

Each growth phase of a long wave tends to be linked to a particular type of organisation of production, with associated technology, labour process and location of industry. The initial industrial revolution was led by cotton, coal and iron in comparatively small factories and mines in Britain. The next phase after 1848 was associated with steam and the spread of railways and extended to Europe and the US. After 1890 heavy, science-based industries, like chemicals, steel and electricity, became dominant and Britain was already starting to become an industrial backwater. After 1945 cars and flow production set the tone. Each form of organisation and labour process is initially stimulative setting the growth process in motion through multiplier and linkage effects. But as it develops and reaches maturity this stimulus ceases. Demand for new investment goods drops, and the form of organisation and the location and structure of existing fixed capital become an obstacle to further change. The slump both destroys the old forms and creates space for the new to grow. The processes involved are slow but fundamental; they extend beyond products and processes of production through the concentration and centralisation of capital, the international division of labour, and the forms of state regulation.

It is a long-wave slump that we are currently experiencing. Old industries, steel, cars, shipbuilding, are contracting in the old industrial centres, and are being re-established in the newly industrialised countries, particularly in Asia and Latin America. Old forms of regulation, management and work organisation are being destroyed and new forms developed. New technologies associated with electronics and bio-technology are being established. Since there is no mechanism to promote planned adjustment, the changes come about in a chaotic and costly way in an environment of business failure and mass unemployment. It is a slow process taking fifteen or twenty years, reflecting the anarchy of market forces and the individual decisions of national and multinational firms whose primary concern is restoring profit, not planning social adjustment. Planning, either by firms or governments, is made more difficult by the great uncertainties associated with the changes in technology, location and organisation, and investment decisions whether public or private become more than usually hazardous.

1.2.4 Cyclical Downturns

In 'normal' times, i.e. in the absence of major turbulence or depression, the long-term growth path is more obvious and the planning of investment and production easier. But even then capitalism shows regular swings in accumulation. In the 19th century there was a seven- to ten-year pattern in the level of output, with production falling in the slump. From 1945 to 1973 there was a three-to-five year pattern in the rate of growth of output, with growth declining in the recession. Profitability, employment and investment show matching patterns, although not exactly in phase with output. In the 19th century this oscillating pattern in trade reflected movements in export markets, imbalances between investment producing sectors (Department I) and consumption producing sectors (Department II) and financial forces. Since World War II the pattern of state intervention has played a major role in the cycle.

In Britain, in better times when unemployment was never above a million, this 'stop-go' cycle was seen as a major problem, a failure of government management of the economy. In fact, UK fluctuations were smaller than in most other countries, and the real problem was that these were around a lower rate of growth. In any event, there is little evidence that smooth steady growth is the normal or natural path of capitalist development; whether induced by government or triggered by other interactions, fluctuations are necessary for the working of the system. Booms encourage investment, risk-taking and expansion. Recessions drive the inefficient out of business, enforce cost cutting and reduce the bargaining power of labour. Alternate stop and go is then necessary to obtain the benefits of both. The unstable rhythm is a natural part of the process by which the market system operates. Capitalists must accumulate and grow in order to survive, but the health of the system requires bankruptcy to drive out the inefficient and unemployment to maintain capitalist strength against the workers. The antagonism between these two needs is resolved by fluctuations and regulated by the rate of profit.

1.3 MECHANISMS

1.3.1 Introduction

We have seen how crisis, by breaking the circuits of capital, disrupts the processes of accumulation in the spheres of exchange, production and distribution. Although the form of the crisis can be characterised by the dominant break, its effects operate in all three spheres. In this section, the mechanisms involved in the disruption of the processes of exchange, production and distribution will be examined in a little more detail in order to explain: (a) how accumulation itself creates barriers to further expansion; (b) how these barriers generate crisis; and (c) how crisis temporarily removes these barriers.

In any account of these mechanisms the rate of profit or of surplus value plays a crucial role, it is the main regulator of the accumulation process (see Mohun, ch. 2). Capitalists only invest to make or to protect their profits, if they do not expect profits they will hold on to their money and not invest. If they do not invest they reduce the demand for products, and so the profits of other capitalists. This stops the others investing, so setting off a cumulative downwards process, similar to that caused by a Keynesian 'multiplier–accelerator' interaction. Orthodox neoclassical economics does not allow for such instability. Rather than starting from a capitalist who advances money for commodities, in order to produce other commodities which can be sold for money, it starts from an economic agent with an endowment of commodities who exchanges them for a preferred set of commodities using money. In this framework there can be no cumulative excess supply, since every supply, i.e. sale of commodity, creates a demand. But recognising that production is for profit not need, changes our perception of the dynamics of the system.

Within the Marxist framework, therefore, anything associated with accumulation which causes the rate of profit to fall, can cause capitalists to cease to invest. This reduces their demand for labour power and means of production. It cuts the sales of other capitalists, drives down the rate of profit, and so depresses accumulation even further. This answers our second question. Any factor within the accumulation process which pushes down profits or expected profits will cumulatively disrupt accumulation sending the system into crisis. This shift can be very abrupt; as expectations change, prospects get re-evaluated, and markets suddenly switch. When capitalists decide that conditions have altered for the worse, catastrophic shifts get rapidly transmitted through the system. This leads to a sharp fall to a much lower level of economic activity consistent with the new prospects.

Why then does accumulation eventually cause the rate of profit to fall? Three major mechanisms have been suggested, elements of which are in Marx's work. These mechanisms are: (a) imbalances created in the process of exchange by realisation problems (section 1.3.2); (b) imbalances in the process of distribution caused by changes in relative class strengths (section 1.3.3); (c) imbalances in the process of production resulting from increases in the organic composition of capital (section 1.3.4). Economists, and not just Marxist ones, have a somewhat unfortunate tendency to espouse monocausal explanations. Thus these three mechanisms are often presented as alternative and competing theories of crisis. The three theories are labelled (respectively) 'Underconsumptionist', 'neo-Ricardian' and 'Fundamentalist'. In fact, all three processes operate, each one produced by a specific form of disproportionality that arises in the course of accumulation. After reviewing the three approaches briefly, this section will conclude with a discussion of the general role of disproportionality, which arises because capitalism cannot maintain all the necessary conditions for continuous accumulation.

1.3.2 Realisation

In discussing above the circuit of capital, we assumed that the capitalist could realise the surplus value generated in production as profit. That is, the commodities produced with value $c + v + s$ could be exchanged for a sum of money of equivalent value M'. This requires that there is a market for the output. Many have argued that capitalism is plagued by a problem of markets, and so is beset by overproduction and excess capacity. Their theories are reviewed by Bleaney (1976). The most sophisticated version of the argument is in Baran and Sweezy (1968), but in one form or another it predates Marx, and is often traced back to before Malthus.

In order to maximise profits, capitalists force the wages of workers as low as possible; but if wages are kept down and workers cannot afford to buy the output produced, to whom will the capitalists then sell their goods? This produces a contradiction between exploitation in production, which requires low wages, and realisation in exchange, which requires high wages to provide a market. Various ways out of this problem have been suggested. Malthus used this as an argument for the need for an unproductive rentier class which would acquire luxuries and maintain demand. But what characterises capitalism and gives it such dynamic is that capitalists do not consume most of the surplus, they plough it back buying more labour power and means of production. As long as they go on doing this, there is no realisation problem because they provide a market for themselves. Capitalists then earn what they spend. But if real wages remain constant and output grows, it requires an ever-increasing share of investment to maintain this process.

Others have emphasised external markets: non-capitalist societies sucked into the system by imperialist expansion or wasteful government demand, like military expenditure. Lack of such markets, it was argued, produces massive excess capacity with stagnant demand and mass unemployment, as in the 1930s. Baran and Sweezy (1968) argued that this was only avoided in the post-war period by waste such as high military expenditure which absorbed the surplus generated. But this inevitable tendency to stagnation is not an essential part of Marx's argument, for as long as capitalists keep investing the system can grow. The difficulty is that capitalists invest only in the expectation of profit; and because capitalism is an anarchic system, there is no social mechanism to ensure that just the right amount of investment will always be made. When investment fails, the system sinks into slump and crisis. The restructuring of capital during the slump by removing the excess capacity – a process which may take a long time – raises the rate of profit on new investment, thus permitting further growth.

1.3.3 Distributional Struggle

As accumulation proceeds, capital expands; the reserve army of labour, those unemployed and reserves in agriculture or households, is depleted and workers become scarce. Wages are bid up, the share of profit falls, and investment slows. The system goes into crisis and slump; unemployment increases; and the reserve army of labour is recreated. Labour saving investment also adds to the reserve army. This weakens the working class power, allowing the rates of exploitation and profit to be raised, and encouraging accumulation to begin once more. A good example of this type of argument is Glyn and Sutcliffe (1972).

The process does not depend merely on the rate of unemployment. The strength of working class political and industrial organisation plays a major role. Nor is the conflict merely over the wage rate, but often, more importantly, about conditions of work and control of the labour process.

1.3.4 Rising Organic Composition of Capital

At first sight it might appear that capitalism can escape from its dependence on labour by mechanisation, which both reduces the need for workers and increases the reserve army, thus reducing labour's strength. But mechanisation itself reduces the rate of profit. The value of output produced is given by $c + v + s$, while the rate of profit is the ratio of the surplus generated to the capital advanced or invested, $c + v$. That is

$$r = s/(c + v)$$

The rate of exploitation, e, is the ratio of the amount of surplus generated to the amount of labour used, i.e.

$$e = s/v.$$

The degree of mechanisation is measured by the organic composition of capital, k, the ratio of the other means of production to labour

$$k = c/v.$$

Dividing the top and bottom lines of the formula for the rate of profit by v puts it in terms of the rate of exploitation and the organic composition of capital. The rate of profit is then given by

$$r = e/(k + 1)$$

A higher k is associated with a lower r. This is just a definition, but it expresses an important aspect of capitalist reality. For a given amount of surplus generated, the larger the investment the lower the rate of profit. Marx argued that because of competitive pressures, the need to reduce labour inputs and the need to adopt new technologies, the organic composition would increase through time, and thus the rate of profit would have a tendency to fall.

However, he also pointed to a range of counteracting tendencies. The rate of exploitation could be increased, either by increasing absolute surplus value by lengthening the working day, etc. or by increasing relative surplus value, through higher labour productivity. Technical progress in capital goods production could reduce their cost, so that, although there was a greater mass of constant capital, the labour time required to produce them, and thus their value was less (see Mohun, ch. 2). The rising organic composition of capital and these counteracting tendencies do not work smoothly in harmony. Mechanisation and increasing capital intensity put downward pressure on the rate of profit, eventually stopping accumulation and sending the system into crisis. During the crisis the rate of exploitation is raised, capital is restructured, the cost of means of production reduced, thus easing the pressure on profit and allowing accumulation to recommence. The argument has been presented here in a simple form, Fine and Harris (1979) elaborate it extensively.

1.3.4 Disproportionality

In each of the explanations above, we saw that the process of accumulation leads to certain imbalances, or disproportionalities. These can be between supply and demand, between relative class powers or between capital and labour in production. In each case these imbalances put downward pressure on the rate of profit. This undermines the motive for investment, brings accumulation to a halt, and throws the system into crisis. The crisis then has the effect of restructuring capital and eventually eliminating the imbalances at least for a time. In fact, this process is much more general than this. Capitalism needs a range of conditions to ensure that smooth expansion occurs. These include adequate supplies of cheap raw materials; a compliant labour force; available markets; an appropriate balance between different sectors of production; and a range of state regulatory functions. The ultimate source of crisis is that capitalism contains no social mechanisms adequate to ensure that these necessary conditions for expansion are maintained. The unbounded nature of private accumulation exhausts these conditions, so that some bottleneck inevitably occurs in the course of sustained expansion. This curtails profitability and investment, and generates crisis.

Given that crisis results from uneven development, the creation of imbalances between the need for either labour, or markets, or means of production and what is available, the form of any particular crisis will depend on the nature of the primary constraint. Likewise the frequency of crises and the length of the period of restructuring will vary depending on the constraint. A reduction in the growth of output and a rise in the rate of unemployment, which lasts a year or two, as in the traditional trade cycle recession, may be enough to depress real wages, weaken short term bargaining power of workers, and enforce competitive discipline on less efficient firms. However, it will have a relatively small effect on the underlying structure of social relations and fixed capital. The fixed nature of plant and equipment, and of infrastructure, like transport and utilities, means that firms are locked into a particular pattern. Given their past heavy investments and the facilities that have grown up around them, it is more profitable to pursue the same path, than to write it all off and start up again on a completely new track. For instance, British capitalists have been repeatedly criticised for lack of entrepreneurship and for their refusal to adopt new technologies, products, or production processes. However, a range of detailed studies (e.g. Sandberg, 1981) now indicate that this did not result from some psychological failure or lack of achievement motivation. It resulted from the fact that given their position, maintaining the old ways was more profitable than developing the new. The old plant was available, the old systems were in operation, and social structures, such as adequate supplies of cheap skilled labour and established markets, supported old styles. Of course, for a competitor starting from scratch abroad, the options were quite different. Without the benefits of existing leadership, the new technology was more profitable; and over the long run it would come to dominate the old, leading to the eventual displacement of British firms, and the general decline of the British economy.

Restructuring capital to remove the imbalances may take a very long time, as the British example illustrates. During this period accumulation proceeds elsewhere. Adjustment is slowed by the rigidity and longevity not only of material structures, like fixed plant and equipment, but of social structures (see Urry, ch. 5). Capital is not a thing, not just money and machines, but a social relationship. The money and machines become capital when used to produce profit by people, as competitors, employers, financiers, etc., in specific social relationships. Gordon *et al.* (1983) refer to these patterns of relationships as the 'Social Structure of Accumulation'. They include the systems of labour relations, state regulation, socialisation, and national and international finance which organise the usual patterns of interaction. They also include the structures mediating raw material supply, the quantity and quality of labour supplied, and political conflict. These are essential to allow expansion, cannot be directly produced by capital for profit, and are as fixed and long-lived as any factory. Restructuring capital means restructuring this matrix of social relations.

We thus have a varied mix of necessary conditions for growth which are eroded by expansion and reconstituted by crisis. The severity of the current crisis reflects the number and nature of the conditions that have failed. This is discussed in detail in chapter 13 of Aaronovitch and Smith (1981). The scale of the barriers is such, that it seems unlikely that sustained expansion could proceed before the end of the decade. Even then, it is not inevitable, since the preconditions for this are only necessary not sufficient, and are social and political, as well as economic.

1.4 CONCLUSION

The brief survey in this chapter has suggested that crisis is an inherent part of the dynamic of capitalism. Accumulation erodes the conditions necessary for it to proceed. This produces imbalances or disproportionalities which depress the rate of profit, driving the system into crisis. The form of crisis is determined by the nature of the imbalances and how they disrupt the circuit of capital; the duration of crisis is determined by the length of time necessary to restructure capital. Despite their fraternal disputes about the exact mechanisms involved and the relative weight to be given to different factors, most Marxists have accepted this sort of analysis as an explanation of the erratic pattern of capitalist accumulation. Where they have differed more sharply is what the implications of this analysis are for the future course of capitalism. One group, whom we might call the 'economic determinists', argue that crisis will eventually destroy the system. The final form of crisis is then the ultimate collapse of capitalism under the weight of its economic contradictions. The opposite group, the 'revisionists', argue that by state regulation to prevent the development of the imbalances and disproportionalities, crisis can be avoided and smooth expansion maintained.

Neither the 'determinist' nor 'revisionist' extrapolation from the theory seems justified either on historical or theoretical grounds. The historical evidence suggests not only that capitalism is very resilient, able to adjust to overcome economic limitations, but also that it remains crisis prone, unable to avoid sharp breaks in the accumulation process with all the disruption these entail. But this is also what the theoretical analysis would lead us to expect. What both drives accumulation forward and makes crises inevitable is the anarchic and antagonistic nature of capitalism as a mode of production. It is anarchic in being based on the individual private decisions of capitalists producing for profit. Apart from market forces, which despite their power have obvious limitations, capitalists have no social mechanism for ensuring either the consistency of their decisions or the maintenance of conditions they cannot produce themselves. State intervention partially fills this need for social regulation to offset the anarchy of the market. But despite the effectiveness of state intervention in many spheres, managing demand and finance, regulating labour and trade, its power remains constrained by the antagonistic nature of capitalism. The system is based on antagonism both between capitalists in competition for markets and resources, and between classes in conflict over the organisation of production and distribution. The consequence of these antagonisms is the contradiction between private appropriation and social production which underlies the inability of the State to maintain indefinitely harmonious conditions of expansion. Although the inability of capital or State to ensure the continuous maintenance of the social and economic structure for accumulation makes economic crisis inevitable, it does not necessarily make it terminal. The antagonism between labour and capital is political and ideological, as well as economic. The economic determinists are right insofar as capitalism can be destroyed, because its economic contradictions produce a political opposition; a working class movement that can displace it. But the economic contradictions are a necessary but not sufficient condition. Economic crisis will not dislodge the system unless there is the political mobilisation to push it out.

GUIDE TO FURTHER READING

A discussion of the role of crisis in Marx's writing can be found in the 'Introduction' by Ernest Mandel to the 1981 Penguin edition of volume 3 of *Capital*. He also briefly discusses the history of its various 'mono-causal' versions. Fine and Harris (1979) examine the different theoretical approaches to crisis in some detail, though from a somewhat partisan position. Wright (1978) and Harvey (1982) both consider crisis theories in a wider context. Aaronovitch and Smith (1981) review the historical and empirical pattern of recent crises, both internationally and within Britain. Rowthorn (1980) explains the inflationary form that crisis has taken in the last decade. Although neither use a Marxist perspective, Kindleberger (1978) and Maddison (1982) give good historical and statistical accounts of financial crises and long waves respectively.

REFERENCES

Aaronovitch, S. and Smith, R. P. (1981), *The Political Economy of British Capitalism* (London: McGraw-Hill).
Baran, P. and Sweezy, P. (1968), *Monopoly Capital* (Harmondsworth: Penguin).
Bleaney, M. (1976), *Underconsumption Theories* (London: Lawrence & Wishart).
Fine, B. and Harris, L. (1979), *Rereading Capital* (London: Macmillan).

Glyn, A. and Sutcliffe, R. (1972), *British Capitalism, Workers and the Profit Squeeze* (Harmondsworth: Penguin).
Gordon, D. M., Weisskopf, T. E. and Bowles, S. (1983), 'Long Swings and the Nonreproductive Cycle', *American Economic Review*, 73, ii, pp. 152-7.
Harvey, D. (1982), *The Limits to Capital* (Oxford: Blackwell).
Kindleberger, C. P. (1978), *Manias, Panics and Crashes* (London: Macmillan).
Maddison, A. (1982), *Phases of Capitalist Development* (Oxford University Press).
Rowthorn, B. (1980), *Capitalism, Conflict and Inflation* (London: Lawrence & Wishart).
Sandberg, L. G. (1981), 'The Entrepreneur and Technological Change', in R. Floud and D. McCloskey (eds), *The Economic History of Britain Since 1700*, 2 vols, (Cambridge University Press), vol. 2, pp. 99-120.
Wright, E. O. (1978), *Class, Crisis and the State* (London: New Left Books).

2 Value Theory*

SIMON MOHUN

2.1 INTRODUCTION: POLITICAL ECONOMY AND FORM ANALYSIS

In 1859, Marx, sketching his intellectual autobiography, remarked that in his critique of Hegelian philosophy fifteen years or so earlier, he had concluded that

> legal relations as well as forms of state are to be grasped neither from themselves nor from the so-called general development of the human mind, but rather have their roots in the material conditions of life, the sum total of which Hegel... combines under the name of 'civil society', that however the anatomy of civil society is to be sought in political economy. (Marx and Engels, 1950, vol. 1, p. 328)

Consequently, Marx devoted most of his time as an exile in London to the study of political economy. At the heart of his approach was a determination of the evolution of civil society via class antagonisms; classes being defined in terms of differential access to the possession and control of the surplus product, which under capitalism followed from differential access to the possession and control of the means of production. He argued that the immediate producers, historically dispossessed of the means of production, are compelled to put their labour-time at the disposal of those who do possess the means of production. The latter can compel the immediate producers to work for longer than is

---

* I would like to thank Susan Himmelweit, Sonja Ruehl and the editors of this book for helpful comments on an earlier draft.

necessary to reproduce their subsistence; consequently, the labour which is surplus to the consumption requirements of the immediate producers is appropriated by those who possess the means of production. For Marx, this basis of coercive property relations determines the development of capitalist society. More generally, the form in which the surplus product is appropriated periodises social development into different modes of production. Thus he commented: 'What distinguishes the various economic formations of society – the distinction between, for example a society based on slave-labour and a society based on wage-labour – is the form in which this surplus labour is in each case extorted from the immediate producer, the worker' (Marx, 1976, p. 325).

It follows from this approach that Marxian political economy must focus on 'form-analysis'; if the forms which labour and surplus labour take define historically specific modes of production, then their changing forms must define the subject matter of political economy. However, the way in which surplus labour was extracted in, for example, slave and feudal modes of production was transparently clear. Despite the many differences between the two, both rested on physical coercion and the rule of force, and surplus labour took the form of working directly for the slave-owner or feudal lord without any remuneration at all. Capitalism is clearly rather different; coercion is (normally) economic, hidden behind the apparent freedom of exchange, laws of the market replace the rule of force, and surplus labour appears as a sum of money in the form of profit. It is not obvious how and why surplus labour should take this form, nor is its evolution through time at all clear. Since these are not issues in pre-capitalist societies, Marx considered political economy to be specifically the study of *capitalist* societies.

Accordingly, Marx did not seek to formulate a general theory of economics valid for all societies at all times. As early as 1847 he was quite explicit in observing that 'Economic categories are only the theoretical expressions, the abstractions of the social relations of production' (*The Poverty of Philosophy*, in Marx and Engels, 1976, p. 165). And twenty years later he repeated that the categories of the economics, or political economy of his day 'are forms of thought which are socially valid, and therefore objective, for the relations of production belonging to this historically determined mode of social production' (Marx, 1976, p. 169).

In order to show the historical transience of capitalism, Marx had to identify and determine the evolution of the laws of motion of capitalist society. Consequently, his economic work necessarily involved a critique of the economics of his day, for, to the extent that such an economics was bound up with the dominant relations of production, it was impossible for it to identify those trends leading to the overthrow of capitalist relations of production, or, more weakly, to recognise itself as historically specific.

Marx's critique of political economy was constructed around his explanation for the dominance of money relations in capitalist society. Money was the form and the only form in which social validation was bestowed upon the products of labour, and as such was the general form of appearance of 'value'. Hence to analyse the specificity of capitalism, he had to show why products of labour were expressed as values, in terms of money, and why the measurement of labour in terms of time was expressed in terms of the magnitude of the value of the product, as a price. Conversely, when the economics of his predecessors (classical political economy) talked of value and its magnitude, Marx claimed that it had failed to ask precisely these questions, and so treated an historically specific and transient mode of production as the natural and eternal form of social production. Marx's value analysis was thus crucial to his joint project of identifying the dynamic of the capitalist mode of production, and of exposing the inadequacies of classical political economy.

Such classical political economy had culminated in the work of David Ricardo; and since Ricardo had founded his analysis on a labour theory of value, there is considerable controversy concerning the relationship of Marx's work to Ricardo's. One way or another, this controversy lies at the heart of all the major issues of current (and not so current) debate in Marxist economics, and consequently this chapter is structured around the relationship of Marx's work to Ricardo's. The first section outlines the logical difficulties of Ricardian value theory, together with Marx's methodological criticisms of it, and this is followed by a second section giving an account of Marx's value theory. The themes of these two sections are then brought together in order to provide a taxonomic overview of modern debates in value theory. Finally, a short conclusion indicates some implications of current positions for future work.

The debates which this chapter considers all fall within a

broadly Marxist terrain. Critical positions from an anti-Marxist perspective are not here considered. Most of these find their inspiration in the work of Böhm-Bawerk (1949, originally published in 1896). His attack on Marxian value theory, which he saw as little different from Ricardian theory, was based on his positivist reading of Marx's method, a reading which found Marx's arguments circular and his results devoid of meaning. Böhm-Bawerk's critical focus on Marx's explanation of prices (the transformation problem) and his consequential rejection of Marxian value theory *tout court* have structured most of the 20th-century debates for supporters and opponents of Marx alike, to such an extent that it is only comparatively recently that the conventional wisdom concerning Marx's relation to Ricardo has been questioned, and attempts made to characterise Marx's method in terms different from the positivism of neoclassical economics.

However, one current of thought (Cutler *et al.*, 1977–78) has developed and refined Böhm-Bawerk's critique of Marxism, and in particular his attack on value theory, from an epistemological perspective whose genealogy is derived from the Althusserian tradition (see Urry, ch. 5). This epistemology claims to attack all epistemologies which privilege certain categories as 'essential', in terms of which all other categories claim their meaning and significance. Examples of such privileging might be assertions concerning the primacy of the economy, or an ontology of labour, or that some concept of visible labour 'represents' something else, underlying and invisible, called 'value', in terms of which it is explained. Attacks on such (real and imagined) essentialism have made little headway in Marxist economics, and modern debates in the subject make little reference to them, perhaps because there is so much resonance between such attacks and those of neoclassical economics.

2.2 RICARDIAN VALUE THEORY AND MARX'S CRITIQUE

The tradition of classical political economy culminated in Ricardo's attempt to determine rigorously the laws which regulated the distribution of the total social product between rent, wages and profits, accruing to landlords, workers and capitalists respectively. Such distributional categories clearly comprise the total inclusive costs of production, for the revenue derived from the sale of commodities must be sufficient to pay wages to the workers employed in their production, rent to the owner of the land on which production takes place, leaving profit for the capitalist who owns the means of production and organises the process of production. Adam Smith had previously determined 'exchangeable value' or price by simply adding together the total costs of production (leaving him with the result that, since costs are themselves the prices of inputs, prices are determined by prices). But Ricardo generalised a view of Smith's about earlier societies and considered that the 'exchangeable value' of a commodity was determined by the total quantity of labour expended in its production, both directly, and indirectly via its embodiment in the means of production used to produce the commodity in question.

Whereas Smith had determined price in terms of the remuneration of labour, Ricardo determined price in terms of the quantity of labour employed. This entailed the objective existence of 'value in exchange' *prior* to its distribution as wages, rent and profit. With rent determined by the relative fertility of land, a change in the wage rate could only lead to a change in the opposite direction in the rate of profit (as long as the total quantity of labour employed remained constant). Whereas for Smith a change in wages necessarily involved a corresponding change in the prices of the products of labour, for Ricardo a change in wages could only affect the division of the product between classes.

The importance of this lay in the contention that economic growth, or accumulation, was determined by the quantity of profits available for investment by the capitalist class. In order to conceive of such a sum of money, it must first be determined how heterogeneous commodities can be reduced to a homogeneous entity through their valuation. Commodities had to be valued, both relatively to each other and absolutely, in order that *what* is to be distributed could be determined prior to the analysis of the laws governing its distribution. Hence Ricardo's theory of value – his labour theory of value – logically had to precede his theory of distribution.

However, the way in which profits accrue to capitalists is through their earning a rate of profit on the capital they have advanced. Such a rate of profit is competitively determined; in pursuit of maximum profits, capital tends to move from sectors of lower profitability to sectors of higher profitability, and this will tend to raise the rate of profit in the former and lower it in the latter. Hence in equilibrium all capitals will earn the same rate of profit. Ricardo quickly discovered that this process of distribution affected his theory of valuation in such a manner as to cast some doubt as to whether he was correct in separating his theories of value and distribution.

The effects of distribution upon valuation emerged in Ricardo's analysis of the effect of a rise in wages. If all capital advanced in the form of means of production is used up in exactly one production period (all capital is circulating capital of identical durability), then the price level cannot be affected. But if the durabilities of capitals differ, typically some means of production lasting for longer than one production period (some capital is fixed capital), then prices will be affected. The effects will depend upon the durability of the means of production and their weight in the production process relative to labour. For the extent to which labour is embodied in durable means of production will affect the length of time that must elapse before the capitalist receives a return on his outlay. Thus, if two capitalists employ identical quantities of labour, but differently distributed in time (as between direct labour and labour embodied in durable means of production), they will, according to Ricardo's theory, produce commodities of equal value. However, the capitalist whose total production period is shorter must earn more profit and hence a higher rate of profit than the other capitalist (since the prices of their commodities by hypothesis are the same). But since competition equalises the rate of profit across different production processes, the price of the more slowly produced commodity must rise, in order that the capitalist who has tied his capital up for longer, can stay in business. Thus Ricardo determined that in the event of a general rise in the wage rate, the profit rate would fall, and given the existence of different durabilities of capital, the prices of 'labour-intensively' produced commodities would rise, and the prices of 'capital-intensively' produced commodities would fall, both relative to that commodity whose price does not change. Such a commodity would be one produced by a capital whose circulating and fixed components, and their durabilities, were exactly average for the economy as a whole. This commodity would then constitute an 'invariable standard of value'.

For Ricardo then, 'exchangeable value' was determined both by total labour embodied in the production of a commodity and by the temporal pattern of that embodiment. The latter Ricardo regarded as 'comparatively slight in its effect' (Ricardo, 1951, p. 36), modifying but never superseding the former, which he continued to regard as 'the nearest approximation to truth, as a rule for measuring relative value, of any I have ever heard' (1951, p. xl). But it was only an approximation, for Ricardo could not account for 'exchangeable value' in terms of labour in production, without conceding some determination of 'exchangeable value' in terms of the temporal structure of capital advanced via the distribution of profits in exchange.

So Ricardo began his analysis with the determination of the magnitude of value by labour time, and proceeded to discover that other economic relations and categories contradicted this basis in labour time. Rapidly arriving at such a contradiction forced him into assertions or beliefs that his starting point was nevertheless correct; yet he had no justification for such assertions. There was no way he could reconcile his labour theory of value with a cost-summation account of equilibrium price; he could only assert that the contradiction did not matter very much in practice. But to found a political economy on the separation of the theories of value and distribution, and then to discover that such a separation could not be strictly justified, was hardly a secure basis for the Ricardian labour theory of value, and, as the 19th century progressed, this theory of value was replaced in economic orthodoxy with a theory of price resting on the contribution of all the different 'factors of production'. In other words, Ricardo's emphasis on determination by labour was abandoned in favour of supply and demand analysis in competitive markets.

Marx was scathing in his condemnation of this development in economic orthodoxy, because he regarded competition as the process whereby the tendential laws of capitalist development were imposed as a coercive force upon individual capitals. Appeals to competition could not explain these tendential laws themselves, and consequently any theory of political economy founded on competition would always have a tendency to degenerate into an ideological apologia for the status quo. He considered that only a labour theory of value could explain what he called 'the intrinsic connection existing between economic

Value Theory

categories or the obscure structure of the bourgeois economic system' (Marx, 1969, p. 165). In order to justify this claim, he had to account for the logical contradiction in Ricardo between a labour theory of value and the consequences for price of the competitive equalisation of the rate of profit. Marx approached this through an argument that Ricardo had failed either to conceive or to account for the historical specificity of the mode of production he was analysing. This had occurred in two related ways.

First, Ricardo was solely concerned with the magnitude of value, and did not examine at all

> the form – the peculiar characteristic of labour that creates exchange-value or manifests itself in exchange-values – the *nature* of this labour. . . . Hence he completely fails to grasp the connection between the determination of the exchange-value of the commodity by labour-time and the fact that the development of commodities necessarily leads to the formation of money. Hence his erroneous theory of money. (Marx, 1969, p. 164)

How is labour-time transformed into money? Failure to account for the historical specificity of the capitalist mode of production involves a failure to account for historically specific forms, such as, for example, the money-form of the product of labour. Tendencies towards universality within particular, historically determined relations of production are misconceived as tendencies towards an atemporal universality, implying that a particular social order is misinterpreted as the universal natural order of things.

Secondly, Ricardo introduced competition (via the equalisation of the rate of profit) at the outset of his analysis, thereby presupposing the full development of historically specific relations of production. In the first chapter of his work,

> not only are *commodities* assumed to exist – and when considering value as such, nothing further is required – but also wages, capital, profit, the general rate of profit and even . . . the various forms of capital as they arise from the process of circulation. (Marx, 1969, p. 168)

Developed categories of political economy, deriving from

developed relations of the capitalist mode of production, are simply *juxtaposed* by Ricardo with their basis in labour time, generating the result that this basis is inadequate as a sole determinant. Instead, Marx considered that Ricardo should have *derived* the apparent discrepancies from their basis in labour-time itself, in order to show 'how matters stand with the contradiction between the apparent and the actual movement of the system' (Marx, 1969, p. 166).

Accordingly, through his critique of classical political economy, Marx had to provide a justification for Ricardo's assertion that labour-time was the source of 'exchangeable value', even when it appeared in fact not to be so. And he had to demonstrate how and why the products of labour took historically specific forms. But to do so was not to render consistent and complete Ricardian value theory; it was rather to overturn it. For Ricardo was only concerned with 'exchangeable value' or 'value in exchange': the quantitative determination of the ratios in which commodities exchange against one another. But there were logically prior questions to these concepts: why do commodities have a value in exchange at all? What was the nature, or the substance, of this value? For Marx, these questions could neither be properly posed nor answered without an understanding of the historical conditions under which the products of labour became commodities, to be bought and sold in markets for sums of money. In turn, this required a specification of the labour which gave commodities a value, and a specification of the forms which such values took.

Marx, therefore, had to determine precisely what the labour was which gave commodities value, whose duration, measured in terms of time, gave that value a measure as exchange-value, which in turn took the form of money. Moreover, such a specification had to be historically specific, in order that he could show that value relations were relations quite specific to capitalism, indeed that their history comprised the history of capitalism.

2.3 MARXIAN VALUE THEORY

Marx began his account of value theory in terms of the commensurability of commodities. Through their distinguishable, physical properties, commodities are useful, or have use-value, and these use-values are realised in consumption. In this, commodities are no different from any sort of product of labour. But commodities also are bought and sold; they exchange against other commodities in determinate proportions and hence have exchange-value. As such, they are commensurable one with another despite their heterogeneity, and what renders them commensurable is that they are all products of labour. The objectification of labour in commodities gives those commodities value. Exchange-value is only a form of appearance of value, appearing when one commodity is exchanged for another.

However, this is not a contingent but a *necessary* form of appearance of value. In order that heterogeneous commodities can be commensurated, Marx considered that they must be able to express their value in something which is different from each of them, yet common to all of them. The value of a commodity has to be expressed through its exchange with another commodity, hence in the physical form or use-value of another commodity; accordingly, social development singles out one commodity whose function is to act as equivalent of the values of all other commodities. Such a 'universal equivalent' is the money-commodity, and in this manner exchange-value is derived from value as its money-form. The opposition between use-value and value, contained within the commodity, is thereby externalised as an opposition between commodities and money, value obtaining a form of appearance different from its commodity form. While abstract labour is materialised in all commodities, its universal form of appearance is as money.

Not only does this ground an understanding of money firmly within the theory of value, but it also provides a basis for the theory of ideology. For if value appears as something different from what it really is, objectified in commodities and realised as money, then it *seems* to belong outside of and separate from production itself. Purposive productive activity takes the form of relations between its results: commodities and money in the market-place. Consequently, human activity is dominated in the capitalist mode of production by its results: the products of labour dominate the producers themselves (through the 'laws of the market') and social relations between people take the form of commodity relations between things. Such 'commodity fetishism' explains the illusions of participants in capitalist society not in terms of simple mistakes, but as consequence of the fact that the social relations of capitalism really do appear as market relations between things. This conclusion of Marx's value theory, namely that capitalism presents itself as something different from what it 'really' is, was of considerable epistemological importance for him, for he defined 'science' as the theorisation of this underlying reality together with the processes whereby such a reality generates the appearances of the world, appearances which systematically mislead their participants as to the nature of their world (on human consciousness in Marx, see also Urry, ch. 5; Barański, ch. 9). By contrast theories which see in appearances the whole nature of the phenomena to be investigated had, for Marx, little explanatory power. This was why he regarded theories based on competition as inadequate and ultimately apologetic: it was the underlying reality which was crucially important.

But for Marx the underlying reality is not simply that commodities are values because they are products of labour. Just as commodities are both use-values and values, so the labour which produces commodities can be considered according as to whether it produces use-values or values. The use-value of a commodity concerns its properties as a particular commodity, which require quite specific acts of labouring activity for their production. Marx called this aspect of labour 'useful' or 'concrete labour'. By contrast, the aspect of labour which renders a commodity a value has nothing to do with any specific act of labour, but is rather labouring activity as such, considered quite independently of the specific forms it might take in particular production. Marx called this aspect of labour 'useful' or 'concrete value.

Hence what the process of exchange does is to commensurate heterogeneous labouring activities. In a society based on private property, these activities are private, separated from one another, employed in particular production processes. As such, an individual commodity is merely the objectification of the labour of its own *particular* production process, and cannot claim to be *universally* representative. Private, independent labours can only have a social, dependent character if they express themselves in a particular commodity which directly represents to all other commodities their value-equivalence. Money is accordingly objectified, universal labour-time, representing the private and concrete labours of independent individuals as social and abstract labour. Consequently, human labours are commensurated through the commensuration of commodity values; the measure of abstract labour (in terms of its duration, i.e. 'socially necessary labour-time') appears as a quantitative value relation between commodities; and social relations between commodity producers appear in the relations between their products. Thus the opposition between individual and universal labour-time is the same as that between the commodity as use-value and the commodity as value: individual labour-time can only become universal labour-time through objectification of this opposition in the marketplace, the money-form of value representing to all commodities their social existence as products of abstract labour.

It remained for Marx to determine how money becomes capital, how the expansion (or valorisation) of value occurs. The typical transaction of a commodity-producing society would appear to depend upon a specialisation of the division of labour. People specialise in the production of those commodities in which they have a comparative advantage. Those commodities which are surplus to their own requirements are sold for money, which can be used to purchase needed commodities which they do not produce themselves. Assuming no systematic fraud or deception, such a free exchange economy ('a very Eden of the innate rights of man . . . the exclusive realm of Freedom, Equality, Property and Bentham', Marx, 1976, p. 280) is characterised by the exchange of value-equivalents, and there is no way in which any participant can leave the market with a greater value than she/he entered it. Hence there is no room in exchange for the creation of value, nor for its accumulation in the hands of one class at the expense of another – indeed there are no classes at all. 'Selling in order to buy' cannot therefore accurately characterise the dynamics of capitalism, and the typical transaction must accordingly be its obverse: 'buying in order to sell (dearer)'.

Such a set of transactions cannot succeed in explaining the expansion of value, if attention is confined solely to the ways in which an initial stock of money is used to purchase commodities, and to the fact that commodities are then sold so that more money accrues than was started out with, for in the exchange of value-equivalents no value expansion can occur. Hence the origins of this expansion must lie in the nature of the use-values of the commodities purchased in the first phase of the transaction. Use-values are realised in consumption. So there must be some commodity which the money-owner purchases in the market (at its full value, by hypothesis), the process of whose consumption has the peculiar property of creating more value than that commodity had itself in the market. Such a commodity is labour-power, the capacity to work. Individuals sell their labour-power for a wage. The purchaser realises the use-value of labour-power by causing it to be consumed *in a production process*. The consumption of labour-power is the production of commodities whose value, realised in sale, is greater than the value of the labour-power (plus material inputs used up) engaged in production, and the extra value (unpaid labour) is a surplus-value accruing to the money-owner as an expansion of her/his money holdings. While to the owner of the commodity labour-power, money in the form of the wage is acting as the means of her/his survival, and selling in order to buy does accurately describe the situation, to the money-owner money is acting as money-capital, and the self-expansion of value, or valorisation of value, through buying in order to sell denotes the money-owner as a capitalist.

Three preconditions are necessary in order for this situation to obtain. First of all, the worker – the owner of the commodity labour-power – must be free of all social and juridical constraints concerning the disposition of her/his labour-power, in particular of all feudal restrictions inhibiting the growth of labour markets. Secondly, the worker must not have the means of working so that the products of her/his labour are her/his own property to be disposed of as desired; the worker must be dispossessed of all means of livelihood so that she/he is forced into the labour market as the only means for her/his survival. And thirdly, the capitalist must, in the first instance, accumulate sufficient resources so as to be able to employ labour (and of course deny the means of that accumulation to workers). For, as Marx remarks,

> nature does not produce on the one hand owners of money or commodities, and on the other hand men possessing nothing but their own labour-power. This relation has no basis in natural history, nor does it have a social basis common to all periods of human history. It is clearly the result of a past historical development, the product of many economic revolu-

tions, of the extinction of a whole series of older formations of social production. (Marx, 1976, p. 273)

This 'past historical development' is essentially one of the forcible dispossession of the majority of the population from their means of subsistence (typically the expropriation of peasants from the land; but see Pearce, ch. 3), forcing people into the labour-market in order to survive. Marx called this process the 'primitive' or 'primary' accumulation of capital, and with it the commodity-form of the product of labour becomes universal. For this reason, that it is only through the market that access to a subsistence base is possible, capitalism is often called a system of universal, or generalised, commodity production.

On this basis of the valorisation of value, the dynamics of the capitalist mode of production can be theorised. Capital only exists in the form of many capitals, whose mutually competitive relations impose upon each their common nature as a coercive social relation. Each capital is concerned to maximise the surplus-value accruing to it, which, prior to legal limitations on the length of the working-day, entailed objectifying in commodities as much labour as possible. With the gradual imposition of such legal limitations from the middle of the 19th century onwards, any given working population could only produce a constant value per day. This value had both to compensate capitalists for the capital they had advanced as wages to purchase labour-power, and to provide them with surplus value. (Capital advanced as means of production transfers its value to the product, and so can be ignored in this analysis.) Then, the only way in which surplus-value can be increased is through a reduction in the value of labour-power. Marx termed this the production of relative surplus-value.

Now the value of labour-power is defined, like the value of any other commodity, in terms of the labour materialised in it; it is accordingly the value of all those commodities which the worker consumes so as to be able to sell her/his labour-power afresh at the beginning of each production period. Hence reducing the value of labour-power involves reducing the values of any or all of these consumption commodities. Given the definition of value, the only way in which the value of a commodity can be reduced is to objectify less labour in it; since abstract labour is measured in terms of its average duration, then the 'socially necessary labour-time' required to produce the commodity in question must be reduced. For a given quantity of labour-time, more commodities must be produced, which in turn involves an organisation of the production process to this end.

The production process is one of labour adding new value to the value of raw materials with the help of various instruments of production. As soon as the motion of the latter is rendered mechanical rather than manual (the principal technical feature of the industrial revolution), then both productive potentialities are enormously enhanced, and control over the production process is removed from the immediate producers. Workers, that is, are gradually de-skilled into appendages of mechanised production processes whose rhythm is controlled by the capitalist. However, of a given capital advanced on inputs, more can be spent on instruments of production only if less is spent on labour-power. Consequently, workers are expelled from a production process which is increasingly 'capital-intensive', thereby forming a 'reserve army of labour', fluctuations in the size of which are determined by the rhythm of accumulation. Hence as capital accumulates, less and less relatively is spent on labour-power and more and more on the instruments of production.

This, according to Marx, is the central dynamic of capitalism and is enforced on individual capitals through competition. For if one capital innovates and thereby achieves a competitive edge for its commodities, other capitals are compelled to follow suit, and the initial gains of the innovator through the undercutting of her/his rivals are thus competed away. If the innovation happens to be in the production of commodities which directly or indirectly form part of the equivalent of the value of labour-power, then all capitals will eventually benefit, as, relative to each other, the value of labour-power falls and surplus-value rises. If the innovation happens to be in the production of some other commodity, only the innovator gains, and then only temporarily (although a conceivable permanent gain might be a greater market share). Accordingly, there is always a motive for each individual capitalist to cheapen commodities by raising labour productivity; such a subjective aim is generated by the coercive force of competition, the movement of individual capitals relative to one another; and this movement in turn is the way in which the immanent nature of capital manifests itself.

In summary, capital 'has an immanent drive, and a constant

Value Theory

tendency, towards increasing the productivity of labour, in order to cheapen commodities and, by cheapening commodities, to cheapen the worker himself' (Marx, 1976, pp. 436–7). This requires that less capital be advanced on labour-power relative to that advanced on means of production, thereby producing a 'relative surplus population'. And since the transformation of money into capital via the appropriation of surplus-value renders all capital accumulated surplus-value, and since all surplus-value is unpaid labour, then the domination of capital over labour is the domination of unpaid labour over paid labour. Thus the dynamic of the capitalist mode of production is ultimately expressed in the contradictory dialectic of paid and unpaid labour, of workers as living labour and of instruments of production as dead or objectified labour, of value, in other words, and use-value.

However, if Marx could thus formulate the dynamics of capitalism in a way which lay beyond the reach of classical political economy, this suggests that his value theory is rather different from the classical labour theory of value. Such an assessment lies at the heart of modern controversies in value theory, as also does the specification of that difference. It is these that must now be considered.

2.4 VALUE AND VALUE-FORM

Perhaps the most enduring controversy within Marxian economics concerns the extent to which Marx's account of the relationship of the form of value in exchange to its content in production can account adequately for capitalist competition. This controversy is known as the 'transformation problem', and it has arisen in the following way.

In Volume One of *Capital*, Marx's focus was on the production and accumulation of surplus-value; since valorisation is common to all capitals, no matter how they might otherwise differ (in location, size, use-value of output and so on), each capital is considered only from the perspective of what it is that all capitals have in common. Capital so considered is called 'capital-in-general' by Marx, or 'capital as such'. Further, Marx assumed equivalence in exchange: all commodities exchange at prices (exchange-values) equal to their money values (i.e. the abstract labour materialised in a unit of each commodity divided by the abstract labour materialised in a unit of the money-commodity).

This assumption is made because Marx wanted to focus on the identification of the origins of surplus-value even if all commodities did exchange at their money values; hence he wanted to ignore transfers of value through unequal exchange in the market (although that is a possibility too).

However, when he analysed how surplus-value was distributed through the competitive process, an understanding of capital as a basically homogeneous category was no longer sufficient. Competing capitals had to be differentiated, and for any given rate of surplus-value, capitals with a greater proportion of workers to raw materials and instruments of production (variable to constant capital) would produce more surplus-value, and hence earn a higher rate of profit. But competition tendentially equalises the rate of profit across competing capitals, and this necessarily implies that commodities cannot exchange at prices equal (or proportional) to their money values. Accordingly, Marx constructed an algorithm whereby each capital produces surplus-value according to the quantity of variable capital employed, but receives a portion of the total surplus-value according to the quantity of variable plus constant capital employed. The mechanism whereby this redistribution occurs is through a systematic deviation of prices from money values, such that each capital, regardless of how it is divided into constant and variable components, earns the same rate of profit. Marx called the prices which equalised profit rates in this way 'prices of production'. While surplus-value has been redistributed in this process, nothing has changed in the aggregate; hence at the level of capital-in-general, nothing is altered, and the dynamics of capitalist production presented in volume 1 of *Capital* hold good. In particular, aggregate surplus-value remains objectified unpaid labour.

However, there is a major difficulty with this account. If the prices of commodity outputs are transformed into prices of production, then insofar as those outputs become inputs to production processes, or elements of workers' subsistence bundles, the components of constant and variable capital can no longer be treated as exchanging at prices equal (or proportional) to their money values. Input values in money terms, that is, must be similarly transformed into prices of production. But if this is done, then it is, in general, impossible rigorously to maintain all of Marx's results concerning the invariance of value aggregates, and the issue at once arises of the extent to which this damages the account of capitalism presented in volume 1, and hence the framework of value analysis itself. In what sense, for example, is aggregate surplus-value in money terms redistributed, if aggregate profit is different from aggregate surplus-value? And how can profit be attributed to unpaid labour-time if the sum of prices of production is different from the sum of money values?

There is no agreement among Marxist economists on how to confront this problem. Broadly speaking, proposed resolutions fall into one of two camps, Ricardian or post-Ricardian, on the one hand, and anti-Ricardian, on the other. The terminology is of course indicative of the extent to which Marxian value analysis is conceived by each camp to be different from that of Ricardo, and thereby of the extent to which value analysis is seen as central to the analysis of capitalist social relations. The issues are fundamental ones, and at the risk of some over-simplification, can be further clarified by discussing each of the two camps in turn.

2.4.1 Ricardian and Post-Ricardian Positions

Beginning with von Bortkiewicz (1949; 1952, both originally published in 1907) and culminating with Seton (1957) is an approach which assumes that workers consume a given wage bundle of commodities which is sufficiently small that production of a surplus product is physically possible. Assuming the technology of the economy is known, if the wage-bundle of commodities is given, then so is the labour-time embodied in those commodities, and a general model of production can be constructed whose solution determines the prices of all commodities and an equilibrium rate of profit. However, while aggregate variable capital is held invariant in the transformation, the same transpires not to be true of aggregate surplus-value, and it therefore becomes quite problematic to claim that surplus-value arises out of unpaid labour-time.

This latter aspect was further clarified by the work of Sraffa (1960). What Sraffa showed was that if the real wage and the technological data (i.e. the input-output structure) of the economy are known, then no further information is required to determine equilibrium prices and a rate of profit. Further, using the same data, Sraffa showed how such prices could be interpreted in terms of dated wage costs, and he constructed an artificial, composite commodity which could act as an invariable standard of 'value', thereby enabling a separation between the theory of price determination and the theory of distribution. Now this was precisely the problem on which the Ricardian theory of value had foundered. It was also the problem which Marx considered he had solved in his transformation procedure, but had not in fact done so. In the face of a logical contradiction between a labour theory of value and the requirements that an equilibrium rate of profit makes of price, it turns out that, first, such prices of production *cannot* be derived on the basis of Marx's assumptions, and, second, that they *can* be derived from technological and real wage data alone. The labour theory of value is thus deemed unnecessary and indeed redundant to the analysis of capitalism. The latter should rather be conducted in physical terms with prices interpreted in terms of dated wage costs if desired.

While Steedman (1977) and Hodgson (1980) have polemicised most vigorously in favour of these conclusions, it is also noteworthy that the major representatives of a previous generation of Marxist economists came largely to accept them in their later works (Dobb, 1973; Meek, 1973; 1977). The substantive difference between Ricardian and Marxian value theory was that the latter had a qualitative dimension that the purely quantitative Ricardian theory lacked. Marx's great merit in this interpretation was to have provided a sociology of class exploitation (via his distinction between labour and labour-power) with which to underpin Ricardian theory; now, with the abandonment of value theory, the challenge is to construct a theory based on physical quantities within which such a sociology of class struggle around exploitation remains meaningful, and which can also discover the dynamics of capitalism.

Little progress has been made to date in this latter direction, although of course this does not foreclose future possible development. However, critics of this school, which has come to be labelled 'neo-Ricardian', argue that there is little prospect of future development as long as an equilibrium methodology is maintained. They argue that neo-Ricardianism is continually in danger of being subsumed by positivism, since making no distinction between appearance and reality, it leaves no room for contradictions between the two, and indeed for contradictions more generally as the driving force of a dialectical methodology.

Value Theory

In particular, critics of this school argue that the value theory which is abandoned is Ricardian rather than Marxian, and they point especially to what they see as the very different role of labour in the two systems.

2.4.2 Anti-Ricardian Positions

For anti-Ricardians, (for example, Fine, 1980; 1982; de Vroey, 1981; 1982; Himmelweit and Mohun, 1981; 1984; Weeks, 1981) it is insufficient to treat value as simply embodied labour, because such a procedure cannot locate the historical specificity of the class relations of capitalism. It is a mode of analysis which can be applied to all societies in which labour occurs, and hence there is a tendency for a theory of a particular society to degenerate into a theory for all societies. For value to be a category specific to and determining of capitalism, it must have a dominating reality within capitalism. Marx's abstract labour must accordingly be understood as the theoretical reflection of a real process, of a social reality, which is something quite different from a means of aggregation. Marxian abstract labour is a different category from Ricardian embodied labour; the latter is a simplifying assumption of dubious validity, whereas Marxian abstractions are real ones. It is some account of these real abstractions which underpins the anti Ricardian position.

Influenced by the interpretations of Marx in Rubin (1972) and in Rosdolsky (1977), anti-Ricardians do not regard value relations as emerging out of the development of capitalist labour processes as workers are de-skilled and fragmented into simple and interchangeable components of such processes. Rather, anti-Ricardians see value relations as emerging out of the way in which private and independent concrete labours are commensurated through exchange of the products of capitalist labour processes. Since capitalism, as an historically specific mode of production, is a system of commodity producers based on private property, who are quite independent of one another, the question arises, in such a system, of how private labour becomes social labour. The answer is seen to lie in Marx's analysis of the money-form of value. For the only way in which the private labour which is materialised in a product can be treated as social labour is through the value of the product as commodity achieving a form which is independent of the commodity itself. That is, the opposition between use-value and value within the commodity is externalised through exchange as an opposition between commodities and money, between concrete labours and directly social labour. Advocates of this position argue that only this approach provides the answer to the questions of why in the capitalist mode of production the objectification of labour in commodities gives those commodities value, and why the measurement of that labour in terms of its duration *must* be expressed as value-magnitudes in the form of money.

Embodied labour theorists fail precisely to give commodities a form of value which is different from their natural physical forms. In this, they share a common ground with the classical political economists, who, Marx had argued, treated the form of value,

> as something of indifference, something external to the nature of the commodity itself. The explanation for this is not simply that their attention is entirely absorbed by the analysis of the magnitude of value. It lies deeper. The value-form of the product of labour is the most abstract, but also the most universal form of the bourgeois mode of production; by that fact it stamps the bourgeois mode of production as a particular kind of social production of a historical and transitory character. If then we make the mistake of treating it as the eternal natural form of social production, we necessarily overlook the specificity of the value-form, and consequently of the commodity-form together with its further developments, the money-form, the capital-form etc. (Marx, 1976, p. 174, n. 34)

Anti-Ricardians thus see value analysis as critical to any determination of the historical specificity of capitalism and its laws of motion.

What then of prices of production, the more developed money-form of value than that which Marx uses in *Capital*, volume 1 to determine the dynamics of capital-in-general? Three different positions can be found in the anti-Ricardian literature as solutions or resolutions of the 'transformation problem'. One sees nothing whatsoever wrong with Marx's solution, claiming that attempts to amend it are symptomatic of revisionist/reformist political positions with respect to capitalist society. Such 'fundamentalist' writings (for example, Williams, 1975; Yaffe, 1975) were very influential in the early 1970s in forcing their readers to come to terms with Marxist fundamentals, but notoriously failed to develop much purchase on the empirical analysis of a world of competing capitals.

A second position uses the abstract rather than embodied labour perspective to solve the transformation problem. Instead of holding the real wage constant in the process of equalising the rate of profit (the neo-Ricardian procedure), these writers hold the rate of surplus-value (defined in aggregate value terms) constant. This amounts to holding constant both the socially necessary labour-time that a unit of money represents, and total surplus-value. In these solutions (see Foley, 1982; Lipietz, 1982), the role of value theory in demonstrating that surplus-value results from unpaid labour is maintained, and an interpretation of the money wage in terms of an unchanged abstract labour equivalent is also maintained. The former is of course essential. But the latter makes sense too, even if the bundle of commodities which the wage can purchase changes across the transformation (as in general it may actually do), because labour-power is not a commodity like other commodities; it is not a commodity produced under capitalist relations of production, and hence there is no reason to transform its money value into a price of production. With this understanding of prices as forms of value, the way is open to develop a more concrete theory of price in which market prices fluctuate around prices of production. The way is also open to attempt empirical estimates of how the rate of surplus-value has fluctuated over time as an illustration of the dynamics of capitalism. And a basis is also laid for the construction of a crisis theory which has empirical reference (see Smith, ch. 1). The difficulty with this last point, however, is that the value of constant capital in general will not remain the same across the transformation process, and this problematises the role of changes in the composition of capital in determining the dynamics of capitalism.

A third position (Fine, 1980, ch. 6; 1982, ch. 3; Himmelweit and Mohun, 1981; 1984) also uses an abstract labour perspective, but focuses on the way in which Ricardo failed to render coherent any distinction between value and the form in which it appeared as exchange-value, forcing contradictions between the two to appear as inconsistencies within his theory. In contrast, Marx emphasised the distinction between value and its form, which gave him a basis both for deriving exchange-value from value and for incorporating within his analysis the real tensions generated by capitalist competition. This latter point sounds like a nonsensical procedure, and indeed it is, from the perspective of a methodology of axiomatic deduction. But it is precisely the use of such a methodology that is what is wrong with Ricardo's analysis: he presumes that labour is an homogeneous entity whose labour-times in production can simply be aggregated and, given the value of money, compared with price. But labour is obviously not a homogeneous entity. And when it turns out that labour-time of production, and, given the value of money, price do not in general correspond, the axiomatic resolution of Ricardo's problem is straightforward: his labour theory of value must be abandoned in the analysis of those societies for which it is not a convenient simplification, in order to formulate a theory of price which is not beset by inconsistency.

But what if consistency in the theory can only be achieved at the expense of its purchase on reality? What if there really are two conflicting ways of calculating values, according to labour-time on the one hand, and according to total capital advanced on the other? Then any theory which axiomatically rejects one in favour of the other might in itself be a logical, consistent theory, yet with little relevance to the explanation of capitalism. Indeed, holding to either way of calculating values, at the expense of the other, generates a theory in which historical explanation is not possible, since the theory must apply to all societies in which labour occurs (the first way of calculating values) or in which prices occur (the second way). A theory of a particular society, capitalism, thereby becomes a theory for all societies. Paradoxically then, all ways of resolving Ricardo's inconsistency by excising one way of calculating values must themselves be founded on a retreat from the explanation of an historically specific reality.

It follows from this discussion that Marx's method of abstraction is not an axiomatic method of successive approximations. It is rather a use of simple, abstract concepts whose unfolding development reproduces in his theory the contradictions of a complex reality. The increasing complexity of the analysis as exchange, distribution and competition are explained does not involve the rejection of the simple, abstract concepts, but rather their development in ways which reproduce the class relations of capitalism in all their complexity. In order for this to be possible, the abstract concepts must themselves have a *real* existence.

This has strong implications for the concept of abstract labour, and hence value. Marxian value theory is not concerned with the aggregation of homogeneous labour-times; its focus is rather on the problem of how heterogeneous, private, concrete labours in production can be commensurated in exchange. This is not an invented problem; it is a real one, and its resolution is also a real one. Marx's abstract labour is not an arbitrary mental generalisation, but theoretically encapsulates a real process fundamental to capitalism. The reduction of concrete labours to abstract labour is a real abstraction, performed by the process of exchange, thereby mediating the contradiction between use-value and value. Once money is rendered independent of commodities, a means for comparing and evaluating different concrete labours, so the form of value achieves a certain independence from value itself, and the transformation process is interpreted qualitatively in terms of the contradictions such independence involves. This means that the 'transformation problem' is not treated as a theory of price formation, but as an expression of the conflict between competing principles of value calculation.

Insofar as a quantitative theory of price formation is required, then in static terms the second anti-Ricardian position is not incompatible with this third position. But a static analysis of price formation sits oddly with a method of abstraction whose purpose is to reveal and reflect the contradictory dynamics of an evolving mode of production, and in this sense it remains an open question whether the second or the third anti-Ricardian position will prove the more fruitful basis for the analysis of the dynamics of capitalism.

2.5 CONCLUSION

The relation between Ricardo and Marx, on the one hand, and the precise characterisation of Marx's method of abstraction, on the other, are the themes underlying all controversies in value theory. But exegesis and taxonomy are of little account in and of themselves; the challenge is to show how a particular interpretation can be used in practice. What then is the use of value theory?

The post-Ricardian tradition argues straightforwardly that value analysis is useless, an impediment to the analysis of capitalism. Little has been successfully put in its place, however, and much effort within this tradition is devoted to the study of linear models of equilibrium price systems, with attempts to relax stringent assumptions concerning the availability of alternative techniques of production (the choice of technique problem) and concerning the number of different outputs of each production process (joint production and the problem of fixed capital). Apart from some assumptions which are seen as mildly eccentric by neoclassical orthodoxy, this tradition is easily incorporated within mainstream, neoclassical economics.

The anti-Ricardian tradition argues that Marx's value analysis should not be interpreted as simply an improvement upon Ricardo's, as the culmination of 'classical political economy' prior to its overthrow in the 'marginalist revolution' of the 1870s and the establishment of modern, neoclassical economics. Rather, value analysis is retained, and is seen as essential to the analysis of capitalism. But much more effort has been put into determining these conclusions than in developing value analysis, particularly the category of the value-form, so that analytical accounts of the post-war development of capitalism can be attempted. Some interesting accounts do exist, but their eclecticism (Mandel, 1975) or their opacity (Aglietta, 1979) beg very many questions precisely because of their lack of concretisation of the underlying theory. Furthermore, value theory narrowly conceived is not sufficient, since an explanation of the evolution of capitalism requires theories of accumulation, of competition, of distribution, of the state, of imperialism, and of crisis. Broadly speaking, and with different emphasis, anti-Ricardians see the development of value theory as the development of these theories – this points to the large amount of work which remains to be done.

GUIDE TO FURTHER READING

The Classic Texts

For Ricardo's value analysis, it is best to refer to the first chapter of the original (Ricardo, 1951, originally published in 1817); the edition cited has a very useful introduction by Sraffa. Marx's

Value Theory   55

value analysis in a narrow sense is contained primarily in the first three chapters of *Capital*, vol. 1 (Marx, 1976, originally published in 1867), with earlier formulations and anticipations of his work scattered through his notebooks, published as the *Grundrisse* (Marx, 1973). His critique of Ricardo occurs at the end of the first chapter of *Capital*, vol. 1, and also in *Theories of Surplus Value*, Part 2, ch. 10 (Marx, 1969). But in a more inclusive sense, Marx's value analysis is developed through all three volumes of *Capital*, and there is no substitute for starting at the beginning with the prefaces to volume 1, and proceeding through all three volumes (Marx, 1976; 1978; 1981). Finally, Marx's analysis of the 'transformation problem' is in *Capital*, vol. 3, Parts 1 and 2 (Marx, 1981).

Marx wrote very little explicitly on his method. There are asides running right through *Capital* and the *Grundrisse*; in a more focused form there are also section 1 of chapter 2 of *The Poverty of Philosophy*, in volume 6 of the Marx–Engels *Collected Works* (Marx and Engels, 1976), the Introduction to the *Grundrisse*, and the *Notes on Wagner* (both in Marx, 1975).

Commentaries

For accounts which place Marx *within* the tradition of classical political economy, see Meek (1973; 1977) and Dobb (1973). The standard mathematical account of the transformation problem is in Seton (1957), and its implications for Marxian economics in a variety of areas are polemically drawn out by Steedman (1977).

General accounts which emphasise Marx's critique of classical political economy include Rubin (1972), Rosdolsky (1977) and Pilling (1980). A 'fundamentalist' account of the transformation problem can be found in Yaffe (1975), while Lipietz (1982) and Foley (1982) provide complementary resolutions of the transformation problem from an abstract labour perspective. Dostaler (1982) also usefully summarises the debate from this perspective. Different elements of the third anti-Ricardian position are in Gerstein (1976), Fine (1980, ch. 6; 1982, ch. 3) and Himmelweit and Mohun (1981; 1984). Other useful studies are Baumol (1977) and Colletti (1977).

Comprehensive collections of articles embracing most of the received positions within Marxian value theory are the one by

Steedman *et al.* (1981), and those edited by Schwartz (1977), and Elson (1979). Lastly, on method, two recent interesting accounts are those by Ilyenkov (1977; 1982); these form a marked contrast with the reasoning of Cutler *et al.* (1977-78).

REFERENCES

Aglietta, M. (1979), *A Theory of Capitalist Regulation* (London: New Left Books).
Baumol, W. J. (1977), 'The Transformation of Values: What Marx "Really" Meant (An Interpretation)', *Journal of Economic Literature*, 12, i, pp. 51–62.
Böhm-Bawerk, E. von (1949), *Karl Marx and the Close of his System*, P. M. Sweezy (ed.) (New York: Augustus M. Kelly).
Bortkiewicz, L. von (1949), 'On the Correction of Marx's Fundamental Theoretical Construction in the Third Volume of *Capital*', in P. M. Sweezy (ed.), *Karl Marx and the Close of his System* (New York: Augustus M. Kelly) pp. 197–221.
—— (1952), 'Value and Price in the Marxian System', *International Economic Papers*, 2, pp. 5–60.
Colletti, L. (1977), 'Some Comments on Marx's Theory of Value', in J. Schwartz pp. 458–73.
Cutler, A., Hindess, B., Hirst, P. and Hussain, A. (1977–78), *Marx's Capital and Capitalism Today*, 2 vols, (London: Routledge & Kegan Paul).
Dobb, M. (1973), *Theories of Value and Distribution Since Adam Smith* (Cambridge University Press).
Dostaler, G. (1982), 'Marx's Theory of Value and the Transformation Problem: Some Lessons from a Debate', *Studies in Political Economy*, 9, pp. 77–101.
Elson, D. (ed.) (1979), *Value: the Representation of Labour in Capitalism* (London: CSE Books).
Fine, B. (1980), *Economic Theory and Ideology* (London: Edward Arnold).
—— (1982), *Theories of the Capitalist Economy* (London: Edward Arnold).
Foley, D. K. (1982), 'The Value of Money, the Value of Labor Power, and the Marxian Transformation Problem', *Review of Radical Political Economics*, 14, ii, pp. 37–47.
Gerstein, I. (1976), 'Production, Circulation and Value: the significance of the "Transformation Problem" in Marx's Critique of Political Economy', *Economy and Society*, 5, pp. 243–91.
Himmelweit, S. F. and Mohun, S. (1981), 'Real Abstractions and Anomalous Assumptions', in I. Steedman *et al.* pp. 224–65.
—— (1984), 'Abstraction, Assumption and Commensuration', in G. Dostaler (ed.), *Théorie de la Valeur et Formation des Prix* (Paris: Maspéro).
Hodgson, G. (1980), 'A Theory of Exploitation Without the Labor Theory o Value', *Science & Society*, 44, iii, pp. 257–73.
Ilyenkov, E. V. (1977), *Dialectical Logic* (Moscow: Progress).
—— (1982), *The Dialectics of the Abstract and the Concrete in Marx's 'Capital* (Moscow: Progress).
Lipietz, A. (1982), 'The So-called "Transformation Problem" Revisited', *Journa of Economic Theory*, 26, pp. 59–88.

Mandel, E. (1975), *Late Capitalism* (London: New Left Books).
Marx, K. (1969), *Theories of Surplus Value*, Part 2 (London: Lawrence & Wishart).
—— (1973), *Grundrisse* (Harmondsworth: Penguin).
—— (1975), *Texts on Method*, T. Carver (ed.) (Oxford: Blackwell).
—— (1976), *Capital*, vol. 1 (Harmondsworth: Penguin).
—— (1978), *Capital*, vol. 2 (Harmondsworth: Penguin).
—— (1981), *Capital*, vol. 3 (Harmondsworth: Penguin).
Marx, K. and Engels, F. (1950), *Selected Works*, 2 vols (London: Lawrence & Wishart).
—— (1976), *Collected Works*, vol. 6 (London: Lawrence & Wishart).
Meek, R. L. (1973), *Studies in the Labour Theory of Value*, 2nd edn (London: Lawrence & Wishart).
—— (1977), *Smith, Marx and After* (London: Chapman & Hall).
Pilling, G. (1980), *Marx's 'Capital': Philosophy and Political Economy* (London: Routledge & Kegan Paul).
Ricardo, D. (1951), *On the Principles of Political Economy and Taxation*, P. Sraffa (ed.), (Cambridge University Press).
Rosdolsky, R. (1977), *The Making of Marx's 'Capital'* (London: Pluto Press).
Rubin, I. I. (1972), *Essays on Marx's Theory of Value* (Detroit: Black & Red).
Schwartz, J. (ed.) (1977), *The Subtle Anatomy of Capitalism* (Santa Monica: Goodyear).
Seton, F. (1957), 'The Transformation Problem', *Review of Economics Studies*, 24, pp. 149–60.
Sraffa, P. (1960), *The Production of Commodities by Means of Commodities* (Cambridge University Press).
Steedman, I. (1977), *Marx After Sraffa* (London: New Left Books).
Steedman, I, et al. (1981), *The Value Controversy* (London: Verso).
Vroey, M. de (1981), 'Value, Production and Exchange', in I. Steedman et al. pp. 173–201.
—— (1982), 'On the Obsolescence of the Marxian Theory of Value: a Critical Review', *Capital and Class*, 17, pp. 34–59.
Weeks, J (1981), *Capital and Exploitation* (London: Edward Arnold).
Williams, M. (1975), 'An Analysis of South African Capitalism – Neo-Ricardianism or Marxism?', *Bulletin of the Conference of Socialist Economists*, 4, i.
Yaffe, D. (1975), 'Value and Price in Marx's *Capital*', *Revolutionary Communist*, 1, pp. 31–49.

3 The Agrarian Question*

RICHARD PEARCE

3.1 INTRODUCTION

The genealogy of the term 'agrarian question' stems primarily from the debates within the German Social Democratic Party in the late 19th century over political strategy with regard to the peasantry, culminating in Kautsky's classic *Die Agrarfrage* (1899). Engels also can lay some claim to originating the expression in his 'The Peasant Question in France and Germany' (1950a).

The appropriate term might better be 'agrarian problem', since the substantial literature which can now be subsumed under this heading represents, to a considerable extent, attempts to reconcile the specificities of agricultural activity to Marxist methodology. The conceptual tools of Marxist political, social and economic investigation have been developed through analysis of the genesis and dynamic of industrial capitalism, particularly manufacturing industry, while the organisation of production of agriculture was, and remains in much of the world, essentially pre-capitalist. Even where agrarian production may be described as capitalist, its organisation still manifests qualitative differences from other industries, making its analysis, in many respects, less straightforward from within the Marxist rubric. In addition, agriculture is an industry unlike any other in terms of its strategically crucial role, particularly with regard to the emergence of industrial capitalism.

Section 3.2 of this chapter outlines in more detail the 'peculiarities' of agricultural organisation and attempts to elabo-

---

* I wish to thank Zyg Barański, Terry Byres, Jayati Ghosh and John Short for helpful comments on an earlier draft of this chapter. Responsibility for what lies herein is entirely my own.

rate on why this industry merits attention. The contributions of both Marx and Engels to the discussion of these issues are sparse, with the partial exception of Marx's analysis of 'ground rent'. The classic texts on agrarian topics are those by Kautsky (1899) and Lenin's 'The Development of Capitalism in Russia' which first appeared at the turn of the century (Lenin, 1973a), both often described as the first applications of Marx's method to agriculture. These fundamental works are reviewed in Section 3.3.

Section 3.4 takes up the themes of contemporary debates and provides the core of this chapter. Two principal issues are discussed. Firstly (sub-section 3.4.1), the problem of categorising production relations within capitalist agriculture. In many respects the genesis of agrarian capitalism has not taken the path which the classical model predicted. Wage-labour has tended to diminish or disappear, rather than becoming generalised, and simple commodity production has proved extremely resilient in the face of rapid technological change. Apart from the problems for political analysis posed by the survival of small-scale family farms, there are important theoretical issues involved here, since the appropriateness of a Marxist analysis of agriculture is called into question.

The second theme frequently overlaps with the first, but focuses more directly on pre-capitalist agriculture and the likely paths of development of agrarian capitalism (sub-section 3.4.2). The importance of these debates to contemporary political strategy is much greater, since they relate to countries where agriculture occupies the majority of the population. The principal topics here concern the *modus operandi* of class formation within the peasantry, and, once more, problems associated with categorising small-scale producers. The question of possible and constructive alliances between an emergent working class and sections of the peasantry provides the underlying purpose of this debate.

The final section suggests by way of conclusion where the strengths and weaknesses of Marxist approaches to agrarian issues lie, and where future effort might most fruitfully be concentrated. I believe that a Marxist approach has much to contribute to the analysis of agrarian problems, but that a preoccupation with abstract, as opposed to empirical concepts, has tended at times to misdirect this contribution.

3.2 THE PARTICULARITY OF AGRICULTURE

Much of the interest occasioned by the agricultural sector arises through its role in the genesis of industrial capitalism. The emergence and consolidation of capitalism within any social formation has perennially been concomitant with a widening of the economic base, bringing about an expansion of the range and quantity of products produced. It is widely accepted amongst Marxists that such precursive changes in the conditions and relations of production will be first initiated within the non-agricultural sectors of production. It is only at a later stage and in response to the growing demands of a burgeoning industrial base, that the agricultural sector itself becomes permeated by capitalism. This is not to say that pre-capitalist agriculture may not perform a crucial role in both the genesis and early growth of industrial capitalism, but rather that the demands made upon it by the latter will eventually necessitate and bring about its transformation (see, for example, Byres, 1977).

To elaborate these points requires reference to the concept of sectoral surplus. This may be defined as that quantity of resources produced within any sector in excess of that quantity necessary to reproduce it, i.e., in excess of *necessary* consumption and investment expenditure. Any such surplus may be dissipated within the agricultural sector by an expropriating class, or may be used to develop and sustain productive activity in other sectors. The surplus may be transferred in the form of financial capital, wage goods, raw materials or labour; and the mechanisms involved, voluntary or involuntary, may include various forms of taxation, including direct appropriation, price manipulation or the spontaneous transfer of investible funds or labour. This sectoral process may be instrumental, during the emergence of industrial capitalism, in facilitating so-called primitive accumulation (Marx, 1974, pp. 667–724), but, in any case, as the relative significance of the non-agricultural economy grows, so do its demands upon agriculture to sustain an increasing surplus.

The dynamics of capitalism, therefore, imply that production relations within agriculture eventually will be transformed in order to facilitate advances in agricultural productivity. If such changes are blocked in any way, the likely results will be upward pressure on the prices of wage goods and/or raw materials, a squeeze on profits and accumulation, and the generation of industrial stasis (for example, see Byres, 1982; and in general see Smith, ch. 1 and Mohun, ch. 2).

It is widely recognised amongst political economists that the organisation of agricultural production is qualitatively different to that of other forms of productive activity, and that this 'difference' necessitates modifications to analytical processes pertinent to investigations of, for example, manufacturing industry. A brief discussion of these specificities of agriculture will provide a foundation for the remaining sections.

In the first place agricultural activity is the most essential productive activity undertaken by human beings in that it provides, or is capable of providing, the prime necessities for the self-reproduction of the species, namely, food, clothing and shelter. Thus the acquisition of control over the means of production provides the most concrete assurance of survival for the individual or for the individual household. The desire to maintain such control in the face of alienating forces is, therefore, likely to be greater than in the case of other means of production. This factor may considerably impede the process of change within the industry, where that process entails a redistribution of productive assets and concomitant change in class relations. In addition, it makes any distinction between production for use and production for exchange less than clear-cut in some cases, since a part, at least, of agricultural production could be utilised for either of these, this part varying on account of circumstances which are often unpredictable, brought about, for example, by yield variations and price movements.

Secondly, given that the nature of agricultural production is biological, and as such is subject to the uncertainties associated with vagaries of climate and disease, the possibility of predicting the outcome of productive activity is less than with most other industrial activities. This is not to say that all productive activity is not subject to the risks associated with commodity production, but only that in agriculture these risks are much greater. These characteristics imply that some activities, particularly those concerned with livestock production, may not as readily yield economies of scale relative to industrial production, since managerial diseconomies may be more difficult to surmount. An example of such diseconomies is the importance of the timeliness of managerial decisions. Much agricultural activity requires frequent adjustment and response to variations in environmental conditions. In addition, the existence of greater risk increases the opportunity cost of investment and slows down the rate of accumulation within the sector.

A third peculiarity of agriculture, again related to its biological character, is the length of time involved in the productive activity itself. This will vary from daily production in the case of milk and eggs, through seasonal time-lags in the case of arable crops, to years in the case of some meat and forestry products. The longer the productive cycle, the greater the risk associated with production and the higher the opportunity cost if investible funds are tied up in the activity. Again, this will tend to deter agricultural investment, since it decreases its relative profitability.

In view of these particularities it is not surprising that Marxist research has concentrated on the structural conditions necessary for raising agricultural productivity and on the concomitant implications of these for production relations within agriculture. Debate has focused on scale in its several guises; in particular on farm size, and the extent to which agriculture will mirror other departments of production in the processes of concentration and centralisation as a consequence of accumulation and competition. Furthermore, if relations of production provide a constraint to agricultural growth, and therefore require transformation if that constraint is to be broken, then the need for an adequate and meaningful theorisation of agrarian class relations becomes essential. For example, if the concern is with the development of capitalism within agriculture, then it is axiomatic that there must exist a consistent set of definitive conditions which describe such a phenomenon. From this standpoint it is possible to observe existing production relations within agriculture, and draw conclusions concerning the extent of capitalist penetration and the likely path of future change. If the Marxist method is to provide a satisfactory approach to an analysis of change within agriculture, then its conceptual categories must be consistent with empirically observed trends, and must be sufficiently flexible to encompass the different possible manifestations of particular phenomena.

3.3 THE CLASSICAL MARXIST POSITION

Specific references to agrarian issues are not plentiful in Marx's writings. Primarily concerned with the genesis and analysis of the capitalist mode of production in general, particularly its English variant, the agricultural sector is treated more for its role in spawning industrial capitalism, for example, through the provision of labour to burgeoning industries (Marx, 1976, Part Seven), and as a laggard in the historical process. The initial impact on agriculture of the development of capitalism occurs through the separation of agricultural and industrial activity, both hitherto taking place within the rural household. This releases labour from the rural sector facilitating large-scale urban factory production. This separation for Marx was necessary and temporary. Necessary in the sense that separation of activities facilitated the revolutionising of productive forces within both activities, and temporary since he envisaged a reconciliation as a characteristic of more advanced modes of production (Marx, 1976, Part Seven).

Throughout his work Marx was deeply influenced in his thinking on agrarian issues by English conditions, where the peasantry had long disappeared, and relatively large-scale, wage-labour based tenant farming had emerged. He consequently maintained a belief in the technical superiority of large-scale agriculture and viewed peasant agriculture as an anachronism. His main references to agrarian issues stemmed from a polemic with Lassallian socialists in the mid-1870s concerning the revolutionary potential of peasant farmers (see the 'Critique of Gotha Programme', in Marx and Engels, 1950). Whilst not rejecting the idea of progressive alliances between the peasantry and the industrial proletariat, Marx repudiated the idea that a cooperative agriculture, based on small-scale peasant units of production, could be compatible with either capitalism or socialism.

The bulk of his analysis of agriculture, however, occurs, almost incidentally, within his discussion of the theory of rent in the third volume of *Capital* (Marx, 1981, Part Six). Here his principal objective is not directly concerned with agrarian issues *per se*, but with the capitalist mode of production in its totality, and with the underlying role played by surplus value in precipitating crises and contradictions within that mode.

His analysis is part critique, part development of Ricardo's theory of differential rent, and so Marx distinguishes between differential rent I and II. Differential rent I constitutes that part of surplus profits derived from the uneven productive powers of land. With market value of produce determined by production on the least fertile land in use, those possessing more fertile land will derive excess profits through the deviation between the individual value of production and its social market value. Differential rent II is derived in similar fashion through the unequal applications of capital to land. Marx considered that the uptake of capital using techniques within agriculture would be slow and uneven due to the limited mobility of land. Thus producers using an above average quantity of capital per unit of land, and therefore deriving greater land productivity, would obtain greater profits. The analytical distinction between these two forms of differential rent has been criticised by some modern commentators; but an important corollary of this analysis is that differential rent, acquired through opportunities to produce with relatively lower costs of production, is a consequence of the character of agricultural production, that is, production significantly dependent on a limited and variable factor of production, namely, land.

Marx further distinguishes between differential and absolute rent. Absolute rent comprises surplus profit derived from the relatively slow development of capitalism within agriculture, resulting in the organic composition of capital (that is the ratio, in value terms, of capital and labour power used in production (c/v)) being lower than in industry. Given that surplus value (s) provides the source of profit and is derived from labour only, the rate of profit $(s/c + v)$ will be greater the lower the organic composition, assuming that the rate of surplus value (s/v) is equal between industries. If potential investment in new land is limited, then higher rates of profit in agriculture cannot be eliminated. Thus absolute rent will tend to disappear as capital permeates agricultural production and c/v rises on a par with other sectors. An important distinction between the two forms of rent is that differential rent will persist irrespective of the advent of agrarian capitalism.

Absolute rent can be described as a monopoly rent derived through ownership of a limited and essential element in production, and it can be argued that this monopoly factor is one that underlies all forms of rent (Ball, 1980; see also Fine, 1979; 1980). In fact, the question of ownership focuses attention on Marx's major concern in his analysis of ground rent, that is, the distribution of surplus value, and the opportunity for non-capitalist landowners (rentiers) to derive a part of surplus profit, thus reducing the rate of accumulation and capital formation in agriculture. This would, at least in part, explain the relative 'backwardness' of the sector. Marx, however, was here, as elsewhere, influenced to an inordinate degree by the 'English model', where a separation between land ownership and agricultural capital was commonplace. But this is not typical of most agricultures, either in the past or in the present. He did not explore in any depth, therefore, other possible causes for this 'backwardness'. He did investigate rather briefly the nature of pre-capitalist rents, such as labour rents and sharecropping, but generally devoted relatively little time to the analysis of peasant agriculture.

Rent theory nevertheless provides an important underlying theme for much of the discussion of agrarian issues to be surveyed (on rent, see also Short, ch. 7). Rental payments derive, at least in part, from the monopolistic control of a limited, essential and significant component of the means of production. The opportunity for owner-occupiers to bolster profits through appropriation of *de facto* rents (i.e., surplus derived from landownership) provides one explanation of the persistence of small-scale producers within capitalist agriculture. In addition, land rent, either in the form of labour, product or money, is the major mechanism of surplus transfer in pre-capitalist agriculture. Any discussion, therefore, of agrarian transition, that is, of the supplanting of pre-capitalist relations of production with capitalist relations and concomitant forms of surplus transfer, must take account of the changing significance of land rent and of the resulting implications for the control of resources. At the theoretical level this remains a relatively unexplored topic, although the work of Patnaik (1983) represents an interesting exception.

As is suggested above, Marx seems to have had a very low opinion of the productive potential of the peasantry. He also regarded the peasants as inherently conservative in outlook and politically reactionary on account of their individualistic lifestyle and motivation. Certainly there is evidence of such views within his writing (Mitrany, 1951), but others within the Marxist tradition would regard this reputation as unfounded and based on misinterpretations which fail to take account of the political purpose of his work (Duggett, 1975). The crucial issue for Marxists here is whether the peasantry can be seen as a potential ally of the working class in revolutionary struggle. Certainly in some discussions of this question, he castigates their 'backwardness' and 'lack of vision' (Marx, 1934). Elsewhere, however, particularly when commenting on countries where the peasantry still constituted an overwhelming majority of the population, for example, Tsarist Russia, he appears more optimistic with regard to their potential as radical allies of the working class (Marx, 1953). Engels too shows a similar ambivalence in his discussions of France and Russia (Engels, 1950a; 1950b).

Although their views of the peasantry reveal some inconsistencies, neither Marx nor Engels ever waivered from the belief in the technical superiority of large-scale farming and its ultimate substitution for peasant forms of production. While both viewed the disappearance of this 'anachronism' as an historical necessity, their work had relatively little to say regarding the processes through which this supersedence was to come about. These themes were developed by Kautsky and Lenin in what have come to be regarded as the classic texts on the agrarian question. Their different, but complementary work has been described as an extension to agriculture of Marx's thinking with regard to industry. Others criticise this view, however, suggesting that when the political contexts in which Kautsky and Lenin wrote are taken account of, their work can be seen more broadly within a Marxist tradition, rather than mere literal adaptations of the letter of Marx (for example, Hussain and Tribe, 1981).

Kautsky's *Die Agrarfrage* was a response to debates between 'revisionists' and 'orthodox' Marxists within the German SPD during the late 19th century (a condensed English version of this work can be found in Banaji, 1976a). In arguing the 'orthodox' case he distinguished between overall trends within agriculture and specific manifestations of its organisation, maintaining that the general direction was, and would continue to be towards the development of large-scale, capital intensive production employing wage-labour. His adversaries, particularly David (see Hussain and Tribe, 1981, p. 102), considered small-scale production to be technically more efficient due to the peculiarities of agricultural production (for example, uncertainty associated with climate and the production cycle), and would therefore prove to be the typical model within capitalism. They further argued that household production of this type was compatible with socialism, since it did not involve the employment of wage-labour.

Kautsky was concerned to show that large-scale agriculture was technically more efficient and sought to explain the persistence of household production as both temporary and at the same time compatible with large farms employing wage-labour. He attributed the survival of small farms to the limited supply of land in the context of private property which inhibited the potential for the expansion of large farms, and to the household nature of production which provided the opportunity for households to reduce consumption in order to survive as producing units. Furthermore, a temporary mutuality of interest between large and small farms arose when small farmers sold their labour to their large-scale competitors, supplementing the supply of cheap rural labour, whilst providing small farmers with additional means of livelihood. Nevertheless, Kautsky argued that smallholders would eventually disappear due to population pressure within the household and the increasing competition from large farms, both of these factors leading to impoverishment and to industrial based wage employment. The superior technical efficiency of large farms, which is instrumental in this process, is derived from their lower costs of production. These are achieved through more economic use of indivisible inputs, such as machinery and other fixed capital equipment, and through other economies of scale obtained via increased division of labour and superior access to markets.

There was little real evidence, at the time Kautsky was writing, that such a concentration of landholding was under way in German agriculture, but this in no way detracts from his thesis, since he was concerned with identifying the general direction of events rather than predicting short-term specificities. I believe, nevertheless, that several qualifications must be added to Kautsky's approach. Firstly, the notion of efficiency is a difficult one to define without specifying particular contexts, and the superior productivity of labour associated with investment in agricultural machinery may not, of necessity, be in the interests of capital when there is a plentiful supply of cheap labour. Secondly, the linking of scale to land area can be misleading, since investment can be land, as well as labour augmenting. Finally, he fails to refute the possibility that diseconomies of scale, arising from the 'special' features of agricultural production, may render any scale economies superfluous.

While Kautsky was primarily concerned with the likely

organisation of production typical of agrarian capitalism, Lenin was more preoccupied with its emergence from pre-capitalist forms of production. He defines two polar developments, with the possibility of intermediate combinations, effected with or without direct State intervention, although always with a minimum of state acquiescence. These are the 'estate' path, whereby pre-capitalist agricultural estates are transformed into large-scale capitalist farms employing wage-labour without any radical redistribution of land taking place. Examples of this model include 19th-century Germany (Lenin, 1973b) and today parts of Latin America (Harris, 1978). The other possibility is the 'peasant path', whereby capitalist enterprises emerge from within the peasantry through a process of socioeconomic differentiation. The latter provides the more common genesis of agrarian capitalism both currently and in the past, and is a process accelerated by land reform measures (Lenin, 1973c; and see also de Janvry and Ground, 1978).

The classic text on differentiation is Lenin's 'The Development of Capitalism in Russia' (Lenin, 1973a). This detailed analysis of Russian agrarian (and other) data purported to demonstrate that by the end of the 19th century the capitalist mode of production was already well advanced within the Russian economy. It contained extensive evidence to support his thesis that even within agriculture the seeds of capitalism were already growing. The primarily political purpose of this work is well documented (Hussain and Tribe, 1981). It nevertheless remains the model upon which many other investigations have been built. Lenin's thesis is that given a peasantry where household activities for self-consumption govern decision-making – the so-called 'middle peasantry' – persistent intrusion of commoditisation will bring about the increasing fracture of this category into rich (large) and poor (small) peasants, with the former finally becoming capitalist farmers and the latter reduced to rural proletarians. The principal vehicles in this process are the opportunities and insecurities provided by the market, and the most common cause of proletarianisation occurs through market dependence, debt and subsequent loss of land. There are likely to be many stages along this route, with the impoverished peasantry forced into the labour market before entirely losing their land. Lenin was undogmatic concerning the 'pure' status of the rural proletarian, acceding that small parcels of land may be retained indefinitely. He was also careful (*contra* Kautsky) not to define his categories in terms of land area alone, stressing the importance of possessing other means of production as well as production relations (for example, labour hiring, wage earning) in determining categories.

Like all the work of the Marxist 'classics', the literature described in this section should be viewed primarily as work appropriate to and conditioned by contemporary circumstances and problems. Although certain of their insights are as appropriate now as when the texts were written, these contributions are mainly important as precursors of the more detailed and sophisticated debates reviewed in the following section.

3.4 CONTEMPORARY APPROACHES TO AGRARIAN ISSUES

3.4.1 Properties of Agrarian Capitalism

Agricultural production, as a proportion of gross national product, has continually declined during this century in many countries, and particularly since 1945 and the onset of the so-called 'technological revolution'. At the same time productivity, whether in terms of unit area or unit labour costs, has increased substantially, to the extent that a relatively declining sector has been more than able to meet the needs of its burgeoning industrial and service populations. Since qualitative technological changes have revolutionised agricultural production, early Marxist predicitons have been borne out. Equally significantly, however, production relations have not been transformed in the manner anticipated. The persistent and ever-increasing incidence of household based farming activity within mature capitalist economies (e.g. EEC, USA, Japan), and the failure of large-scale farming to become pervasive in some more newly industrialised countries (Greece, Portugal, Spain) have led some people to question the usefulness of orthodox Marxist analysis with respect to agriculture.

Vergopoulos (1978) uses evidence from Greece to argue that household production best serves the interests of 'urban' capitalism. The essence of his argument is that this 'deformed' agrarian capitalism facilitates higher rates of accumulation within industry, primarily by maintaining a low market value of agricultural production, thus providing cheaper wage goods and/or raw materials. This low market value is obtained through household producers being prepared to respond to falling incomes, caused, for example, by adverse movements in the intersectoral terms of exchange, by intensifying the family labour input and thus increasing output. This phenomenon is frequently accompanied and reinforced by increasing indebtedness on the part of those households which borrow in order to finance capital investment. This investment provides further demand for industrial products. Thus, it is maintained, such an income squeeze increases the productivity of household farms over that of larger, wage-labour based units of production, leading to the greater technical efficiency of small-scale production. In fact, such a response is not new and was anticipated by Kautsky, but the argument that such developments will lead to superior competitiveness and persistence of small-scale production is directly antithetical to his thesis. A corollary to this 'productivity increasing immiserisation' is that existing wage-labour based farms, capitalist in the orthodox sense, seek to lower costs through labour saving investments to the extent that many are converted into household based simple commodity producers. The concluding view of the development of capitalism within agriculture, therefore, is not of a sector mirroring the organisation of industry, but of one characterised by relations of simple commodity production, a process advanced rather than reversed by the development of productive forces.

Further theoretical attempts to explain this persistence of household based productive units come from, *inter alios*, Djurfeldt (1981). Like Vergopoulos he maintains that simple commodity producers, relative to wage-labour farms, are more able to survive declining profitability, because they operate according to a different decision-making process. Being household producers rather than capitalist profit maximisers, they respond to adverse terms of exchange movements by intensifying production in order to maintain household income. Capitalist (wage-labour based) producers, on the other hand, transfer investments to more lucrative targets to agro-industries such as processing, fertiliser manufacture, etc. Djurfeldt bases his argument on an analysis of Marx's rent theory, claiming that international trade in grain in the 19th century led to a reduction in the market value of agricultural produce and consequently to a fall in differential rents. This heralded the demise of capitalist farming and the growth of simple commodity production.

His interpretation of rent theory has been criticised by Winter (1982) for confusing absolute and differential rent, yet nevertheless his contention that investment will flow into industries ancillary to agriculture rather than into farm production is a valid one in the light of contemporary evidence. Winter further argues that, in the context of owner occupation, the concomitant capitalisation of rent (surplus profit) will drive up land prices and further buttress household producers against competition from profit maximising potential capitalists.

Sympathetic criticism of Djurfeldt is provided by Raikes (1982), who argues that it is the nature of the labour process in agriculture which deters large-scale investment through the creation of diseconomies of scale. This argument reflects the particularities of agricultural production discussed in Section 3.2.

Mann and Dickenson (1970) also make a significant contribution to this debate. They argue that the persistence of simple commodity production can be explained by a distinction between production time and labour time, given that for many activities the production process involves long periods of inactivity (for example, the maturing of cereal crops between field operations). This problem is compounded by the seasonal and irregular flow of commodities, which therefore require storage, or by the temporarily uneven nature of market activity where the product is perishable. They reinforce their argument by suggesting that much agricultural research is geared towards reducing the distance between production and labour time.

The fact that, in many cases, household based organisation or simple commodity production remains prevalent in capitalist agricultures is incontrovertible, and the above paragraphs have outlined the major interpretations put forward for explaining their survival. Nevertheless, two important issues remain unresolved. First, whether the apparent persistence of simple commodity production is merely a temporary hiccup in a long-term trend towards concentration within agriculture; and second, if household production is the norm within capitalist agriculture, what are the implications for exploitation and accumulation both inside and outside the sector?

With regard to the first issue, Mouzelis (1976) indicates, in a critique of Vergopoulos' work, that one should distinguish in analysing this question between specific conjunctures and trends. The paths to capitalist development in agriculture are likely to be many and varied depending on particular historical circumstances and class formations. What appears as a function of industrial capitalism may be supportable only on a temporary basis, particularly if this function is obtained through progressive relative immiserisation of the peasantry. In addition, this functional relationship can only be sustained if the peasantry can meet the increasing demands of industrial capital. Given the limits to productivity implicit in these social relations (the problems of acquiring an investible surplus to finance advances in technology), he argues that such relationships may eventually disintegrate.

The second issue is more complex. The major contribution comes from Friedmann (1980), who distinguishes between simple commodity producers (SCPs) and peasant producers, the status of the former dependent on competition, commodity production and factor mobility. Simple commodity reproduction 'deepens' rather than 'resists' commoditisation, and requires constant adaption to changing market conditions and technological developments. In this way simple commodity producers are totally integrated into the capitalist mode of production. Conversely none of these conditions apply in full to peasant production. However, these SCPs are not capitalists, since their relations of production are based on a union rather than a separation between direct producers and means of production. It would be incorrect, she argues, to speak of capitalist social relations in this context, and therefore of capitalist exploitation, and it is theoretically correct to suggest that no accumulation (in the Marxist sense) takes place. But deepening commodity relations bring with them, through competition, the necessity of constantly expanding the material basis of production. Such expansion requires an investible surplus, and the source of this surplus must be identified and explained.

This investment fund, I would suggest, could in some contexts be based on self-exploitation, that is, by the voluntary reduction of consumption to below the level of the average wage. But the majority of SCPs in industrialised countries certainly earn more than the average wage. Investible surplus can only be obtained, in their case, through the conditions of exchange involving mechanisms which, in other circumstances, will be used to transfer a surplus from agriculture. Whether or not this constitutes exploitation is more than a semantic point, since exploitation, in a Marxist sense, has a material basis in production and can only be mediated rather than actualised through exchange. But this mediation implies that material exploitation is taking place. One must conclude that SCPs, to the extent that they are remunerated above the level of the average wage, are benefiting by the terms of exchange which redistribute surplus value to them from an industrialised working class via a class of industrial capitalists. To the extent, therefore, that simple commodity production prevails within agriculture, agrarian social relations of production are not strictly capitalist, but are dependent on capitalist relations of production obtaining within the wider mode of production.

3.4.2 Emergence of Capitalist Agrarian Relations

Notwithstanding the problems associated with characterising a capitalist agriculture, the question still needs to be answered as to how this might emerge from within peasant-based social formations. As suggested above, Lenin's work on differentiation has been, and remains, extremely influential in this respect, although it is also the subject of controversy. A significant critique of his thesis emerged from outside the Marxist tradition, from the Chayanovian school. This critique is especially important for the responses it has brought from Marxist commentators, which have led to the clarification of formerly inadequately investigated areas.

In his *Theory of Peasant Economy*, Chayanov (1966), working on pre-Revolution Russian data, denied the inevitability of socio-economic differentiation (increasing stratification in terms of control over means of production) amongst peasant producers, brought about by agricultural commoditisation, a process that would lead eventually to the disintegration of the peasantry into the distinct classes of large-scale capitalist farmers and of rural proletarians. He argued, on the contrary, that changes in landholding structure were cyclical in nature responding to family life cycles and to the consumption demands of the household. Not unlike the revisionists of the German SPD debate, as well as some contemporary Marxists, he believed that household labour-based agrarian production possesses superior attributes to wage-labour based organisation on account of the producers' consumption satisfying, rather than profit maximising objective function, together with its enhanced motivation of labour and lack of supervision costs in production. Thus family based holdings, the scale of which will be determined by the size of the household, are more able than capitalist farms to produce independently of market conditions by varying consumption levels and work intensity. For Chayanovians these 'family labour farms' will survive the inroads of the market and resist any tendency towards concentration; and supporters of this view stress the advantages of vertical integration through production and marketing cooperatives over horizontal integration.

Whilst some Marxists have implicitly taken on board the central tenets of the Chayanovian approach (such as Vergopoulos and Djurfeldt discussed above), the majority have attacked his work both for its theoretical and empirical assumptions. Whilst both Patnaik (1979) and Harrison (1975) have called into question his use of data, others have sought to demonstrate contradictions within his thesis. The main target of Marxist attacks is the notion of a persistently independent peasantry inhibiting the development of capitalist relations within agriculture. Central to this argument is the fate of the 'middle peasant' category, those who typically neither purchase the labour of others nor sell their own, and who provide the archetypal producer for the Chayanovians, but who, in the Leninist view, appear the most vulnerable to the destructive powers of the market.

If peasant farm organisation persists in the manner suggested by Chayanov, then, I would argue, attempts to theorise it lead to conceptual problems associated with a peasant mode of production – a peasant based form of organisation which is independent of, yet articulated with, industrial capitalism. It is this assumption of independence, implying an ability to reproduce the unit of production based on household labour alone, which provides the weak point in the argument. As Littlejohn (1977) and others (for example, Ennew et al., 1977) argue, in a context where both output and means of production are increasingly commoditised, the ability to reproduce the household unit becomes more and more dependent on the wider economy, while the form of organisation must remain insulated from the vicissitudes of the market if it is to remain stable. So peasant production is both affected by its integration into the national economy (through labour and commodity market opportunities, access to technological improvements, etc.), yet unaffected in its basic nature. The central characteristic of the household labour farm is the unity of producing and consuming units, therefore, this unity must remain intact in the face of market penetration. It must depend, in favourable years, on a leisure preference limiting consumption and/or accumulation and, in unfavourable years, on a lack of alternative means of remuneration. In particular, the destabilising influence of indebtedness on the landholding structure will be intensified by commoditisation. It is unacceptable, therefore, to suggest, as a general conclusion, that the structure of peasant organisation will remain unaffected by the rationale of the market once it has become dependent on it. Thus attempts to rationalise the persistence of simple commodity production inside the capitalist mode of production need to look elsewhere than at the tenacious nature of the household labour farm and its subjective equilibrium.

While I believe that the volume of literature generated through the debate between Chayanovians and Marxists greatly exaggerates the importance of Chayanov's thinking, it has led to a more flexible view amongst Marxists of the rationale behind peasant decision-making. This is a view which is more prepared to take account of leisure preferences in contexts where survival is relatively secure (for example, see Hyden, 1980), although such circumstances are, in practice, increasingly rare. Along these lines an attempt is made by Banaji (1976b) to integrate the work of Chayanov, Kautsky and Lenin. He maintains that the Chayanovian notion of a subjective equilibrium between drudgery of work and utility of income, underlying the organisation of production, explains a process of 'labour intensification for lower pay' in response to economic pressure. Corollaries to this process are indifference on the part of peasants to objectives concerning labour productivity, and to the potential for expanding the consumption fund (the quantity of goods available for household use) through increased farming intensity. He attempts to use survey data from India to support his thesis. Assuming a correlation between family size and holding size, it is axiomatic that middle size farms should have the highest level of work intensity, since they possess the highest consumer to worker ratio. Banaji attempts to demonstrate this, for example, through analysis of cropping patterns. His concern is not to counterpose cyclical to socioeconomic differentiation, but to reconcile the two. Banaji's work is interesting, but not entirely convincing, mainly because of his basic assumption that any correlation between family size and farm size is demographically caused. Certainly there is little evidence from Asia to justify such an assumption, and the appropriateness of applying Chayanovian concepts to that part of the world where land scarcity is a general phenomenon seems to be slight.

Although notions of demographic differentiation are of limited value, Marxists have nevertheless considered it pertinent to consider the processes through which classes emerge from within a relatively homogeneous peasantry.

Possible mechanisms whereby the integration of peasants into the wider economy leads to social differentiation are outlined by Bernstein (1979). Stressing that whilst there will be no single manner in which the process of commoditisation occurs, the general process will take the form of an increasing replacement of need fulfilment through use-value production by dependence on exchange. Household reproduction increasingly involves relations between the individual household and the market, rather than relations within the household itself. Thus, while simple commodity production persists, it becomes subject to a 'simple reproduction squeeze'. This 'squeeze' occurs through an inability to reproduce the household production unit with the existing level of productive forces in the face of the vagaries of climate, disease and infertility, and through the fact that the material means of production are in limited supply. It forces the purchase of more productive and expensive means of production with no guarantee of equivalent return for the now commoditised output. Reproduction becomes dependent on good fortune and the terms of exchange, greatly increasing the vulnerability of the household to forces outside its control. The greater the extent to which simple commodity reproduction becomes dependent on exchange, the greater the possibility of adverse circumstances leading to a 'cycle of indebtedness'.

Thus the previous uniformity of the conditions of reproduction of the peasantry is altered to a state in which the possibilities of impoverishment and aggrandisement become central. Those least endowed with resources are forced increasingly to sell their labour power, while others, through the increasing translation of

The Agrarian Question

wealth into capital, are able to enhance their position in relation to the market and to engage in a cycle of expanded reproduction.

As Bernstein, following Lenin, implies, the sale of labour power does not in itself constitute capitalist social relations. Equally relevant is the extent to which the object of production is translated into accumulation and expanded reproduction. Even where socioeconomic differentiation is apparent, the transition to agrarian capitalism may be an extremely slow or still-born process. Certainly most social formations in the less industrialised parts of the world provide evidence of a polyglot of social relations within agriculture, which seldom conform to classical interpretations of capitalism. This has led to some debate concerning the categorisation of agrarian social relations, particularly with regard to the South Asian sub-continent. The question whether the capitalist mode of production is already dominant, is emergent or dormant within Indian agriculture has been the subject of intense controversy and considerable intellectual endeavour. Three main arguments run through the literature: the emergence of capitalist farmers from a 'rich' peasantry, and related to this the conceptual problems involved in distinguishing the two; the precise nature of a rural proletariat; and the categorisation of modes of production within agriculture.

This controversy emerged out of the work of Rudra (1970), who hypothesised a set of conditions which a producer must simultaneously meet to be described as capitalist. Finding no evidence of the presence of these conditions, he concluded that capitalism had yet to emerge within Indian agriculture. Patnaik (1972) responded by maintaining that for farmers to conform to Rudra's conditions would imply that the transition was already complete. The important issue for her was whether there existed a *tendency* towards the emergence of capitalist farmers. She argued that while a complex interaction between capitalist and non-capitalist relations within Indian agriculture was emerging, it was a 'distorted' development with no straightforward teleological solution. Her principal point was that labour was not fully 'free', in the double sense of being both free to sell labour power and divested of means of production, since it was effectively bonded to agricultural employers through the lack of alternative opportunities. In addition, the condition of wage-labour was insufficient to ensure the existence of capitalism. For this to obtain it was also necessary for accumulation to take place through appropriation and investment of surplus value. This was not possible while usury, trade and landlordism remained the common forms of surplus utilisation. Her work led to an exchange with Chattopadhyay (1972), who maintained that capitalism exists wherever generalised commodity production through wage-labour prevailed.

This exchange led to a wide-ranging debate and to a plethora of attempts to categorise the 'agricultural mode of production'. The political implications of this argument are important and evident (and are effectively summarised by Harriss, 1980), since its conclusions will influence both the feasibility and the desirability of particular class alliances. Marxists have similarly analysed agrarian relations and the conceptual status of the peasantry in Latin America (for example, see Latin American Perspectives, 1978). The debate on India led to several hypotheses concerning production relations varying from capitalist to semifeudal and to those specific to a 'colonial' mode of production. A good example can be found in the work of Banaji (1977). He defines as rural proletarians, those household producers 'subsumed' by markets which facilitate, through the transfer of surplus, the process of capital accumulation in other sectors. As a result of this, they obtain the status of generators of surplus labour typified by wage-labour production. Following Marx's distinction between formal and real subsumption of labour to capital (Marx, 1982, 'Appendix'), he describes these producers as 'pre-formally' subsumed. Although in part a device to enable agrarian relations to be characterised as 'capitalist', this thesis does raise the vexed question of 'centre-periphery' relations, and the extent to which the interests of international capital are best served by household based agrarian production. Evidence from Latin America, at least, suggests that a subservient and often rack-rented peasantry is harnessed to the process of accumulation as the supplier of cheap wage goods and the buttress for the reserve army of labour (de Janvry and Garramon, 1977). It is probable that a similar process exists in parts of East Africa (Cowen, 1981).

At the same time, if these peasant producers are only partially and not fully integrated into commodity production they cannot be categorised as simple commodity producers. In such circumstances what relations of production do prevail within agriculture? Attempts to categorise these as 'feudal' or 'semi-feudal', only overcome the problem terminologically, and in fact raise a host of problems of definition best left undisturbed. Similarly, sub-categorisation of the peasantry into 'semi-proletarians' or 'proto-capitalists' is equally inadvisable. True, production may take place under the auspices of a combination of capitalist and pre-capitalist relationships, but these will be varied and heterogeneous, and to generalise them simply as 'semi-feudal' seems to me to miss the point that the majority of peasantries in the periphery are increasingly penetrated by markets dominated by industrial and financial capital. The particular nature of any transaction will be determined by its own historical conjuncture, and attempts to categorise agricultural modes of production or articulations of modes of production can only lead to an unhelpful theoretical rigidity or multiplicity of conceptual terms reminiscent of Weberian ideal types.

In my view the concept of mode of production is an abstract concept unsuitable for concrete verification and analysis. All social formations are now dominated by the capitalist mode of production and contain within them relations of production which are both capitalist and dominant, and non-capitalist and symbiotic or contradictory. The important issue for Marxists is not to make categorical generalisations, but to facilitate awareness of specific common class interests and contradictions, and to analyse their changing nature. Relations of production within pre-capitalist agriculture are particularly complex and variable. For example, sharecropping is extremely widespread (see the collection of articles in Byres, 1983) and occurs in a wide range of contexts where it functions as a mechanism facilitating surplus transfer; but, as I have argued elsewhere (Pearce, 1983), the character of production relations in terms of tenant subordination varies considerably. This non-uniformity, based, for example, on the degree of tenant control over means of production in general, may be compounded by differential access to credit and to input and product markets. As Bhaduri (1977) has demonstrated, the size of rental payments *per se* may give no real indication of the degree of surplus extraction in those places where sharecroppers are subjected to additional appropriation through usury and trade by landlords who are also acting as moneylenders and/or merchants. Such 'interlocking' of channels of exploitation through the combination of landlordism with merchant and usury capital ('antediluvian' capital) is not only common, but also very specific in the form it takes. The extent to which this 'interlocking' occurs, however, will help to determine the resilience of precapitalist production relations in the context of their transition to agrarian capitalism. Attempts to categorise such relationships using sweeping generalisations will only create the possibility of policy or strategy decisions which are frequently inappropriate.

The characteristics of transition are nowhere more apparent than in the literature on the so-called 'green revolution' (see Byres, 1981, for a useful bibliography). A complex combination of seeds, chemicals and, frequently, technological hardware, this 'revolution' in productive forces has caused existing production relations to be rapidly modified in many instances as those parties controlling access to resources seek to avail themselves of the new profit-making opportunities. The complexities of such interactions are well documented by Byres (1981), and are dependent not only on the attendant relations of production, but also on the extent to which changes in bio-chemical technology (seeds, chemicals, water provision) are accompanied by mechanical innovations. It is probable that in the long run the two cannot really be separated given the nature of ensuing class relations; but where technical factors (relating to soil type, for example) do not predetermine their short-term combination, the speed and appearance of consequent changes in relations of production are likely to vary.

Pre-capitalist agriculture, I should like to suggest, is shaped by a complexity of social and economic interactions which collectively constitute relations of production, whose specificity is produced by particular agro-demographic and cultural factors. A unifying trend is emerging through the relative uniformity of changes in the pattern of productive forces. But a trend does not necessarily represent a transformation, and premature attempts to find uniform classifications of relationships have led to questionable conclusions (such as the identification of agrarian relations as 'feudal' or 'semi-feudal'). A more productive use of the materialist method is to combine an awareness of these trends with an understanding of the variety and complexity of the relationships involved. Recent work by Rudra (1978) and Mitra (1977) are examples of such an approach.

3.5 CONCLUSION

It is clear from the evidence available that, in both mature capitalist and transitional economies, a significant proportion of agricultural commodities is produced on holdings organised on a household or family basis. In many industrialised nations, the survival of these small farms is effectively guaranteed by government protection and subsidies, quite apart from technological and socioeconomic factors which facilitate their persistence. In the 'periphery' impoverished sections of the peasantry cling, with varying degrees of success, to their peasant 'status', often with the active encouragement of the State through redistributive land reforms. Both categories of producer are effectively integrated into a wider capitalist mode of production, because of common interests between household production and the functional needs of capital.

Whether or not these 'needs' will in future require that household production is overwhelmingly superseded by other methods of organising agricultural activity, as anticipated by the orthodox or classical Marxist position, remains to be seen. But whatever the outcome, Marxists would agree that its determination will be by these 'functional needs of capital'. In the light of this, I believe contemporary debates have tended to stress one aspect within agrarian analysis, i.e. relations of production, and have neglected the other, i.e. productive forces. Chayanovian prognostications, although fashionable and powerful in their support for populist rhetoric, do not seem to merit the energy which has been spent in refuting them. Preoccupation with the categorisation of production relations, an approach strongly influenced by Althusserian 'formalism' (see Urry, ch. 5), has led to a relative neglect of issues which historical materialism is most suited to investigate, namely, the *dynamic* interaction between forces of production and the relationships of resource control, surplus generation and distribution. Of course, there are many commentators whose work is exempt from such criticisms, and I have discussed some of these above. Similarly recent work which either implicitly or explicitly focuses on labour processes in agriculture is an encouraging development (see especially Byres, 1981; Bhadhuri, 1983).

I think it fair comment to state that, until recently, agriculture has remained a neglected area of investigation by Marxists. This is perhaps explainable in terms of its neglect by Marx, of the relatively small part which agrarian classes and agrarian production play in the political theatre of industrialised nations, and of the Eurocentrism of much Marxist research. This neglect is unfortunate, since many of the commentators mentioned in this chapter have shown, in my opinion, that Marxism, when its method is used creatively and undogmatically, is far more capable of explaining the *modus vivendi* of agrarian activity and agrarian change than any of the 'orthodox' paradigms which purport to do the same. It has proved particularly useful in demonstrating the uneven and variable impact of changing productive forces on agrarian relations in a manner which highlights both the international and 'macroeconomic' influences at work, and the specificities of local contexts. The work of Banaji (1977) and of Bernstein (1979) provide particularly informative illustrations of this approach.

Future emphasis will, in my opinion, fall increasingly on analyses of the relationship between specific labour processes and the social organisation of production, particularly of household production. This will include studies of the changing status both of simple commodity producers and of that generic category of participants in, and victims of world events, known collectively as peasants.

GUIDE TO FURTHER READING

For those unfamiliar with the principal conceptual categories used in mode of production analysis, a useful starting point is Althusser and Balibar (1970). This book has been very influential, although, in my opinion, the influence has not always been beneficial. A book very much within the Althusserian tradition is Hindess and Hirst (1975). For different and in many ways more rewarding approaches to modes of production, see Cohen (1978) and Corrigan *et al.* (1978).

Surprisingly little has been written, in recent years, on the preoccupations of the classics, particularly Kautsky's. The most useful investigation in this sphere is Hussain and Tribe (1981). As far as contemporary non-capitalist agricultures are concerned, however, there exists a large body of literature within the Marxist tradition. For Latin America two recent books provide a helpful introduction to the subject: Goodman and Redclift (1981) and de Janvry (1981). An excellent work dealing with African perspectives is Kitching (1980). Attention should also be drawn to the *Review of African Political Economy*. As far as Asia is concerned, no single book adequately deals with the problems of this continent, although Mitra (1977) provides a stimulating introduction. There are, however, many useful individual analyses; see especially the two excellent journals: *The Economic and Political Weekly* and *The Journal of Peasant Studies*. The latter also covers much of interest pertaining to all continents.

REFERENCES

Althusser, L. and Balibar, E. (1970), *Reading Capital* (London: New Left Books).
Ball, M. (1980), 'On Marx's Theory of Agricultural Rent: a reply to Ben Fine', *Economy and Society*, 9, pp. 304–26.
Banaji, J. (1976a), 'Summary of Selected Parts of Kautsky's *The Agrarian Question*', *Economy and Society*, 5, pp. 2–49.
—— (1976b), 'Chayanov, Kautsky, Lenin: Considerations Towards a Synthesis', *Economic and Political Weekly*, 11, pp. 1594–607.
—— (1977), 'Capitalist Domination and the Small Peasantry', *Economic and Political Weekly*, 12, pp. 1375–404.
Bernstein, H. (1979), 'African Peasantries: a Theoretical Framework', *Journal of Peasant Studies*, 6, pp. 421–44.
Bhaduri, A. (1977), 'On the Formation of Usurious Interest Rates in Backward Agriculture', *Cambridge Journal of Economics*, 1, pp. 341–52.
—— (1983), 'Cropsharing as a Labour Process', in T. J. Byres (ed.), pp. 88–93.
Byres, T. J. (1977), 'Agrarian Transition and The Agrarian Question', *Journal of Peasant Studies*, 4, pp. 258–74.
—— (1981), 'The New Technology, Class Formation and Class Action in the Indian Countryside', *Journal of Peasant Studies*, 8, pp. 405–54.
—— (1982), 'India: Capitalist Industrialisation or Structural Stasis?, in M. Blenfield and M. Godfrey (eds), *Struggle for Development* (London: John Wiley).
Byres, T. J. (ed.) (1983), *Sharecroppers and Sharecropping* (London: Frank Cass).
Chattopadyay, P. (1972), 'Mode of Production in Indian Agriculture – an Anti-Kritik', *Economic and Political Weekly*, 7, pp. A185–92.
Chayanov, A. V. (1966), *The Theory of Peasant Economy*, edited and introduced by D. Thorner *et al.* (Illinois: Irwin).
Cohen, G. A. (1978), *Karl Marx's Theory of History – a Defence* (Oxford University Press).

Cowen, M. (1981), 'Commodity Production in Kenya's Central Province', in J. Heyer *et al.* (eds), *Rural Development in Tropical Africa* (London: Macmillan) pp. 121–43.
Corrigan, P., Ramsey, H. and Sayer, D. (1978), *Socialist Construction and Marxist Theory* (London: Macmillan).
de Janvry, A. (1981), *The Agrarian Question and Reformism in Latin America* (Baltimore and London: Johns Hopkins University Press).
de Janvry, A. and Garramon, C. (1977), 'The Dynamics of Rural Poverty in Latin America', *Journal of Peasant Studies*, 4, pp. 206–16.
de Janvry, A. and Ground, L. (1978), 'Types and Consequences of Land Reform in Latin America', *Latin American Perspectives*, 5, iv, pp. 90–112.
Djurfeldt, G. (1981), 'What Happened to the Agrarian Bourgeoisie and Rural Proletariat under Monopoly Capitalism?', *Acta Sociologica*, 24, pp. 167–91.
Duggett, M. (1975), 'Marx on Peasants', *Journal of Peasant Studies*, 2, pp. 159–82.
Engels, F. (1950a), 'The Peasant Question in France and Germany', in K. Marx and F. Engels (1950), vol. 2, pp. 420–40.
—— (1950b), 'On Social Relations in Russia', in K. Marx and F. Engels (1950), vol. 2, pp. 49–61.
Ennew, J. *et al.* (1977), 'Peasantry as an Economic Category', *Journal of Peasant Studies*, 4, pp. 295–322.
Fine, B. (1979), 'On Marx's Theory of Agricultural Rent', *Economy and Society*, 8, pp. 241–79.
—— (1980), 'On Marx's Theory of Agricultural Rent: a Rejoinder', *Economy and Society*, 9, pp. 327–31.
Friedman, H. (1980), 'Household Production and the National Economy: Concepts for the Analysis of Agrarian Formations', *Journal of Peasant Studies*, 7, pp. 158–84.
Goodman, D. and Redclift, M. (1981), *From Peasant to Proletarian: Capitalist Development and Agrarian Transitions* (Oxford: Blackwell).
Harris, R. (1978), 'Marxism and the Agrarian Question in Latin America', *Latin American Perspectives*, 5, iv, pp. 2–26.
Harrison, M. (1975), 'Chayanov and the Economics of the Russian Peasantry', *Journal of Peasant Studies*, 2, pp. 389–415.
Harriss, J. (1980), *Contemporary Marxist Analysis of the Agrarian Question in India*, Working Paper No. 14 (Madras: IDS).
Hindess, B. and Hirst, P. (1975), *Pre-Capitalist Modes of Production* (London: Routledge & Kegan Paul).
Hussain, A. and Tribe, K. (1981), *Marxism and the Agrarian Question* (London: Macmillan).
Hyden, G. (1980), *Beyond Ujamaa in Tanzania* (London: Heinemann).
Kautsky, K. (1899), *Die Agrarfrage* (Stuttgart: Dietz).
Kitching, T. (1980), *Class and Economic Change in Kenya* (Yale University Press).
Latin American Perspectives (1978), *'Peasants, Capital Accumulation and Rural Underdevelopment'*, 5, iii and iv.

Lenin, V. I. (1973a), 'The Development of Capitalism in Russia', *Collected Works*, vol. 3 (Moscow: Progress).
—— (1973b), 'The Agrarian Question and the Critics of Marx', *Collected Works*, vol. 5 (Moscow: Progress) pp. 103–22.
—— (1973c), 'New Data on the Laws Governing the Development of Capitalism in Agriculture', *Collected Works*, vol. 22 (Moscow: Progress) pp. 13–102.
Littlejohn, G. (1977), 'Peasant Economy and Society', in B. Hindess (ed.), *Sociological Theories of the Economy* (London: Macmillan) pp. 118–56.
Mann, S. and Dickenson, J. (1978), 'Obstacles to the Development of a Capitalist Agriculture', *Journal of Peasant Studies*, 5, pp. 466–81.
Marx, K. (1934), *The Eighteenth Brumaire of Louis Bonaparte* (Moscow: Progress).
—— (1953), 'Letter to the Editorial Board of "Notes of the Fatherland"', in *Marx and Engels, Selected Correspondence* (London: Lawrence & Wishart) pp. 376–9.
—— (1976), *Capital*, vol. 1 (Harmondsworth: Penguin).
—— (1981), *Capital*, vol. 3 (Harmondsworth: Penguin).
Marx, K. and Engels, F. (1950), *Selected Works*, 2 vols (London: Lawrence & Wishart).
Mitra, A. (1977), *Terms of Trade and Class Relations* (London: Frank Cass).
Mitrany, D. (1951), *Marx Against the Peasant* (London: Weidenfeld & Nicolson).
Mouzelis, N. (1976), 'Capitalism and the Development of Agriculture', *Journal of Peasant Studies*, 3, pp. 483–92.
Patnaik, U. (1972), 'On the Mode of Production in Indian Agriculture', *Economic and Political Weekly*, 7, pp. A145–51.
—— (1979), 'Neo-populism and Marxism: The Chayanovian View of the Agrarian Question', *Journal of Peasant Studies*, 6, pp. 375–420.
—— (1983), 'Classical Theory of Rent and its Application to India: Some Preliminary Thoughts on Sharecropping', in T. J. Byres (ed.), pp. 71–93.
Pearce, R. (1983), 'Sharecropping: Towards a Marxist View', in T. J. Byres (ed.), pp. 42–70.
Raikes, P. (1982), 'Djurfeldt's "What Happened to the Agrarian Bourgeoisie and Rural Proletariat under Monopoly Capitalism?" – a Comment', *Acta Sociologica*, 25, pp. 159–65.
Rudra, A. (1970), 'In Search of the Capitalist Farmer', *Economic and Political Weekly*, 5, pp. A85–7.
—— (1978), 'Class Relations in Indian Agriculture', *Economic and Political Weekly*, 13, pp. 916–23, 963–8, 998–1004.
Vergopoulos, K. (1978), 'Capitalism and Peasant Productivity', *Journal of Peasant Studies*, 5, pp. 446–65.
Winter, M. (1982), '"What Happened to the Agrarian Bourgeoisie and Rural Proletariat under Monopoly Capitalism?" – a Reply to Goran Djurfeldt', *Acta Sociologica*, 25, pp. 147–57.

Part II

Theories of Society

4 Marxism and the British Historiographical Tradition

PAUL CORNER

4.1 INTRODUCTION

When Marx wrote, in his *Eighteenth Brumaire of Louis Bonaparte*, that 'Men make their own history, but not of their own free will' (1973; orig. pub. 1852), he posed a whole series of theoretical problems for the historian in the pursuit of his or her discipline. In Italy, Germany, and to a lesser extent in France, generations of intellectuals responded to the challenge by re-defining their relationship with history and attempting to re-think the mechanisms of the historical process. Novel ideas concerning historical materialism, economic determinism, and the historical role of the working class profoundly affected the vision of history and provoked radical reassessment among a large number of European intellectuals. In Britain, despite the attention which both Marx and Engels had devoted to the condition of the English working class (Marx and Engels, 1971; orig. pub. 1844–45), this sea-change in historical thinking went largely unnoticed. The consequences are, at least in part, still with us; only in recent years have there been significant developments in the direction of change. The extent of these developments is perhaps best measured by reference to two quotations. In 1972 Gareth Stedman Jones provided a caustic and succinct account of the immobility of the British historical tradition: 'the progress of British historiography over the last hundred years provides a spectacular case of arrested intellectual development and conceptual poverty' (1972, p. 96). Yet, little more than a decade later,

Perry Anderson felt able to write, 'Today the *predominant* centres of intellectual production seem to lie in the English speaking world, rather than in Germanic or Latin Europe, as was the case in the inter-war and post-war periods respectively.... The traditional relationship between Britain and continental Europe appears for the moment to have been effectively reversed – Marxist culture in the UK for the moment proving more productive and original than that of any mainland state' (1983, pp. 24–5). This essay will attempt to provide some explanation of this astonishing reversal of roles, at least as far as the British tradition is concerned, and hopes to assess the extent to which Marxism has played and is increasingly playing a decisive part in reshaping British historians' approach to their subject.

4.2 LIBERALISM, POSITIVISM, AND THE BRITISH HISTORICAL TRADITION

Such an assessment cannot but start from the recognition that British historiography has traditionally shown itself to be extremely wary of theory. In the particular case of Marxism, hostility has undoubtedly been generated in the years since World War II by the onset of the Cold War and the facile identification of Marxism with Soviet Communism. But it would be misleading to suggest that this hostility has done anything more than confirm a state of affairs which has its origins much further back, in the intellectual formation of the British liberal tradition in history during the course of the 19th century. The central influence on historians of the 1860s and 1870s was, of course, that of positivism; although it has been rightly observed that, while many historians may have taken their methodology from positivism, they may equally have been relatively unaware of the philosophical basis of their chosen approach (Hobsbawm, 1972, p. 266). This notwithstanding, the immediate impact of positivism on historical study was undoubtedly beneficial in as far as positivism encouraged the historian to look at the methods and practices of the natural sciences and to attempt to apply them where possible to the study of history. The value of this opening to the natural sciences was, however, strictly limited by the fact that the principal model was provided by biological investigation, which placed its emphasis on explanation through the accumulation of observed evidence – a method which could be applied satisfactorily to only certain of the fields which could be considered the legitimate areas of interest for the historian. The positivist approach encouraged above all the belief that uncovering the 'facts' in history would by itself lead to historical explanation. Thus Ranke's famous dictum, that the job of the historian was simply to show 'wie es eigentlich gewesen' (how it really was) – as though the 'facts' would in some way manage to speak for themselves.

Particularly in Britain, positivism was heavily buttressed by liberalism, with its attendant emphasis on the autonomy of the individual and the primacy of individual action in explaining the process of historical change. The kind of history produced reflected this dual approach. History became the accumulation of 'facts' about individuals (generally 'great men') and events, or else it concentrated on institutions through which individuals were seen to act, and in its presentation it was generally narrative and chronological. In Britain, the heavy influence of liberalism also gave rise to a flourishing school of constitutional history, since the liberalism of the British was identified with their constitution. Much of the production was undoubtedly of a high standard in terms of research, even if – as any student of late 19th-century historians knows – inclined to be heavyhanded and tedious, but the philosophical basis of the work, and in particular the question of the relationship of the historian to the material studied, remained obscure. As important, the emphasis on 'facts' and the accumulation of evidence clearly excluded from study many areas of history where 'facts' were not obviously available for collection and collation.

In following the positivist and liberal tradition during the second half of the 19th century, British historians were in large measure reflecting trends which were prevalent throughout Europe. What marks the British tradition as different, is the persistence of this approach beyond the turn of the century. In continental Europe, the shocks to intellectual life represented by the appearance and diffusion of the works of Marx produced a radical reassessment of the historical method (for example, in the work of Labriola, Kautsky, Jaurès, Herr). Historians were presented with a body of ideas which upset the traditional orthodoxy at precisely the time in which rapid industrialisation and the sudden growth of militant working class movements seemed to upset the rather complacent positivist belief in the pursuit of progress. This is not to say that Marxism simply took the place of positivism, although in many areas this was so after 1880; but even where Marxism was rejected, its impact was registered heavily and served to produce new lines of thought which differed greatly from the preceding positivist and liberal traditions.

Such an impact was largely absent in Britain. The weakness of a strong pre-Marxist socialist school of thought undoubtedly meant that Marxism found a less fertile terrain on which to build than in many other areas of continental Europe. Equally the working class threat was felt in a different manner. By the 1880s the British working class already possessed a strong non-Marxist tradition of its own, developed across the struggles of the previous century. It was a tradition very different from that of working class militancy within Europe, as is made readily evident by the fact that Gladstone and Disraeli felt able to make repeated, and often successful bids, for working class support. Where Marxism did appear, as in London with the Social Democratic Federation (SDF) during the 1880s and 1890s, it was notably unsuccessful in organising a coherent labour movement (Stedman Jones, 1971). As a consequence, Marx appeared to have less to say to the British intelligentsia: the system was very much less under attack and existing models of thought, still centred around the positivistic liberalism of the second half of the 19th century, continued to dominate. Historians could remain firm in their belief in liberalism and the pursuit of progress, and in their attachment to a historical methodology based on these precepts.

This situation persisted until the end of the second decade of this century, that is, until the fundamental optimism of 19th-century liberalism was finally shattered by the experience of World War I. Even this experience, though, failed to bring British historiography back into line with the dominant trends in continental Europe. While the work of the major European political scientists and sociologists became more widely known in Britain after the end of the war (especially Mosca, Pareto, Weber, Michels, Durkheim), their methodologies were generally accepted only in part, and they remained distant influences rather than masters. The two most influential figures of the inter-war period in Britain, Tawney and Namier, are in a sense exceptions to this general rule, in as far as Tawney clearly owed a great deal to the religious sociology of Weber, while Namier introduced methodological concepts provided by Pareto's theory of élites and Freud's writings on psychoanalysis. But they remain only partial exceptions because of their failure to stimulate any thoroughgoing revision of the methodological bases of historical study. The implications of much of Tawney's work remained undiscussed; he provided an alternative to Weber, 'an excuse not to read Weber' (Stedman Jones, 1972, p. 106). Namier's methods were followed by an entire school of historians, but they were followed in a generally uncritical manner and without the necessary attention to their intellectual origins. Despite their efforts, therefore, neither Tawney nor Namier succeeded in creating a British historical tradition which was more open to continental influences. The major history schools in Britain reflected the fact that the golden age of liberalism was past, but it remained unclear what was to take the place of that liberalism. 'The demolition of Victorian historical assumptions left history without a centre. Political and constitutional history had provided the main vertebra upon which the ambition of universal history had depended. After the First World War, what had been a solid marble block became a honeycomb. To political history was added economic history, administrative history, ecclesiastical history, army history, navy history, local history, entrepreneurial history, or agricultural history. No attempt was made to fuse this aggregate of specialist routines into a meaningful historical totality' (Stedman Jones, 1972, pp. 106–7). Moreover the great majority of historians of this period – and indeed of subsequent years – remained subject to a method of historical reconstruction which insisted that the historian was bound by his or her evidence and that a pragmatic and empirical approach to historical material constituted the best guarantee of an 'unbiased' history.

4.3 THE ORIGINS OF BRITISH MARXIST HISTORIOGRAPHY

It is only in recent years, since the mid 1950s, that this kind of methodology has come seriously under attack, and Marxist historians have been able to make decisive inroads into the prevailing liberal historical tradition. However, insistence on the general impermeability of the liberal tradition should not be permitted to obscure the fact that these Marxist historians were themselves in many cases the representatives of a very different, but in many ways a very peculiarly British historical tradition – a tradition which, if it had only rarely succeeded in penetrating the formal institutions of higher education, was nonetheless extremely important in determining what British Marxists took from Marx and what use they made of it.

This tradition is itself anything but homogeneous. Marxism was, in a sense, grafted on to a series of different influences already present in British society, albeit often as influences to which only a relatively small minority of the population was subject. The major intellectual current which preceded Marxism and which in many ways provided a fertile base from which Marxism could grow, was that of radicalism and democratic dissent, both aspects of a body of thought deeply rooted in the British tradition. The main tenets of this current of thought – the defence of the individual against authority, a passionate belief in social justice, and a rejection of the hierarchical bases of British society – provided obvious meeting points with certain of the tenets of Marxism. Historians writing from a radical or dissenting standpoint produced material which was in many ways compatible with the emphases provided by Marxism. The result was what has been termed 'people's history' – a history where the main object of study was the British people, rather than isolated individuals, wars, treaties, etc. This kind of writing is exemplified particularly in the work, published during the 1860s and 1870s, or Thorold Rogers (*Six Centuries of Work and Wages*, 1887) and J. R. Green, whose *Short History of the English People* (1877) has rightly been judged 'a fundamental text for understanding the provenance of "history from below"' (Samuel, 1980, p. 38). It is worth quoting in full a passage from the preface to this volume in order to make clear the priorities present in 'people's history': 'The aim of the following work is defined by its title; it is a history not of English Kings or English Conquests but of the English People . . . I have preferred to pass lightly and briefly over the details of foreign wars and diplomacies, the personal adventures of kings and nobles, the pomp of courts, or the intrigues of favourites, and to dwell at length on the incidents of that constitutional intellectual and social advance in which we read the history of the nation itself. It is with this purpose that I have devoted more space to Chaucer than to Creasy, to Caxton than to the petty strife of Yorkist and Lancastrian, to the Poor Law of Elizabeth than to her victory at

Cadiz, to the Methodist revival than to the escape of the Young Pretender.'

Early Marxist historians such as Hyndman, Connolly and Johnston, had little difficulty in following in this tradition. From it they took many of its perspectives and causes, limiting themselves usually to increase the revolutionary element in the interpretation. Marxist history at this time – the last quarter of the 19th century – was very much 'people's history' in the radical and dissenting tradition. Ironically, this foundation produced not studies of industrial society or of the tensions of 19th-century capitalist development, but works which tended to an idealisation of the past. The central point of focus was that moment when the 'people' were assumed to have lost their independence – with enclosures – and the peasant and the artisan played the major role in these histories. This tendency undoubtedly owed something to the utopian socialism of Robert Owen, but equally it reflected a common belief that peasant society had been freer and more just than was that of industrialised Britain, and that the guild organisations of 15th- and 16th-century artisans had represented a kind of democratic organisation of labour which was totally absent in capitalist society. In the words of H. M. Hyndman, the organiser of the Marxist SDF, 'the fact still remains that the common working Englishman of the 15th century fared better and was in every respect a more independent vigorous man than his descendent of any later age' (Samuel, 1980, p. 40). Here the early Marxist hatred of existing industrial society is made fully evident.

A further influence on British Marxist historians, not unrelated to the tradition of radical and democratic thought, but distinct from it, is that of non-conformity. Here the links are at times more difficult to uncover. As Raphael Samuel has remarked, 'One is treading here on unknown and almost forbidden territory, where few materials are as yet available and generalisations are necessarily speculative' (Samuel, 1980, p. 42). Yet the connection is immediately apparent when the background of many of the most distinguished Marxist historians is examined. From Belfort Bax and Christopher Hill to E. P. Thompson and Sheila Rowbotham, the strong influence of a Methodist upbringing is easily recognised. Other historians reflect other branches of the protestant, non-conformist tradition. The terms of the transfer to Marxism are difficult to establish, but they would appear to lie in the strength of a dissenting tradition combined with an ingrained concern for the spiritual and physical conditions of life of the working class. Non-conformity gave to British Marxism the dedication of a persecuted sect, an evangelical approach to recruitment, and the moral rigour and discipline characteristic of chapel going workers. And while Marxism was clearly militantly atheistic, there can be little doubt that many historians saw their role as that of the dissemination of a secular faith which bore the hallmarks of self-sacrifice, solidarity, and personal commitment common to the non-conformist cause.

From the historical point of view, the non-conformist influence had very important consequences. Whereas the early Marxist writers had concentrated their attention on the 15th century, and had provided manuals, which, through the activities of the Plebs League (an important Marxist educational organisation) during the first two decades of the century, had strongly influenced workers' educational movements in the direction of peasant studies at the moment of capitalist expropriation, later historians changed the principal focus of attention. Non-conformity and the tradition of radical dissent led straight back to the 17th century. This proved a particularly fertile area for Marxist historiography. The Putney debates and the speeches of Gerard Winstanley seemed to provide a specifically English tradition for communism onto which many of the concepts of Marxism could be readily grafted. In particular the notion of the English Revolution served to indicate that revolutionary politics were not absent from the English tradition; on the contrary, it could be affirmed that revolution lay at the base of post-17th-century British society. In the writings of Christopher Hill these themes have been consistently stressed in a way which has given them a clear relevance for the 20th-century communist movement in Britain (1940; 1949). In so doing, he has neatly combined the traditions of radical dissent and the Puritan Revolution with certain of the distinguishing features of non-conformity to provide a specifically Marxist bridge between the past and the present.

If the influence of non-conformity has sometimes been minimised (and at times volubly rejected), it has been because of the desire on the part of certain writers to place the British Marxist tradition firmly in that intellectual current which undoubtedly does represent a further influence – that of rationalism and freethought. The militant atheism which characterises this current has found it difficult to accept any debt to non-conformity, although it seems more realistic to assume that the influences which brought people to Marxism were several and operated in very different ways. Certainly, scientific rationalism and freethought were powerful forces, particularly during the 1920s and 1930s, in determining the direction of historical study and the interpretation given to that study. In some respects the influence was felt through the writings of scientists and anthropologists, who, concentrating on the themes of evolution and primitive social organisation, dealt severe blows to religious tradition in the name of scientific rationalism and historical materialism (for example, Haeckel, Tylor, Frazer). Such attacks were readily followed by historians, who found in the new interpretations of the origins of life, a stimulus to the reinterpretation of history in rationalist and atheistic terms (for example, Childe, Pascal, Farrington, Robertson). This tendency was reinforced in the years before 1945 by the inspiration provided by the Soviet Union, where it seemed that scientific and technological development was bringing about a truly Marxist idea of progress. Historians were inclined, therefore, to see their task as part of a battle of ideas. Science represented social progress; materialism was opposed to idealism; and the enlightenment provided by scientific rationalism and historical materialism was opposed to the superstition and myth of religion. It is not surprising, therefore, to find that the 16th-century struggles of England against Catholic and absolutist Spain are represented as struggles of enlightenment against obscurantism, just as the fight against fascism also comprehended the fight against a Catholic Church which supported the fascist states. For the communist historians of the 1930s and 1940s, 'science was a metaphor for human achievement, a measure of progress, a crucial lever of change' (Samuel, 1980, p. 80). Moreover the historians also regarded themselves as scientists in the use of Marxist methodology, 'insisting upon the notion of causality in the study of historical phenomena, and relating the accidental and contingent to a causally determined whole' (Samuel, 1980, p. 84). It is interesting to note in this context that the Marxist historical journal *Past and Present*, first published in 1952, carried as its subtitle 'a journal of scientific history'.

4.4 THE EMERGENCE OF A MARXIST HISTORIOGRAPHY

By the 1950s, a clear trend in Marxist historiography had emerged. A small, but intellectually distinguished, group of historians, centred around the Communist Party Historians' Group, had made themselves known for work which, beyond its immediate subject, was generally characterised by attention to what were considered to be the laws of social movement, of 'social dynamics', provided by a careful reading of Marx and Engels. In the work of Christopher Hill, Rodney Hilton and Eric Hobsbawm, the specifically Marxist feature was provided by the search for causality in history within the overall conceptual framework of a total world picture. Deeply committed to scientific rationalism, all three at different times argued the case for a 'progressive' Marxist history, and indicated their belief in this 'progressivism' by masterly and seminal works on the English Revolution (Hill, 1940), the English peasantry (Hilton, 1947), and the British labour movement (Hobsbawm, 1948). The works of all three, recognised generally in the historical profession as eminent contributions to British history, served to put Marxist historiography on the map in a way which had been inconceivable in the 1930s. In particular, their attention to broad social questions served to provide many common points of approach with the more broadly based radical and democratic history of these years, particularly in the field of labour history where Marxist historians had tended to specialise. Yet, while there was undoubtedly a great deal of cross-fertilisation between radical, social democratic history, and Marxist history, the latter remained very much subordinate to the former. Marxist history 'existed as a tributary to a very much broader stream' (Samuel, 1970, p. 37); the most successful works of the 1930s and 1940s, from the point of view of diffusion, had been popularising home educators in the Marxist tradition, while the academic profession remained generally hostile to the products of the more scholarly Marxist historians. This hostility was to continue into the 1950s, at least for the more bitter years of the Cold War. It was a hostility which stifled debate about theory or methodology and which reflected the continuing domination of the liberal individualistic tradition within British academic historiography.

Only towards the end of the decade did it become obvious that

Marxist influence was on the ascendant. With the shocks of 1956 to the Left in part digested, and with the beginnings of *detente*, Marxist methods and emphases began to attract greater attention. This was reflected in particular in an increased disposition among historians to open their study to the influences of sociology and psychology, and in a general tendency to reinforce the place given to economic and social factors in historical explanation. Much of the influence can probably be termed 'vulgar Marxist' (Hobsbawm, 1972, p. 270), in the sense that only certain ideas particularly that of the importance of the economic factor in history – have been absorbed, while many of the ideas more central to the thinking of the mature Marx have been at best only partially embraced (see Urry, ch. 5). This notwithstanding, the importance of the penetration of these ideas cannot be underestimated. They 'represented concentrated charges of intellectual explosive designed to blow up crucial parts of the fortifications of traditional history, and as such they were immensely powerful. Perhaps more powerful than less simplified versions of historical materialism would have been, and certainly powerful enough in their capacity to let light into hitherto dark places' (Hobsbawm, 1972, p. 271).

This 'new light' really began to illuminate the world of history from the beginning of the 1960s. Marxism undoubtedly benefited from the general shift to the Left during this decade, and from the political prominence of nationalist and anti-imperialist struggles in the Third World, which seemed to justify much of the libertarian 'progressivism' of Marxist thinking. At the academic level Marxist history began for the first time to occupy a position of notable importance. A major shot, fired across the bows of traditional historiography, was the appearance in 1963 of Edward Thompson's *The Making of the English Working Class*, a work which has in many ways dominated the British historical field over the last twenty years (see also Lumley and O'Shaughnessey, ch. 10). Thompson's writing is in part important for the depth of its research, but it is chiefly notable, within the context of the British historiographical tradition, for the attention it pays to methodology and the formulation of theoretical concepts. This is nowhere more evident than in his discussion of the key term in the book, that of 'class' itself. Far from seeing class as the static result of conditioning, Thompson emphasises that it is a fluid relationship, a result of a complex interaction between people. 'By class I understand a historical phenomenon, unifying a number of disparate and seemingly unconnected events, both in the raw material of experience and in consciousness. I emphasise that it is a *historical* phenomenon. I do not see class as a "structure", nor even as a "category", but as something which in fact happens (and can be shown to have happened) in human relationships' (Thompson, 1968, p. 9). The stress on flexibility and experience is repeated in another passage: 'class happens when some men, as a result of common experiences (inherited or shared), feel and articulate the identity of their interests as between themselves, and as against other men whose interests are different from (and usually opposed to) theirs' (pp. 9–10). And the clearest definition of all comes, perhaps, in *The Peculiarities of the English*, where Thompson insists that 'class itself is not a thing, it is a happening' (Thompson, 1965, p. 357).

This definition immediately opened the way to a whole new series of emphases in historical enquiry. As a cultural phenomenon, a question of consciousness, class ceased to be subject to the mathematical definitions of economic historians and statisticians; as a phenomenon which clearly grows out of experience, class can no longer be considered a 'pejorative theoretical concept, imposed upon the evidence' (Thompson, 1968, p. 10). It is a definition which in fact greatly enriches the scope of historical enquiry, making it evident that it is the sum total of experience which is decisive and not that of the experience which is necessarily 'progressive' or successful. Thus Thompson himself emphasises the importance of the 'losers' in history in helping to develop the consciousness of class. 'I am seeking to rescue the poor stockinger, the Luddite cropper, the "obsolete" hand-loom weaver, the "utopian" artisan and even the deluded follower of Joanna Southcott, from the enormous condescension of posterity' (1968, p. 13). This produces not simply 'history from below'; it also represents a major elaboration of one of the central concepts of Marx, that of class, in terms which contribute greatly to the further utilisation of the concept.

The impetus given to the study of history by the work of Thompson has been evident in the years since 1963. The redefinition of the concept of class and the attempt to interpret a revolutionary tradition in exclusively English terms has produced a new approach to Marxist history and served to rescue that history from the sometimes arid field of preceding 'labour history'.

In the work of John Foster (1974), Perry Anderson (1980; 1983), and Gareth Stedman Jones (1971), the broader approach to questions of class formation are reflected in full. Both in terms of production, and in terms of reception, Marxist history is now clearly one of the principal schools within the British academic tradition. This school has been further reinforced in recent years by another initiative, again indicative of the renewed force of Marxist studies during the 1960s. 'History Workshop', founded at Ruskin College, Oxford in 1966 has attempted to radicalise both the writing and the consumption of history in significantly socialist ways. Starting from the conviction that the documents of archives and county halls tend to reflect the opinions of persons exercising authority – of judges, organisers, and administrators – and that histories based on these sources have tended to reflect the personal biases of such people, 'History Workshop' has attempted to develop a different methodology – one which permits the ordinary people, the objects of administration, to play a greater role in the writing of their history. It has tried to arrive at a new reading of existing sources, at the discovery of new sources, and, where possible, at the utilisation of the oral accounts of the participants themselves. Centred always on experience 'at the point of production', this methodology has given rise to a new kind of social and cultural history where those, so often neglected by traditional history, have assumed the major roles. This emphasis has produced new subjects for study; 'Childhood in history' was the title of the first workshop; 'Family, Work, and Home' the title of a later meeting. Inevitably the place and role of women has assumed a particular importance: 'There are shelf-fuls of books about factory legislation; not one about factory girls' (Samuel, 1975, p. xvi). This exclusion of women from history, in part because they were rarely organised as a group and therefore presented particular problems for the student, has been one of the central points of attack of the Workshop, reflecting the desire to produce a genuine 'people's history' within a specifically socalist perspective. It is a methodology which certainly runs the risk of fragmentation, with the isolated case divorced from the general, but in many cases it has produced studies which go further towards convincing historical explanation of popular culture and popular movements of resistance than do the more general accounts which often remain at a more superficial level (Samuel, 1975; 1977; White, 1980).

4.5 THE GENESIS OF THEORETICAL DEBATE

As important as the works produced – perhaps in the long run more important – has been the fact that the new impetus to Marxist studies has at last served to generate debate about history within the academic world. The implicit assumptions of the great majority of British historians – assumptions which had dominated historical enquiry for decades – have finally been challenged by a methodology which has attempted to make its conceptual framework explicit from the outset. This has not always been exclusively the work of Marxists. An exception is provided, for example, by E. H. Carr's *What is History?*, published in 1961, in which the author gently chided the historical establishment for assuming that their interpretations in history sprang from the 'facts' and not from the implicit personal values and attitudes of the historians themselves. Although not a Marxist, Carr's refusal to accept a rigid division between interpretation and the 'facts' pointed clearly in the direction in which Marxist historians were also moving, and served to strengthen their case for an increased emphasis on theoretical presuppositions. This emphasis has subsequently been reflected in continuing debate between Marxist historians and between Marxist and non-Marxist historians. The violent polemics which surrounded Thompson's *Making of the English Working Class* provide one example among many which have been generated over the last twenty years. Such debates have been important not only for themselves, but also because they have made evident the central position occupied by theory in the writing of history. In so doing they have helped to break down that impervious empiricism which has for so long characterised the liberal tradition.

In recent years debate has also intensified through the appearance of new influences. During the 1970s the French structuralist school made significant inroads into the theoretical debate taking place in Britain. The anthropological work of Levi-Strauss (1965) provided important methodological lessons for British Marxists, while the seminal writings on Marx of Louis Althusser provided a further impetus to the elaboration of a Marxist theory of history (1969; 1970). Equally important perhaps was the 'discovery' of Gramsci in Britain, made possible by the appearance of the English translation of his early writings and *Prison Notebooks* (1971; 1977; 1978). Gramsci's emphasis on the concept of hegemony and on the importance of ideas and consciousness in obtaining that hegemony greatly illuminated the relationship between base and superstructure – a point left notoriously unclear by Marx himself (see also for these and subsequent points Urry, ch. 5; Baranski, ch. 9; Lumley and O'Shaghnessey, ch. 10). It provided a new place of departure for Marxist studies of culture, and once again reinforced the tendency to develop theoretical precepts as a precondition of historical study. If at a political level the writings of Gramsci have sometimes been oversimplified ('All we need to do is gain hegemony'), for the historian they have provided an invaluable insight into the network of relationships which characterise the exercise of power within contemporary society.

It is the French structuralists, and in particular Louis Althusser, who have provided the most recent cause for a thoroughgoing review of Marxist theory among historians in Britain. Works like *For Marx* and *Reading Capital* achieved considerable success during what has been described as the 'Althusserian moment' of the late 1960s and early 1970s. In part the attention paid to Althusser reflected a trend, carried forward during the 1960s by certain British Marxists and by the *New Left Review* in particular, to criticise the British tradition in the name of an allegedly more sophisticated and more fully developed continental Marxist tradition. Detractors of this tendency sought to defend themselves from what they saw to be the seductions of the Left Bank. In his *Peculiarities of the English*, Edward Thompson was at pains to protect the specifically English tradition in which English Marxism was rooted and to reject those interpretations which took so much from continental influence. But it has been the recent contribution of Thompson in *The Poverty of Theory* (1978) which has served to make the dividing lines totally clear. Thompson's work is both a spirited defence of historical materialism, as he perceives it, and a caustic attack on the abstractions and idealism of Althusser and his followers. The central point of this attack is related to Althusser's accusation that history is necessarily a form of empiricism in as far as it is produced by empirical techniques of investigation. His position has been carried to its logical conclusions by certain of his followers, in this case British, when they write 'Marxism, as a theoretical and political practice, gains nothing from its association with historical writing and historical research. The study of history is not only scientifically but also politically valueless' (Hindess and Hirst, 1975). From this it follows that theory is all important, and more crucially, that theoretical formulations are not related to the objects of their study. As Althusser writes, 'We should say the same of the science which concerns us most particularly – historical materialism. It has been possible to apply Marx's theory with success because it is "true"; it is not true because it has been applied with success' (Althusser, 1970, p. 59). Theory for Althusser, therefore, is bound to precede application; moreover that theory is in no way related to the question of its application to the raw materials of history itself.

Thompson directs his attack on Althusser to what he sees as the fundamental misunderstanding of the way history is written or of the way in which theoretical formulations about history are arrived at. Central for Thompson is the fact that Althusser's position confuses the empirical mode of investigation common to all historians, with the ideological formation, empiricism. Consequently he is quite unable to envisage that kind of enquiry which seeks to examine one of the principal tenets of Thompson's position, namely, the importance of 'experience' in forming both social being and social consciousness. In putting his emphasis here, Thompson in fact returns implicitly to many of the points made in the introduction to *The Making of the English Working Class*. If class is a 'happening', the result of a given situation *and* of the way people respond to and modify that situation, then it is clearly essential that any theory should take into account the *dialogue* between social being and social consciousness. Althusser, Thompson argues, has no way of handling or of evaluating 'experience'; as a consequence his structuralism is static and certainly not in line with Marx's own interest in discovering the dynamic of society. This accusation of stasis is further reflected in Thompson's contention that 'Althusser's conceptual universe has no adequate categories to explain contradiction or change – or class struggle'. Hence Althusser is also silent about other important categories, 'among them "economic" and "needs"', and is therefore, 'unable to handle except in the most abstract and theoretical way, questions of value, culture – and political theory' (Thompson, 1978, p. 197).

It is obvious that Thompson is not arguing against theory as such, but against a kind of theorising which he regards as fundamentally detrimental to the practice of the historian. He is in fact at pains to elaborate his own theory of historical materialism which again takes up many of the themes made both implicitly and explicity in his earlier writings. The originality of his contribution lies in the fact that, while his work is firmly rooted in the 'material', Thompson avoids the pitfalls of vulgar Marxism and of rigid economic determinism, in order to provide a theoretical position which is sufficiently flexible to allow precisely for that dialogue between social being and social consciousness which is at the centre of his insistence on the category of 'experience'. The significance of 'experience' is clearly stated:

> Experience walks in without knocking at the door, and announces deaths, crises of subsistence, trench warfare, unemployment, inflation, genocide. People starve: their survivors think in new ways about the market. People are imprisoned: in prison they meditate in new ways about the law.

And the relationship between social being, social consciousness and experience is made equally clear:

> changes take place within social being which give rise to changed *experience*: and this experience is determining, in the sense that it exerts pressures upon existing social consciousness, proposes new questions, and affords much of the material which the more elaborated intellectual exercises are about. (Thompson, 1978, pp. 200–1)

Such passages provide a persuasive theory of historical materialism, which is intended to explain historical change at all levels, encompassing both what is given in any situation and what is susceptible to the agency of man. It thus attempts to overcome that apparent dichotomy between agency and determination, and to provide a subtle and flexible theory of the process of historical change.

Thompson is not, of course, without his critics. For many, his category of 'experience' is both too subtle and too flexible. While accepting as welcome Thompson's attempt to refute the Althusserian position, where classes become mere 'bearers' of the historical process and the historical process itself a process 'without a subject', critics have argued that 'experience' must of necessity contain both real and ideological elements and that the use of a single category for what is in reality a highly complex process of interweaving is more likely to confuse than to illuminate (Hall, 1981; Johnson, 1981). In particular, Thompson has been accused of 'creeping culturalism' in the weight he has given to agency and consciousness within the historical process through the adoption of the category of 'experience' (Anderson, 1980). Thompson himself, in a reply to his critics, has attempted to refine his use of 'experience', arguing that it can be divided between 'experience 1' (lived experience) and 'experience 11' (perceived experience), and that 'experience 1' 'exerts a pressure on the whole field of consciousness [which] cannot be indefinitely diverted, postponed, falsified or suppressed by ideology' (1981, p. 406). This defence, while attempting to meet the central problem of the relationship between structural conditions and individual consciousness, is scarecely adequate at a formal level, however. As Stuart Hall has commented, 'You do not facilitate the difficult process of thinking the relation *between* two terms by naming them with the *same* concept' (Hall, 1981, p. 384).

At an even more fundamental level, Thompson has been accused of paying inadequate attention to Marx's own definition of historical materialism, the thesis that the contradiction between the forces of production and the relations of production is the deepest spring of long term historical change. In particular it has been argued that the category of 'experience', in addition to the other problems which it presents, provides no clear dynamic of change in the way Marx's insistence on the laws of motion of capital do (Anderson, 1980). This criticism also clearly embraces Thompson's view of class, rooted for him in consciousness rather than in man's 'objective place in the network of ownership relations' (Cohen, 1978, p. 73). In the case of both accusations, Thompson is faced by the more traditional face of Marxism; his defence is clearly that in formulating new categories he is not attempting to override these views but rather to find ways of interrogating historical evidence in areas where the traditional Marxist, largely dominated by the emphasis on political economy, has few and inadequate tools at his disposition.

For the moment the debate has subsided, at least in part because Althusser's more extreme positions have been generally considered to be untenable and Thompson's polemic has therefore lost a good deal of its sting. Indeed the ramifications of the debate have tended to centre more around Thompson's position (socialist–humanist or Marxist?) than around the original subject of the argument. Clearly no solution has been reached, even if the various positions taken up within the debate have been clarified through the process of discussion. As Anderson has remarked, 'The actual terrain tilled by the historian lies somewhere between a confinement to structural changes and an infinity of human behaviour. It is not a matter of reproach that neither Thompson nor Althusser should have resolved one of the oldest and most obdurate puzzles in the philosophy of history' (Anderson, 1980, p. 14). Yet the discussion itself has clearly been of great value, precisely because it has served to indicate to a general audience the problems involved in the writing of history, and the particular contribution which Marxism is able to make in tackling those problems. And, within the general confusion, advances have certainly been made. That Marxism-as-system which relied heavily on economic determinism and which was characteristic of much early Marxist history has clearly been superceded by a far more sophisticated approach to the phenomenon of historical change. The encounter with structuralist–functionalist interpretations of society has been beneficial in helping Marxists define better their attitude to the fundamental structures of society, but equally it has forced Marxists to stress that where structuralists and functionalists tend to be static in their analysis of society, Marxism is capable of explaining the springs of historical change. The virtue of Marxism would seem to be, therefore, that it is capable of explaining both the static and the changing within society. This recognition, in no way a product of the present debate but made more generally evident by it, has led to greater attention being paid to the relationship between base and superstructure and to the general problem, evident throughout Thompson's work, of the determinants and the role of consciousness in producing historical change.

4.6 MARXIST HISTORY TODAY

What, then, can be said in conclusion about the place of Marxism in the study of history today? No definitive answer can be given to this question, precisely because, as the pages above indicate, the theories of Marxists themselves with regard to their practice are still – necessarily – a matter of discussion and debate. But certain points can be made. That illusion of 'value free' history so dear to the British school of historiography, for so long dominated by liberal and purely empiricist ideas, has clearly been shattered during the last twenty-five years. This is in no way to say, of course, that Marxism has become the dominant influence within the British historical tradition – far from it – but it is to say that even non-Marxists no longer find it possible to ignore questions of methodology and in particular to avoid asking themselves questions about the way they interrogate their evidence. This may be in part a consequence of a general decline in confidence in the liberal values of a post-imperial power, but it has certainly also been a partial result of the discussion which Marxist methodology has provoked within the British academic tradition.

Secondly it has to be said that Marxism itself has seen a radical change in its emphases over recent years. That triumphalistic progressivism characteristic of certain of the historians of the 1930s and 1940s has given way to a vision of change which is far less convinced of the evolutionary march of history in a positive direction. Attention is now paid less to the high points of the struggles of the working class, fulfilling as it seemed its historical mission, and more to the less obviously central subjects of working class development, such as the role of the aristocracy of labour or of the lumpen-proletariat. This has represented in fact an abandonment of any linear view of history and a recognition that, while the materialist explanation of cause remains valid, the various elements of historical enquiry may not necessarily combine to form any single unified picture. In part this has represented a strength in as far as it has permitted a much greater diversification of enquiry than was the case when labour history remained central. Studies of family, crime, the role of women in society, now concern the Marxist historian much more nearly (Fox-Genovese, 1983). But the abandoning of any linear view of the progress of history is also indicative of the state of Marxist studies in history today; for, if the vitality of the school of younger Marxist historians cannot be put in doubt, the theoretical position which inspires them is undoubtedly less homogeneous than it has been in the past. Far from being a set system, therefore, Marxism has become for the historian a point of departure which can lead in diverse directions, many of which were until recently no more than on the edge of Marxist analysis. There are many virtues in this increased flexibility from the point of view of historical study, but not the least is perhaps the fact that a less rigidly linear Marxism offers more points of contact with non-Marxist writers.

And this, for a methodology which has until recently been shunned by the majority of British historians, is of great importance.

GUIDE TO FURTHER READING

Interesting essays, which provide a good introduction to the subject (and on which the first sections of this essay are largely based), are Hobsbawm (1972), Stedman Jones (1972) and Samuel (1980). Samuel's article is still to be completed and the second part should be a valuable contribution if pitched at the same level as the first. Thompson (1978) is, of course, essential to the understanding of current polemics, and there are interesting contributions to the debate from Hall (1981), Johnson (1981; 1982) and McLennan (1981), and a lively rejoinder from Thompson himself (1981). Anderson (1980) makes some acute observations on the state of British Marxist historiography and further defines his position in a more recent work (1983). A good point of comparison with much of the above is provided by the cogent and forceful work of Cohen (1978), even if this study represents a more orthodox approach to Marxism. For those interested in reading history, rather than historiographical and theoretical debates, Thompson (1968) is an essential starting point, while Samuel (1975; 1977) and White (1980) show the strengths of the History Workshop approach to history. An excellent bibliography on women's history can be found in Fox-Genovese (1983).

REFERENCES

Althusser, L. (1969), *For Marx* (London: Allen Lane Penguin).
—— (1970), *Reading Capital* (London: New Left Books).
Anderson, P. (1980), *Arguments within English Marxism* (London: Verso).
—— (1983), *In the Tracks of Historical Materialism* (London: Verso).
Cohen, G. (1978), *Karl Marx's Theory of History: a Defence* (Oxford: Clarendon Press).
Foster, J. (1974), *Class Struggle and the Industrial Revolution* (London: Methuen).
Fox-Genovese, E. (1982), 'Placing Women's History in History', *New Left Review*, 133, pp. 5–29.
Gramsci, A. (1971), *Selections from the Prison Notebooks* (London: Lawrence & Wishart).

—— (1977), *Selections from Political Writings 1910–1920* (London: Lawrence & Wishart).
—— (1978), *Selections from Political Writings 1921–1926* (London: Lawrence & Wishart).
Hall, S. (1981), 'In Defence of Theory', in R. Samuel (ed.), *People's History and Socialist Theory* (London: Routledge & Kegan Paul) pp. 378–85.
Hill, C. (1940), *The English Revolution* (London: Lawrence & Wishart).
—— (1949), *The Good Old Cause: the English Revolution of 1640–1660* (London: Lawrence & Wishart).
—— (1958), *Oliver Cromwell 1658–1968* (London: Routledge & Kegan Paul).
Hilton, R. (1947), *The Economic Development of Some Leicestershire Estates in the 14th and 15th Centuries* (Oxford University Press).
Hindess, B. and Hirst, P. (1975), *Pre-capitalist Modes of Production* (London: Routledge & Kegan Paul).
Hobsbawm, E. J. (1948), *Labour's Turning Point 1880–1900* (London: Lawrence & Wishart).
—— (1962), *The Age of Revolution: Europe 1789—1848* (London: Weidenfeld & Nicolson).
—— (1972), 'Karl Marx's Contribution to Historiography' in R. Blackburn (ed.), *Ideology in Social Science* (Glasgow: Fontana/Collins) pp. 265–83.
Johnson, R. (1981), 'Against Absolutism', in R. Samuel (ed.), *People's History and Socialist Theory* (London: Routledge & Kegan Paul) pp. 386–96.
—— (1982) 'Reading for the Best Marx: History Writing and Historical Abstraction', in R. Johnson, G. McLennan, B. Schwarz, D. Sutton (eds), *Making Histories* (London: Hutchinson) pp. 153–201.
Levi-Strauss, C. (1965), *Anthropologie structurale* (Paris: Plon).
Marx, K. (1973), 'The Eighteenth Brumaire of Louis Bonaparte', in *Surveys from Exile* (Harmondsworth: Penguin) pp. 143–249.
Marx, K. and Engels, F. (1971), *Articles on Britain* (Moscow: Progress).
McLennan, G. (1982), 'E. P. Thompson and the Discipline of Historical Context', in R. Johnson, G. McLennan, B. Schwarz, D. Sutton (eds), *Making Histories* (London: Hutchinson) pp. 96–130.
—— (1982), 'Philosophy and History: Some Issues in Recent Marxist Theory', in *ibid*, pp. 133–52.
Samuel, R. (ed.) (1975), *Village Life and Labour* (London: Routledge & Kegan Paul).
—— (ed.) (1977), *Miners, Quarrymen and Saltworkers* (London: Routledge & Kegan Paul).
—— (1980), 'Sources of Marxist History', *New Left Review*, 120, pp. 21–96.
—— (ed.) (1981), *People's History and Socialist Theory* (London: Routledge & Kegan Paul).
Stedman Jones, G. (1971), *Outcast London* (Oxford University Press).
—— (1972), 'History: The Poverty of Empiricism', in R. Blackburn (ed.), *Ideology in Social Science* (Glasgow: Fontana/Collins) pp. 96–115.
Thompson, E. P. (1965), 'The Peculiarities of the English', in R. Miliband and J. Saville (eds), *The Socialist Register*, 2; reprinted in E. P. Thompson, *The Poverty of Theory*.

—— (1968), *The Making of the English Working Class*, 2nd edn (Harmondsworth: Penguin).
—— (1978), *The Poverty of Theory and Other Essays* (London: Merlin).
—— (1981), 'The Politics of Theory', in R. Samuel (ed.), *People's History and Socialist Theory* (London: Routledge & Kegan Paul) pp. 396–408.
White, J. (1980), *Rothschild Buildings: Life in an East End Tenement Block 1887–1920* (London: Routledge & Kegan Paul).

5 Social Theory*

JOHN URRY

5.1 SOME THEMES IN MARX AND ENGELS' SOCIAL THEORY

There is no doubt whatsoever that the writings of Marx and Engels represent a colossal intellectual achievement; they are arguably the most significant single contribution to the analysis of the social relations characteristic of industrial capitalist societies. Their works dwarf those of later Marxists and of later social analysts. Their contribution is even more remarkable given the fact that it was produced in something of an intellectual vacuum. No contemporary of theirs either shared or even understood most of their work, and many of their writings were unpublished when Marx died in 1883 (see Anderson, 1976, ch. 1). Clearly there was an important political context for this work, but even this was intermittent, and indeed their work was produced *before* either the organisation of large industrial working classes into trade unions, or the emergence of the major socialist/social democratic political parties.

Three features of their writings are of particular relevance to contemporary social theory. First, there is the method of 'critique'. This involves working through existing conceptions and theories and identifying their inadequacies, but it also involves both the understanding of the social relations and class interests which gave rise to such conceptions, and the attempt to preserve certain positive features of this earlier work within the newly derived theory (see Sayer, 1981). In particular, Marx and Engels subjected classical political economy to such a critique. They

---

* I am very grateful for the comments of Nick Abercrombie, Zyg Barański, Scott Lash, Larry Ray, John Short and Sylvia Walby on the first draft of this chapter.

criticised those theories which commenced analysis from a hypothetical isolated individual (the 'Robinson Crusoe' of some classical economics), or from typical individuals whose needs, abilities and preferences are presumed to be independent of the social relations within which they live and work. Such 'individualistic' conceptions, which resulted from the emerging liberal capitalism of 19th-century Britain, were criticised by Marx in terms of his materialist conception of history. This involves the view, not merely that there is a material world comprised of matter or dependent upon matter for its existence, but that this world is itself created through human labour. It is labour, the objectifying of oneself in material objects, which is the means by which human beings create themselves as truly human and distinguish themselves from animals. These human powers are developed through these processes of labour which serve to transform nature. They are necessarily social activities, formed in and through either direct or indirect social relations with others (see Avineri, 1968; Rubin, 1972).

Marx further argues that these social relations are historically variable — in other words, different forms in which labour produces material objects give rise to further distinctive sets of political, social and ideological relations. It is therefore incorrect to postulate unchanging economic laws which are applicable to all societies (see also Mohun, ch. 2). For example, Marx criticised the utilitarian theory of Jeremy Bentham for assuming that 'the modern petty bourgeois, especially the English petty bourgeois, is the normal man' and that 'whatever is useful to this peculiar kind of normal man . . . is useful in and of itself' (Marx, 1976, p. 759ff, originally published in 1867). It is incorrect to develop laws of economic and social life based on the workings of a single variety, for example, that of 19th-century capitalist Britain. Moreover, Marx argued that the specific *social* relations of material production govern the manner in which *things* enter into the process of production. In capitalist societies, a machine like the spinning jenny is only to be viewed as capital because of its specific function within capitalist relations of production, that is, the relations between capital, on the one hand, and wage-labour, on the other. The properties of any group of workers or of any piece of machinery are not natural but stem from the particular social relations of production within which they are located. And further, Marx argued that much conventional analysis, which focused either on the isolated *individual*, or on the *natural* productivity of labour or capital, was fundamentally flawed because it concentrated upon 'superficial' or 'phenomenal' features of social and economic life, and failed to penetrate to the deeper, underlying 'real relations' (see Geras, 1971; Cohen, 1972; and Mepham, 1972). This argument is supported both by the general claim that no science could proceed if appearances (for example, air as an undifferentiated substance) were not explained in terms of the real relations (air as in fact made up predominantly of oxygen and nitrogen), and by the specific claim that appearances and reality diverge under capitalist relations because of the fetishism of the commodity-form. Under capitalism people are not connected to each other directly, but indirectly through the transfer of things, commodities, for exchange. People enter production relations as commodity-owners and this attributes to these things a distinct social form (see Rubin, 1972). At the same time, however, these relations between things (capitalist 'markets') constrain and coerce individuals who both fail to see that such determining relations between things are in effect the exchange of different amounts of labour-time, and who improperly attribute natural properties to material objects rather than tracing 'the formation of the social forms of things from the production relations among people' (Rubin, 1972, p. 25).

The second major contribution made by Marx and Engels to contemporary social theory is in terms of their analysis of these different 'production relations among people' or 'modes of production'. In *Capital* Marx laid bare the laws of motion of the capitalist mode (CMP), laws which derive from two absolutely central contradictions. There is that between, on the one hand, the *material* process of production, involving the progressive development of the productive forces, the economising of labour through technical innovation, and the massive expansion in the physical production of commodities by means of other commodities; and, on the other hand, the *social* process of production with the dominance of valorisation, production for profit rather than for need, the heightened fragmentation and dehumanisation of labour, and the dominance of machinery and of the objective laws of capitalist production. Hence, the development of the capitalist mode of production entails an increase in the mastery of nature by human labour, but this mastery is realised in a distorted, dehumanising and contradictory social form (see

Cohen, 1978, ch. 4). There is the contradiction structured by the appropriation by capital of the surplus-labour in the form of value which has been created by the labour of the workers (on value theory, see Mohun, ch. 2). Wage-labourers are forced to sell their labour-power to one capitalist or another for as much as possible, while capitalists are forced to maximise the extraction of surplus-value from the workers employed. Hence, capital, which consists of a band of 'hostile brothers' competing with each other, and wage labour are placed in implacable opposition to each other and, although the form of this may vary, the contradiction cannot be overcome without a change in the dominant social relations. Marx argued in 1847 that even if in the long run both profit and wages rise, there is still conflict between the two, since 'there is at the same time a widening of the social chasm that divides the worker from the capitalist, an increase in the power of capital over labour, a greater dependence of labour on capital' (Marx, 1933, p. 39). In the *1844 Manuscripts* Marx analysed how this domination of capital resulted in the alienation of the labourer from the means of production, from the work process, from the products of labour, and from the very species-being of labour itself which is to realise one's potentialities for creative and authentically social labour (1959b; and see Avineri, 1968; Ollman, 1971; see also Barański, ch. 9).

Thirdly, Marx and Engels contributed to the analysis of the social and political relations of various forms of society. They argued, in particular, that it is necessary to transcend the illusion that the object of philosophy is philosophy itself. Traditional materialist philosophies (including Feuerbach, for example) had all lacked the activist, practical element which is necessary in order not merely to comprehend the world but to change it. However, the precise implication of this proposed unity of theory and practice was left unclear, since philosophy would only be able to shape a new form of society, once it was sophisticated enough to comprehend reality satisfactorily. Certainly Marx wished to argue that it is through the practical activity of workers, rather than mere philosophical contemplation, that social change will come about. It is the organisation of workers that transforms them from a class-in-themselves to a class-for-themselves. The very process of association is itself educative, as workers come to *know* that they are exploited and that the present form of society is historically contingent. Other workers come to be seen not as competitors but as fellow workers. Theory or philosophy should develop out of these struggles and not just from the economic conflict but especially from the *political* movement. The working class would be literally forced to defend itself as a class and, in so doing, to bring about the transformations necessary to redeem all of humanity. Marx considered that the increasing concentration of workers in progressively centralised factories and cities, reductions in the skill content of an increasingly homogenised capitalist labour process, the disappearance of the petty bourgeoisie, the increasing polarisation between labour and capital, the growing relative immiseration of workers, and the heightening of the crisis-ridden tendencies of the capitalist economy spreading worldwide, would all strengthen the power of the working class through revolution to realise the socialised potentialities which are latent within capitalism (see Avineri, 1968, ch. 6).

Central to Marx's analysis here was that of ideology; however, he did not maintain a consistent theory, presenting both a fetishism-based theory and a class-based theory (see Urry, 1981, ch. 4; more generally, see Larrain, 1983). And even within the latter there are two different formulations employed (see Cohen, 1978; Larrain, 1979; Abercrombie, 1981). On the one hand, Marx said that it is social being that determines social consciousness, in other words, that each class through its relationship to the means of the production and its general conditions of existence develops a particular class culture or ideology. Different classes have distinctive 'social beings', different material circumstances, and hence different interests. They thus develop separate ideologies relating to the specific interests that they articulate. On the other hand, Marx said that the economic base produces a specific superstructure, a system of state and legal apparatuses, and forms of ideology that hold the society together. The 'real foundation' gives rise to a 'legal and political superstructure', and 'definite forms of social consciousness'. If we consider these forms of social consciousness we find that the ideas of 'the ruling class are in every epoch the ruling ideas'; thus 'the class which is the ruling material force of society, is at the same time its ruling intellectual force' (Marx and Engels, 1968, p. 61, originally published in 1846). Ideology in this scheme is viewed negatively, it functions to limit or frustrate the mobilisation of class practices; while in the first model it is viewed positively as the expression of class interests. Thus, the two metaphors 'being-consciousness' and 'base-superstructure', are not equivalent to each other and give rise to differing conceptions of ideology (see also Barański, ch. 9).

5.2 THE GOLDEN AGE

Marxist social thought from the death of Marx in 1883 to the death of Stalin in 1953 passed through first, what Kolakowski (1978) calls, a 'Golden Age' and then underwent the major 'Breakdown' under Stalin. It was only to revive again in a distinctively different and more academic form after Stalin and especially after 1968. Very brief mention will now be made of a few of the important contributions to social theory which were developed in the 'Golden Age' – they can be divided into the economic, the political, and the ideological.

Apart from the studies at the end of the 19th century of agrarian transformation by Kautsky (1970) and by Lenin (1964; for both, see Pearce, ch. 3), the most important innovations in economic analysis involved the investigation of the global and structural changes in the CMP. Rosa Luxembourg maintained that Marx had failed to analyse satisfactorily the problem of overproduction, since he had believed that compound reproduction would continue with capitalists collectively providing the market for the means of production produced by each other (1951). Luxembourg maintained that this was not the case and that there had to be markets external to both departments of production capable of absorbing commodities at a rate consistent with the pattern of accumulation. She thought that this would be provided by the non-capitalist market in the rest of the world and this would enable the realisation of the profits of mature capitalism. However, as capitalist production spread to more and more of the world economy then this would progressively exhaust these possibilities and hence would lead to the breakdown of capitalism on a world scale (see also Smith, ch. 1).

Rudolf Hilferding produced in 1910 the first systematic analysis of finance-capitalism (1981). He argued that, as capital was increasingly concentrated, it became progressively more difficult to ensure sufficient mobility of capital for an average of profit to be secured. Banks therefore developed to mobilise capital on a large scale. They minimised competition between units of productive capital, they maximised profits, and they developed industrial monopolies. 'Finance-capital' was then taken to be a new form of the CMP with productive capital subordinated to bank-capital, and with a financial oligarchy as the new ruling class (see Thompson, 1977, for further discussion). Lenin relied both on this and on J. A. Hobson's *Imperialism* to argue in 1916 that the highest stage of capitalism emerged with the export of capital, the division of the world amongst monopolistic leagues of international capitalists, and the territorial division of the world amongst the Great Powers (Lenin, 1968). 'Imperialism' was seen as the monopoly stage of capitalism which *contra* Kautsky's 'ultra-imperialism' heightened the likelihood of military conflict between the monopoly-dominated nation-states, encouraged the working class to challenge the imperialist structuring of the world economy, and strengthened the likelihood of the imperialist chain breaking at the 'weakest link' (see Lane, 1981, ch. 2).

While these economic analyses built upon the legacy of Marx and Engels, there was no similar corpus of political work on which to build (see discussion in Anderson, 1976, ch. 1). Of the three most important sets of writings on this latter question, those by Lenin on the vanguard role of the revolutionary party have of course been the most historically influential (see 1963, originally published in 1901–2, and 1969, originally published in 1917). He argued that the party could not be regarded as merely the servant of a spontaneous workers' movement, but must function as the vanguard and organiser bringing Marxist analysis *to* that movement. The party would be comprised of revolutionary intellectuals and constituted as a small, centralised and disciplined organisation (on the origins of this notion see Kolakowski, 1978, p. 389). Clearly such a political organisation was ideally suited to challenging the Tsarist State in Russia, but Lenin failed to provide much analysis of the kind of political organisation appropriate to challenging certain West European states. This absence was clearest in *State and Revolution*, where Lenin's emphasis upon the unevenness of imperialist development should have made him more aware that there would be important variations in the appropriate political organisation of the working class (see Anderson, 1976, p. 116; Lane, 1981, pp. 62–3). Trotsky also analysed the Russian Revolution in terms of combined and uneven development, in other words, that societies do not follow each other in the same order, they develop unevenly, and that elements from different 'stages' of development may be combined to produce a particular 'correlation of forces'. Writing of 1905, Trotsky talked of the contrast between 'the primitive savagery of the northern forests, where men eat raw fish and worship trees, to the most modern social relations of the capitalist city', and of the 'most concentrated industry in Europe, based on the most backward agriculture in Europe' (1972, p. 44; originally published in 1910). A crucial consequence of this situation was that there were not separate stages of revolution, but that there was a process of 'permanent revolution' derived from the particular complex of uneven and combined social forces (see Knie-Paz, 1978). Gramsci dealt specifically with these differences between the forms of struggle appropriate to the frontal confrontation, or war of movement in the East, especially Russia, and the protracted, multi-frontal war of position in the West. In both cases he argued the need to analyse the particular balance of coercion and consent within a particular conjuncture, and the necessity for the proletariat to establish hegemonic leadership within civil society (1971); and see the essays in Mouffe, 1979; Buci-Glucksmann, 1980). Gramsci provided a most penetrating analysis of the changing character of Western societies:

> The massive structures of the modern democracies both as State organisations, and as complexes of associations in civil society, constitute for the art of politics as it were the 'trenches' and the permanent fortifications of the front in the war of position: they render merely 'partial' the element of movement which before used to be 'the whole' of war etc. (1971, pp. 242–3)

The main contribution to a social theory of ideology in this period was published in 1923 by Lukács in his analysis of reification (1971). He argued that the essential feature of capitalism was the fetishism of commodities, the main effect being to reify social relations which acquire a 'phantom objectivity'. They take on the appearance of autonomous, all-embracing and rational relations between things. Society and history appear not as the products of social activity, but as alien and impersonal forces determining human behaviour. In particular, there is a process of rationalisation in which each individual worker becomes a merely mechanical element incorporated into a mechanical system. This spread of rationalisation and calculability extends to all spheres of social life penetrating the organisation of science and the 'very depths of man's physical and psychic nature' (Lukács, 1971, p. 101). The only social basis for overcoming reification is provided by the proletariat whose imputed, if not actual class consciousness is true, because it is both the product and the producer of history. Its interests are truly universal and, because it is at the very centre of bourgeois society, it can and will develop the knowledge of its entire workings (see also Barański, ch. 9).

5.3 CONTEMPORARY DEBATES

Since the death of Stalin in 1953 there has been an enormous explosion of Marxist work and debate within Western capitalist societies and the Third World, but not in Eastern Europe (see Bahro, 1978, for an important exception). As a result such work is to an important extent the product of defeat rather than of success. Moreover, it has been located particularly within Western universities where, as Anderson shows, professional philosophers have played an extraordinarily important role in its development (1976, pp. 49–50). Partly the growth of such work was activated by the general availability, in particular, of Marx's *Economic and Philosophical Manuscripts* (EPM) and the *Grundrisse*. A profound discussion developed during the Long Boom over the 'alienating' character of work and more general social experience; while the widespread collapse of the Western economies since the early seventies encouraged a more economically focused debate over the changing character of the 'exploitative' relations of capitalist society. It is, moreover, important to realise that the growth of such work and related political practice resulted from the emergence of a substantial new social grouping deriving its power from the possession of higher education credentials and having interests partly at odds with those of both workers and capitalists (see Abercrombie and Urry, 1983, Part 2, on the 'service class'). Partly this explains why much of the debate has been concerned with the nature of the 'capitalist state' (see Jessop, 1981) and with the forms of 'bourgeois ideology' (see Larrain, 1983), topics discussed elsewhere in this book (see ch. 6, Dunleavy). In the following analysis of 'social theory' I will consider: (a) methodology; (b) the labour process and social class; and (c) problematising class. This last section will contain various suggestions as to future topics and areas of debate.

5.3.1 Methodology

One important tradition which kept alive a kind of pessimistic Marxism during the 'Breakdown' between the late 1920s and the 1950s was the Frankfurt School or Critical Theory (see Jay, 1973; Held, 1980). In *Negative Dialectics* Adorno elaborated the concept of 'non-identity' thinking (1973). This involves an immanent criticism of the object, for example, by examining contradictions between the object's idea of itself and its actual existence, and between the object and the concept that is formed of it (see 1973). According to Adorno, Marx's analysis of commodity fetishism well illustrates the method of 'negative dialectics'. This is because Marx showed that there is a false identity between 'things' and certain 'social properties'. This fetishism results from the universalisation of the exchange principle, which in turn stems from an identity between the non-identical (that is, social classes). By penetrating the appearance of society and perceiving the underlying non-identical social relations of production, negative dialectics points towards the values and potentialities at present unfulfilled within existing objects. Marcuse, although more influenced by the *EPM* than *Capital*, takes up similar themes, especially in his notion of the dialectic; in *Reason and Revolution* he says that the dialectical pattern 'represents, and is thus "the truth of", a world permeated by negativity, a world in which everything is something other than it *really* is, and in which opposition and contradiction constitute the laws of progress' (1960, p. 49). This progress results from the fact that: '*All things are contradictory in themselves* . . . "Contradiction is the root of all movement and life", all reality is self-contradictory. Motion especially, external movement as well as self-movement, is nothing but "existing contradiction" ' (1960, p. 147). In *One-Dimensional Man* Marcuse elaborated a sustained critique of one-dimensional society and thought (1964; and see *Eros and Civilisation*, 1966, for an attempted synthesis of Marx and Freud). Such one-dimensional forms are characterised by a spuriously happy consciousness based upon false needs and the belief that the real is rational, that there is no separation between essence and appearance, that there is no such thing as 'dialectical logic', and that technological rationality is a new and all-pervasive form of subordination and control. This critique of technology, and of the positivist philosophy of science which buttresses it, has been further developed by Habermas (see 1971; and the papers in Adey and Frisby, 1976). Amongst much else, he has attempted to recast historical materialism in terms of the forms of interaction and communication characteristic of different stages of historical evolution, as well as the typical modes of organisation of work and production (see 1979; and Thompson and Held, 1982). He has also discussed the concept of a 'legitimation crisis' characterising late 20th-century advanced capitalist societies, whereby the state increasingly fails to attract and maintain popular support (see 1976).

However, the most historically influential development within Marxist social theory within the recent period (since 1956 until the late 1970s) has been 'Althusserianism', and especially the methodological and theoretical debates initiated by Althusser within, and on the margins of, the French Communist Party (see 1969 and 1971; and also Althusser and Balibar, 1970). Central to Althusser's approach was his notion of a problematic, the system of basic interrelated concepts which fit together to form the conceptual framework of a particular science. Such a system has as its focus a given object which is constituted in thought. Any such problematic is determined as much by the questions that it neglects as by the questions that it poses. An individual term only acquires meaning when it is located within such a problematic; and the same term, for example, alienation, embedded in a different problematic will have a different and possibly non-scientific meaning. Althusser was particularly concerned to elaborate the 'epistemological break' in Marx's writings, that watershed when Marx first employed the distinction between labour and labour-power and the concept of surplus-value. Althusser viewed the 'discovery' of the latter as analogous to the discovery of oxygen in chemistry; in each case the conceptual innovation ensures scientificity. Moreover, he argued that the texts written by a single author do not necessarily exhibit a unity. Each text has to be 'read' symptomatically, so that it becomes possible to identify the underlying system or problematic which is working within the text to produce a particular surface effect (cp. Macherey's methods of analysis, Barański, ch. 9). The problematic in each text produced by a single author will not necessarily be the same.

Althusser, and 'Althusserians' more generally have identified and criticised the 'empiricist' character of many apparently scientific texts. Empiricism, according to Althusser, is based on the following three propositions: (a) the starting point for science is the given, observable, concrete object; (b) knowledge is to be seen as the extraction of the *essence* of this real object by abstraction and idealisation; and (c) models are developed to represent this essence that has been abstracted from the inessential features of the concrete object. In opposition to this, Althusser argued in *For Marx* and *Reading Capital* that there is a complete disjuncture between real processes and thought processes, and that knowledge is situated entirely within thought. Theoretical work proceeds from a raw material, it consists of a process of production, by which a given raw material is transformed into knowledge. However, the raw material involved is not the real concrete, but rather the pre-existing theories, notions, information, etc. in the field. Thus, if we take any particular scientific concept, for example, the feudal mode of production, this is the product, not of generalisation from historically given feudal societies, but is rather the product of theoretical work, from the place that concepts occupy in a given and determinate field of concepts. This then involves theoretical forms of proof and demonstration; and science can never be a question of matching the given real with the theoretical.

It is furthermore not merely a question of choosing between alternative epistemologies, whether empiricist or scientific. This is because there are no pure concrete objects, or elements of experience, or facts of history. There is nothing that is simply given to knowledge, since even what appear to be the more elementary facts, are in essence the product of definite practices (ideological/ scientific) conducted under specific conditions. Facts, so-called, are thus produced and never simply exist. What is essential is the *scientific* production of 'facts' and 'theories', and this involves rigorous and explicit theoretical work as opposed to non-theoretical 'empiricist' ideology. For example, Poulantzas subjected Miliband's *The State in Capitalist Society* to such a critique, since it confronted pluralist political science on its own empiricist terrain, rather than developing a rigorously scientific theory of the capitalist state and of its objective relations with other structures within capitalist social formations (see Miliband, 1969; Poulantzas, 1969 and 1973; and Althusser's 1976 self-criticism of his 'theoreticist' tendencies).

Althusserians maintained that there were two levels of theoretical work: first, the theory of different modes of production – each such mode consists of an articulated combination of economic, political and ideological structures; and second, the concept of each particular 'real-concrete object' – that is, of each social formation (or society) in which two or more modes are always present and in which the relations of dominance/subordination between the different modes are analysed. In each social formation there are, as mentioned above, three different levels or structures; these structures are not to be seen as given essences which enter into external relations with each other, but constitute an articulated combination in which each presupposes the other two. Any particular social formation is highly complex and Althusserians specifically reject economistic theories in which changes in the economic base are taken to produce more or less equivalent changes in the super-structure. They especially object to those theories in which developments in the economic base are seen as propelling all societies inexorably towards a predetermined classless end-state. Each of these three structures has its own specific effectiveness and relative autonomy, and it is possible to develop theories of each of them; for example, in *Political Power and Social Classes* we find Poulantzas' regional theory of the political structure. What though, it may be asked, remains of the conventional Marxist doctrine that the economy is determinant in the last instance? Althusserians distinguish between determination and dominance, so that while the economic is always determinant, it is not always the dominant instance within a given structure. Rather, it determines which structure, the economic, or the political, or the ideological, is dominant within a given mode or social formation. In simple societies, Godelier argues that ideology in the form of kinship is dominant (1967), while in competitive capitalism Poulantzas maintains that economics is dominant, and that in monopoly capitalism it is politics, in the form of the state, which is dominant (1973).

The final point to note here is that Althusserians typically treated agents as 'bearers' of the economic, political and ideological structures, a position which led to E. P. Thompson's critique in the *Poverty of Theory* (1976) (see also Corner, ch. 4). *Inter alia* Thompson argued that (a) Althusser inappropriately generalises from the manner in which philosophers work, that is through conceptual/theoretical critique, and ignores the historian's encounter with historical documentation; (b) Althusser does not distinguish properly between 'empiricism' and 'empirical method' so that while the former can be criticised the latter cannot, to do so is to prioritise the conceptual and is therefore idealist; (c) the concepts then of historical materialism should be properly seen as *historical*, as changing and changeable in relationship to historical process and investigation, hence *Capital* is the source of historical hypotheses, not the attainment of Marxist science; (d) Althusser in particular neglects the absolutely central category of *experience*, and especially of class experiences which arise at the intersection of determination and self-activity – as Thompson had earlier shown, classes make themselves as much as they are made (1968; and see Calhoun, 1982); (e) Althusser's much-vaunted anti-Stalinism is nothing of the kind (it is in fact a reconstructed Stalinism), especially since it is 'socialist humanism' which is taken by Althusser to constitute the 'main enemy' – Thompson argues that if we erroneously think of people as 'bearers' of structures, then we will act towards them as though their political activity does make little or no difference; and (f) Althusserianism has given rise to a remarkable obsession with the concept of the 'mode of production' which both ignores detailed historical work on different societies and reinforces an academic élitism in which even Philosophy is equated with the class struggle (it enables academics to 'engage in a harmless revolutionary psycho-drama' (1978, p. 378); for a discussion of Althusser and Thompson, see Johnson, 1979; Warde, 1982; on 'modes', see Taylor, 1979, in relation to development, and Delphy, 1977, in relation to gender inequalities).

It is ironic that two of the writers most taken to task by Thompson were Hindess and Hirst. In *Pre-Capitalist Modes of Production* they wrote the most distinctive contribution to Althusserianism in Britain (1975). However, within a couple of years they broke with that tradition arguing against, amongst other things, the concept of a 'mode of production' (and in favour of that of 'social formation'); the law of value; and the thesis that there are 'class-essences' which are merely waiting to be expressed, and that specific forms of political calculation and organisation are not of autonomous significance (1977; Cutler, Hindess, Hirst and Hussain, 1977 and 1978; and see also Hirst, 1976; Hindess, 1983). Indeed, in the UK at least, Althusserianism dislodged a previously pervasive economic reductionism, raised the general level of methodological debate, and legitimated a diversity of political struggles within each of the 'relatively autonomous' structures (see the journal *Politics and Power* on the last point).

Althusserianism also revived interest in Marx's later works and particularly in *Capital*, and this was especially so outside economics (which had always focused on that work anyway). Althusser's work redirected attention away from Marx's earlier 'humanist' writings and indeed from the notion that arguments for socialism are moral or ethical rather than scientific. In Britain this gave rise to two further sets of writings where Marx's scientific methodology, especially in his later works, has been explored. These are 'theoretical realism' and 'technological determinism'.

The former concerns a much more general debate about the nature of science and of 'the possibility of naturalism'. In Bhaskar it is also placed in the context of a controversial transcendental argument in which it is argued we have to reason from the effect, science, to the conditions of its existence, namely, that (a) there exists a world of enduring and transfactually active mechanisms (such as modes of production) which are independent of and prior to our knowledge of them, and (b) the knowledge yielded by science is indeed knowledge of (a) (see Bhaskar, 1975; 1979; Hillel-Ruben, 1977, pp. 101–2; O'Hagan, 1982, pp. 244–5). It is then argued that, since science does exist, so the conditions of its existence (a) and (b) must also exist. Thus science involves the description of these enduring and transfactually active mechanisms. Other 'realists' or 'theoretical realists' (Keat and Urry, 1975/1982; Benton, 1977; Sayer; 1979; Outhwaite, 1983; all influenced in part by Harré, 1971; Harré and Madden, 1975) do not accept this transcendental argument, but more generally argue for a modified naturalism. A realist science involves describing these enduring mechanisms whose powers are contingently realised in observable events. Ontologically there are, on the one hand, structures or mechanisms possessing certain powers, and, on the other hand, specific events which may be contingently recorded through what Bhaskar calls the 'transitive' concepts of science. Theoretical realism involves rejecting the claims that the 'observable' enjoys ontological and epistemological privilege, that science can be characterised in terms of the deductive-nomological or similar logical models, and that we should dispense with notions of natural necessity in favour of a roughly Humean concept of causation.

It has further been argued by theoretical realists that Marx's later writings represent one of the most substantial contributions to the establishment of a realist social science. There have been two main versions of this argument. On the one hand, Keat and Urry (1975) and Benton (1977) argue that Marx commences analysis through the development of the theory of different modes of production – each mode being conceptualised as a causally powerful structure based on a distinct mechanism of surplus-labour production and appropriation. Marx then analyses the articulation between these modes to explain the surface features of given societies, as he puts it, to reconstitute the concrete as a 'rich totality of many determinations and relations' (Marx, 1973, p. 100). It should be noted that this 'reconstitution' is highly complex, since the interdependence between causally powerful entities involves some modification of each entity (see Keat and Urry, 1982, pp. 245–6). Sayer, by contrast, argues against the importance of the concept of a mode of production (1981). He maintains that Marx always begins with the phenomenal appearances (not though as the basis of inductive generalisations) and then, through a dialectical critique, posits various mechanisms which would, if they existed, explain how and why the observed phenomena take the form that they do. Sayer thus emphasises the empirical, comparative and critical aspects of Marx's realism.

The most distinctive recent British contribution to Marxist social theory is G. A. Cohen's 'technological' interpretation of historical materialism (1978). He argues that the forces of production are to be categorically distinguished from the relations of production, that only the latter constitute the economic base of society, that the productive forces are primary, that these forces functionally explain the character of the economic relations, that capitalism develops because the productive forces cannot develop within the pre-existing structures, and that the superstructure has the character it does, because it confers stability on the production relations. Probably the most distinctive of Cohen's claims are that (a) Marxism's central explanatory propositions are 'functionalist', and (b) functionalism is a legitimate mode of explanation. (a) has been fairly systematically argued for within the literature on the capitalist state; while (b) is less usual and contradicts recent orthodoxy in social theory (see the debate between Cohen, 1982, and Elster, 1982). *Inter alia*, Cohen argues that, if we seek to explain a given social phenomenon in terms of its functional consequences, then it is unlikely that there are such a wide range of alternative phenomena that would have the *same* functional consequences as that phenomenon in *that* society. Indeed, if we were able to identify a phenomenon that did have roughly the same consequences, we might still be able to explain not the presence of the phenomenon itself, but rather why some phenomenon exists which does meet that particular function. In other words, we may be able to establish the need for a 'dominant ideology', but not for any *particular* 'dominant ideology' (1978, ch. 9; but see Abercrombie, Hill and Turner, 1980).

5.3.2 The Labour Process and Social Class

The last fifteen or so years have seen a most impressive mushrooming of Marxist-influenced analyses and studies of specific classes and class structures (see also Dunleavy, ch. 6; Short, ch. 7; Lumley and O'Shaughnessey, ch. 10). However, up to the publication of Braverman's *Labour and Monopoly Capital* in 1974, many of these were of a general sort concerned with explaining why revolutionary consciousness and action had not developed within the traditional working classes of Western Europe and the USA. There were a number of explanations advanced: (a) the growth of a labour aristocracy and the effects of this in converting the nascent labour movement to social democracy (see the critique of this position in Moorhouse, 1978); (b) the development of specific ideological formations resulting from the particular combination of landed and capitalist classes (on the 'peculiarities' of British development, see Anderson, 1964); (c) the strength of a more general 'dominant ideology' particularly working via the 'incorporation' of the worker through notions of individual achievement, equality of opportunity and the freedom of the individual (see Abercrombie, Hill and Turner, 1980, generally on such arguments); (d) the development of the welfare state, which has locked the working class into bureaucratised, individualised and oppressive structures of state provision (see

Ginsburg, 1979); (e) the emergence of a 'dual consciousness' amongst workers that was generally based on forms of 'pragmatic acceptance', and only occasionally on direct perception of 'class oppression' (see Blackburn, 1967); (f) and the decline in the importance of the old, manual, working class and the growth in significance of a new technical intelligentsia, the 'new working class' (see Gorz, 1967; Mallet, 1975; see Mann, 1973, on a number of these points). Generally speaking, Marxist studies of the workplace during this period re-emphasised the fundamentally 'alienating' quality of work (see for example, Friedmann, 1955; Beynon, 1973).

Braverman's discussion of the capitalist labour process transformed the terms of the analysis (see Braverman, 1974; 1976; Burawoy, 1978; Edwards, 1979; Littler; 1982, Wood, 1982). He argued that it is the accumulation of capital that fundamentally determines the organisation of the labour process, and in particular the tendency for labour to become progressively fragmented and deskilled, and for the work of 'conception' (mental labour) to be separated off from 'execution' (manual labour) and to be embodied within functionally separate management structures. These developments occur because of the tremendous savings in the cost of labour-power that capital can thereby obtain. Braverman demonstrates that through the so-called Babbage-principle, capital is progressively able to obtain *precisely* those quantities and qualities of labour-power that it in fact requires (see Babbage, 1832). The more that the labour process is fragmented, the greater the ability of capital to avoid purchasing 'unnecessarily' skilled labour to undertake deskilled work. Braverman proceeds to analyse the nature of 'monopoly capitalism' and the consequential forms of deskilling particularly of previous 'craft' occupations (see Cutler, 1978, on Braverman's over-emphasis on early capitalist labour as craft-based).

His thesis that the accumulation of capital is, through the processes of deskilling, generating a necessarily larger, less divided, and stronger working class has been challenged by a large number of theoretical and substantive analyses. *Inter alia*, it has been shown that (a) Braverman-type 'direct control' of the labour process is only one amongst a number of 'managerial strategies' (see Friedman, 1977; Edwards, 1979); (b) the employment of different strategies depends in part at least upon different forms of work organisation and resistance (see Friedman, 1977; Burawoy, 1978); (c) such forms of organisation have important effects in dividing the workforce – such divisions do not stem simply from the process of accumulation (see Penn, 1982); (d) there are crucially important new forms of skill and control which are generated by accumulation and which are not simply 'deskilled' (see Jones, 1982, on numerically controlled machine tools, for example); (e) there are important historical and comparative variations in the forms and degree of deskilling of the labour process through 'scientific management' (see Littler, 1982; Abercrombie and Urry, 1983, ch. 6); (f) Braverman underemphasises the internationalisation of the accumulation process, which means that the 'deskilled' labour force is divided up within spatially distinct national territories (see Fröbel, Heinrichs and Kreye, 1980; Abercrombie and Urry, 1983, ch. 4); and (g) there are absolutely crucial bases of working class division especially around gender and ethnicity which make any class homogeneity unlikely (on the former, see Hartmann, 1979; Walby, 1983; on the latter, see Rhodes and Pearn, 1981).

Possibly the most controversial section of Braverman's book concerns his arguments about the deskilling of the 'middle classes'. To some degree he elaborates here a view which goes back to Marx, who spelled out a number of processes by which 'the labour-power of these people is therefore devaluated with the progress of capitalist production' (Marx, 1959a, p. 300; and see Klingender, 1935). This 'proletarianisation' position has been further developed by Carchedi, who through a very complex analysis of the functions of what he calls 'global capital' and the 'collective labourer' elaborates the changing importance of different processes of proletarianisation (1977; Abercrombie and Urry, 1983, ch. 4). There are, though, a number of important studies which argue against any of these proletarianisation-theses-studies which commence from Marx's further comments about how the middle class will grow in size and how 'only one third of the population [will] take a direct part in material production, instead of two thirds as before' (Marx, 1919, p. 189; for a discussion of this, see Abercrombie and Urry, 1983, ch. 4). Nicolaus argued that such an expansion of unproductive workers is necessary in order to consume the ever-growing, absolute surplus generated by capitalist development (1967). Poulantzas maintained that there is a substantial 'new petty bourgeoisie', determined by economic, *and* political *and* ideological structures, and which has a class position at odds with both capital and labour (1975). Johnson argued that at least certain professions will be unlikely to be proletarianised; this is where their power rests on forms of knowledge which cannot be simply expressed and codified in technical terms – such 'indeterminate' bodies of knowledge characterise professions which are components of the capital function (1977). The Ehrenreichs extended the analyses of the professions to argue that there has developed, in the USA at least, a distinctive 'professional-managerial class' based upon the possession of a college degree, who function to reproduce capitalist culture and class relations. This new class has given rise to quite distinct forms of politics which disrupt previously structured politics between capital and labour (see Ehrenreichs, 1979a; 1979b; and Walker, 1979, more generally, as well as Abercrombie and Urry, 1983, chs 5, 7 and 8). Finally, E. O. Wright maintained that not all positions in the division of labour are class-positions – many are in fact to be viewed as 'contradictory class-locations' (1978).

5.3.3 Problematising Class

Although the studies very briefly summarised in the previous section vary considerably, they do share a number of assumptions: (a) that class relations are always the most important determinant of the social and political practices of a given society; (b) that each class possesses a distinct essence which ultimately will be realised; (c) that the organisation of at least capitalists and workers into distinct classes is relatively unproblematic, and that once they are established as a class-for-itself they simply remain as such; and (d) that these relations between classes transcend most spatial and historical variations within and between different capitalist societies.

However, a number of Marxist-influenced writers have recently challenged these assumptions in a variety of ways (see also Dunleavy, ch. 6; Short, ch. 7; Lumley and O'Shaughnessey, ch. 10). Firstly, it has been argued by Skocpol that revolutionary change cannot be understood simply in class terms, or indeed in ways in which the 'state' can ultimately be reduced to class (1979). She argues for a 'realist' and 'organisational' approach to the state, whereby states are *actual* organisations controlling or attempting to control territories and people. She argues that in the investigation of revolutionary change it is necessary to examine the contradictions within the existing potentially autonomous state and the international system of states, as well as the relationship between states and dominant/subordinate classes. She maintains that revolutions cannot occur simply because classes are organised 'for-themselves', or because a given state is no longer 'legitimate'. Revolutions only occur when the existing state, as part of an international system of interdependent states, collapses. Otherwise, a state can remain quite stable if its coercive organisations remain 'coherent and effective' (1979, p. 32).

Second, Przeworski amongst others argues that the basic assumptions of Marx's theory of class itself should be dispensed with (1977). This basic problematic involves defining the 'class-in-itself' at the level of the economic base, and the class-for-itself at the level of the 'superstructures' (and see Stark, 1980; Abercrombie and Urry, 1983. ch. 8). This position is erroneous because the economic structure does not produce unambiguous social classes 'superstructurally'. This is partly because the structural determinations are not in fact outside the class struggles which they are meant to explain. Indeed the nature of such struggles is such, that they in turn affect the very conditions which supposedly structure such struggles in the first place. Moreover, struggles are not just a question of 'releasing' or 'expressing' class's true essence, since much struggle in fact involves the very attempt to establish class as the relevant category of organisation and struggle. Class organisations will thus be temporally and spatially discontinuous, and in part underdetermined by the 'structures'. They will depend in part upon the dynamic interrelations between classes which are to a certain extent theoretically unpredictable (see Montgomery, 1979).

Third, much recent Marxist debate has been concerned with the conditions under which social classes are organised as collective actors. This issue was posed in a distinctive fashion by Olson, who argued that it was in a sense irrational for workers to engage in class actions since 'a worker who thought he would benefit from a "proletarian" government would not find it rational to risk his life and resources to start a revolution against the bourgeois government' (this is because of the 'free-rider' problem; see 1965, p. 106). Elster, in his highly original *Logic and*

Society, argues that Marxist analysis does indeed need game theory to investigate such issues, but says that Olson is wrong to postulate an invariant 'free rider' preference structure (see 1978 generally; 1982, p. 484). Elster considers 'universal cooperation', collective action, will develop and be successful: (a) the more that actors *perceive* that there is some kind of contradiction characterising their society; (b) the lower the *'communicational distance'* (a function of geographical distance plus transport technology) between the members; (c) the lower the rate of *turnover* of class members; and (d) the greater the degree to which such contradictions are *reversible* (1978, pp. 134–50; more generally see Lash and Urry, 1984). Offe and Wisenthal have elaborated the contrasting logics of collective action of capital and labour (1980; Abercrombie and Urry, 1983, ch. 8). They argue *inter alia* that the only way in which the organisations of labour can be systematically sustained (let alone enhanced) is through the existence of a 'collective identity' which deflates the standards by which the costs of membership are assessed, and in which the lack of immediate success is seen as of only minor significance. They also argue that it is crucial for labour to sustain 'dialogical' associations where the activities and views of the membership are represented, discussed and embodied, and where there is a continuous process of communicating within the membership about the appropriate means and objectives. In order that labour can identify its real interests, relatively undistorted communication is necessary between all the membership – the sort of communication which does not occur within what Offe and Wisenthal term 'monological' associations which characterise both the organisations of capital and increasingly those of labour (on 'communication' their views are influenced by Habermas; see the collection in Thompson and Held, 1982). Calhoun has explored some of the spatial variations in collective communication and action in Britain in the early years of the 19th century, and argues that such conditions were in fact best met within older, more traditional communities of artisans and similar workers whose whole existence was threatened by the development of capitalist relations (1982, especially ch. 8).

A fourth area in which class has been re-examined has been in that of ideology. Poulantzas regularly insisted that classes did not 'carry' around ideologies on their backs (1973, p. 202). Ideologies are not simply class ideologies. Laclau has taken this further by arguing that classes should be defined as 'the poles of antagonistic production relations which have no *necessary* form of existence at the ideological and political levels' (1977, p. 159). There are a number of implications to these positions, namely that classes cannot be thought of at the ideological and political levels by way of a process of reduction, but only in a process of articulation; that such articulation depends upon non-class contents – interpellations and contradictions – which constitute the raw material on which class ideological practices operate (see Part III); that classes (within production) and empirically observable groups do not necessarily coincide; and that there is a further objective determination besides classes which is that of the relationship the 'people'/the 'power bloc'. Specific analyses have then to be constructed as to the articulation between contradictions of class and of the people/the power bloc. The latter enables us to analyse the relative continuity of popular traditions, as well as the various ways in which popular forces and notions can be appropriated or reappropriated by different social classes. Hall has demonstrated how the contradiction between the people/the power bloc has been neutralised by the 'New Right', which is, through Reagan/Thatcher, apparently acting with and for the people especially against the State (1980, p. 177).

Finally, although it is clear that Marxism has made a major contribution to contemporary social theory, there are a number of crucial developments which at least raise the issue of whether it will continue to be appropriate to the analysis of the emerging form of Western societies, which are increasingly characterised by the declining significance of manufacturing industry and of the 'industrial classes' of Western capitalism; by the increased importance of 'service' industry, of a 'new middle class' of women within the labour force; by the heightened significance of 'social movements' oriented around either non-production based single issues or around gender, ethnicity or other popular democratic interpellations; by the development of consumption-based politics focused upon issues like housing, transport, energy and consumer affairs; by the extension of an enormously elaborate 'civil society', in some sense intermediate between production relations and the state; and by an increasingly ineffective state – albeit one with increased powers – which is unable to control multinational capital, or to overcome fiscal crises, or to be able to act 'legitimately' (see, for example, Mandel, 1975; Habermas, 1976; Dunleavy, 1980; Hobsbawm, 1981; Urry, 1981, 1983).

All the major social theories were born within industrial capitalism. They are all in some sense theories of industrial societies. But what of the future? What kind of social theory will be appropriate to the societies at present emerging in the First World, to the 'former industrial societies' of which the UK is a leading example? I would argue that this development will reinforce tendencies which are already undermining the distinctiveness and clarity of Marxism within the developed capitalist societies. Will it not be, as Kolakowski predicted in 1969, that:

> the concept of Marxism as a separate school of thought will in time become blurred and ultimately disappear altogether, just as there is no 'Newtonism' in physics, no 'Linnaeism' in botany, no 'Harveyism' in physiology, and no 'Gaussism' in mathematics. What is permanent in Marx's work will be assimilated in the natural course of scientific development? (p. 204)

GUIDE TO FURTHER READING

For Marx's own life and works, see McClellan (1973); for more detailed examinations, see Rubin (1972) and Cohen (1978). For influential analyses in the Golden Age, see Hilferding (1981); Lenin (1968); Gramsci (1971); Lukács (1971). Kolakowski (1978) presents an exhaustive if antagonistic survey of Marxist thought, while Anderson (1976) offers an interesting interpretation of this. On recent debates, see Marcuse (1964) on philosophy; Althusser (1969) on epistemology; Poulantzas (1973) and Jessop (1982) on the state; Habermas (1976) on ideology and legitimation; Braverman (1974) on the labour process; and Mandel (1975) on the overall development of 'late capitalism'.

REFERENCES

Abercrombie, N., Hill, S. and Turner, B. (1980), *The Dominant Ideology Thesis*, (London: Allen & Unwin).
Abercrombie, N. and Urry, J. (1983), *Capital, Labour and the Middle Classes* (London: Allen & Unwin).
Adorno, T. (1973), *Negative Dialectics* (New York: Seabury Press).

Adey, G. and Frisby, D. (trans.) (1976), *The Positivist Dispute in German Sociology* (London: Heinemann Educational Books).
Anderson, P. (1964), 'Origins of the Present Crisis', *New Left Review*, 23, pp. 26–53.
—— (1976), *Considerations on Western Marxism* (London: New Left Books).
Althusser, L. (1969), *For Marx* (Harmondsworth: Penguin).
—— (1971), *Lenin and Philosophy and Other Essays* (London: New Left Books).
—— (1976), *Essays in Self-Criticism* (London: New Left Books).
Althusser, L. and Balibar, E. (1970), *Reading Capital* (London: New Left Books).
Avineri, S. (1968), *The Social and Political Thought of Karl Marx* (Cambridge University Press).
Babbage, C. (1832), *On the Economy of Machinery and Manufacturers* (London: Knight).
Bahro, R. (1978), *The Alternative in Eastern Europe* (London: New Left Books).
Benton, T. (1977), *Philosophical Foundations of the Three Sociologies* (London: Routledge & Kegan Paul).
Beynon, H. (1973), *Working for Ford* (Harmondsworth: Penguin).
Bhaskar, R. (1975), *A Realist Theory of Science* (Leeds: Alma).
—— (1979), *The Possibility of Naturalism* (Hassocks: Harvester).
Blackburn, R. (1967), 'The Unequal Society', in R. Blackburn and A. Cockburn (eds), *The Incompatibles: Trade Union Militancy and the Consensus* (Harmondsworth: Penguin).
Braverman, H. (1974), *Labour and Monopoly Capital* (New York: Monthly Review).
—— (1976), 'Two Comments', *Monthly Review*, 28, pp. 119–25.
Buci-Glucksmann, C. (1980), *Gramsci and the State* (London: Lawrence & Wishart).
Burawoy, M. (1978), 'Towards a Marxist Theory of the Labour Process: Braverman and Beyond', *Politics and Society* 3–4, pp. 247–312.
Calhoun, C. (1982), *The Question of Class Struggle* (Oxford: Blackwell).
Carchedi, G. (1977), *On the Economic Identification of Social Classes* (London: Routledge & Kegan Paul).
Cohen, G. (1972), 'Karl Marx and the Withering Away of Social Science', *Philosophy and Public Affairs*, 1, pp. 182–203.
Cohen, G. A. (1978), *Karl Marx's Theory of History* (Oxford: Clarendon).
—— (1982), 'Reply to Elster on "Marxism, Functionalism, and Game Theory" ', *Theory and Society*, 11, pp. 483–95.
Cutler, A. (1978), 'The romance of "labour" ', *Economy and Society*, 7, pp. 74–95.
Cutler, A., Hindess, B., Hirst, P. and Hussain, A. (1977–78), *Marx's Capital and Capitalism Today*, 2 vols (London: Routledge & Kegan Paul).
Delphy, C. (1977), 'The Main Enemy: a Materialist Analysis of Women's Oppression', *WRCC*.
Dunleavy, P. (1980), 'The Political Implications of Sectoral Cleavages and the Growth of State Employment: Part I: the Analysis of Production Cleavages', *Political Studies*, 28, pp. 370–83.
Edwards, R. (1979), *Contested Terrain* (London: Heinemann Educational Books).
Ehrenreich, J. and E. (1979a), 'The Professional-Managerial Class', in Walker (ed.), pp. 5–45.
—— (1979b), 'Rejoinder', in Walker (ed.), pp. 313–54.

Elster, J. (1978), *Logic and Society* (Chichester: John Wiley).
―― (1982), 'Marxism, Functionalism, and Game Theory', *Theory and Society*, 11, pp. 453–82.
Friedmann, G. (1955), *Industrial Society* (New York: Free Press).
Friedman, A. (1977), *Industry and Labour* (London: Macmillan).
Fröbel, F., Heinrichs, J. and Kreye, O. (1980), *The New International Division of Labour* (Cambridge University Press).
Geras, N. (1971), 'Essence and Appearance: Aspects of Fetishism in Marx's *Capital*', *New Left Review*, 65, pp. 69–85.
Ginsburg, N. (1979), *Class, Capital and Social Policy* (London: Macmillan).
Godelier, M. (1967), 'System, Structure and Contradiction in "Capital"', *Socialist Register*, pp. 91–119.
Gorz, A. (1967), *Strategy for Labour* (Boston: Beacon Press).
Gramsci, A. (1971), *Selections from Prison Notebooks* (London: Lawrence & Wishart).
Habermas, J. (1971), *Knowledge and Human Interests* (London, Heinemann Educational Books).
―― (1976), *Legitimation Crisis* (London: Heinemann Educational Books).
―― (1979), *Communication and the Evolution of Society* (London, Heinemann Educational Books).
Hall, S. (1980), 'Popular-Democratic vs Authoritarian Populism: Two Ways of "Taking Democracy Seriously"', in A. Hunt (ed.), *Marxism and Democracy* (London: Lawrence & Wishart) pp. 157–85.
Harré, R. (1971), *The Principles of Scientific Thinking* (London: Macmillan).
Harré, R. and Madden, E. (1975), *Causal Powers* (Oxford: Blackwell).
Hartmann, H. (1979), 'Capitalism, Patriarchy and Job Segregation by Sex', in Z. Eisenstein (ed.), *Capitalist Patriarchy and the Case for Socialist Feminism* (New York: Monthly Review) pp. 206–47.
Held, D. (1980), *Introduction to Critical Theory* (London: Hutchinson).
Hilferding, R. (1981), *Finance Capital* (London: Routledge & Kegan Paul).
Hillel-Ruben, D. (1977), *Marxism and Materialism* (Hassocks: Harvester).
Hindess, B. and Hirst, P. (1975), *Pre-Capitalist Modes of Production* (London: Routledge & Kegan Paul).
Hindess, B. and Hirst, P. (1977), *Mode of Production and Social Formation* (London: Macmillan).
Hindess, B. (1983), *Parliamentary Democracy and Socialist Politics* (London: Routlege & Kegan Paul).
Hobsbawm, E. (1981), 'The Forward March of Labour Halted', in M. Jacques and F. Mulhern (eds), *The Forward March of Labour Halted* (London: New Left Books).
Jay, M. (1973), *The Dialectical Imagination* (London: Heinemann Educational Books).
Jessop, B. (1982), *The Capitalist State* (Oxford: Martin Robertson).
Jones, B. (1982), 'Destruction or Redistribution of Engineering Skills?; The Case of Numerical Control', in S. Wood (ed.), pp. 179–200.
Johnson, R. (1979), 'Histories of Culture/Theories of Ideology: Notes on an Impasse', in M. Barrett *et al* (eds), *Ideology and Cultural Production* (London: Croom Helm) pp. 49–77.
Johnson, T. (1977), 'The Professions in the Class Structure', in R. Scase (ed.),

Industrial Society: Class, Cleavage and Control (London: Allen & Unwin) pp. 93–110.
Kautsky, K. (1970), La Question Agraire (Paris: Maspero).
Keat, R. and Urry, J. (1975/1982), Social Theory as Science (London: Routledge & Kegan Paul).
Klingender, F. D. (1935), The Condition of Clerical Labour in Britain (London: Martin Lawrence).
Knie-Paz, B. (1978), The Social and Political Thought of Leon Trotsky (Oxford University Press).
Kolakowski, L. (1969), Marxism and Beyond (London: Pall Mall).
—— (1978), Main Currents of Marxism: the Golden Age (Oxford University Press).
Laclau, E. (1977), Politics and Ideology in Marxist Theory (London: New Left Books).
Lane, D. (1981), Leninism: a Sociological Interpretation (Cambridge University Press).
Larrain, J. (1979), The Concept of Ideology (London: Hutchinson).
—— (1983), Marxism and Ideology (London: Macmillan).
Lash, S. and Urry, J. (1984), 'The New Marxism of Collective Action: Critical Analysis', Sociology, 18, pp. 33–50.
Lenin, V. I. (1963), What is to be Done? (Oxford: Clarendon).
—— (1964), The Development of Capitalism in Russia (Moscow: Progress).
—— (1968), Imperialism, the Highest Stage of Capitalism (Moscow: Progress).
—— (1969), The State and Revolution (Moscow: Progress).
Littler, C. (1982), The Development of the Labour Process in Capitalist Societies (London: Heinemann Educational Books).
Lukács, G. (1971), History and Class Consciousness (London: Merlin).
Luxembourg, R. (1951), The Accumulation of Capital (London: Routledge & Kegan Paul).
Mallet, S. (1975), Essays on the New Working Class (St. Louis: Telos Press).
Mandel, E. (1975), Late Capitalism (London: New Left Books).
Mann, M. (1973), Consciousness and Action among the Western Working Class (London: Macmillan).
Marcuse, H. (1960), Reason and Revolution (London: Routledge & Kegan Paul).
—— (1964), One-Dimensional Man (London: Routledge & Kegan Paul).
—— (1966), Eros and Civilization (Boston: Beacon).
Marx, K. (1919), Theorien Über den Mehrwert, vol. 1 (Stuttgart: Dietz).
—— (1933), Wage-Labour and Capital (London: Lawrence & Wishart).
—— (1959a), Capital, vol. 3 (London: Lawrence & Wishart).
—— (1959b), Economic and Philosophic Manuscripts of 1844 (Moscow: Progress).
—— (1973), Grundrisse. Foundations of the Critique of Political Economy (Harmondsworth: Penguin).
—— (1976), Capital, vol. 1 (Harmondsworth: Penguin).
Marx, K. and Engels, F. (1968), The German Ideology (Moscow: Progress).
McClellan, D. (1973), Karl Marx: His Life and Thought (London: Macmillan).
Mepham, J. (1972), 'The Theory of Ideology in Capital', Radical Philosophy, 2, pp. 12–9.
Miliband, R. (1969), The State in Capitalist Society (London: Weidenfeld & Nicholson).

Mouffe, C. (ed.) (1979), *Gramsci and Marxist Theory* (London: Routledge & Kegan Paul).
Montgomery, D. (1979), *Workers' Control in America* (Cambridge University Press).
Moorhouse, B. (1978), 'The Marxist Theory of the Labour Aristocracy', *Social History*, 3, pp. 61–82.
Nicolaus, M. (1967), 'Proletariat and Middle Class in Marx: Hegelian Choreography and the Capitalist Dialectic', *Studies on the Left*, 7, pp. 22–49.
O'Hagan, T. (1982), 'Althusser: How to be a Marxist in Philosophy', in G. H. R. Parkinson (ed.), *Marx and Marxisms* (Cambridge University Press) pp. 243–64.
Ollman, B. (1971), *Alienation. Marx's Conception of Man in Capitalist Society* (Cambridge University Press).
Olson, M. (1965), *The Logic of Collective Action* (Cambridge: Harvard University Press).
Outhwaite, W. (1983), *Concept Formation in Social Science* (London: Routledge & Kegan Paul).
Penn, R. (1982), 'Skilled Manual Workers in the Labour Process, 1856–1964', in Wood (ed.), pp. 90–108.
Poulantzas, N. (1969), 'The Problem of the Capitalist State', *New Left Review*, 58, pp. 67–78.
—— (1973), *Political Power and Social Classes* (London: New Left Books).
—— (1975), *Classes in Contemporary Capitalism* (London: New Left Books).
Przeworski, A. (1977), 'Proletariat into a Class: the Process of Class Formation from Karl Kautsky's "The Class Struggle" to Recent Controversies', *Politics and Society*, 7, pp. 343–401.
Rhodes, E. and Pearn, M. (eds) (1981), *Discrimination and Disadvantage in Employment* (London: Harper & Row).
Rubin, I. I. (1972), *Essays on Marx's Theory of Value* (Chicago: Black & Red).
Sayer, D. (1981), *Marx's Method: Ideology, Science and Critique in "Capital"* (Brighton: Harvester).
Skocpol, T. (1979), *States and Social Revolutions* (Cambridge University Press).
Stark, D. (1980), 'Class Struggle and the Transformation of the Labour Process', *Theory and Society*, 9, pp. 89–130.
Taylor, J. (1979), *From Modernization to Modes of Production* (London: Macmillan).
Thompson, E. P. (1968), *The Making of the English Working Class* (Harmondsworth, Penguin).
—— (1978), *The Poverty of Theory* (London: Merlin).
Thompson, G. (1977), 'On the Relationship Between the Financial and the Industrial Sectors of the UK Economy', *Economy and Society*, 6, pp. 235–83.
Thompson, J. B. and Held, D. (eds) (1982), *Habermas: Critical Debates* (London: Macmillan).
Trotsky, L. (1972), *1905* (Harmondsworth: Allen Lane).
Urry, J. (1981), *The Anatomy of Capitalist Societies* (London: Macmillan).
—— (1983), 'De-Industrialisation, Classes and Politics', in R. King (ed.), *Capital and Politics* (London: Routledge & Kegan Paul) pp. 28–48.
Walby, S. (1983), 'Women's Unemployment, Patriarchy and Capitalism', in *Socialist Economic Register 1983* (London: Merlin) pp. 99–114.

Walker, P. (ed.) (1979), *Between Labour and Capital* (New York: Monthly Review).
Warde, A. (1982), 'E. P. Thompson and "Poor" Theory', *British Journal of Sociology*, 33, pp. 224–37.
Wood, S. (ed.) (1982), *The Degradation of Work?* (London: Hutchinson).
Wright, E. O. (1978), *Class, Crisis and the State* (London: New Left Books).

6 Political Theory

PATRICK DUNLEAVY

6.1 INTRODUCTION

This chapter discusses how contemporary Marxist writers have analysed liberal democratic politics in the advanced capitalist societies. It thus falls far short of a review of all Marxist political theory, since it leaves on one side the classical Marxist preoccupations with the prospects and mechanisms of revolutionary change (Miliband, 1977), and more recent work on the political process in less developed countries. Some restriction is clearly inevitable in dealing with a field of the richness and sophistication of Marxist political thought. But the particular justification for focusing on the 'normal' political process in advanced capitalism is that it has constituted 'the basic historical impasse that was the origin and matrix of Western Marxism itself' (Anderson, 1976, p. 80).

Marxist theory in the post-war period has been acutely sensitised to the resilience of liberal democracy as a political form, aware of the dangers of bureaucratisation and Stalinism in allegedly socialist alternatives, and conscious too of the extent to which post-war political practice by Western left-wing parties has moved away from reliance on classical Marxist strategies (Heydebrand, 1981, p. 91). One result of this changed perspective has been a more explicit reappraisal of political life under advanced capitalism:

> Bourgeois democracy is crippled by its class limitations, and under constant threat of further and dramatic impairment by conservative forces, never more so than in an epoch of permanent and severe crisis. But the freedoms which, however inadequately and precariously, form part of bourgeois democracy are the product of centuries of unremitting popular

struggles. The task of Marxist politics is to defend these freedoms; and to make possible their extension and enlargement by the removal of their class boundaries. (Miliband, 1977, p. 190)

Linking this reappraisal to new kinds of political analysis has provoked some stimulating changes in Marxist thought. But three central analytic problems remain unresolved. First, there is still a major difficulty in using the theory of class struggle to try to decode the patterns of political beliefs, alignments and conflicts observable in most liberal democratic input politics (such as party competition or the interest group process). Many working people simply do not seem to perceive their interests or to act politically in the ways in which Marxist theory predicts they should. The classical Marxist texts develop an asymmetric model of how class action and class conflict should dominate the political scene. Much recent work has been directed towards understanding from within a Marxist method why this has not been the case. Second, there is perennial controversy about the mechanism by which state intervention in liberal democracies operates to foster the accumulation process and to stabilise the social formation. In particular, the ways in which the analysis of state intervention should be meshed into an account of dominant class control mechanisms remains problematic. Third, Marxist political thought remains very much at the level of a holistic theoretical critique of liberal democracy. There has been no movement towards producing a theoretical basis for the applied prescriptive programmes for action implied in the quotation from Miliband.

6.2 POLITICAL CONFLICTS AND CLASS STRUGGLE

Any Marxist must insist upon the pre-eminence of divisions between social classes in understanding capitalist social relations. But equally most recent writers deny that observable political conflicts can be simply 'reduced' to straightforward struggles between social classes. Struggle is instead said to be 'mediated' and displaced along diverse pathways, appearing in hard-to-recognise forms and in unexpected locations. Obviously the potential for theoretical and practical self-deception involved in trying to uncover a process of class conflict underlying quite different-seeming political appearances is considerable. Two main stages are involved in reaching a more analytically based solution: (a) reappraising traditional Marxist class categories; and (b) developing a class-based explanation of why social class mobilisations form only one component in liberal democratic input politics.

6.2.1 Contemporary Class Categories

In the *Communist Manifesto* Marx and Engels claimed: 'All previous historical movements were movements of minorities, or in the interests of minorities. The proletarian movement is the self-conscious, independent movement of the immense majority in the interests of the immense majority' (Marx–Engels, 1969, p. 92). This historically and practically important claim has been called into question by over a century of change in the social structure of advanced industrial societies, which until recently was not matched by any comparable development in Marxist social class categories. Since 1970, however, a large volume of work has re-examined the questions of how to define social classes and of the potential appeal of a socialist movement (see Crompton and Gubay, 1978). A purist stream, represented by Poulantzas in some of his writings (1973; 1975), attempts to restrict the working class to manual workers, not engaged in supervisory roles and working in productive (i.e. manufacturing) industry. This definition connects closely with the dual criterion suggested by the labour theory of value, that workers are both exploited and have surplus value expropriated from them. But as Wright (1978) demonstrates, only one in five of the contemporary US employed workforce meet these stringent criteria. Even dropping the criterion of 'productive' employment does not enlarge the proletariat beyond one in three employees. Equally the main consequence of the purist strategy is to inflate the intermediate social class categories between the proletariat and the bourgeoisie to around 70 per cent of the total workforce.

A second strategy focuses on the 'economic identification' of classes, looking in particular at the 'global functions of capital' ('the work of control and surveillance', supervision and management) involved in the social organisation of the labour process (Carchedi, 1977). There are hybrid intermediate groups of wage earners performing some of these functions, and internally divided between those whose work tasks closely align them with the interests of capital, and those who are partly engaged in productive work (and hence have surplus value extracted from them). Applying a version of this categorisation to the USA, Wright (1978) identifies a potentially mobilisable bloc of working people accounting for 70–80 per cent of the labour force. A half to two-thirds of this group are unambiguously working class (wage earners without supervisory roles), while the remainder have higher levels of work autonomy or some labour-control functions. Those not mobilisable include owners of capital, the petit bourgeoisie and upper echelon controllers of labour. Although these proportions obviously vary considerably from one society to another, this kind of class schema preserves the essential Marxist claim that a working class political movement represents majority interests in a way which more orthodox accounts do not.

6.2.2 Class Analysis of Political Conflicts

However, broadening the definition of the working class to include manual and non-manual workers across all sectors, also makes it harder to explain internal divisions within classes. Intra-class divisions in the enlarged working class constitute some of the most obvious features of contemporary liberal democratic politics. Perhaps the least plausible option open to Marxist writers is to acknowledge the problem, but at the same time to take refuge in the assertion that somehow (given appropriate crisis conditions, for example) objective social classes still influence the political process, despite appearances to the contrary. Thus Miliband argues:

> The working class is much more divided than the dominant class. It is divided (and not merely differentiated) in terms of occupation and skill, of sex, race, in some instances religion, often in terms of political perceptions, positions and choices. *There is nothing 'inherent' or ineradicable about these divisions*; but they do exist and cut across class lines, oppose worker to worker, and erode or annul class solidarity. This is clearly of the greatest importance in relation to the capacity of the working class to defend itself and to advance its demands. *But it cannot be taken to*

undermine the objective character and existence of the working class as a social entity whose being is not dependent on the class perceptions (or absence of class perceptions) of those who constitute that class. (Miliband, 1982, p. 10; my emphasis)

Most modern Marxist work recognises that this is an inadequate response. Three more developed explanations have been put forward. The first strategy is to try and retrieve an inclusive class analysis by respecifying social class definitions to incorporate references to political and ideological alignment. A second option is to modify class analysis to incorporate 'within-class' categories with partially divergent social interests. The third strategy is to modify class analysis in a far more fundamental way, by acknowledging the existence of cross-class bases for political mobilisation and alignment.

Class-inclusive explanations develop from Marx's own distinction between the situation of a 'class in itself' (defined by its position in production relations), and a 'class for itself' (defined by consciousness of its common real interests and its alignment around an effective political movement). Writers pursuing this insight argue that it is 'reductionist' to expect any direct or unmediated connection between class positions in the production system and political mobilisations and conflicts (Przeworski, 1977). Looking for a one-to-one link between class and alignment suggests that somehow political and ideological phenomena could automatically be read off from economic phenomena.

Class-inclusive explanations accordingly stress that there are different levels or modes in which class conflict becomes manifest. At the most basic economic level there is a class structure – an ensemble of contradictory locations to which are linked 'fundamental interests' in the maintenance or supercession of the capitalist mode of production. The first stage in the emergence of class conflict is a process of class formation which concerns whether or not social classes come into being as effective foci of political action and ideological awareness. Various aspects of the organisation of advanced capitalist societies are seen as acting to inhibit class formation, especially the operations of economic markets and associated ideologies of competition, the individualising juridical and representational conceptions of liberal democracy, and the actions of state ideological agencies, which for some authors include a whole battery of social institutions, such as the family, religion, labour movements, etc. (see Crompton and Gubay, 1978). Class formation is logically prior to the emergence of class struggle between opposed social classes, which centres around their fundamental interests and hence calls into question the basic social arrangement of capitalism.

Wright (1978) makes this analysis more complicated by stressing that there may be different changes going on at all three levels – structure, class formation and class struggle. Where the working class is dragged into a deeper level of class struggle by changes in other classes' behaviour – for example, because of a broad-based attack on wage levels mounted by employers during a recession – then this experience can radicalise people quite quickly. For example, in the USA in the 1930s the New Deal emerged out of capital owners' assault on working class living standards following the Wall Street crash. However, most of the time non-dominant social classes tend to be poorly organised, since the sectional 'immediate interests' they have within a capitalist society diverge markedly from their overarching 'fundamental' interests in superceding that society.

There seem to be two major problems with class-inclusive explanations. First, it is unclear whether the two-stage process of class formation and class struggle applies equally to all social classes, or differentially to non-dominant classes, especially the working class. In some formulations, Wright suggests that state intervention is a major way in which working class formation is inhibited, while the class organisation of capital owners is enhanced. But how then are we to understand the divisions between capital owners themselves? If these conflicts are perhaps not as serious as the internal fragmentation of the working class, they are nonetheless pervasive and prominent aspects of contemporary Western societies with apparently significant impacts on state policy-making.

Second, the fundamental/immediate interest distinction does not genuinely help to take further the analysis of why some workers adopt communist politics, some socialist politics, and others neither. It merely *redescribes* the situations to be analysed without illuminating them any further. For example, to say that the Italian working class is more 'formed' than that in the USA is just another way of saying that the former votes in large part for a Communist Party, but the latter does not. The danger here is that a particularly tendentious way of restating empirical differences displaces any grounded analytical discussion of how these differences come into existence.

Within-class explanations go beyond class-inclusive explanations by trying to explain where 'immediate interests' inhibiting class formation originate. In addition, they attempt to classify intra-class conflicts in a systematic fashion, ranking them in importance and providing a detailed analytic (as opposed to simply a descriptive) account of how they differ from and relate to conflicts between social classes.

A first key concept introduced is that of a 'class fraction', i.e. a section of one class which has distinctive interests, is well organised to express these interests, and generates its own political movement or party in order to project its interests to the state (Poulantzas, 1973; 1975). Class fractions are very visible and long-lasting phenomena. Examples frequently cited are divisions between monopoly capital owners or corporations and other sections of the bourgeoisie, or divisions between industrial, commercial and finance capital. Class fractions are large-scale social divisions – they cannot apply to single interest groups or industries. The criterion of relation to a political movement or party is quite a restrictive one in this respect.

Second, Poulantzas identifies 'class strata', where there is a less obvious or formalised internal cleavage in a social class, and one which is relatively transient or based in rather specific historical circumstances. Class strata are not capable of sustaining autonomous political organisations or generating distinctive modes of expressing their interests politically. Conflicts between class strata are important though because of their impact on overarching class-based political organisation. For example, divergent interests between 'skilled' and 'semi-skilled' manual workers, or between 'craftsmen' and 'general workers', have historically been very significant in structuring the overall development of the British trade union movement.

Third, there are instances of 'displaced class conflict', where a small element in overall class conflict becomes associated with some other basis for social differentiation. For example, Westergaard and Resler (1976) suggest that a spurious association of class inequalities with racial differences occurs in Britain, where particularly unpleasant and exploited working class roles have come to be disproportionately filled by coloured people. They deny that coloured people form any sort of 'underclass' or that in any fundamental sense racial divisions modify class interests and conflicts.

Last, within-class explanations acknowledge the existence in particular classes of 'social categories' whose positions are not based in production situations and hence do not directly relate to capital/labour conflicts. Good examples are the armed forces and the state bureaucracy in many industrialising societies, categories which may have political importance at specific developmental junctures, especially where capitalist societies move away from liberal democracy into 'exceptional' regimes.

The gains made by within-class explanations are considerable in some areas. The approach has been applied by Poulantzas (1973; 1978) to develop a complex account of the relationship between the capitalist state and a 'power bloc' composed of different classes and class fractions (together with some residual elements from former modes of production) operating under the leadership of a hegemonic class fraction of the bourgeoisie. It can also permit a head-on approach to the difficult task of formulating a developed Marxist account of the persisting importance of fascist regimes and dictatorships in modern capitalism (Poulantzas, 1974). And as Parkin (1979) points out, within-class conflicts are defined by the specific development of social relations in each nation state (in contrast to the quite general character of class struggle across all capitalist societies). Hence they absorb much of the explanatory burden of adapting Marxism's generalised theory of the origins of political conflicts to particular historical circumstances.

But there is a fundamental methodological problem in this approach. Since reference to political alignments and behaviour is incorporated into the *definition* of fractions, strata, and other salient social categories, any attempt to 'explain' political phenomena in terms of interactions between within-class groupings rapidly becomes tautologous. They thus fail to be useful in explaining why one thing happens rather than another. Thus, if the British labour movement remains resolutely social democratic in approach (because of the attitudes of skilled workers' unions), one says that this reflects the impact of a skilled manual stratum upon class practice. And this is bound to be true, since it is precisely this impact which allowed the existence of the stratum to be identified in the first place. Clearly there is a danger here that no empirical phenomena need remain 'unexplained', since the apparatus of within-class categories can simply be adjusted to incorporate it (see Saunders, 1979, ch. 4).

Cross-class explanations' essential innovation is to move away from a specific account of this or that internal division in a particular social class in a particular country. Instead they focus on generalised lines of cleavage which affect multiple classes in similar ways across several or many capitalist countries. *Ad hoc* appeals to 'immediate interests' or single-country explanations give way to a more integrated account of the forces which prevent class interests from more clearly structuring political beliefs, alignments and conflicts in contemporary capitalism.

Two bases which create cross-class interests have been identified across several capitalist societies. The first of these is the segmentation of capital into sectors. There has been a progressively greater differentiation in post-war economic and social life between: (a) the large-firm, corporate sector, deploying advanced technology, undertaking major investment projects, exercising considerable monopolisitic or oligopolistic control over its product markets, and employing its workforce in large plants and organisations; and (b) the small-firm, market sector, where the scale of investment is less, productivity growth is correspondingly lower, where firms are price takers subject to competitive pressures in product markets, and where the workforce is highly fragmented in multiple locations and tiny workplaces and perennially vulnerable to unemployment (Bluestone, 1972).

Of course, this sort of distinction has been made before by many kinds of Marxist and liberal writers. But the distinctiveness of cross-class explanations is their insistence that once a fragmentation takes place between types of capital, then this line of cleavage will tend to be reproduced in other social classes as well. The capital sectors approach 'allows us to analyse the segmentation of the workforce in theoretical terms pertinent to the workings of the production system as a whole. ... At the most general level, capital sectors structure the manner in which class and occupation determine economic returns. In turn, class and occupation have logical priority over individual traits brought to the labour market' (Hodson, 1978, p. 478). The main political corollaries of class segmentation between capital sectors is that the unionised workforces in the corporate sector enter into a 'class compromise' with employers, bottling up productivity gains in higher wages and insulating themselves from inflation. Unorganised workers in small firms may then move to the right under the threat of inflationary wage drift (O'Connor, 1973; Habermas, 1976). The second basis for cross-class cleavages is the impact of state intervention on the social structure. Effects here include the growth of state employment, the emergence of consumption sectors, and divisions between the working and state-dependent populations. Because state sector workers are differentially unionised in many Western countries and can protect their living standards despite low rates of productivity growth, the relative price of public services and hence the tax-take by the state may be pushed up over time (O'Connor, 1973; Gough, 1979). The fiscal stress created can lead to anti-statist reactions by private sector workers (Best and Connolly, 1977). Similarly state intervention in consumption may create cross-class cleavages around tax/subsidy issues between those involved in public collective forms of consumption and those involved in apparently private or individualised forms of consumption (Castells, 1973; 1979). This effect is especially prominent in those countries where state agencies directly produce outputs such as housing, transport or health care, and where there is a high level of fragmentation between public and commercial provision. Similarly, divisions between working and state-dependent populations can create new bases for conflict, because modern welfare systems of taxation and transfer payments overwhelmingly redistribute resources *within* classes – from those in employment to the elderly, the sick, the disabled and the unemployed (see Westergaard and Resler, 1976). Widening income taxation increasingly places acute burdens on low paid workers, while the reduced income gap between them and the state dependent population can seem to impugn the basic value of their working lives (see Sennet and Cobb, 1977).

The overall impact of capital sectors segmentation and state intervention is to constitute powerful cross-class bases for political alignment and action, which certainly have begun to have a major impact on voting behaviour in some Western countries such as Britain (Dunleavy, 1979; 1980). But it also finds expression in other forms including strong sectoral patterns of industrial action and of support for anti-statist social movements.

While the account of cross-class cleavages given above does not seem to be exposed to major methodological problems, it provides at best a very limited grip on internal class divisions. For example, it can get a slightly better grip on racial conflicts in so far as they involve consumption sector effects – such as the concentration of coloured people differentially in some types of housing or geographical locations. But this still leaves Marxist accounts of ethnic conflicts (including religious, cultural, separatist, and nationalist movements, as well as racial tensions) in a weak and poorly developed form (Parkin, 1979). Marxist writers generally give instrumental interpretations of ethnically based demands, as when Miliband explains nationalist movements in terms of a 'drive to statehood'. 'There is nothing mysterious about this; it simply marks a recognition that "sovereignty", however limited it may be, makes possible the fulfilment of aims which would otherwise be unattainable' (1977, p. 101). Such accounts simply seem incommensurate with the scope and intensity of ethnically based conflicts, even when linked to developed accounts of the ideological themes associated with such movements as nationalism (Nairn, 1978; see also Short, ch. 7).

Finally it is important to notice that there are a number of propositions being discussed by Marxist writers which are much more vaguely specified than the cross-class explanations considered here, and which consequently seem to float dangerously between cross-class and non-class patterns of explanation. A good example is provided by Jessop's account of a politico–ideological dimension of social tension which he labels 'officialdom versus people' conflicts:

> The 'people' comprise those agents who are subject to state intervention and 'officialdom' comprises the agents of intervention. The exact composition of 'the people' will depend on the form and range of state intervention (since it is this that establishes the pertinence of categories such as taxpayer, criminal, citizen, conscript, licensee, pupil, pensioner, and supplementary benefit claimant). This poses the problem of the heterogeneity and pluralization of 'the people'. It must also be stressed that the unity of 'officialdom' can[not] be taken for granted and that different public agencies and agents can respond in contrasting ways to 'popular' demands and interests as well as to various class demands and interests. (Jessop, 1982, p. 249)

Jessop argues that 'popular-democratic' struggles are present in multiple forms in all liberal democracies, although they will always acquire a 'class pertinence' after some period. Jessop is further prepared to envisage cases 'where "officialdom-people" relations constitute the principal contradiction in a society and class antagonisms assume a secondary role' (1982, p. 251). He does, it is true, associate these situations with the existence of 'exceptional' regimes, arguing that 'on the introduction or restoration of democratic rule . . . class relations acquire greater significance'. But this must still be counted an astonishing point for a Marxist writer to accept. Nor does Jessop make any falsifiable claims about what will happen as a result of 'officialdom/people' conflicts. In some circumstances 'popular/democratic' forces may have a progressive, socialist character; but in other cases they recruit people into supporting the regressive anti-statist populism of the Thatcherite variety.

6.3 CLASS DOMINATION AND THE ROLE OF THE STATE

Just as liberal democratic input politics cannot easily be decoded in terms of class struggle, so there are problems for Marxist writers in deciphering state policy outputs in terms of the domination exercised by capitalist interests within Western societies. The core of the problem revolves around the 'relative autonomy' of the state, that is to say, the extent to which the state apparatus is directly influenced by capitalist interests in making policy decisions. If the state apparatus is explicitly run by the bourgeoisie in its own interests, then it has no significant autonomy, functioning merely as the 'executive committee' of the bourgeoisie. But this picture cannot easily apply to many Western societies, especially those with socialist or social democratic governments. Nor does it seem a plausible interpretation of state policy-making even in more overtly plutocratic political systems, such as that of the USA. Finally, of course, such a stance confronts intractable problems in explaining why the state apparatus not infrequently intervenes against the wishes of many or most capital owners, or why state policy changes, in particular, towards making concessions to working class demands. If, on the other hand, the state apparatus is not directly controlled by the bourgeoisie, then it is vital to be able to explain the mechanisms by which it nonetheless takes actions which are supportive of capitalism as a social system.

Three main strategies have developed to try and analyse this inter-relationship. These are: (a) an instrumentalist view, concentrating on fairly direct causal mechanisms by which the dominant class might secure control over the state apparatus; (b) a 'balance of class forces' model, grounding the analysis of state policy-making in a detailed account of the struggle between social classes; and (c) a structural account, stressing the determination of state intervention along lines functional for the maintenance and development of the accumulation process and capitalist social relations.

6.3.1 Instrumentalism

The instrumentalist view of state policy is still the best known of the Marxist accounts (Miliband, 1969; 1982; Greenberg, 1979). It stresses that owners of capital, even if they cannot completely control, may nonetheless exert a very large measure of direct influence upon state policy-making. Four kinds of evidence are cited in support of this view. First, capital and corporate interests exert major political influence directly by buying commercial control of the mass media, via advertising and command over other specialised skills (e.g. legal skills) (see Lumley and O'Shaughnessey, ch. 10), by superior interest organisation, and by lavish funding of right wing political parties. Second, the state apparatus is manned either directly by personnel drawn from the bourgeoisie or by people from non-dominant classes normally aligned with owners of capital. Both types of officials are orientated towards defending and enhancing capital owners' interests because of their background, education, social values, ideological attachments, social position and organisational contacts. Third, capital interests control economic resources of crucial significance for any government, and use their leverage systematically to cripple left-wing governments' economic policies, and to inhibit their chances of election or re-election. The mechanisms invoked here all revolve around the holding back or shifting of investments, and can include short run 'investment strikes', foreign exchange or stock market panics, and capital movements across national boundaries or within a country to penalise left governments or sub-national governments. Fourth, the configuration of state policy reveals a consistent attempt to defend capital interests, underpinning business investment and research and development, socialising costs of production, and structuring social arrangements so as to maintain or enhance the dominance of bourgeois interests and capitalist social relations.

Hence the distinctive mode of operation and apparent institutional separation of the state from business or the bourgeoisie is largely illusory. State responsiveness to capital interests is secured directly by capitalists' involvement in the political process, by personnel and ideology linkages between capital owners and the state élite, and by the use of corporations' economic and organisational resources. The apparent separateness of state institutions reflects primarily: (a) the need for an organisational form capable of reconciling the partially divergent interests of different capital fractions; and (b) the need to take a 'long look' at trends of societal development, rather than being limited to the sectional, possibly inexpert, and notoriously short-run estimates of 'optimal' policy made by capital owners themselves. Liberal democratic political institutions also generate more differentiated and effective strategies for 'containing pressure' from non-dominant social classes than the repressive 'exceptional' regimes which have from time to time displaced them.

There are a number of reasons why instrumental explanations have been of declining significance in recent Marxist theory. They have seemed increasingly unsatisfactory because they do not provide a developed explanation of how the state apparatus can at times intervene against capitalist interests, while remaining dominated by them. Nor have instrumentalist accounts aged very well. In the period up to the 1970s, instrumentalism became widely known because more than any other Marxist approach it appeared to possess an articulated anti-pluralist argument. Certainly this is a crystal clear motivation in Miliband's work (1969). But in the 1970s pluralism metamorphosed into neo-pluralist thought, where much of the élite theory and Marxist critique of liberal democracy is accepted, but is incorporated into an argument that advanced industrial societies could not be run otherwise (see Galbraith, 1969; Lindblom, 1977; Dahl, 1982 for different variants of neo-pluralist thought). Equally élite theory approaches have changed to stress the dominance of an autonomous state élite (Nordlinger, 1981), while a vigorous 'new right' anti-pluralism has emerged as a major stream in liberal thinking (see Tullock, 1975). Against all of these new developments instrumentalism seems tired and out-of-date, still combating an implausible classical pluralism long since abandoned by its erstwhile defenders (see especially Miliband, 1982).

6.3.2 The Balance of Class Forces Model

Explanations of state policy-making in terms of a 'balance of class forces' have developed from some hints dropped by Marx (1852) and Engels (1852) to the effect that, where bourgeois and proletarian forces are relatively balanced, then scope exists for the state apparatus holding the balance between them to act in a rather more self-directed fashion. The direction of intervention will still obviously be towards the stabilisation of capitalism and the preservation of social cohesion. But the detailed policy mechanism used, and the type of change effected, may nonetheless reflect extensive state concessions to working class mobilisation and to manifest social unrest.

The popularity of this rather vaguely specified model is easy to underestimate because it tends to be deployed primarily in detailed historical analyses, especially of turning points in labour movement history, such as the introduction of public housing in Britain or the inter-war and post-war growth of state welfare systems in many countries (Piven and Cloward, 1971; 1977; 1982; Dickens, 1977). Much conventional Marxist work emphasises historical studies, which are supposed to connect better with historical materialism, especially in the current climate of reaction against the 'theoretical excesses' of structuralism (Thompson, 1978; see also Corner, ch. 4 and Urry, ch. 5). But two problems arise. First, because it is so vaguely specified, the 'balance of class forces' model seems to have seriously anti-theoretical implications, eschewing altogether any developed account of the general relations between the state apparatus and socio-political groupings. Second, the model's association with historical studies can often be an excuse for simply avoiding the difficulties of giving a Marxist analysis of *contemporary* liberal democratic politics.

Finally the 'balance of class forces' model contains a mode of explanation which is rather clearly suited for 'myth-building' academic work of a kind which from time to time appeals to more activist Marxist writers. Particularly applied to periods of state concessions to working class or radical movements, the model works backwards from the scale of concessions made to an estimate of the commensurate degree of working class pressure judged necessary to have provoked them. But characteristically the model provides no criteria or methodology by which the existence of a requisite level of successful class struggle can be established. There appears to be no way of assessing the force of pressure on the state apparatus except through the policy changes to be explained.

6.3.3 Functional Accounts

Functional explanations of state policy-making have been put forward by a wide range of Marxist writers – ranging from those committed to very orthodox views (Gough, 1979), to structuralist writers (Castells, 1973), to exponents of much looser Marxist schemas, such as the 'legitimation crisis' school (O'Connor, 1973; Habermas, 1976). Common to all of them is an attempt to specify a set of functional imperatives or constraints acting upon the state apparatus, so that public policy changes support the maintenance and future development of capitalism. In all cases, *part* of the explanation of state action is the function that intervention serves. But bitter controversy surrounds the claims of Cohen (1980) that a *wholly* functional explanation (put forward without any accompanying causal account) will be necessary or useful in establishing a Marxist analysis of the state.

The common core of virtually all contemporary Marxist functional accounts is the claim that state intervention is directed to two goals, fostering greater capital accumulation and domestic economic growth (the accumulation function), and preserving social cohesion and an impression of capitalist social arrangements as inevitable and desirable (the legitimation function). In O'Connor's account of state expenditures, there is a three-way split producing a separate category of 'expenses' for socially necessary state activities (such as policing) which do not directly enhance profit potential. But in most other versions such elements are assimilated into the legitimation function, along with a wide range of necessary services supporting social life. The accumulation and legitimation functions are commonly viewed as contradictory or in tension, with the configuration of state policy shifting in emphasis from one to another in response to changing priorities indicated by the sequencing of economic/fiscal or political/ideological crises. The separate development of crisis tendencies across these two fields is sometimes seen as quasi-cyclical (especially in structuralism; Heydebrand, 1981), and sometimes seen as a process of displacement (with crises 'resolved' in one area being exported into the other). Habermas (1976) and Offe (1983), for example, suggest that state intervention to manage economic crisis tendencies leads to the internalisation of contradictions as 'rationality crises' in state policy-making. The tension between welfare state interventions supporting social cohesion and the requirements of the accumulation process leads in turn to fiscal strains, which may precipitate legitimation failures when existing public service levels are cut back.

The distinction between accumulation and legitimation functions has been a productive one in terms of giving Marxist approaches an analytic grip upon state institutional arrangements. Influential work in the late 1970s developed a Marxist notion of 'corporatism' (see Jessop, 1982). This literature stresses the emergence of separate institutional forms for handling economic, production and external relations policy areas of central significance for capital interests, and operating in ways quite distinct from those used in managing broader social policy areas of less direct importance for accumulation. In Jessop's (1982) conception, corporatist policy-making creates networks which effectively by-pass all representative political institutions – leaving them only secondary policy issues and details to pick over and reformulate. Similarly the 'dual state thesis' argues that the state apparatus can manage the accumulation/legitimation tension by creating an institutional dualism between different tiers of government. Production/accumulation functions are increasingly centralised while consumption/legitimation functions remain with peripheral agencies. Central/local relations within the state apparatus hence become a crucial mechanism for regulating the balance of state policy-making (see Saunders and Cawson, 1983).

An important aspect of these more applied analyses of state policy-making has been the attempt to link them up with various Marxist strategies for analysing input politics. Jessop's distinction between class-based and 'popular/democratic' conflicts (see above) is to a considerable extent one between class conflicts going on *within* the sphere of corporatist policy-making, and those conflicts which try to supercede or attack the hegemony of this sphere of state action. Similarly exponents of the dual state thesis have attached it to one type of cross-class explanation of input politics, with centralised production locations seen as influenced by class-based mobilisations of social interests, but localised consumption policy areas influenced by conflicts between fragmented consumption sectors (Saunders and Cawson, 1983).

Despite their popularity in the 1970s, Marxist functional accounts have confronted some acute difficulties in developing beyond their original insights. The dichotomy between accumulation and legitimation functions is not in itself enough to distinguish a Marxist approach to the state, contrary to the impression given by many current Marxist approaches to state theory (see Jessop 1982). Neo-pluralists, such as Burnham (1982, p. 75) have no difficulty in accepting that these functions exist, and that they are centrally conditioned by the economic substructure of social organisation. The problem for Marxist writers is to get a more specific grip on state policy-making. One common way forward is to try and articulate the accumulation/legitimation distinction. Here theorists take as a starting point some particular economic or social requirement of the capitalist mode of production (such as the nature of commodity consumption, the process of circulation of capital, or the need to raise the rate of exploitation of labour) and try to *derive* from this requirement by logical analysis the necessary form of state apparatus and state intervention which will ensure that it is successfully met. Since Marx's original texts deal with a very complex *system* of relations and inter-dependencies, there are a great many necessary conditions which can serve as possible starting points for such 'state derivationist' accounts. Each of these produces a somewhat different distribution of emphasis on aspects of state activity falling under the accumulation or legitimation functions, with a corresponding range of characterisations of state policy-making as primarily repressive/exploitative or manipulative/concessionary (for a wide-ranging review, see Jessop, 1982).

Straddling the gap between these theoretically pure exercises in 'form derivation' and the descriptive accounts given by instrumentalist or by 'balance of class forces' writers are a number of more productive positions. Both Poulantzas and Offe, for example, consider in different ways the special situation of multiple constraints which defines the limits of state action under capitalism. For Poulantzas (1973) the central problem of the state's 'relative autonomy' is to manage simultaneously under the contradictory pressures and constraints set up by changes in distinct economic and politico-ideological structures. For Offe (1972; 1975; 1984) the advanced capitalist state is bound to attempt complex 'productive' or social engineering kinds of intervention. Such efforts are frustrated in large part, because a capitalist state has to insulate itself from any genuinely participatory or democratic control, and hence can never acquire the information or co-operation necessary for effective decision-making (see Habermas, 1971).

Running through all Marxist functional accounts, apart from the 'form derivation' school, is a persistent problem in identifying which are the necessary and which are the contingent features of capitalist state intervention. One feature of the theoretical systems advanced in the 1970s has been the distinctive slants accorded to necessary features of the capitalist state by West German, French or Anglo-American Marxists. Carried over into more applied work (such as the rapidly burgeoning field of urban political sociology; see Short, ch. 7), such ethnocentric theorising quickly attracted fierce criticism for the confusion of analytic 'levels' which it involved (e.g. Duncan (1981) attacking Castells, 1973 and 1979).

The second basic strategy for articulating functional accounts is to define a relatively complex grid of accumulation and legitimation roles which may be pursued by a capitalist state apparatus under particular conditions. Major changes in state policy are ascribed to the development of capitalist economies through particular 'stages' or periods, each characterised by the hegemony of a dominant class fraction and its associated bloc of interests. In particular, shifts in the economic base, through a sequence of competitive, monopoly, state-monopoly, and post-welfarist forms of capitalism evoke appropriate state policy responses, respectively *laissez-faire*, welfare state, and recommodification forms of intervention. The problems here are fairly well known. There are almost as many schemas for periodisation as there are types of Marxist analysis, both in the classic Marxist texts, and in newer schools of thought. Explaining shifts in state policy by referring to periodisation schemas almost automatically broadens the analysis and puts it into such a long time perspective that contemporary political analysis becomes almost an afterthought. Changes of 'stage' or period are especially hard to identify in any well-grounded theoretical manner for the contemporary era. These two problems have combined to give Marxist functional accounts a reputation for tautologous or unfalsifiable reasoning. For example, welfare state interventions are ascribed to a state-monopoly phase of advanced capitalism, which they in turn partly define (Offe and Ronge, 1975).

6.4 UNDERSTANDING STATE ORGANISATION

One general problem of all Marxist approaches to the state deserves special mention, namely that they often seem to be purely critical in content. It is difficult to see what prescriptive implications might be worked out from much of the macro-theory which has dominated Marxist discussions of the role of the state. At one level, this is unsurprising. Detailed prescriptive extensions of the theory of the state might imply that there existed some set of institutional changes within the current (capitalist) mode of production which could effectively stabilise or legitimise social arrangements. Marxist writers of course dispute such claims, just as they are keen to avoid formulating new political practices which might tend to further entrench existing exploitative social arrangements. They stress also that institutional changes within the state apparatus do not emerge as a result of academic theorising, but are rather the products of much broader socio-economic developments. And the sifting process built into the political system under capitalism is such that any proposed piecemeal reforms in state organisation are liable to be distorted so as to support the capitalist system they attempt to modify.

But the absence of prescriptive Marxist theory is disturbing for two reasons. First, holistic theoretical critiques tend to distance recent Marxist thought from effective contact with political practice, even in those European countries where large Communist parties exist. In this specialised sense, the linkage between theory and practice becomes fatally attenuated, quite apart from the extent to which Marxist writers are directly or personally engaged in current politics. The dominant mood of much recent

Marxist theory has been one of fatalism, even of despair (Heydebrand, 1981). Second, many modern Marxist schools of thought declare their commitment to preserving liberal democracy, while extending its scope to break down its class boundaries (see the quotation from Miliband above). But such a position begins to look very thin if there is no developed body of ideas which Marxist theory can point to as providing an action programme for this task.

Lenin's *State and Revolution* casts a heavy shadow here. Writing in 1917, Lenin tried to come to grips with the problem of bureaucracy in the modern state, as part of a wider attempt to explain how the transition to socialism could take place. His solution was to dismiss the Weberian model of bureaucracy as one specific to a capitalist mode of production. Instead he claimed that under socialism the potential would exist and could be actualised for a sweeping democratisation of state administration, which would open up the way for coercive state organisations progressively to wither away. But in practice, these pronouncements became simply an ideological cloak behind which a massive Soviet state and party bureaucracy was constructed. Nothing in the existing practice of state socialist societies gives any reason to suppose that any progress has been made towards devising more genuinely liberating forms of state organisation or decision-making. The absence of a prescriptive element in current Western Marxist state theory must therefore give rise to the suspicion that little has changed here either – that in effect no worked-out ideas for extending the scope of 'bourgeois democracy' currently exist.

Of course, a number of proposals have been floated by European left parties influenced by Marxist thought. These have included greater decentralisation of national government powers to regions or localities, and the need to extend and qualitatively transform 'participation' procedures. But such proposals are not well grounded in Marxist theory, and they sit very uneasily alongside the strategic arguments of other Marxist writers. For example, there is a powerful case for supporting secessionist movements, because of their potential for radicalising the political environment of otherwise conservative nation states (Nairn, 1978), rather than backing regional autonomy or devolution. Similarly a strong case can be made for the view that state policy concessions are primarily won in response to overt or incipient social unrest, rather than as a result of formalised participation processes (Piven and Cloward, 1977).

But there are a few more hopeful signs in this area. Some work has begun to be done in a radical or a Marxist vein on developing a theory of organisations, on re-evaluating the role of professions in policy making (Johnson, 1972; Larson, 1977), and on resolving long-running practical conundrums – such as the circumstances in which sub-national government agencies can offer a viable institutional base for developing socialist policy solutions under capitalism (Boddy and Fudge, 1984). But a great deal of progress still needs to be made, if Marxist political science is to be credible in confronting the burgeoning liberal prescriptive literature. In particular, Marxist and socialist writers more generally have so far been tied into reacting defensively to new right institutional initiatives, such as privatisation, budget and manpower cutbacks, and changes in the technology of public service delivery systems. Western Marxists appear to have been caught unprepared by the organisational strategies which the Thatcher and Reagan administrations have adopted, and have reacted in part by standing pat on a defence of the status quo. Paradoxically then, the left in practical politics has fetishised at least some of the welfare state institutions which modern Marxist theory has been intent on criticising.

All Marxist work on the theory of the state has at some point to confront the undeniable problem of preserving liberal democracy under socialism, and avoiding the rampant bureaucratisation and authoritarianism which characterises contemporary state socialist societies. For Western Marxists this is especially difficult, since the initial context of any piecemeal transition to socialism will be a fundamentally capitalist society. Some discussion of what authentically socialist and genuinely democratic institutions would look like, is obviously overdue.

GUIDE TO FURTHER READING

There are, unfortunately, no good book-length introductions to alternative Marxist perspectives on the contemporary politics of advanced industrial states, although Ralph Miliband (1977) provides a discussion of older themes. Perry Anderson (1976) is indispensable material on the background to recent theories, lucidly and sympathetically written. Making progress from here is then chiefly a matter of sampling some of the major writers' work. Highly recommended books must include: O'Connor (1973), Habermas (1976), Poulantzas (1978), Wright (1978), Castells (1979), Offe (1983). For those already well versed in Marxism and anxious to learn more particularly about orthodox variants of state theory, Jessop (1982) provides an unnecessarily complicated account.

REFERENCES

Anderson, P. (1976), *Considerations on Western Marxism* (London: New Left Books).
Best, M. and Connolly, W. (1977), *The Politicized Economy* (Lexington, Mass: Heath).
Bluestone, B. (1972), 'Capitalism and Poverty in America', *Monthly Review*, 24, pp. 65–71.
Boddy, M. and Fudge, C. (eds), (1984), *Local Socialism?* (London: Macmillan).
Burnham, W. (1982), 'The Constitution, Capitalism and the Need for Rationalized Regulation', in Goldwyn and Schambra, pp. 75–91.
Carchedi, G. (1977), *On the Economic Identification of Social Classes* (London: Routledge & Kegan Paul).
Castells, M. (1973), *The Urban Question* (London: Edward Arnold).
——— (1979), *City, Class and Power* (London: Macmillan).
Cawson, A. and Saunders, P. (1983), 'Corporation, Competitive Politics and Class Struggle', in R. King (ed.), *Capital and Politics* (London: Routledge & Kegan Paul) pp. 8–27.
Cohen, G. (1980), *Karl Marx's Theory of History* (Oxford University Press).
Crompton, R. and Gubay, J. (1978), *Economy and Class Structure* (London: Macmillan).
Dahl, R. (1982), *Dilemmas of Pluralist Democracy* (New Haven, Conn.: Yale University Press).
Dickens, P. (1977), 'Social change, housing and the state', in M. Harloe (ed.), *CES Conference on Urban Change and Conflict* (London: Centre for Environmental Studies).
Dunleavy, P. (1979), 'The Urban Bases of Political Alignment', *British Journal of Political Science*, 9, pp. 409–43.
——— (1984), 'The Political Implications of Sectoral Cleavages and the Growth of State Employment', *Political Studies*, 26, pp. 364–83 and 527–49.
Duncan, S. (1981), 'Housing Policy, the Methodology of Levels and Urban Research', *International Journal of Urban and Regional Research*, 5, pp. 231–54.
Engels, F. (1852), 'Revolution and Counter-Revolution in Germany', in *Karl Marx and Friedrich Engels: Collected Works, Volume II* (London: Lawrence & Wishart, 1979) pp. 3–96.
Galbraith, J. (1969), *The New Industrial State* (Harmondsworth: Penguin).
Goldwyn, R. and Schambra, W. (1982), *How Capitalistic is the Constitution?* (Washington: American Enterprise Institute).
Gough, I. (1979), *The Political Economy of the Welfare State* (London: Macmillan).
Greenberg, E. (1979), *Understanding Modern Government* (New York: John Wiley).

Habermas, J. (1971), *Towards a Rational Society* (London: Heinemann).
—— (1976), *Legitimation Crisis* (London: Heinemann).
Heydebrand, W. (1981), 'Marxist Structuralism', in P. Blau and R. Merton (eds), *Continuities in Structural Inquiry* (London: Sage).
Hodson, R. (1978), 'Labour in the Monopoly, Competitive and State Sectors of Production', *Politics and Society*, 8, pp. 429–80.
Jessop, R. (1982), *The Capitalist State* (Oxford: Martin Robertson).
Johnson, T. (1972), *Professions and Power* (London: Macmillan).
Larson, M. (1977), *The Rise of Professionalism* (Berkeley: University of California Press).
Lindblom, C. (1977), *Politics and Markets* (New York: Basic Books).
Marx, K. (1852), *The Eighteenth Brumaire of Louis Bonaparte*, in *Karl Marx and Friedrich Engels: Collected Works* (London: Lawrence & Wishart, 1979) pp. 99–188.
Marx, K. and Engels, F. (1969), *The Communist Manifesto* (Harmondsworth: Penguin).
Miliband, R. (1969), *The State in Capitalist Society* (London: Weidenfeld).
—— (1977), *Marxism and Politics* (Oxford University Press).
—— (1982), *Capitalist Democracy in Britain* (Oxford University Press).
Nairn, T. (1978), *The Break-up of Britain* (London, New Left Books).
Nordlinger, E. (1981), *On the Autonomy of the Democratic State* (Cambridge, Mass.: Harvard University Press).
O'Connor, J. (1973), *The Fiscal Crisis of the State* (New York: St Martin's Press).
—— (1981), 'The Fiscal Crisis of the State Revisited', *Kapitalistate*, 9, pp. 41–62.
Offe, C. (1975), 'The Theory of the Capitalist State and the Problem of Policy Formation', in L. Lindberg et al. (eds), *Stress and Contradiction in Modern Capitalism* (Lexington, Mass.: Heath).
—— (1983), *Contradictions of the Welfare State* (London: Hutchinson).
Offe, C. and Ronge, V. (1975), 'Theses on the Theory of the State', *New German Critique*).
Parkin, F. (1979), *Marxism and Class Theory: a Bourgeois Critique* (London: Tavistock).
Piven, F. and Cloward, R. (1971), *Regulating the Poor* (New York: Pantheon).
—— (1977), *Poor People's Movements* (New York: Pantheon).
—— (1982), *The Class War* (New York: Pantheon).
Poulantzas, N. (1973), *Political Power and Social Classes* (London, New Left Books).
—— (1974), *Fascism and Dictatorship* (London: New Left Books).
—— (1975), *Classes in Contemporary Capitalism* (London: New Left Books).
—— (1978), *State, Power, Socialism* (London: New Left Books).
Przeworski, A. (1977), 'Proletariat into Class: the Process of Class Formation from Kautsky's "The Class Struggle" to Recent Debates', *Politics and Society*, 7.
Saunders, P. (1979), *Urban Politics* (London: Hutchinson).
Sennet, R. and Cobb, J. (1977), *The Hidden Injuries of Class* (Cambridge University Press).
Thompson, E. (1978), *The Poverty of Theory* (New York: Monthly Review Press).
Tullock, G. (1975), *The Vote Motive* (London: Institute of Economic Affairs).
Westergaard, J. and Resler, H. (1976), *Class in a Capitalist Society* (Harmondsworth: Penguin).
Wright, E. O. (1978), *Class, Crisis and the State* (London: New Left Books).

7 Human Geography and Marxism*

JOHN R. SHORT

7.1 INTRODUCTION

Human geography is an academic discipline whose central focus is the analysis of the relationships between the environment and society, spatial structure and social process. Since the 1960s the discipline has come into contact with Marxism and particularly the Marxist inspired work on the relationships between environment, space and society. My concern in this chapter is not with picking out the environmental issues and spatial themes implicit or explicit in classical Marxist thought. This has been done elsewhere (see Parsons, 1977; Sandbach, 1980; Quaini, 1982). Moreover, there has not been an agreed set of classical Marxist arguments which have been used to guide subsequent work, it is much more a case of creative readings of classical Marxist texts by successive generations. My aim, therefore, is to show how this area of contemporary scholarship has been transformed by the use of Marxist theory and how this theory has in turn been re-evaluated.

The contact has been brought about by scholars bridging the gap between geography and Marxism. As an exemplar, we can consider the work of David Harvey who has been one of the most influential scholars of recent years. His first book was *Explanation in Geography* published in 1969 at a time of intense debate within human geography. *Explanation* informed and reflected this debate which concerned the nature of method in quantitative social science. The book begins by drawing a distinction between

---

* I am grateful to Zyg Barański and John Urry for comments on an earlier draft.

philosophy and methodology. We can draw a distinction, Harvey argues, between our beliefs and our values. The book is concerned with the methods of analysis rather than the object of analysis, and Harvey's main aim is to harness the, then growing, quantitative, model building approach. And he wants to do this by formulating criteria for judging the soundness of arguments. The book is essentially concerned with understanding the process of scientific explanation. The best way to achieve this explanation is through the use of a deductive approach involving the use of models to suggest hypotheses which can then be verified. The testing of hypotheses allows the construction of theory which in turn provides the basis for subsequent models and hypothesis testing. *Explanation in Geography* is fundamentally an argument for the adoption of the deductive approach in geography.

The context for his next book, *Social Justice and the City* (1973), was very different. The wider changes were the end of the long post-war economic boom and the beginnings of conflict fracturing along lines of race and class. The cities were the loci of discontent and crisis. Within the discipline a growing need was felt for geography and geographers to say something about current issues and contemporary problems (Johnston, 1979). Again, Harvey reflected and to some extent informed the debates. *Social Justice* began by taking up the same initial questions as *Explanation*: the separation between philosophy and methodology. This time, however, Harvey argued that this distinction should be avoided, because the method of analysis conditions the object of analysis; method and objective are not independent. *Social Justice in the City* is really two books. The first part, entitled, 'Liberal Formulations', is concerned to focus geographical enquiry on socially relevant topics concerning the urban system, the redistribution of real income and social justice. The second part, 'Social Formulations', marks a distinct epistemological break. Now ideas are seen to be derived from a particular context and social justice cannot be discussed in the abstract, instead it must be placed within the consideration of the nature of the wider society. The concept of the city is radically altered. Rather than being a thing in itself, an independent object of enquiry the city is seen as one element mediating and expressing wider social processes. Through considerations of Marxist rent theory, the history of urbanism and the notions of paradigm shifts, and consequent social science research, Harvey's main aim in the second part is to show the relationship between the city and society from the perspective of historical materialism.

Harvey's third book which followed on from a series of papers, which I shall discuss later, was published in 1982 under the title of *The Limits to Capital*. Now the concern is nothing less than to provide a re-exposition and extension of Marx's original analysis of capitalism, to rewrite Marx's *Capital*, with even the exposition closely mirroring the initial intent. Chapter 1, for example, begins with the discussion of commodities, use-values and exchange values. Significant 'extras' include chapters on the prediction of spatial configurations and crisis in the space economy of capitalism. As a whole the book is marked by a functionalist tinge, it is strong on capital, weak on its limits. However, it still constitutes a major statement of Marxist commitment.

Harvey's particular route of intellectual inquiry is unique, but it does encapsulate the broad nature of the shift in the discipline of human geography as a whole, which now has to consider Marxism even if only to dismiss it (for example, Eyles, 1981), and mirrors to a varying extent the biographies of a significant number of other scholars. There is now a vigorous radical group, the Union of Socialist Geographers, and specific journals – *Antipode, International Journal of Urban and Regional Research, Society and Space, Herodote* – which include work by Marxist geographers. If one definition of an intellectual group is internal dissension, then the radical geographers are no exception, with debates already appearing on the interpretation of 'true' radical theory and practice (see, for example, the argument between Peet, 1977; 1981 and Smith, 1979; 1981). There is thus no one party line in this academic venture, but a series of different traditions sharing a common concern with the relationship between Marxist theory and certain issues. In the following pages I will survey four of the main issues.

7.2 SOCIETY AND NATURE

7.2.1 General Approaches

The relationships between society and nature, people and environment was a significant, if often implicit theme in classical Marxism. It is of much more explicit concern in contemporary debates. The Marxist position has been developed in response to two general approaches.

The *nature in people* approach seeks to show the biological basis of social action and human behaviour. Herbert Spencer, was an early exponent of this approach. He sought to show how social behaviour could be considered using ecological principles, and it is to Spencer, not Darwin, that we owe the phrase 'the survival of the fittest'. This biological basis has been a consistent theme in social theory from the Chicago school of Burgess and associates, to the recent elaborations of human ecology (Hawley, 1971) and more popular works of Robert Ardrey (1967) and Desmond Morris (1967; 1977; 1979). Ardrey, for example, seeks to demonstrate the imperative of territoriality in understanding human action, while Morris has sought to link human action to basic biological drives and impulses.

In the *nature on people* approach the emphasis is placed on the role of nature in influencing social behaviour. This approach covers a range of opinion from a crude environmental determinism, to a more subtle approach which stresses the primacy of nature in people/environment relationships. This approach stretches from the work of Robert Malthus to the 'limits of growth' argument of contemporary neo-Malthusians.

The Marxist approach has charted a path between the biological determinism of the first and the environmental determinism of the second. Much of classical and contemporary Marxism has been concerned with the repudiation of these approaches. Not only are they identified as intellectually inadequate, but their ideological function is made explicit. The *nature in people* approach, for example, is seen as a biologising of social behaviour, because not only is the rich diversity of social behaviour reduced to that of mere surface phenomena, but social actions are given the tag of 'natural', relating to unchanging biological principles and so beyond human emancipation. Thus, while Spencer gives a biological justification for capitalist competition, Ardrey biologises private property. Social institutions and practices are read back from a biological basis and thus seen as eternal verities, rather than as the product of social relations (compare Mohun, ch. 2).

The criticism of the *nature on people* argument has a long history in Marxist thought. At a number of points in his many writings, Marx attacks the writings of Malthus who had sought to show that the food resources limited population increase. When population pressed against these limits the result, according to Malthus, was misery and starvation, which were 'natural' checks to bring the population–environment relationship back to stability. Malthus went on to argue that the appropriate policy towards the lower classes should be one of benign neglect, since poverty was a natural state of affairs. Not surprisingly, Marx rejected this argument and sought to show how it was 'an apologia for the existing state of affairs in England'. The seeming limits of nature were in fact the ideological justification for the limitations of a social system.

The Marxist approach has sought to stress the dialectical relationship between people and nature. History is seen as the story of the interaction between people and the external environment. The creative power of humanity is affirmed by Marxists and nature bears the stamp of human imprint. But the relationship with nature is part of the social relationship between people. The form of social relations shapes the people environment relationships, while the human capacity to transform nature constitutes an important element in the totality of social relations. Marx uses the term, mode of production, to refer to both social relations and the relations of production, which can be defined as the ability to transform the external environment. The people–environment relationship is thus not considered in the abstract by Marxist writers, but as part of the more general discourse on social relations.

7.2.2 The Production of Nature

From the Marxist perspective it follows that there is no such thing as an external environment independent from social activity. The human production of nature takes two forms.

First, nature is produced by the successive effects of human activity, from the clearing of forests to the production of micro climates. This point has been made by many writers but, where Marxists differ from other scholars is in stressing the primacy of the relations of production in the evaluation and production of nature (see Smith and O'Keefe, 1980). In seeking to stress the social dynamic of people/environment relations, Marxist inspired work has been concerned with drawing the links between capital accumulation and environmental degradation. Walker (1979), for example, identifies circuits of resources in which elements of the external world are perceived, appropriated and turned into the commodity form. In the simple case a direct relationship is drawn between the relations of production and the drive for profit, on the one hand, and environmental degradation, on the other. 'The mode of perceiving nature, under the rule of private property and money is a real contempt for, and a practical degradation of nature' (Marx, 1964, p. 37, originally published in 1844). More recently, Marxists have criticised those arguments which use a socially neutral language of technological progress to explain the increase in pollution. The ecological crisis, it is argued, is not caused by the tyranny of progress, 'the ones responsible are the monopolies, the corporations, they have made enormous profits while they pollute and destroy our environment. . . . The major victims are the working people, who suffer the effects of pollution every minute of their lives' (Hall, 1972, p. 7). A major difficulty with this argument, which reads off environmental degradation from the dominant capitalist mode of production, is the existence of widespread pollution in, what Bahro (1978) has termed, actually existing socialist societies. The existence of such environmental degradation suggests a structural similarity between both capitalist and socialist, industrialising and industrialised societies, and creates difficulties for a simple Marxist schema in which explanatory primacy is afforded to the relations of production.

Second, nature is reproduced through the images of the environment employed in literature and cinema, mass media and all cultural forms (see also Barański, ch. 9; Lumley and O'Shaughnessey, ch. 10). An important element in, what we may call, the cultural materialist school, has sought to identify the links between environmental images and social interests in art (Barrell, 1980; Rosenthal, 1982), poetry and literature (Williams, 1973). England with its large scale urbanisation and complex rural mythology, intensively capitalist agriculture and deep anti-urbanism has been a rich area for study. Williams (1973), for example, shows how the concepts of city and country were used by English writers against the background of agricultural enclosure and large scale urbanisation and capitalisation. In particular, Wiener (1981), in a survey of England from 1850 to 1980, discusses the struggle between radicals and conservatives to lay claim to the legacy of old rural England. He suggests that the anti-urbanism of the middle and upper classes was part of a decline in what he terms the industrial spirit. The employment of environmental images was not merely a product of social change, 'the English countryside became a social and cultural force. The abundance of historical associations and natural beauty with which the English countryside had been endowed by previous centuries was not an unmixed blessing for the nation. Like the existence of a vast overseas empire, it encouraged English opinion to retreat into a less demanding world, like the fixed industrial capital created by early economic sucess, the impressive cultural capital embodied in the scenery and buildings of the country help to commit Britain to its past and to an essentially antique self-image' (Wiener, 1981, pp. 79–80).

7.2.3 Population and Resources: The Limits to Growth?

An important strand in the development of Marxist thought has been the elaboration of arguments against those who take the population-resources equation as a set of fixed relations. We have already noted that Marx criticised Malthus for his apologia of the existing social system dressed up as the limitations of the natural world. Contemporary Marxists have responded in similar vein to the neo-Malthusian reasoning of the more recent 'limits to growth' arguments. The argument, which saw its fullest articulation in the late 1960s and early 1970s (see Ehrlich and Ehrlich, 1970; Meadows *et al.*, 1972), stated that population growth was coming up against the limits of the world's carrying capacity and that food production would be unable to support the ever increasing population; increasing demand through population and industrial growth was reducing the non-renewable resources of the earth, and increasing pollution levels caused by population and industrial growth were harming the planet. The answer to these problems, according to many commentators, lay in stabilising population growth and reducing the levels of industrial growth. The basic answer therefore was to slow down growth. Criticisms of these arguments have been many. Subsequent studies have questioned the empirical basis of many of the forecasts, but the Marxists' response has been to question the very assumptions of the arguments. They have argued that overpopulation, scarcity and pollution are socially determined, the so-called limits to growth are not the barriers of nature but the product of social practice. It is not so much the crude population number-quantity of resources ratio that matters, but the way the resources are evaluated, produced and distributed. Resources in capitalist world economy are evaluated and produced according to profit, not human need. This contradiction explains why American farmers can be paid to destroy their crops while a significant proportion of the world's population goes hungry. It thus follows that the answer does not lie simply in limiting population but in transforming the social system. The emphasis on crude numbers and 'natural' factors in the limits to growth argument is at best incorrect and at worst a justification for the status quo, as the no growth society becomes the no change society, freezing patterns of ownership and distribution of life chances. As Harvey (1974) notes, 'the overpopulation and shortage of resources arguments can be used as powerful ideological levers to persuade people in acceptance of the status quo and of authoritarian measures to maintain it' (p. 274). Nor does the answer lie in the crude technological fix arguments of better science and more efficient technologies: 'The solution to environmental problems depends therefore not merely upon reforming the science and technologies available but transforming the social relations of production – production of policy, technology and knowledge itself' (Sandbach, 1980, p. 223). Marxists are not alone in making this point. Their unique contribution is to stress that the solution lies in taking common control over the means of production.

7.2.4 Environmentalism and Socialism

The 1960s and 1970s witnessed the emergence of an important social movement in Western Europe and North America, the development of environmental groups. This environmentalism was a broad and diverse movement covering environmental determinists, conservatives, liberals and socialists – all with an increasing awareness of the environmental costs of economic growth in general and the nature of environmental degradation in particular. The reaction of Marxist commentators to this phenomenon has varied over time. In the early days many were rightly sceptical of the conservative and reactionary elements in environmentalism. It was also noted that much popularised ecology appealed to harmony, balance and symbiosis, and overlaid a 'deep seated wish for the reimposition of control and authority through consensus and social cohesion' (Lowe and Warboys, 1978, p. 199). The message to shift collective attention from the 'merely' political to the 'main' biological aspects of the human situation reintroduced biologism in a new guise.

The environmental movement was seen by many Marxists simply as a middle class response to economic growth. This interpretation tended to question the existence of a purely ecological crisis, preferring to see the movement as the articulated demands of the middle and upper classes for environmental security and peace often at the cost of working class jobs. In recent years however there has been a more subtle interpretation of environmental issues, as shown in the establishment of the Socialist Environment and Resources Association in 1973 and in a fusion of left-wing and environmental groups in most Western European countries. The most effective has been the Green Party in West Germany. There are now a large number of writers who accept the existence of an ecological crisis linking its cause and solution to the language and politics of contemporary Marxism (Illich, 1973; 1978; 1981; Gorz, 1980; Croall and Sempler, 1980; Croall and Rankin, 1981; Bahro, 1982). This new attitude to environmentalism has in turn caused a reinterpretation of Marxism, because a consistent theme, in early Marxist theory and socialist rhetoric throughout the 19th and 20th centuries, has been the potential of human ingenuity in comparison to its limited articulation in capitalist society. The promise of plenty on the basis of industry organised on socialist principles has been a resonant theme throughout socialist propaganda over the years. The solution to poverty was seen to be a more affluent, better organised, bigger and better economic growth machine.

This new interpretation has asked Marxists not only to think about the relations of production but to consider the forces of production. In according more attention to the technostructure, Bahro (1982) and others are shifting attention away from the notion of unlimited expansion towards general emancipation, because, as they see it, socialism should not be simply concerned with managing the economic growth machine better than the capitalists, but with dismantling and completely replacing it by an economic system sensitive to ecological considerations and human needs. The recent work of Bahro recalls the concerns of William Morris. This intellectual fusion of environmentalism and socialism has its political parallel, 'the socialists need the Greens, for survival is a pre-condition for them to attain their traditional goals; the Greens need the socialists, for survival can only be ensured by disconnecting the motor of monopoly competition' (Bahro, 1982, p. 22).

7.3 SPACE AND SOCIETY

The concern with space and location has long been a central concern in human geography. It has not been an explicit focus in Marxist thought. Human geographers and others with a concern with space and an interest in Marxism have been attempting to combine the two (Gregory and Urry, 1984). The starting point has been a rejection of those approaches which see space either as a blank page simply inscribed with human activity or as an external factor above, beyond or outside society. In viewing the relationship between space and society as a dialectical one, Gregory (1978, p. 121) notes that we 'need to recognise . . . that social structures cannot be *practiced* without spatial structures, and *vice versa*'. Within this general framework, if we 'view location as a fundamental material attribute of human activity but recognise that location is socially produced. The production of spatial configurations can then be treated as an 'active moment' within the overall temporal dynamic of accumulation and social reproduction' (Harvey, 1982, p. 374).

The Marxist critique of existing approaches to spatial configurations has involved a rejection of purely spatially based explanations. Linguistic usage in this area is interesting. The use of spatial adjectives and nouns – the regional problem, the problem of the inner city, the division of the world into rich north and poor south – is often used in conjunction with an approach which places the explanatory emphasis on place and location. The problems are thus seen as place specific, arising from the spatial organisation of society and not from the social organisation of space. There is circular reasoning at the basis of this approach, as the problems of peripheral regions are seen to be their peripherality, the problem of the inner city areas is where they are, and the north is rich because of where it is while the south is poor because it has southern type attributes. To place the explanatory emphasis in this manner is to spatialise issues, to deny or misrepresent their social significance. In contrast Marxist and Marxist-inspired writings on world development, regional structures and spatial behaviour have attempted to link social and spatial considerations, to see the social production of space and the spatial reproduction of society as an interrelated process. Work on the uneven development at the world scale, for example, has attempted to stress the development of underdevelopment, rather than seeing the cause of world poverty in lack of resources or climatic factors or in theories which stress the inadequacy of Third World societies (Buchanan, 1972; Amin, 1974; Brookfield, 1975; Blaut, 1976; Frank, 1981). Analysis of regional structures has focused on the combined processes of capital accumulation and government policy, and on how regional structures in turn shape subsequent accumulation, while regional alliances shape government policy (Holland, 1976; Lebas, 1977; Walker, 1978; Carney et al., 1980; Peet, 1980; Clark, 1981). The critique of existing location theory has involved a rejection of the possibility of autonomous location theory independent from analysis of the nature of society and the type of economy in which firms and workers make decisions (Walker and Storper, 1981; Storper and Walker, 1983). The main thrust has been 'to establish the link between locational behaviour, changing patterns of employment and developments at the level of the process of capital accumulation' (Massey, 1981, p. 226).

We can consider some of the more detailed work by looking at the relationship between space and accumulation and space and reproduction.

7.3.1 Space and Accumulation

If capital accumulation is seen as a space-time phenomenon, then we can see more clearly the role of space as an active moment. The peaks of the long waves of the Kondratieff cycles, for example, can then be seen as a bunching of innovations and investments which have definite spatial outcomes (see Smith, ch. 1). Each peak sees the development of new forms of technology and new labour processes which lead to re-evaluations of nature and locational attributes. During the industrial revolution in Britain, for example, coal fields and deposits of iron-ore became valuable commodities and, given restricted transport technology, locations close to these sites became highly prized. Capital investment was attracted to these sites, because given the prevailing forces of production, these were the sites of greatest profitability. Gregory (1982) provides a detailed case study of spatial structure and social process in the early industrial revolution, while Dunford and Perrons (1983) provide a more general historical geography of the development of British capitalism.

In any one cycle of capital accumulation there is the production of spatial structure. Patterns of fixed capital investment and labour power distribution provide the decision-making context for successive cycles. Space is not only continually structured but also shapes the basis for capital restructuring. Massey (1978) has characterised the relationship as a series of waves of capital accumulation. Capital responds to the uneven distribution of conditions for accumulation and creates new transport routeways, new spatial divisions of labour, and this transformed spatial structure in turn guides the flow of successive waves of capital accumulation.

Recent years have seen a geography of restructuring with implications for the restructuring of space and social relations. There have been improvements in transport which 'annihilate space with time' and the introduction of mass production techniques. These characteristics have been utilised by capital, which is increasingly organised in large international conglomerates and thus able to make locational decisions in a world-wide context. The criteria of locational decision-making vary by sector. International variations in wages, for example, provide the context for making decisions concerning factories with mass production techniques. The newly industrialising countries, for example, South Korea, Singapore, have all been the site of multi-national investment because of the cheap and relatively docile workforces. Research and development (R & D) establishments in contrast require highly skilled labour generally only available in the richer developed countries. There is a concentration of R & D facilities in the more favoured regions of the developed world, for example, southeast England and high amenity towns of the United States. The net result has been for a pattern of disinvestment from the older industrial cities and regions of the developed world with consequent effects on sections of labour. In the USA, for example, there has been the growth of the Sunbelt and the decline of the Frostbelt (Perry and Watkins, 1977), while Doreen Massey (1984) examines the decline of the old industrial cores in Britain as a response to spatial readjustment and industrial restructuring.

Location is not only a relative attribute. given the nature of private property, it is bought and sold as a commodity. Recent Marxist work has sought to refurbish Marx's writing on land and location while also applying his methods to the contemporary scene.

The starting point has been the critique of the concept of rent used in standard location studies. Rent is seen in the dominant neo-classical framework as a harmonious allocative device sorting out land uses within the context of general equilibrium. In criticising this concept of rent, Harvey (1973; 1974) resurrected Marx's three categories of differential, monopoly and absolute rent (see also Pearce, ch. 3). Although there has been a vigorous detailed debate over the exact definition and validity of the different categories (see Bassett and Short, 1980), the main thrust of the Marxist argument has been to show that rent is a social relationship arising from the power afforded to landowners by private ownership; rent is a payment to private property with the amount being fixed by the relative bargaining power between landowners, producers and consumers. The balance obviously varies by economic sector and by location. Through the development of rent theory, the locational aspects of traditional Marxist concerns on accumulation and reproduction have been elaborated (see Harvey, 1982, ch. 11).

The nature of land ownership obviously affects the perception and utilisation of land as a commodity. In their work on land ownership in Britain, Massey and Catalano (1978) have identified three types of land ownership: former landed property, industrial land ownership and financial land ownership, each with differing characteristics and attributes. For former landed property, which involves the church, crown estates and landed aristocracy, land is used as a basis for profit seeking activities, although other social and symbolic considerations are also important. For the second category, which includes owner occupier farmers, construction companies and the manufacturing sector, land is simply an element of their operation. In some of these sectors, however, the relationship to land is not quite so simple. Construction companies which have large land holdings can reap speculative gains at times of increasing land prices. The distinction between land as a prerequisite for construction and as an investment in its own right can become blurred. The relationship of the farmer to the land is a complex one. Land is a factor of production but often notions of stewardship effect commodity relations. However, the rise of large agribusiness and associated reshaping of agricultural landscapes marks a move towards a more purely commodity relationship. For the final category of financial land ownership, which includes the pension funds, banks and property companies, land is a commodity to yield investment returns. The growth of these financial institutions and their involvement in land and property markets has been a subject of considerable research (see, for example, Plender, 1982), but the hallmark of the specifically Marxist contribution to this field has been to concentrate on identifying definite circuits of capital and noting their implications for investment in other sectors (Thompson, 1977; Minns, 1982). The academic concern with land and property investment has had political corollaries. A number of commentators have sought to inform political debates concerning public control over land and investment (Massey *et al.*, 1973). A consistent theme of much radical thought and some Labour Party practice in Britain has been the attempt to capture development gains of land transactions for the local communities. In the early 1970s, in the wake of the property boom, much interest was focused on land nationalisation, but the resultant Community Land Act of 1975 was a poor shadow of the original scheme.

7.3.2 Space and Social Reproduction

Space is not only a site for capital accumulation, it is also the scene for social reproduction. Social relations vary over space and spatial relations modify social patterns. As Urry (1981) notes, 'social practices are spatially patterned, and . . . these patterns substantially effect these very social practices' (p. 456).

The relationship between space and social practice has been mainly considered through the nexus of the uneven development of capitalism. The onset of capitalism has involved a radical transformation of the socio-spatial structure. New factories have been built, existing social relations have been modified and transformed, and cities and regions have been tied into a world capitalist market by commodity relations and increased transport networks. All this development has been an uneven one. A number of scales can be identified.

(a) At the world scale a distinction has been made between the core of the world economy, made up of the rich capitalist countries, and the peripheral social formations, often known as the Third World. The semi-periphery is an intermediate classification. This structure is reproduced in social relations and transformed by political practice. Perhaps the single most important contribution has come from Lenin (1965; first published in 1917) who argued that the relative stability of the core derived from the high wages paid to sections of labour. The creation of a labour aristocracy in the core with a material interest in social democratic parties was possible because of the exploitation of the periphery. The epicentre of revolution in the later stages of capitalism, according to Lenin, shifted from the core to the periphery. In large measure, the historical experience of the 20th century would seem to verify this hypothesis. Revolutions, as Marxists use the term, have very largely been confined to the periphery and semi-periphery. However, in those areas the picture has been varied, as capitalist uneven development has taken place against a varied background, from the feudal relations of Latin America to the tribal histories of Africa and to the kingdoms of Southeast Asia. The result is a complex mosaic of social formations in which class relations vary and the potential for revolutionary ideologies is not restricted to the urban working class (Alavi and Shanin, 1982).

(b) At the regional scale the analysis has focused on two interrelated topics. First there has been the general work on nationalism (Nairn, 1977; Short, 1982, especially ch. 4; Anderson, 1983). Classical Marxism never dealt very satisfactorily with nationalism. The feeling has persisted amongst Marxist scholars that nationalism was somehow a blind alley or even worse a diversion from the main class struggle. The most important work of recent years to question this assumption has been that of Nairn (1977), which sought to establish an explanatory framework for discussing nationalism. In essence nationalism, according to Nairn, arises when cleavages of uneven development are overlain with differences in culture, language and opportunities. Nationalism is the cultural vehicle used to mobilise popular support against perceived inequality and an attempt to transform the structuring of space. Nairn's work has been widely criticised, Hobsbawm (1977) repeats the old Marxist charges, while others have noted that his work concentrates on nationalism in areas with lower than the national average income and restricted economic opportunities which ignores, for example, the case of Catalonia and the Basque country in Spain where higher regional incomes are found but nationalism still flourishes. Despite its perhaps too simple assumptions on the link between uneven development and nationalism without a more detailed analysis of mediating factors, Nairn's work constitutes an important reference point. Anderson (1983) has developed our understanding of some of these factors in his analysis of language and information dissemination.

Second, there have been the more specific studies of the way capital accumulation and consequent social relations vary within particular regions. This has involved general statements (Lipietz, 1977) and analyses of local economies which pay particular attention to the role of the state, patterns of ownership and the effect of restructuring on the local social structure (Castells and Godard, 1974; NTCDP, 1978; MSRG, 1980; Simon, 1980). Although varying in detail, all these studies highlight the important differences between regions and local labour markets not only in terms of economic structure, but also in terms of social relations, political attitudes and political practice. In Britain, for example, because of difference in class composition there are clearly some regions, such as South Wales and Central Scotland, which are more radical than others (Cooke, 1983a). These differences are part cause and part effect of cycles of accumulation as capital partly creates and partly responds to these differences in the conditions for accumulation across space and over time.

(c) In the simplest Marxist model two classes are formed in relation to the ownership/non-ownership of the means of production. Although the relationship between political and class interests is a contentious issue within Marxism (see Urry, ch. 5; Dunleavy, ch. 6), for present purposes the important point to note is that traditionally politics is almost entirely linked with ownership and production. But in recent years there has been an emergence of the politics of consumption, especially that tied to particular locations. Much human activity is firmly rooted in small local territories. The area of residence is as much a place of socialisation as workplaces, indeed for some sections of the population, especially those engaged in non-waged work, it is of greater importance. The rise of local political movements, such as residents groups, community associations and environmental groups has seen the growth of local political practices seeking to shape urban structure and local social relations (Short, 1984). The growth of community actions and neighbourhood politics has been the source of some controversy in Marxist studies. Crudely, two alternatives have been suggested. On the one hand, there are those who see it either as an epiphenomenon to the main capital–labour cleavage (Harvey, 1976). Such analyses, in seeking to see community politics as incidental to the essential politics, fail to understand the reason for and consequences of consumption politics. But because the politics of consumption have a real material basis (see Saunders, 1978) and real political effects (Dunleavy, 1980), there are those, on the other hand, who, while accepting the basic Marxist frameworks, see community politics as a legitimate form of political practice and a real basis for social cleavages, social mobilisation and social change. The most recent work of Castells (1983) takes this line of argument to its furthest extent, by arguing that mobilisation based on residence and consumption is as, if not more important than that based on work and production.

7.4 MARXISM AND THE METROPOLIS

The city had a special place in Marx's thought, since it was the built form of industrial capitalism. From his writings and especially those of Engels (*The Housing Question*, *The Condition of the English Working Class in 1844*), we can identify two themes. The first was that the city was not something separate from the wider society. This now seems obvious but for many 19th- and 20th-century observers the sheer pace and scale of urbanisation seemed to have a life of its own. There was the development of a separate urban discourse which treated the city separate from society and abstracted urban matters from wider social concerns (Smith, 1980; Saunders, 1981). This tradition is echoed, when contemporary commentators discuss the urban crisis, the inner city problem, etc. separately from a fuller understanding of society. The label of urban or of inner city often seems to spatialise rather than socialise issues. Those working within the Marxist tradition reject the urban specific approach.

The second major theme was the radical potential of the city. For Marx and Engels the city was pregnant with socialist consequences. The concentration of workers in cities gave the potential for collective experience to be translated into socialist practice. The process of urbanisation saved people from the 'idiocy of rural life'.

The growing social tension within the city in the 1960s and 1970s stimulated both academic and government concern, which formed a platform and provided institutional space for an explosion in Marxist inspired writings on the city (Harvey, 1973; Pickvance, 1976; Castells, 1977; 1979; 1983; Harloe, 1977; Tabb and Sawyers, 1978; Bassett and Short, 1980; Scott, 1980; Dear and Scott, 1981; Harloe and Lebas, 1981; Mingione, 1981; Simmie and Lovatt, 1983; Short, 1984; and in the papers regularly published in the journals, *International Journal of Urban and Regional Research* and *Society and Space*). From this huge literature I will discuss briefly two major themes.

7.4.1 The City and Capital

A major theme of Marxist urban studies has been to unravel the relationship between the dynamics of capital accumulation and the production of built form. Two strands can be identified. The first is concerned with the city as a setting for capital–labour relations. Gordon (1978), for example, seeks to demonstrate within a general model of urbanisation and capitalist development in the United States how industrial suburbanisation was partly a response by capital to the increasing power of the working class within the city. Clark (1981) shows more generally how spatial decentralisation of production and the emergent division of labour within sectors are used as bargaining strategies by firms in their dealings with labour.

A second strand has drawn on the work of Baran and Sweezy (1966), who within an underconsumptionist model (see Smith, ch. 1) sought to show how, for the United States, investment in the built form was an important investment outlet which delayed the long-term tendency towards stagnation. The state had a key role in underwriting and stimulating this process with infrastructural investments and conducive social and economic policies. The link between capital and built form was firmly established in this model. This strand has been developed by Harvey (1978) who identifies two circuits of capital. The primary circuit involves investment in the production of commodities, while the second circuit involves investment in fixed capital items, for example, roads, buildings, etc. Investment in the second circuit provides a temporary solution to the crisis of over-accumulation in the primary circuit. In this way Harvey ties in the production of the built environment with circuits of capital and the recurring crisis of capitalism. However, the process of profit equalisation would seem to be a more appropriate explanation of shifts between the two circuits, since it does not involve an *a priori* assumption of underconsumption or over-accumulation. The main weakness of this whole line of work is to see the production of particular types of built form as neatly dovetailed to the needs and interests of capital. Much Marxist analysis of suburbanisation has been particularly guilty of this error, seeing the suburbs as neatly meeting the needs of capital accumulation, while also providing the ideal form for social and political reproduction. The more sophisticated treatments are aware of the contingencies. Walker (1981) for example notes:

> The construction of urban space is clearly a *constitutive* process ... not a phenomenon to be relegated to an unmaterial, reflective superstructure ... the social relations of the mode of production set limits and create pressures for a certain kind of spatial organization, but they do not determine spatial relations in any unique, non-contradictory or unidirectional way. Indeed, spatial relations are part of the internally structured whole of a mode of production. (p. 384)

But the problem remains of analysing the production of built form within a deterministic approach while also being sensitive to contingent factors. This is a problem central to Marxism as an explanatory theory of how history evolves and why particular spatial configurations emerge. Recent work has begun to identify the specific agents involved in the production of urban space. Boddy (1981), for example, analyses the growth of the property sector, that nexus of financial institutions and property companies which invest in and administer the secondary circuit, while Ambrose and Colenutt (1975) consider the case of property development in London and Brighton. The most interesting development of Marxist urban studies is the move away from the grand ahistorical generalisations towards a much more detailed analysis of specific agents operating in real time.

7.4.2 The City and Community

In their concern with the city as a scene for the wider reproduction of social relations Marxist writers have focused on two topics. First there has been a concern with class structure and residential segregation. The attempt has been made to integrate theories of residential differentiation with those of social stratification and class formation. Harvey (1975), in developing Giddens' (1973) ideas, sees residential differentiation as an important secondary force of social stratification: residential areas provide a common background of shared experiences, a locale for the maintenance and production of life styles, attitudes to work and education. Social inequalities and social images are produced and reproduced in the urban mosaic of the city. In essence Harvey sees a functional link between residential differentiation and the reproduction of a class based society. Residential differentiation functions in two senses in this schema: (a) it is secondary to the basic capital–labour division formed at the workplace and leads to community consciousness rather than class consciousness which vitiates class struggle; (b) the different neighbourhoods reproduce the different elements of the labour force with their varying levels of skill, attitudes and aspirations. However, the role of residential segregation is more complex than Harvey's scheme allows. Sharply differentiated residential areas may produce intra-group cohesion. The transformation of this cohesion into inter-class conflict depends on a whole series of contingent factors which may lead to either 'accommodative reaction, or ... a powerful practice of revolt' (Katznelson, 1979, p. 232). Harris (in press), for example, notes the range of political consequences arising from similar patterns of residential segregation, while Katznelson provides a detailed case study drawn from the United States. He convincingly argues that the strength of residential segregation along ethnic cleavages in the USA is one reason behind the lack of class-conscious labour policies.

The second topic has been a concern with the city itself as a scene for social and political struggle. Harvey (1976) sees a broad conflict between a landed fraction of capital, whose revenue comes from landownership, a construction fraction of capital, and labour with the state acting as a referee between the three, albeit with the interests of capital predominant in its deliberations. This crude framework ignores conflicts between different social groups, between the local and central state, and by reducing such issues to the crude production based capital–labour dichotomy ignores the specificity of consumption based conflicts. A more sophisticated analysis has been developed by Castells (1977; 1978). The starting point is to conceptualise the city as a scene of collective consumption. Items of collective consumption include transport, housing health services, education, etc. which are not produced by the market but which are necessary to the reproduction of labour power. Since the state provides these goods and services, issues of collective consumption become questions of political power encompassing the competing demands of various fractions of capital, consumers, residents and labour. Castells distinguishes between urban struggles, which arise when those affected either by changing demand or perceived levels of provision of items of collective consumption become mobilised, and urban social movements. Demonstrations against increases in urban transport fares, for example, would constitute an urban struggle. These struggles become urban social movements when, under the dominance of the working class they seek a disruption of existing property arrangements and a transformation of dominant political practice. Castells' work has been the centre of intense debate (for example, Saunders, 1979; 1981; Short, 1982) and his early work has been particularly criticised for its mechanistic quality, in which contradictions simply call forth urban struggles. In his later work, however, Castells (1983) employs a more cross-cultural historical framework sensitive to temporal contingencies and social variation.

These two topics highlight the conservative and radical aspects of urbanisation. At a superficial level residential differentiation would seem to vitiate class consciousness, while urban social movements may provide the platform for new widely-based struggles. But these bold remarks need severe qualifications. The effect of marked residential differentiation can have many outcomes ranging from accommodation to revolt. And many urban struggles are concerned with parochial matters, defending local turfs often at the expense of residents in other parts of the city. The politics of location is often an attempt at community self-interest rather than social advancement. The relationship between city, community and society is not simply one of either radicalising action or quiet deference. In the creation of some alternative cultures and in certain community groups whose actions reinforce social inequalities (for example, suburban groups set up to restrict further growth), the relationship is one of subversive quietism and conservative action.

7.5 THE CAPITALIST STATE AND SPACE

Other chapters of this book will be dealing explicitly with Marxist interpretations of the state (see especially, Dunleavy, ch. 6). In this section I will therefore only touch upon those selected facets of the state in which space and location constitute active moments. For general discussions see Johnston (1982); Short (1982); and Clark and Dear (1984).

7.5.1 The State and Space

Two aspects of the relationship between state and space have been identified by those working in the Marxist tradition. First, there has been some consideration of the state as a spatial entity. Since the boundaries of the state incorporate territory varying in character, the state has different issues, problems and responses in different parts of its territory. The practice of state regional planning for example, has been conceptualised as a mediated response to the varying demands of fractions of capital and

Human Geography and Marxism

sections of labour in different parts of the country (Castells, 1975; Dunford *et al.*, 1981).

The second related concern has been with nationalist movements and regional struggles. The interest here, as we have discussed earlier, has been to draw on the links between uneven development, consequent regional policies, and secessionist and nationalist struggles (Nairn, 1977; Carney, 1980). This work has drawn attention to the material preconditions for the articulation of regional conflicts, but has sometimes degenerated into a crude materialism which makes a mechanistic connection between uneven development and secessionist movements. However, there are analyses which are aware of both the cultural framework and the economic basis, and are as sensitive to the historical context as to the nature of the current economic climate (Anderson, 1983). Unless this type of framework is adopted it is difficult to explain those instances where uneven development is marked, but secessionist movements are weak, for example, in the USA.

7.5.2 Central and Local States

In most countries of the world there are a variety of territorial subdivisions of the state apparatus. In general we can identify a central state and a whole series of local or non-central states. The relationship between central and local has been seen by one commentator as a direct, unmediated one in which the local state performs similar types of roles to those of the central one in maintaining accumulation and ensuring legitimation (Cockburn, 1977). But this interpretation fails to note the specificity of local state forms or the existence of real conflicts between central and local state (see Duncan and Godwin, 1982a). In the more recent, non-functionalist perspective now emerging, the local state in capitalist societies is seen as an arena for struggle whose form is shaped by the competing demands found in a society dominated by a capitalist mode of production (see Byrne, 1982; Cooke, 1982; Duncan and Godwin, 1982b).

Particular attention has focused on the local state in urban areas. Saunders (1980) makes a distinction between the urban local state sensitive to local pressure, more democratic and more concerned with social welfare expenditure, and the central state

188 Theories of Society

concerned with aiding capital accumulation and more involved in corporate compromises. In the United Kingdom attention has focused on the increasing tension between central and local government. Behind this seemingly central-local dispute are competing social demands on public expenditure (Bassett, 1982; Boddy, 1983). In the United States the history and consequences of the metropolitan fragmentation of local government have been a prime source of concern (O'Connor, 1973; Markusen, 1978). Particular attention has focused on the resultant fiscal crisis faced by many urban authorities which has been seen as a process of attempting to legitimise the redirection and restructuring of local spending (Marcuse, 1981; Friedland, 1982).

7.5.3 Urban Planning

The state regulated restructuring of urban space affects social relations and social relations are restructured through and in urban planning. The starting point for Marxist analysis of urban planning has been the critique of those approaches which see it as a purely technical exercise informed by professional practice (Fainstein and Fainstein, 1979; Roweis, 1981; 1983; Cooke, 1983b; Forester, 1983). Planning is rooted within a context of material interests and state policies and urban planning is not socially neutral, it is a state activity firmly rooted in the tensions and forces operating on the state in capitalist societies. Now there are some Marxist inspired views of urban planning which see it simply as an aid to capital. However, this functionalist perspective ignores the historical evolution of planning, the changing boundaries of legitimate state action and the mediation of professional ideologies and human agency in the planning sphere.

The weakness of this particular Marxist contribution has been the failure to locate wider debates about the state and state apparatus within empirically informed studies of what planners do and what are the redistributional consequences of planning. More concrete analysis of concrete situations is urgently required if we are to move beyond either journalistic snapshots of individual cities or insipid theorising.

7.6 CONCLUSIONS

There are no simple conclusions which can adequately summarise the range of material covered in this chapter. I will restrict myself therefore to three remarks.

(a) The most important Marxist contribution to the analysis of the relationship between society and space has been to question the existence of ecological limits or environmental constraints independent from social relations and human activity. Increasingly, however, non-Marxists are making the same statement. The specific contributions unique to Marxism has been to insist on the primacy of the relations of production in shaping the nature of the people-environment relationship. And as we have shown this position is problematic.

(b) The use and elaboration of Marxist economic theory has enlivened location based studies of capital accumulation, social reproduction, and urban structures, while an important spatial component and dynamic has been added to the largely aspatial traditional Marxist schemes which prioritised time over space. In the developing area of space–time studies of economic systems, social formations and urban form, Marxism has acted, not as a catalyst causing change while itself remaining untouched, but as an ingredient which itself has been transformed in the process of intellectual development.

(c) The assumption that the adoption of a Marxist perspective *per se* gives a privileged insight is one that cannot be sustained. The divisions within Marxism and the inadequacies of classical Marxism all cast doubt on the ability of a Marxist paradigm, on its own and as presently constituted, to provide a complete explanatory framework for social phenomena. In human geography, as in many other disciplines, Marxism has been almost entirely associated with structural Marxism; enabling all Marxist perspectives to be consistently defined by most commentators as structuralist approaches (see Johnston, 1983). The rise and more recently the fall of structural Marxism from its pre-eminence is mirrored in current debates (Duncan and Ley, 1982). There is now an emerging concern with the creative role of human agency

(Giddens, 1981; Gregory, 1981; Sayer, 1983; Thrift, 1983) and growing interest in social divisions based on race and gender (McDowell, 1983). These concerns are taking many academics, sympathetic to Marxism, beyond the constraints of structuralist perspectives in particular and the confines of contemporary Marxist theory in general. The results could be a radical reshaping of human geography and a subversive transformation of Marxism.

GUIDE TO FURTHER READING

A very useful bibliographical guide is provided by Russell King in his translation of Quaini (1982). Harvey (1982) provides the most sustained general Marxist perspective, while an indication of the development away from structural Marxism towards a concern with human agency can be seen by comparing Castells' two studies on the urban question (1977; 1983).

On the relationship between Society and Nature the most readable work is Croall and Sempler (1980), while Bahro (1982) attempts to link up socialism and environmentalism.

Massey (1984) provides an example of a Marxist inspired perspective on capital accumulation. Work on the spatial context of social reproduction and social relations is only just being developed, but see Short (1984) and Gregory and Urry (1984) for a range of readings.

There is a large variety of works on the city and Marxism. For an international range see Pickvance (1976), Bassett and Short (1980), and Dear and Scott (1981).

REFERENCES

Alavi, H. and Shanin, R. (eds) (1982), *An Introduction to the Sociology of 'Developing' Societies* (London: Macmillan).
Ambrose, P. and Colenutt, B. (1975), *The Property Machine* (Harmondsworth: Penguin).
Amin, S. (1974), *Accumulation on a World Scale: a critique of the Theory of Underdevelopment* (New York: Monthly Review Press).
Anderson, B. (1983), *Imagined Communities* (London: Verso).
Ardrey, R. (1967), *The Territorial Imperative* (London: Collins).
Bahro, R. (1978), *The Alternative in Eastern Europe* (London: New Left Books).
—— (1982), *Socialism and Survival* (London: Heretic Books).

Baran, P. and Sweezy, P. (1966), *Monopoly Capital* (Harmondsworth: Penguin).
Barrell, J. (1980), *The Dark Side of the Landscape* (Cambridge University Press).
Bassett, K. A. (1982), 'Which Way for Labour Councils?', *Local Government Studies*, 8, pp. 8–13.
Bassett, K. A. and Short, J. R. (1980), *Housing and Residential Structure* (London: Routledge and Kegan Paul).
Blaut, J. M. (1976), 'Where Was Capitalism Born?', *Antipode*, 8, pp. 1–11.
Boddy, M. (1981), 'The Property Sector in Late Capitalism: the Case of Britain', in M. Dear and A. J. Scott (eds), *Urbanization and Urban Planning in Capitalist Society* (London: Methuen).
—— (1983), 'Central-local Government Relations: Theory and Practice'. *Political Geography Quarterly*, 2, pp. 119–38.
Brookfield, H. C. (1975), *Interdependent Development* (London: Methuen).
Buchanan, K. (1972), *The Geography of Empire* (Nottingham: Spokesman Books).
Byrne, D. (1982), 'Class and Local State', *International Journal of Urban and Regional Research*, 6, pp. 61–82.
Carney, J. (1980), 'Regions in Crisis: Accumulation, Regional Problems and Crisis Formation', in J. Carney, R. Hudson, and J. Lewis (eds), *Regions and Crisis* (London: Croom Helm).
Carney, J., Hudson, R. and Lewis, J. (eds) (1980), *Regions in Crisis* (London: Croom Helm).
Castells, M. (1975), *Sociologie de l'Espace Industrial* (Paris: Anthrropus).
—— (1977), *The Urban Question* (London: Edward Arnold).
—— (1978), *City, Class and Power* (London: Macmillan).
—— (1983), *The City and The Grassroots* (London: Edward Arnold).
Castells, M. and Godard, F. (1974), *Monopolville* (Paris: Mouton).
Clark, G. L., (1981), 'The Employment Relation and Spatial Division of Labour, A Hypothesis', *Annals of the Association of American Geographers*, 71, pp. 412–24.
Clark, G. and Dear, M. (1984), *State Apparatus* (London: Allen & Unwin).
Cockburn, C. (1977), *The Local State* (London: Pluto Press).
Cooke, P. (1982), 'Class Interests, Regional Restructuring and State Formation in Wales', *International Journal of Urban and Regional Research*, 6, pp. 187–204.
—— (1983a), 'Regional Restructuring: Class, Politics, and Popular Politics in South Wales', *Society and Space*, 1, pp. 265–80.
—— (1983b), *Theories of Planning and Spatial Development* (London: Hutchinson).
Croall, S. and Rankin, W. (1981), *Ecology for Beginners* (London: Writers & Readers).
Croall, S. and Sempler, K. (1980), *Eco-Socialism in a Nutshell* (London: Writers & Readers).
Dear, M. and Scott, A. J. (eds) (1981), *Urbanization and Urban Planning in Capitalist Society* (London: Methuen).
Duncan, J. and Ley, D. (1982), 'Structural Marxism and Human Geography: a Critical Assessment', *Annals of the Association of American Geographers*, 72, pp. 30–59.
Duncan, S. S. and Godwin, M. (1982a), 'The Local State: Functionalism, Autonomy and Class Relations in Cockburn and Saunders', *Political Geography Quarterly*, 1, pp. 77–96.

—— (1982b), 'The Local State and Restructuring Social Relations: Theory and Practice', *International Journalism of Urban and Regional Research*, 6, pp. 157–86.
Dunford, M., Geddes, M. and Perrons, D. (1981), 'Regional Policy and the Crisis in the UK: A Long-run Perspective', *International Journal of Urban and Regional Research*, 5, pp. 377–410.
Dunford, M. and Perrons, D. (1983), *The Arena of Capital* (London: Macmillan).
Dunleavy, P. (1980), *Urban Political Analysis* (London: Macmillan).
Ehrlich, P. R. and Ehrlich, A. H. (1970), *Population, Resources, Environment* (San Francisco: W. H. Freeman).
Eyles, J. (1981), 'Why Geography Cannot be Marxist: Towards an Understanding of Lived Experience', *Environment and Planning A*, 13, pp. 1371–88.
Fainstein, N. I. and Fainstein, S. S. (1979), 'New Debates in Urban Planning: The Impact of Marxist Theory Within the United States', *International Journal of Urban and Regional Research*, 3, pp. 381–403.
Forester, J. (1983), 'The Geography of Planning Practice', *Society and Space*, 1, pp. 163–80.
Frank, A. G. (1981), *Reflections on the World Economic Crisis* (London: Macmillan).
Friedland, R. (1982), *Power and Crisis in the City* (London: Macmillan).
Giddens, A. (1973), *The Class Structure of the Advanced Societies* (London: Hutchinson).
——(1981), *A Contemporary Critique of Historical Materialism* (London: Macmillan).
Gordon, D. M. (1978), 'Capitalist Development and the History of American Cities', in W. K. Tabb and L. Sawyers (eds), *Marxism and the Metropolis* (New York: Oxford University Press).
Gorz, A. (1980), *Ecology as Politics* (Boston: South End Press).
Gregory, D. (1978) *Ideology, Science and Human Geography* (London: Hutchinson).
Gregory, D. (1981), 'Human Agency and Human Geography', *Transactions of the Institute of British Geographers New Series*, 6, pp. 1–18.
—— (1982), *Regional Transformation and Industrial Revolution* (London: Macmillan).
Gregory, D. and Urry, J. (1984) (eds), *Social Relations and Spatial Structures* (London: Macmillan).
Hall, G. (1972), *Ecology, Can We Survive Under Capitalism?* (New York: International Publishers).
Harloe, M. (ed.) (1977), *Captive Cities* (London: John Wiley).
Harloe, M. and Lebas, E. (eds) (1981), *City, Class and Capital* (London: Edward Arnold).
Harris, R. (in press), 'Residential Segregation and Class Formation in the Capitalist City', *Progress in Human Geography*.
Harvey, D. (1973), *Social Justice and The City* (London: Edward Arnold).
—— (1974a), 'Class Monopoly Rent, Finance Capital and the Urban Revolution', *Regional Studies*, 8, pp. 239–55.
—— (1974b), 'Population, Resources and the Ideology of Science', *Economic Geography*, 50, pp. 256–77.
—— (1975), 'Class Structure in a Capitalist Society and the Theory of Residential Differentiation', in R. Peel, P. Haggett and M. Chisholm (eds). *Processes in Physical and Human Geography: Bristol Essays* (London: Heinemann).

—— (1976), 'Labor, Capital and Class Struggle around the Built Environment in Advanced Capitalist Countries', *Politics and Society*, 6, pp. 265–94.
—— (1978), 'The Urban Process Under Capitalism', *International Journal of Urban and Regional Research*, 2, pp. 101–31.
—— (1982), *The Limits to Capital* (Oxford: Blackwell).
Hawley, A. M. (1971), *Urban Society: an Ecological Approach* (New York: Ronald Press).
Hewitt, K. (ed.) (1983), *Interpretations of Calamity* (London: Allen & Unwin).
Hobsbawm, E. (1977), 'Some Reflections on "The Break-up of Britain" ', *New Left Review*, 105, pp. 3–23.
Holland, S. (1976), *Capital Versus the Regions* (London: Macmillan).
Illich, I. (1973), *Tools for Conviviality* (London: Boyars).
—— (1978), *The Right to Useful Employment and Its Professional Enemies* (London: Boyars).
—— (1981), *Shadow Work* (London: Boyars).
Johnston, R. J. (1979), *Geography and Geographers* (London: Edward Arnold).
—— (1982), *Geography and the State* (London: Macmillan).
—— (1983), *Philosophy and Human Geography* (London: Edward Arnold).
Katznelson, I. (1979), *City Trenches: Urban Politics and the Patterning of Class in the United States* (New York: Pantheon).
Lebas, E. (1977), 'Regional Policy Research: Some Theoretical and Methodological Problems,' in M. Harloe (ed.), *Captive Cities* (London: John Wiley).
Lenin, V. I. (1965), *Imperialism, the Highest Stage of Capitalism* (Moscow: Progress).
Lipietz, A. (1977), *Le Capital et Son Espace* (Paris: Maspero).
Lowe, P. and Warboys, M. (1978), 'Ecology and the End of Ideology', *Antipode*, 10, pp. 12–21.
Marcuse, P. (1981), 'The Targeted Crisis: on the Ideology of the Urban Fiscal Crisis and its Uses', *International Journal of Urban and Regional Research*, 5, pp. 330–55.
Markusen, A. (1978), 'Class and Urban Social Expenditure: a Marxist Theory of Metropolitan Government', in W. K. Tabb and L. Sawyers, (eds), *Marxism and the Metropolis* (New York: Oxford University Press).
Marx, K. (1964; orig. 1844), *On the Jewish Question in Karl Marx Early Writings*, translated and edited by T. B. Bottomore (New York: McGraw Hill).
Massey, D. (1978), 'Regionalism: Some Current Issues', *Capital and Class*, 6, pp. 102–25.
—— (1981), 'The UK Electrical Engineering and Electronics Industries: the Implications of the Crisis for the Restructuring of Capital and Locational Change', in M. Dear, and A. J. Scott (eds), *Urbanization and Urban Planning in Capitalist Society* (London and New York: Methuen).
—— (1984), *Spatial Divisions of Labour* (London: Macmillan).
Massey, D. B., Barras, R. and Broadbent, T. A. (1973), 'Labour Must Take Over Land', *Socialist Commentary*, July.
Massey, D. and Catalano, A. (1978), *Capital and Land* (London: Edward Arnold).
McDowell, L. (1983), 'Towards an Understanding of the Gender Division of Urban Space', *Society and Space*, 1, pp. 59–72.

Meadows, D. H., Meadows, D. L., Runders, J. and Behrens III, W. W. (1972), *The Limits to Growth* (New York: University Books).
MSRG (Merseyside Socialist Research Group) (1980), *Merseyside in Crisis* (Manchester Free Press).
Mingione, E. (1981), *Social Conflict and the City* (Oxford: Blackwell).
Minns, R. (1982), *Take Over the City: the Case For Public Ownership of Financial Institutions* (London: Pluto).
Morris, D. (1967), *The Naked Ape* (London: Jonathan Cape).
—— (1977), *Man Watching* (London: Jonathan Cape).
—— (1979), *Gestures* (London: Jonathan Cape).
Nairn, T. (1977), *The Break-up of Britain* (London: New Left Books).
NTCDP (North Tyneside Comunity Development Project) (1978), *North Shields: Living With Industrial Change* (London: Community Development Project).
O'Connor, J. R. (1973), *The Fiscal Crisis of the State* (New York: St. Martin's Press).
Parsons, H. L. (1977), *Marx and Engels on Ecology* (Westpoint, Conn.: Greenwood Press).
Peet, R. (1977), 'The Development of Radical Geography in the United States', *Progress in Human Geography*, 1, pp. 64–82.
—— (1980), 'Capital Accumulation and Regional Crisis in Western Europe', *Environment and Planning A*, 12, pp. 1317–24.
—— (1981), 'Spatial Dialectics and Marxist Geography', *Progress in Human Geography*, 5, pp. 105–10.
Perry, D. and Watkins, A. J. (eds) (1977), *The Rise of the Sunbelt Cities* (Beverly Hill: Sage).
Pickvance, C. G. (ed.) (1976), *Urban Sociology: Critical Essays* (London: Tavistock).
Plender, J. (1982), *That's The Way the Money Goes: the Financial Institutions and the Nation's Savings* (London: Andre Deutsch).
Quaini, M. (1982), *Geography and Marxism*, R. King (ed.) (Oxford: Blackwell).
Rosenthal, M. (1982), *British Landscape Painting* (Oxford: Phaidon).
Roweis, S. (1981), 'Urban Planning in Early and Late Capitalist Societies: Outline of a Theoretical Perspective' in M. Dear and A. J. Scott (eds), *Urbanization and Urban Planning in Capitalist Society* (London: Methuen).
—— (1983), 'Urban Planning as Professional Mediation of Territorial Politics', *Society and Space*, 1, pp. 139–62.
Sandbach, F. (1980), *Environment, Ideology and Policy* (Oxford: Blackwell).
Saunders, P. (1978), 'Domestic Property and Social Class', *International Journal of Urban and Regional Research*, 2, pp. 233–51.
—— (1979), *Urban Politics: a Sociological Interpretation* (London: Hutchinson).
—— (1980), 'Local Government and the State', *New Society*, pp. 550–1.
—— (1981), *Social Theory and the Urban Question* (London: Hutchinson).
Sayer, A. (1983), Review of A. Giddens, *A Contemporary Critique of Historical Materialism*, *Society and Space*, 1, pp. 109–17.
Scott, A. J. (1980), *The Urban Land Nexus and the State* (London: Pion).
Short, J. R. (1982), *An Introduction to Political Geography* (London: Routledge & Kegan Paul).
—— (1984), *The Urban Arena* (London: Macmillan).
Simmie, J. M. and Lovatt, D. (1983), *Marxism and Cities* (London: Macmillan).

Simon, R. M. (1980), 'The Labour Process and Uneven Development: the Appalachian Coalfields 1880–1930', *International Journal of Urban and Regional Research*, 4, pp. 46–71.
Smith, M. P. (1980), *The City of Social Theory* (Oxford: Blackwell).
Smith, N. (1979), 'Geography, Science and Post-positivist Modes of Explanation', *Progress in Human Geography*, 3, pp. 356–83.
—— (1981), 'Degeneracy in Theory and Practice: Spatial Interactionism and Radical Eclecticism', *Progress in Human Geography*, 5, pp. 111–18.
Smith, W. and O'Keefe, P. (1980), 'Geography, Marx and the Concept of Nature', *Antipode*, 12, pp. 30–9.
Storper, M. and Walker, R. (1983), 'The Theory of Labour and the Theory of Location', *International Journal of Urban and Regional Research*, 7, pp. 1–43.
Tabb, W. K. and Sawyers, L. (eds) (1978), *Marxism and the Metropolis* (New York: Oxford University Press).
Thompson, G. (1977), 'The Relationship between the Financial and Industrial Sectors in the United Kingdom Economy', *Economy and Society*, 6, pp. 235–83.
Thrift, N. J. (1983), 'On the Determination of Social Action in Space and Time', *Society and Space*, 1, pp. 23–57.
Urry, J. (1981), 'Localities, Regions and Social Class', *International Journal of Urban and Regional Research*, 5, pp. 455–73.
Walker, R. (1978), 'Two Sources of Uneven Development under Advanced Capitalism: Spatial Differentiation and Capital Mobility', *Review of Radical Political Economy*, 10, pp. 28–37.
—— (1979), Editor's introduction to special issue on natural resources and environment, *Antipode*, pp. 1–16.
—— (1981), 'The Theory of Suburbanization: Capitalism and the Construction of Urban Space in the United States', in M. Dear and A. J. Scott (eds), *Urbanization and Urban Planning in Capitalist Society* (London: Methuen).
Walker, R. and Storper, M. (1981), 'Capital and Industrial Location', *Progress in Human Geography*, 5, pp. 473–509.
Wiener, M. J. (1981), *English Culture and the Decline of The Industrial Spirit 1850–1980* (Cambridge University Press).
Williams, R. (1973), *The Country and the City* (London: Chatto & Windus).

Part III

Cultural Theory

8 Linguistics*

GIULIO LEPSCHY

8.1 INTRODUCTION

This chapter examines theories and statements about language which, at various times, have been considered representative of 'Marxist linguistics'; it thus studies an episode in our intellectual tradition which already has its own, interesting albeit modest, niche in the history of Marxism as well as of linguistics.

It does not deal with another topic, i.e. the centrality of language in society. Language is today widely felt to be a phenomenon of basic social relevance, with the disparities in linguistic ability constituting an effective social barrier, the control on standards of correctness playing an important role in the management of social hierarchies, the power to define meanings being a key element in the overall manipulation of consciousness, and the use of language appearing as a powerful weapon in political and social struggles. The fact that language is felt today (more than in Marx's times) to be a phenomenon which conditions the whole functioning of society is itself a result of the Marxist atmosphere which pervades contemporary culture.

If, on the other hand, we do not have a satisfactory account for these aspects of language, this ought to be laid at the door of linguistics rather than of Marxism. Whether, and how, they can be investigated in a theoretically interesting way, is an open question; but it seems legitimate to assume that it ought to be possible to find in Marxism notions which are relevant for the study of language in society, for questions of language policy, etc.

---

* I am grateful to the following for their comments on a first draft of this paper (this does not imply that they agree with the line I take or with any individual statements): Z. G. Barański, B. Garvin, V. Jones, A. Lavers, A. Momigliano, P. Ramat, L. Rosiello, J. R. Short, J. Stone, S. Timpanaro.

The fact that the works examined in this chapter are rather disappointing from a linguistic viewpoint appears indicative of the fact that the Marxist tradition has been more relevant and effective in its analysis of economic and social questions (of the problems connected with social inequalities, class contrasts, and their solutions) than in its analysis of systems of knowledge and belief and in its attempt to relate them to the economic structure. But only a dogmatic would conclude that the disappointing nature of the linguistic contributions examined in this chapter detracts from the genuine importance of Marx's and Engels's theories.

8.2 MARX AND ENGELS

Marx and Engels did not have very much to say about language, and what they said was mostly marginal to their main concerns. This is confirmed by an examination of the useful compilation of their writings 'On Language, Style and Translation' prepared for the East German Institut für Marxismus–Leninismus (Marx and Engels, 1974). The works which are usually quoted for their observations on language are *The German Ideology* of 1845–46 and *Dialectics of Nature* of 1873–83. In the former we read:

> The production of ideas, of conceptions, of consciousness, is at first directly interwoven with the material activity and the material intercourse of men – the language of real life [Sprache des wirklichen Lebens]. Conceiving, thinking, the mental intercourse of men at this stage still appear as the direct efflux of their material behaviour. The same applies to mental production as expressed in the language of the politics, laws, morality, religion, metaphysics, etc., of a people. (Marx and Engels, 1975 foll., vol. 5, p. 36; 1956–68, vol. 3, p. 26)
>
> The 'mind' [Geist] is from the outset afflicted with the curse of being 'burdened' with matter, which here makes its appearance in the form of agitated layers of air, sounds, in short, of language. Language is as old as consciousness, language *is* practical, real consciousness that exists for other men as well, and only therefore does it also exist for me; language, like consciousness, only arises from the need, the necessity, of

intercourse with other men. (Marx and Engels, 1975 foll., vol. 5, p. 44; 1956–68, vol. 3, p. 30)

Language is the immediate actuality of thought [Die unmittelbare Wirklichkeit des Gedankens ist die *Sprache*]. Just as philosophers have given thought an independent existence, so they were bound to make language into an independent realm.... The philosophers have only to dissolve their language into the ordinary language, from which it is abstracted, in order to recognize it as the distorted language of the actual world [die verdrehte Sprache der wirklichen Welt], and to realise that neither thoughts nor language in themselves form a realm of their own, that they are only *manifestations* [*Äusserungen*] of actual life [des wirklichen Lebens]. (Marx and Engels, 1975 foll., vol. 5, pp. 446–7; 1956–68, vol. 3, pp. 432–3)

These statements have an obvious Hegelian ring, with language being 'the existence of Spirit. Language is self-consciousness existing for others' (Hegel, 1977, p. 395; see also Hegel, 1971, p. 213). It is possible, in fact, to relate the marginality of language in Marx's thought to its peripheral, background position (notwithstanding Simon's (1966) attempt to show its centrality) in Hegel's philosophy (see Bodammer, 1969).

Some twelve years after the *German Ideology*, in the *Grundrisse*, of 1857–58, Marx stresses the social nature of language with words which seem to imply its direct connection with the existence of the community, rather than its dependence on the economic base: 'Language itself is the product of a community, just as it is in another respect itself the presence [Dasein] of the community, a presence which goes without saying [das selbstredende Dasein desselben]' (Marx, 1973, p. 490; 1974, p. 390).

In *Dialectics of Nature* we find a more positivist statement of the origin of language, in connection with work and social interaction. As is well known, this was a theory defended by L. Noiré (1877, pp. 331, 346–7) in his essay on the origin of language. Hegel also discusses work and language in chapter VI, B, I, a of the *Phenomenology*; in chapter V, A, c he comments: 'Speech and work are outer expressions in which the individual no longer keeps and possesses himself within himself, but lets the inner get completely outside of him, leaving it to the mercy of something other than himself' (Hegel, 1977, p. 187).

This is what Engels writes on this question:

> the development of labour necessarily helped to bring the members of society closer together by multiplying cases of mutual support, joint activity, and by making clear the advantage of this joint activity to each individual. In short, men in the making arrived at the point where *they had something to say* to one another. The need led to the creation of its organ; by modulation the undeveloped larynx of the ape was slowly but surely transformed for ever more developed modulation, and the organs of the mouth gradually learned to pronounce one articulate letter after another. (Engels, 1954b, p. 232; Marx and Engels, 1956–68, vol. 20, pp. 446–7)

There appears to be little awareness of the grammatical complexity which characterises language and whose connection with the development of the larynx is far from clear. This was of course not uncommon at the time. Also problematic are the assumptions concerning different degrees of development reached by different languages (and their possible racialist implications) which seem to be involved by statements like the following:

> First labour, after it, and then with it, articulate speech – these were the two most essential stimuli under the influence of which the brain of the ape gradually changed into that of man . . . The reaction on labour and speech of the development of the brain and its attendant senses . . . gave an ever-renewed impulse to the further development of both labour and speech. This further development did not reach its conclusion when man finally became distinct from the monkey, but, on the whole, has continued since to make powerful progress, varying in degree and direction among different peoples and at different times, and here and there even interrupted by local or temporary regression. (Engels, 1954b, pp. 233–4; Marx and Engels, 1956–68, vol. 20, pp. 447–8)

In fact we do not know of any human language which is less 'human', more 'ape like' (whatever that may mean), than another.

There is a lot about individual languages in Marx and Engels, particularly in the latter, from Romansh to Slavic, often with elaborate 'philological' comments (which are unconvincingly argued, see Marx and Engels, 1975 foll., vol. 16, p. 558 on the patois of Piedmont and Lombardy being 'in its inflection, thoroughly Provençal'); and considerable attention is paid to the linguistic situation of certain communities and its exploitation for political purposes (see, for example, Marx and Engels, 1975 foll., vol. 7, pp. 65, 341; vol. 8, pp. 233, 369–70; vol. 14, pp. 157–60, 691).

Marx and Engels were interested both in the traditional questions of 'philosophy of language', and in the new 'colossal, extensive science' (Marx and Engels, 1956–68, vol. 29, p. 583) of comparative philology, in 'the tremendous and successful development of the historical science of language which took place during the last sixty years' (Engels, 1954a, p. 444; Marx and Engels, 1956–68, vol. 20, p. 299). Marx called Engels a 'comparative philologist' (Marx and Engels, 1956–68, vol. 32, p. 265), but, although they frequently quote J. Grimm and some other linguists, they do not appear to have exceptionally up to date information in the field, or to use it in a particularly penetrating way. The main exception to this is constituted by Engels's striking work on the Frankish dialect (1974), which illustrates his ability to make effective use of the individual details for testing general hypotheses; it can be considered to be a forerunner of the methods of modern linguistic geography, and is still highly valued by leading specialists in Germanic philology (see Ramat, 1983).

The questions concerning the relations of the two areas of philosophy of language and of comparative philology, which gradually became sharply separated during the 19th century are not straightforward; see the essay by Jendrejek (1975) on Hegel and Grimm, and by Kolb (1970) on Marx and Grimm. There are in the works of Marx and Engels many passages which can be considered belonging to a field of 'Sprachkritik', in which they (but particularly Marx) make sharp considerations on the ideological implications of certain expressions (*The German Ideology* is full of vivid examples: see the critique of the equivocations on *Eigentum* 'property', *Eigenschaft* 'characteristic feature', *Eigentümlichkeit* 'peculiarity', *eigen* 'one's own', in the commercial and in the individual sense; or on 'speculation' in the commercial and in the philosophical sense, Marx and Engels, 1975 foll., vol. 5, pp. 231, 277; 1956–68, vol. 3, pp. 213, 258) or of certain linguistic-cultural traditions: see the striking letter by Engels to

Marx of 29 November 1873 concerning the translation into French of the first volume of *Capital*:

> With all respect for the art with which this chapter was turned into elegant French, I grieve for the beautiful chapter. Its strength and sap and life have gone to the devil. The possibility for an ordinary writer to express himself with a certain elegance is bought with the castration of language. To produce thoughts in this straitjacket of modern French [in diesem modernen Zwangfranzösisch] is more and more impossible. (Marx and Engels, 1956–68, vol. 33, p. 94)

Engels, who in 1841 had criticised the repulsive mixing of languages which was fashionable and stated that 'the carriage of our thoughts does indeed run better on most roads with German rather than French or Greek horses, a fact which ridicule of the extremes of the puristic trend does not alter' (Marx and Engels, 1975 foll., vol. 2, p. 138), in the 1870s in the *Anti-Dühring* stresses the importance of learning classical and modern foreign languages, and objects to the concentration on the grammar of one's own tongue; Dühring

> wants to do away with the two levers which in the world as it is today give at least the opportunity of rising above the narrow national standpoint: knowledge of the ancient languages, which opens a wider common horizon at least to those people of various nationalities who have had a classical education; and knowledge of modern languages, through the medium of which alone the people of different nations can make themselves understood by one another and acquaint themselves with what is happening beyond their own borders. (Engels, 1954a, p. 444; Marx and Engels, 1956–68, vol. 20, p. 298)

Notwithstanding thorough (Erckenbrecht, 1973) and stimulating (Houdebine, 1977) modern discussions, I can only conclude that what we can learn about language and linguistics from Marx and Engels is not very much, with the possible exception of Engels's work on Frankish, and that one of the main points subsequently discussed in the Marxist tradition, i.e. the relation between language and notions such as class, ideology, base and superstructure, does not find a straightforward solution in the works of Marx and Engels. The attempt on the part of modern authors (such as Calvet, 1977; Houdebine, 1977) to present what Marx and Engels say about language as particularly rewarding from the viewpoint of our contemporary problems, seems to me unconvincing. One may note, however, as has been suggested on several occasions by different scholars, that there may be an interesting analogy between what Marx and Engels do in their interpretation of historical and economic facts, and what modern linguists and structuralists do in their analyses. We can recall Z. Harris who in his 1951 review of Sapir's *Selected Writings*, wrote:

> Leonard Bloomfield remarked to me that in studying *Das Kapital* he was impressed above all with the similarity between Marx's treatment of social behaviour and that of linguistics. In both cases, he said, the activities which people were carrying out in terms of their own life situations (but in those ways which were socially available) turned out to constitute tight patterns that could be described independently of what people were about. (Harris, 1970, p. 722)

Also, Lévi-Strauss (1966, p. 44) found in Marx a paradigm for the use of models in social sciences, and before trying to unravel some difficult ethnological question liked to fortify himself by reading some pages from *The Eighteenth Brumaire of Louis Bonaparte* or *A Critique of Political Economy;* and we may recall Luporini's presentation of *Capital* as a work which is not historical, and even less historicist, but structuralist; not to speak, of course, of Althusser and his interpretation of Marxism (see Urry, ch. 5). But here we have, clearly, a question which concerns not Marxist linguistics, but rather the influence of modern linguistics on structuralism, and the relations between the latter and contemporary Marxism (see below sections 8.6; 8.9; and also Urry, ch. 5; Barański, ch. 9; Lumley and O'Shaughnessey, ch. 10).

8.3 EARLY MARXISTS

The texts which are usually quoted, after those of Marx and Engels, for Marxist linguistics, were written at the end of the last century and the beginning of ours.

Paul Lafargue, the French socialist, and husband of Laura

Marx, published an essay in 1894 on 'The French Language Before and After the Revolution' (see the French text in Calvet, 1977, pp. 77–144). In it he outlined the complex opposition between the language of the aristocracy and that of the bourgeoisie, within their social backgrounds, before, during and after the French Revolution. The revolutionary period marked the victory of the freer, more vigorous language of the bourgeoisie over the more regulated, polished language of the aristocracy. The situation, however, Lafargue explains, is not as simple as this dichotomy might suggest. During the 18th century bourgeois language had been gradually gaining ground; but the ideals of the enlightenment had been expressed by the Encyclopedists in the classical language of the aristocracy. During the revolution the most violent and crude expressions of the common people were exploited demagogically by aristocrats and royalists in their antirevolutionary articles even before they were used by the extreme revolutionaries of the *Père Duchesne*. After the revolution, when there was a puristic backlash, it was often the defenders of the revolutionary ideals who turned with nostalgia to the clarity, precision and sobriety of the language of the ancien régime, while writers like Chateaubriand used effectively the new, colourful, romantic language in order to attack the principles of 1789 and to promote the restoration of Catholic ideals, guaranteeing, with the success of their work, the final literary triumph of the language of the bourgeoisie. Lafargue's essay is lively and interesting, but in many ways inadequate in its treatment of linguistic material and in its etymological considerations (even in relation to the state of Romance linguistics at the time). There are statements of a positivist nature on the need to relate language and society, but the argument does not seem to me theoretically impressive. One may agree with Calvet (1977, p. 28) when he states that Lafargue is '*the* Marxist linguist of the nineteenth century' – but this does not say much for Marxist linguistics.

Lafargue's essay was translated into German by K. Kautsky, who at the beginning of the century was involved in a polemic with O. Bauer on the question of language and nation (see the Italian translation in Formigari, 1973, pp. 107–31). The discussion concerns the obvious problem of Marxist internationalism, and of the precise sense in which, say, German, English and Russian workers belong to the same class, across their different nations, and of the importance of language in defining these notions. Lenin and Stalin (see Formigari, 1973, pp. 133–53) also wrote on the language question, in the context of the 'national question', particularly from a Russian viewpoint, facing the problems of the various nations oppressed by the Russian empire (and with the added specific question of the *Bund*, the league of Jewish workers). Again, practically nothing emerges which is of specifically linguistic, rather than political interest in these discussions.

Lenin has in general very little to say about language, as can be seen from the paucity of references in the index volume which accompanies the Russian complete edition of his works (Lenin, 1958–65, *Spravochnyj tom*, part I, p. 727, s.v. *jazyk*). In his reading of Hegel's logic, he writes: 'History of thought=History of language??' (Lenin, 1958–65, vol. 29, p. 81; Lénine, 1973, p. 87), and he takes up again the question of the relation between language and thought when he accepts that 'in language there is only the *general*' (Lenin, 1958–65, vol. 29, p. 249; Lénine, 1973, p. 261), that 'every word (discourse) already *generalizes*' (Lenin, 1958–65, vol. 29, p. 246; Lénine, 1973, p. 258), and that 'the senses show reality; thought and word, the general' (ibid.). In *Materialism and Empirio-Criticism* he states that sensations and ideas are not conventional signs, symbols, hieroglyphs, as Plekhanov wanted, but, as Engels said, 'copies, photographs, images [*izobrazhenija*], mirror-reflections of things' (Lenin, 1958–65, vol. 18, pp. 244–5; 1947, p. 237).

8.4 MARRISM

During the years which preceded and followed the Revolution there was in Russia an extraordinary flowering of intellectual energy, and language did take a place of honour among the interests of some of the groups which were formed, such as the Moscow Linguistic Circle, with Roman Jakobson, and the Opojaz (*Obshchestvo izuchenija poèticheskogo jazyka*: Society for the study of poetic language). Jakobson and Trubeckoj were later among the main animators of the Prague Linguistic Circle. The Russian Formalists initiated theoretical developments of great interest and originality, which have had belated reverberations in the West over the last twenty years. Marxism was not central to these positions, but it contributed to the powerful animation of the intellectual scene. By the late 1920s the long tragic night of Stalin's version of Marxism had fallen on the Soviet Union. For linguistics it took the rather bizarre shape of Marrism. Nikolaj Jakovlevich Marr, son of a Scotsman and a Georgian woman, from 1902 was professor of Armenian and Georgian philology at St. Petersburg. He was interested in languages (with a remarkable knowledge of Caucasian languages) and in the study of material culture. After the Revolution he developed a 'Marxist' theory of language which in the 1930s was, in typically Stalinist fashion, imposed on the whole of the Soviet Union and virtually cut off Soviet studies from the international developments of linguistics for about twenty years. According to Marr language belongs to the superstructure and therefore is determined by the economic base and reflects its changes; there are no national languages, because all languages are class languages. What was felt to be most offensive by linguists, though, was not so much the adoption of these rather crude principles, as their incorporation into the eccentric 'Japhetic' theory Marr gradually elaborated. Originally he called 'Japhetic' certain southern Caucasian languages, but later he extended the notion to include all pre-Indo-European languages of the Mediterranean basin, found elements of Japhetism in Africa and America, and finally derived Indo-European languages as a successive development of the Japhetic ones. He also came to reject the very notion of the genealogical development of languages, based on the differentiation of an original unit into separate branches, and argued instead in favour of convergence or unification of local dialects into larger units. Between local dialects exchanges of all kinds can occur, so that the notion of language family becomes meaningless, and they can lead to the formation of new features which introduce a 'qualitative' change: hence the idea of an evolution by successive 'stages' (Marr's theory is also known as 'stadial'). The first stage of language is cinetic or manual. This hand language is followed by spoken language, at a tribal, totemic stage, with four monosyllables (*sal, ber, jon, rosh*) which are the basis for all further developments in human speech. As for the language of the future, in a classless society this will be thought itself, freed from the encumbrance of natural matter (see Marr, 1933–7; Thomas, 1957; Borbé, 1974, which includes a German translation of an essay by Marr; Gadet *et al.*, 1979, with fascinating documents, in French translation).

8.5 STALIN'S INTERVENTION

In 1950 a discussion took place in the columns of *Pravda* on questions of linguistics (see Murra *et al.*, 1951). Stalin intervened in it, putting a stop to the dominance of Marrism, and changing overnight the face of Soviet linguistics. He derided and rejected many of Marr's suggestions, and produced some unexpected statements about language from a 'Marxist' viewpoint: (a) language does not belong to the superstructure; the latter consists of political, juridical, religious, artistic, philosophical, etc. views and institutions, whose changes do not imply a corresponding transformation of language. The Russian language has remained basically the same from Pushkin to the present day; it had served capitalism just as well as it now serves the socialist system; (b) language does not have a class character: to believe otherwise is to confuse language and culture; language serves the whole of society and can only be marginally influenced, in the use of individual words or phrases, by class speech habits. National languages belong to the whole nation, and what is characteristic of a class may amount to slang, jargon, dialect, but does not constitute a language; (c) what are the features which characterise a language? Its basic lexical stock and its grammatical structure, a set of abstract rules comparable to those of geometry, which abstracts from concrete objects and defines them in terms of their relations. This does not mean that language should be analysed in isolation from society: on the contrary it must be studied in connection with the history of the people who use it as a means of communication.

Stalin's articles enjoyed an immediate success among linguists abroad, partly because they appeared to represent a return to commonsensical assumptions of traditional linguistics, after the most ludicrous extravagances of Marrism. Those Marxists who were sympathetic to the idealist identification of language and art could not fail to see in Stalin's theses a way of subtracting art from the field of superstructure and so guaranteeing its loftier, more independent character; others were struck by unexpectedly original observations, like the one about the parallelism between grammar and geometry. What was little noted at the time was the unsatisfactory drift of his answers from a Marxist even more than from a linguistic viewpoint as shown by his juggling with a crudely oversimplified picture of the notions of base and superstructure. In the Soviet Union what was, on the surface, a beginning of destalinisation (the critique of the suppression of academic freedom by the administrative enforcement of Marr's theories – but this did not apply to the partly analogous situation of biology, in which the dominance of Lysenko's views lasted a few more years) was embraced with the extravagant unanimity characteristic of the Stalinist atmosphere. It has in fact been suggested (Laurat, 1951), even though the argument was not convincingly developed, that there were hard political reasons behind Stalin's intervention, connected with the spread of Russian cultural imperialism: the attainment of literacy in the different national languages of the Soviet Union (with all the required work of elaboration of alphabets, standardisation of varieties, etc.) was a first step toward Russification (knowledge of Russian being also necessary for the technological development of the country). And the Marrists, with their paleontological preoccupations on the one hand, and their schematic Marxism on the other, had proved unable to perform the empirical, descriptive, pedagogic and organisational work required by the linguistic policy of the State.

For a brief period (until Stalin's death in 1953 and the beginning of destalinisation with the Twentieth Congress in 1956) Soviet linguistics was full of self-criticism as leading scholars denounced their previous allegiance to Marr's mistakes and declared their boundless enthusiasm for Stalin's genial principles. This in turn was followed by a short phase of freer debate, in the Khrushchev years, until 1964, in which Western style structural linguistics was openly examined and practised, and then, from the mid-1960s, by a rehabilitation of Marr and a return to more traditional Soviet concerns. I cannot say that the contributions produced through these violent changes of direction give me the impression of having offered any clarification of the problems of Marxism and linguistics.

8.6 SOVIET STRUCTURALISM

One of the main practitioners of contemporary linguistics, who produced a complex mathematical theory of language, S. K. Shaumjan (now teaching in the United States), attempted, in my opinion rather weakly, in 1961 to show the Marxist–Leninist character of structural linguistics. This is the abstract theory of the *relational* structure of language; a structure is a network of *relations* between objects whose nature is defined, in the context of a given analysis, only by the relevant relations. (For instance, the relations btween b, d, g and p, t, k allow us to define the former as voiced and the latter as voiceless, while m or h cannot in the same way be defined as voiced or voiceless respectively, because they remain outside the structure constituted by the voiced-voiceless relation.) Marx in *Capital* has underlined the distinction between relations and physical substance, with reference to the notion of value, which is also central to linguistic structuralism. Lenin has also clearly stated that the term 'matter' has two different senses, one which corresponds to 'physical substance', and the other to 'objective reality, which is external to consciousness'. This second sense includes also the relations mentioned above, and it is the one according to which Marxism is called materialist. Ergo, structural linguistics is materialist, in this second sense of the term 'matter'. It investigates the laws of language, and, as Lenin pointed out, an essential feature of any scientific law is that 'a law is a relation' (Lenin, 1958–65, vol. 29, p. 138; Lénine, 1973, p. 145). It is interesting to find here (see Shaumjan, 1961 and 1971) considerations, made from the viewpoint of linguistics, not too dissimilar from those which some philosophers in the West were advancing in the same years to prove that Marx was in fact the first structuralist, and that therefore the structuralists could call themselves Marxists.

8.7 VOLOSHINOV AND BAKHTIN

The most interesting contributions to the discussion on Marxism and linguistics came, in the Soviet Union, before, rather than after the establishment of Marrist–Stalinist orthodoxy. They are presented here (together with the following section 8.8), outside their 'chronological' order, because their seminal modernity connects them, over the backward-looking Stalinist discussions, with topics and concerns still alive today. One of the most gifted and eccentric linguists, in those early days of Soviet power, was E. D. Polivanov, of whom Shklovskij (1966, pp. 100, 136) has left a striking pen portrait in his memoirs (see Lepschy, 1977). This orientalist, killed soon after his arrest in 1937, was one of the few who dared to speak up against Marrism and succeeded, as late as 1931, in publishing a collection of articles with the challenging title 'For a Marxist Linguistics', notable for its anti-Marrian stance rather than for a constructive development of the question. Another victim of Stalinist terror, V. N. Voloshinov, had managed to published, in 1929, and in a second edition in 1930, a book which only re-emerged into notoriety during the last ten years, when it was reprinted in the West and translated into several languages. Voloshinov, a teacher at the music conservatory of Vitebsk, belonged, with another victim of the purges of the late 1930s, P. N. Medvedev, with Marc Chagall and others, to a group which has become known as 'Bakhtin's Circle'. M. Bakhtin, the author of two brilliant books (one on Dostoevskij, which appeared in 1929 and the other on Rabelais, which appeared in 1965; see Barański, ch. 9), had some of his works published under the name of his friends, partly because he refused to compromise and accept certain modifications and formulations which were at the time unavoidable. The title of *Marxism and the Philosophy of Language*, and certain parts more directly related to it, belong apparently to Voloshinov, but most of the book, as well as its whole inspiration, is in fact Bakhtin's, and the French translation was published under his name (see Bakhtine, 1977, and the preface by R. Jakobson). The book offers an extraordinarily lively and stimulating discussion of 'reported speech', and in general of the way in which speech presents other speech, talks about it and incorporates it. If we perceive the world through language, we can say that language is inevitably about language as well as about the world. The social generation of speech is reflected within speech itself. Within the word we trace the history of the word. This, which is in my opinion the main and most interesting section of the book, is preceded by two parts in which, again with amazing freshness, we find a presentation of the question of language and ideology. What is ideological must have meaning: it is a *sign*. Without signs there is no ideology. What is ideological inevitably has semiotic value. The word is therefore the ideological phenomenon par excellence. Of course different classes use the same language – but from this Voloshinov draws the conclusion (which is more interesting than the statement formulated by Stalin some twenty years later about language showing, like productive forces, a certain indifference towards classes) that 'signs become an arena of the class struggle'

(Voloshinov, 1973, p. 23). The whole discussion is strikingly well informed about the most recent developments in current research, both on 'indirect free speech', in the last part of the essay, and on contemporary linguistics (including, naturally, Saussure) in the first two sections. There is here an anticipation of modern semiotic studies, as they were going to be developed by the School of Tartu with Lotman and Uspenskij (1973). Of course the 'social *multiaccentuality* of the ideological sign' (Voloshinov, 1973, p. 23) and the delicate examination of the different forms of speech within the speech cannot but be related to Bakhtin's 'polyphony' and the theory of 'intertextuality' as it was reintroduced into modern criticism by Kristeva. What this book is not, in spite of all its novelty and intellectual vigour, is an examination of the question presented in its title.

Even more problematic is the question of Marxism in a thinker of genius of the same years, Walter Benjamin (see Barański, ch. 9), who developed a theological and mystical theory of language, which also purports to be materialist (see Benjamin, 1972–82, vol. 2, pp. 140–57; vol. 4, pp. 9–21; Schweppenhäuser, 1983; Agamben, 1983). His work is becoming more and more influential; but I shall say nothing about it, as it implies questions which are too remote from those discussed in this chapter. But a survey must be mentioned in the present context, devoted to works on the sociology of language, and including other studies beyond this field (Benjamin, 1972–82, vol. 3, pp. 452–80). For similar reasons I shall limit myself to a reference to the work of J. Habermas (1979), who in his discussions of hermeneutics, universal pragmatics, and communicative action, develops theories relevant both to philosophy of language and Marxism (for an examination from a Marxist viewpoint, see Anderson, 1983).

8.8 GRAMSCI AND SOCIOLOGICAL LINGUISTICS

Another author who wrote in very difficult circumstances, this time under fascist rather than communist oppression, is Antonio Gramsci (see also Barański, ch. 9; Lumley and O'Shaughnessey, ch. 10). This man of extraordinary intelligence and integrity, whose political and cultural inheritance is far from having lost its relevance, and the interpretation of whose ideas is still far from obvious, was a student of linguistics at the university of Turin, where he was a pupil of Matteo Giulio Bartoli, a comparative philologist who was converted to some aspects of Benedetto Croce's idealist notion of language as a cultural and spiritual force, with results which were interestingly problematic but not altogether felicitous. Gramsci devoted several of the reflections which fill his *Prison Notebooks* to questions of language, but these do not seem to me to be among the most stimulating of his observations. His notes on grammar appear to suffer from the isolation which was characteristic of Italian culture in those years (in a way that does not apply, as we saw, to Bakhtin/Voloshinov). Paradoxically, one senses that it was not so much his Marxism which influenced his linguistics, but vice versa his ideas on language which were the source of some of the notions he developed within his political and ideological outlook (for instance, the concept of linguistic 'prestige' may have helped him to shape as he did the idea of 'hegemony': see Lo Piparo, 1979; Rosiello, 1982).

His Marxism adds sharpness (obviously, more from the viewpoint of observations on method than of actual research) to the attitude of the French linguistic 'sociological' trend (represented in particular by the great comparative philologist Antoine Meillet) by which he was undoubtedly influenced. It is worth noting that much of what has been produced in the way of a sociological analysis of linguistic facts, which appears to be of interest in the context of Marxism, comes from this school, represented by scholars who were not Marxists, like Meillet. More recently Marcel Cohen (see his 1956 synthesis), notwithstanding his allegiance to Marxism, produced work very much in the same sociological tradition (see on this French school of linguistics Bolelli, 1982, which includes a critical sketch of the questions of Marxist linguistics). With reference to these studies, we may add that the exact way in which language should (according to Marxist, or even non-Marxist sociologists of language) be related to society is not immediately clear. In a well known letter to Joseph Bloch of 21 September 1890 Engels expounds the view that only 'in the last instance [in letzter Instanz]' is the base the determining moment, and that it is not the *only* factor. One of the examples he gives (although it is not clear exactly how it relates with these statements) is that one will hardly succeed in explaining by the economy the origin of the High German

Lautverschiebung 'without making oneself ridiculous [ohne sich lächerlich zu machen]' (Marx and Engels, 1955–68, vol. 37, p. 464). But is it ridiculous because we do not know enough about the origins and reasons for the *Lautverschiebung*, or is it because there is something wrong with this sort of explanation? Meillet (1928, ch. 10) has suggested, for instance, that the noun, in Indo-European, with its different cases, presented notions in different forms depending on circumstances, and this was because Indo-European was the language of aristocrats who wanted more than anything else to be independent chiefs: therefore their language used words with a maximum of autonomy. The noun in Romance, instead, presents a notion in a fixed manner, as it does not use the case system any more; the noun is no longer autonomous, but normalised, as is more suitable to a banalised, simplified language such as Vulgar Latin, fit for uneducated speakers of heterogeneous origin, who had nothing in common any more with the chiefs of the groups who had diffused the ancient Indo-European languages. Is this a legitimate sociological hypothesis? If Marr had proposed it, one can imagine how it would have been treated.

8.9 AFTER FREUD AND SAUSSURE

One of Gramsci's most often quoted thoughts suggests that

> every time that, in one way or another, the language question emerges, this means that a series of other problems is making itself felt: the formation and widening of the ruling class, the need to establish more intimate and secure relations between the ruling groups and the national-popular mass, that is to reorganise cultural hegemony. (Gramsci, 1975, p. 2346 = 1950, p. 201)

This statement, which he refers to the Italian *questione della lingua* (i.e. to the problem which runs through the history of Italian culture, about the variety of language which is most suitable for literary use), could also be applied to the discussions on language which have taken place in the Marxist tradition, and might prove helpful in interpreting the current ones: when some general statement is made about language, we should try to interpret it for what it reveals about social and political conditions as well as for its contribution to linguistics proper. And this applies inevitably also to what Marxists say (see Laurat (1951) on Stalin). Much of what we have been saying is of course dependent on certain assumptions about what can be meaningfully called 'Marxist'. Most of the authors I have quoted have remained, for reasons which are quite obvious (either of chronology, or of cultural bias) extraneous to certain trends in the modern tradition for which the question of language has become central. If one wanted to quote individual names to which this more 'linguistic' attitude can be connected, one should of course mention Freud and Saussure, two figures which are at the root of the structuralist and post-structuralist movement.

For Freud (see, e.g., 1900) language (and not just ordinary language, but also the semiotics of our dreams and of all our actions) does not necessarily mean what it says. Under the manifest meaning there is always a latent one, to be retrieved through a difficult process of interpretation; the nature of the difficulty (the split in the subject caused by the unconscious) is such that often the interpretation must come to us from someone else, and it must come through language, in the form of a discourse which reveals to us what we really meant. Our illness is caused by our inability to say what we mean, and our cure consists in becoming capable of saying it. Language is crucial.

In Saussure (1972) we find a presentation of the sign as consisting of signifier and signified, both belonging to *langue* and being defined in terms of *value*, i.e. on the basis of relations between linguistic units, without recourse to the 'external' world, to the 'extralinguistic' object. This has induced some linguists to concentrate on *langue* 'in and for itself' as one reads at the end of the *Course*, in words which apparently belong to the book's editors, on *langue* as an abstract system of formal values, rather than on *parole* as it is used, in the real world, to communicate, in the context of social relations. Within *langue*, many linguists have preferred to analyse the *signifier*, which lends itself to formal treatment more easily than the signified. And the dominance of the signifier has been increased by the central place it occupies in Saussure's work on poetics and in the modern studies inspired by it.

These questions, presented here in traditional terms, appear in a somewhat different light in contemporary discussions. Language, in these trends, which put together Freudian and Saussurean views following Lacan's lead (1966), is not confidently looked at any more as a means of communication, or as an instrument for the expression of thought, something neutral, or transparent, which allows us to record and transmit without distortion our ideas about reality. Language becomes something much more autonomous, opaque and threatening. It takes over. It does not just shape our thoughts, but it also thinks for us, or rather, we are thought/spoken by our language. The basis of our speech is not our self-consciousness, but our unconscious, which is structured like a language. Our being is marked by a lack, symbolised by the phallus. The phallic signifier expresses the desire of the Other, it refers not to a signified but to another signifier, it represents the subject for another signifier. A word does not have meaning, but meaning is always a word for another word. The formation of the subject takes place through language, society, the symbolic order. According to Derrida our relation to the world is discursive, there is nothing outside the text, and all we can do is try to deconstruct it (see, e.g. 1967a; 1967b). Foucault studies the history of our civilisation in terms of strategies of power which are manifested as 'discursive practices' (see, e.g. 1966; 1969; 1977). Althusser tries to identify the relative autonomy of the superstructure and the 'discursive processes' in which class struggle is embodied (see especially 1970); E. Laclau (1981) has arrived at a notion of the 'poetics of politics' based on the suggestion that we must abandon 'the prejudice that objective social relations have a subjacent logic, distinct and more limited than the possible discursive positions', because it is discourse that 'constitutes reality' (and, with a nice touch of Orwellian newspeak, he calls interpretation 'authoritarian', and the practice of intervening and interrupting 'democratic', throwing out at the same time the distinction between science and political action). This is not out of keeping with some aspects of the new semiotics, discussed by Barthes (see, e.g. 1970; 1977; 1978) and Eco (see, e.g. 1976) which present the world as a system of signs in which the very possibility of 'referring', of relating a word to a thing, a linguistic structure to a complex of denoted facts, appears to evaporate, together with any criterion for distinguishing a true discourse from a false one.

Even though some of the authors I have mentioned consider themselves Marxists, the general drift of their arguments (which are of course very different from each other and are not to be reduced to the same assumptions) may 'seem to compromise materialism', as Callinicos (1982, p. 48) disarmingly observes, going on to stress that Marxists ought not to reject this linguistic 'bias', but to take it seriously, both intellectually and politically. What is in fact very curious is that such patently idealist positions, sometimes laced with mysticism and irrationalism (see the vigorous polemic by Timpanaro, 1975, in his book *On Materialism*; also Anderson, 1983), should have come to be hailed by many of their admirers as a model of what contemporary Marxist materialism ought to be. It appears that, mainly for reasons which are left implicit but are evidently grounded on a dislike of contemporary social systems, many intellectuals opt for the stands which seem to them the most radical and subversive, and presumably owing to the long association between revolutionary attitudes and the Marxist tradition, they feel that their positions, just because they are radical, must also be Marxist and materialist, even when these labels seem most inappropriate.

In particular for the specific topic we are discussing, an intellectual trend has developed which is often considered to represent the most advanced Marxist positions in linguistics, and is in fact inspired by the views mentioned above, especially Lacan's version of Freud, Althusser's notion of ideological formations, Foucault's work on discursive strategies, Kristeva's study of the 'revolution' of the literary language (1969; 1974). Perhaps the most influential author in this area is Michel Pêcheux (1975). Some of the main points emerging from this trend are: (a) semantics, which is normally disregarded, or considered intractable, or studied in a purely formal, language bound manner, by linguists, is in fact a crucial meeting point for linguistics and philosophy (and historical materialism in particular) at which their concerns overlap. The meaning of a word is not predetermined by language (as its phonological or morphological structure), but it is produced by the relation between signifiers (what Lacan calls 'metaphor': a word for another word), as an effect of paraphrase which takes place within a discursive formation. (b) 'Discourse theory' is here the central concern, i.e., the study of 'discursive processes' (see also, Barański, ch. 9). This turns out to be quite different from what linguists do under the label of 'discourse analysis', even though 'discourse theorists' often refer to Harris's work, and some 'discourse analysts' perform their investigations with linguistic techniques but in an ideological key (see Fowler *et al.*, 1979; Kress and Hodge, 1979, inspired by Halliday but referring to Foucault's views; recent linguistic introductions to discourse analysis in Brown and Yule, 1983; Stubbs, 1983). Discourse processes do not refer just to *parole*, to individual 'performance' by a speaker who says what he wants to say and, as it were, by accident uses a certain language. They have to do with the fact that what is, in a sense, one and the same language, appears to be fractured along class and ideological lines. One has to investigate 'discursive formations' or 'interdiscourse' which is bound up with the 'ideological formations' characteristic of a 'social formation' at a given point in the development of the class struggle. (It has in fact been suggested that the very notion of *langue*, of a uniform system common to all individual speakers, is not a naturally given object of investigation, but rather an ideological category internal to the linguistic practices of modern bourgeois society, see Balibar and Laporte, 1974.) (c) The notion of 'subject' must be clarified, by examining the split, in the subject of discourse, between the subject of the enunciation, who holds certain views about what he is saying, and a 'Universal Subject', who is already given and enforces the dominant view about what is being said. As a result of this split, things may be said and at the same time questioned (as in 'What you call Marxist linguistics', for instance). The problematic situation of the subject is illustrated by jokes and paradoxes. The 'accidents' in which language breaks down, puns, equivocations, ambiguities, etc. ought to be treasured, investigated and used effectively against the state's attempts to imprison us in the dominant discourse, outside which there is emargination, reserved for the irrelevant nonsense of the poet, or psychiatric treatment, meted out to the dissident (one recalls the striking picture drawn by Orwell, 1949). The dominant discourse can be subjected to a sort of *Sprachkritik*, of which Marx was a past master, and the results can be rewarding not only in cutting through occasional obfuscation, but also in clarifying questions central to the nature of language.

We may try to give some examples (distorting and banalising, no doubt, the arguments of these authors, in order to try to be intelligible). Pêcheux quotes the joke about the schoolboy who rings the headmaster to excuse himself for an absence, and, when asked 'Who is speaking?', answers, pretending to be his father:

'It's my father.' Here the semantic and syntactic mechanisms seem to be obvious: when Tom Jones says 'my father' and 'Tom Jones's father', the two expressions have the same reference for him, but not for his headmaster; in his phone call he uses an expression which has the intended reference, but disregarding the fact that it shows the subject of the enunciation to be himself and not his father. This is clear with pronouns, and with deictics in general ('here, now', etc.) which refer to the time, place, situation in which the utterance is produced. But it applies to many other elements in what we say. In E. M. Forster's *Where Angels Fear to Tread*, Harriet, bothered by the passengers on an Italian train, states: 'Foreigners are a filthy nation.' The term 'foreigner', which ought to be relative to the speaker in her home territory, becomes used absolutely. One can recall the semantic development undergone by terms like 'native' in the language of European countries with an imperial tradition. Similarly, in the film *A Touch of Class*, Glenda Jackson says irritably to Helmut Berger that foreign films are horrible, and he agrees: 'Yes, particularly English and American ones'; here the point is underlined by the fact that she says it in English, and he answers in German: 'Ja, besonders die englische und amerikanische' (I quote from memory).

How far does this extend in language? Evidently terms like 'good', 'bad', 'big', 'small', 'high', 'low', etc. are relative to the speaker, or refer to standards of normality which inevitably depend on the values and criteria prevailing in one's culture. Will this not apply to everything one says? And if the division into classes is essential in the constitution of any society and its culture, ought the interpretation of any sentence, even apparently the most objective and uncontroversial, not depend on the reference system of the class to whom the speaker belongs? Does then any utterance, to put it crudely, mean different things for different classes?

8.10 CONCLUSION

Many of the works I have mentioned are, in different ways, interesting. But what strikes me, in the context of linguistics, is the poverty of what most of them have to say about language. It is in fact sometimes explicitly stressed that what is in question is not the ordinary concern of linguists (and the implication is: so much the worse for them). Houdebine (1977, pp. 201-2) for instance talks about approaching language as a plurality of signifying practices taking place within history, with the implication of the speaking subject, and adds that what he has in mind is the question of language as a nodal point in which Marxism is intricated, and not language as it can be studied by a particular scientific discipline. So Etienne Balibar (1966, pp. 22-3) stresses that the questions posed by Stalin should be approached not so much by linguistics as by dialectical materialism, in an attempt to distinguish language as the object of study of the former discipline, from language as a social formation to be investigated in the context of historical materialism.

If we assume that language can be studied empirically, like any other phenomenon, we ought to let its students get on with the job, untrammelled by Marxism or any other philosophy, as far as this is possible (this can of course be stated also from a viewpoint sympathetic to Marxism: see Rosiello, 1974, p. 63). The fact that scientific discourse is inevitably ideologically conditioned does not, in this view, affect linguistics any more than other scientific disciplines. This does not imply that linguistics is a 'hard' science, of the same order as physics or biology (although it may be legitimate for linguists to try to make it into one), but rather that, as in any historical, philological, or psychological discipline, one ought to use criteria for the collection, evaluation, interpretation of the evidence, which have their internal logic and their tests for verification or falsification, rather than depend on the external pressure of ideological interests and immediate political concerns. From this angle it does not seem to make sense to ask whether the work of Chomsky, or Labov, or Bernstein is more or less compatible with Marsixm. The question is whether it tells us something interesting about language. There is of course the question of deciding which features of language are biologically determined and which depend on historical conditions, and, among the latter, which ought to be explained sociologically, and which depend on other aspects, from the psychology of the individual to the internal structure of certain linguistic patterns. But here again one ought to expect a Marxist to be interested in getting the factually correct answer, and not in pushing as much as possible into the field of sociological explanations.

It is in fact curious that Chomsky (see, e.g. 1972; 1981), widely known for his left-wing (but anarchist and libertarian rather than Marxist) political positions, has developed a kind of linguistics which is highly formalised and abstract in its techniques and relies on the idealist philosophical tradition, from Descartes to Humboldt; if one looked for a side to it which might be called materialist, one would perhaps find it in its appeal to the innate, biological foundations of language, and not in the social aspect of speech, for which very little interest is shown. On the other hand, to recall the names mentioned above, Labov's kind of sociolinguistics is more popular with linguists than the one practised by Bernstein whose use of Marxist notions is more explicit.

If on the other hand we feel that language escapes this sort of empirical study, and is a phenomenon that involves in a more pervasive way the methods with which we try to investigate it, our own status as subjects of the investigation, and the very constitution of the universe which includes us, language, and everything else, then we may feel that it is a topic more suitable to be studied by philosophy than by linguistics. But this, to refer to the doubts expressed at the beginning, does not seem to me to help to clarify the notion of 'Marxist linguistics', and there is little indication that in such a general and all-embracing approach, intellectually valuable results are likely to be obtained. Our discussion of Marxism and linguistics does not seem to indicate that the foundation of a Marxist linguistics is a particularly rewarding or desirable aim. It does however leave open the question of the contribution that Marxism may make to the study of the function of language in society.

GUIDE FOR FURTHER READING

The main texts by Marx and Engels are collected in Marx and Engels, 1974; in English, marginal for our topic, see the anthology by De la Haye, 1980; a useful general collection in Italian: Formigari, 1973; a more limited one in French, Calvet, 1977; a good Italian edition of Engels's writings on Germanic philology, Ramat, 1974. General surveys in Houdebine, 1977; Marcelllesi and Gardin, 1974; Mounin, 1972. For the individual sections: on Marx and Engels, see Bykovskij, 1934; Erckenbrecht, 1973; Höppe, 1982, Kacnel'son, 1934; Kolb, 1970; Ramat, 1975; 1981; 1983. For Marr: apart from the five volumes of his selected works

(1933-7), see Borbé, 1974; Gadet *et al.*, 1979; Tagliavini, 1951; Thomas, 1957. On Soviet linguistics and Stalin's intervention: the texts in Murra, 1951, in English; in Stalin, 1952; 1968, in Italian; in Balibar, 1966; Calvet, 1977, in French; see Devoto, in Stalin, 1968; Gadet *et al.*, 1979; Laurat, 1951; Lepschy, 1967; Marcellesi, 1974; Rosiello, 1974; Tagliavini, 1951; Timpanaro, 1963. On Polivanov, see Polivanov, 1931; 1974; Gadet *et al.*, 1979; Lepschy, 1977. On Bakhtin and Voloshinov, see Ivanov *et al.*, 1977; Ponzio, 1980. On Gramsci, see Lo Piparo, 1979, Rosiello, 1970; 1982; Salamini, 1981. On French sociological linguistics, see Bolelli, 1982. On modern Soviet semiotics: see Eimermacher and Shishkoff, 1977; Lotman and Uspenskij, 1973; Lucid, 1977; Prevignano, 1979. For the connection with (post-)structuralism, semiotics, deconstruction, etc., see Anderson, 1983; Belsey, 1980; Callinicos, 1982; Coward and Ellis, 1977; Gadet and Pêcheux, 1981; Heath, 1977; Henry, 1977; Houdebine, 1977; Lavers, 1982; MacCabe, 1979; Norris, 1982; Pêcheux, 1975; Ryan, 1982; Timpanaro, 1975; Woods, 1977.

REFERENCES

Agamben, G. (1983), 'Lingua e storia. Categorie linguistiche e categorie storiche nel pensiero di Benjamin', in L. Belloi and L. Lotti (eds), *Walter Benjamin. Tempo storia linguaggio* (Roma: Editori Riuniti) pp. 65-82.
Althusser, L. (1970), 'Idéologie et appareils idéologiques d'état (Notes pour une recherche)', *La Pensée*, 151, pp. 3-38 (also in Althusser, L. (1976), *Positions* (Paris: Editions sociales) pp. 67-125; English translation by B. Brewster, 'Ideology and Ideological State Apparatuses (Notes towards an Investigation)', in Althusser, L. (1971), *Lenin and Philosophy and Other Essays* (London: New Left Books) pp. 121-73).
Anderson, P. (1983), *In the Tracks of Historical Materialism* (London: Verso).
Bakhtine, M. (Volochinov, V. N.) (1977), *Le Marxisme et la philosophie du langage* (Paris: Minuit).
Balibar, E. (1966), 'Marxisme et linguistique', *Cahiers Marxistes Léninistes*, 12-13, pp. 19-25.
Balibar, R. and Laporte, D. (1974), *Le Français national. Politique et pratiques de la langue nationale sous la Révolution française* (Paris: Hachette).
Barthes, R. (1970), *S/Z*, Paris: Seuil (English translation by R. Miller, *S/Z* (London: Cape, 1975)).
—— (1977), *Image-Music-Text*. Essays Selected and Translated by S. Heath ([London]: Fontana).
—— (1978), *Leçon*, Paris, Seuil (English translation by R. Howard, 'Lecture', *Oxford Literary Review*, 4 i, (1979), pp. 31-44).
Belsey, C. (1980), *Critical Practice* (London: Methuen).

Benjamin, W. (1972–82), *Gesammelte Schriften*. Unter Mitwirkung von Th. W. Adorno und G. Scholem herausgegeben von R. Tiedemann und H. Schweppenhäuser (Frankfurt am Main: Suhrkamp).
Bernstein, B. (1971), *Class, Codes and Control*, vol. 1: *Theoretical Studies towards a Sociology of Language* (London: Routledge & Kegan Paul).
Bodammer, Th. (1969), *Hegels Deutung der Sprache. Interpretationen zu Hegels Äusserungen über die Sprache* (Hamburg: Meiner).
Bolelli, T. (1982), 'La scuola linguistica francese', in *Leopardi linguista e altri saggi* (Messina-Firenze: D'Anna) pp. 201–23.
Borbé, T. (1974), *Kritik der marxistischen Sprachtheorie N. Ja. Marr's* (Kronberg Ts.: Scriptor Verlag).
Brown, G. and Yule, G. (1983), *Discourse Analysis* (Cambridge University Press).
Bykovskij, S. N. (1934), 'K. Marks i jazykoznanie', in N. Ja. Marr and A. G. Prigozhin (eds), *K. Marks i problemy istorii dokapitalisticheskikh formacii* (Moskva-Leningrad: OGIZ) pp. 665–94.
Callinicos, A. (1982), *Is There a Future for Marxism?* (London: Macmillan).
Calvet, L.-J. (ed.) (1977), *Marxisme et linguistique: Marx, Engels, Lafargue, Staline* (Paris: Payot).
Chomsky, N. (1972), *Problems of Knowledge and Freedom* (London: Fontana/Collins).
—— (1981), *Radical Priorities*, edited with an Introduction by C. P. Otero (Montréal: Black Rose Books).
Cohen, M. (1956), *Pour Une Sociologie du langage* (Paris: Albin Michel).
Cohen, M. et al. (eds) (1958), *Linguistique, Recherches internationales à la lumière du marxisme*, 7.
Coward R. and Ellis, J. (1977), *Language and Materialism* (London: Routledge & Kegan Paul).
Culler, J. (1983), *On Deconstruction. Theory and Criticism after Structuralism* (London: Routledge & Kegan Paul).
De la Haye, Y. (ed.) (1980), *Marx & Engels on the Means of Communication* (New York-Bagnolet: IG/IMMRC).
Derrida, J. (1967a), *De La Grammatologie*, Paris: Minuit (English translation by G. Chakravorty Spivak, *Of Grammatology* (Baltimore and London: The Johns Hopkins University Press, 1976)).
—— (1967b), *L'Ecriture et la différence*, Paris, Seuil (English translation by A. Bass, *Writing and Difference* (London: Routledge & Kegan Paul, 1978)).
Eco, U. (1976), *A Theory of Semiotics* (Bloomington and London: Indiana University Press).
Eimermacher, K. and Shishkoff, S. (1977), *Subject Bibliography of Soviet Semiotics: the Moscow-Tartu School* (Ann Arbor: Michigan Slavic Publications).
Engels, F. (1954a), *Anti-Dühring. Herr Eugen Dühring's Revolution in Science* (Moscow: Foreign Languages Publishing House).
—— (1954b), *Dialectics of Nature* (Moscow: Foreign Languages Publishing House).
—— (1974), *Storia e lingua dei Germani*. Scritti filologici a cura di P. Ramat (Roma: Editori Riuniti).
Erckenbrecht, U. (1973), *Marx' materialistische sprachtheorie* (Kronberg Ts.: Scriptor Verlag).
Faye, J.-P. (1972), *Langages totalitaires* (Paris: Hermann).

—— (1982), *Dictionnaire politique portatif en cinq mots* (Paris: Gallimard).
Formigari, L. (1973), *Marxismo e teorie della lingua: Fonti e discussioni* (Messina: La Libra).
Foucault, M. (1966), *Les Mots et les choses*. Une *archéologie des sciences humaines*, Paris: Gallimard (English translation *The Order of Things: an Archaeology of the Human Sciences* (London: Tavistock Publications, 1970)).
—— (1969), *L'Archéologie du savoir*, Paris: Gallimard (English translation by A. M. Sheridan Smith, *The Archaeology of Knowledge* (London: Tavistock Publications, 1972)).
—— (1977), *Language, Counter-Memory, Practice*. Selected Essays and Interviews, D. F. Bouchard (ed.) (Oxford: Blackwell).
Fowler, R. *et al.* (1979), *Language and Control* (London: Routledge & Kegan Paul).
Freud, S. (1900), *Die Traumdeutung* (Leipzig & Wien: Deuticke). (See the eighth 1930 edition in *Gesammelte Werke*, vol. II/III (London: Imago, 1942); English translation by J. Strachey, *The Interpretation of Dreams*, in *The Standard Edition of the Complete Psychological Works of Sigmund Freud*, vols 4 and 5 (London: The Hogarth Press and The Institute of Psycho-analysis, 1953).)
Gadet, F. *et al.* (1979), *Les Maîtres de la langue. Avec des textes de Marr, Staline, Polivanov* (Paris: Maspero).
Gadet, F. and Pêcheux, M. (1981), *La Langue introuvable* (Paris: Maspero).
Gramsci, A. (1950), *Letteratura e vita nazionale* (Torino: Einaudi).
—— (1975), *Quaderni del carcere*. Edizione critica dell'Istituto Gramsci. A cura di V. Gerratana (Torino: Einaudi).
Habermas, J. (1979), *Communication and the Evolution of Society* (London: Heinemann).
Halliday, M. A. K. (1978), *Language as Social Semiotic: the Social Interpretation of Language and Meaning* (London: Edward Arnold).
Haroche, C. *et al.* (1971), 'La Sémantique et la coupure saussurienne: langue, langage, discours', *Langages*, 24, pp. 93–106.
Harris, Z. S. (1970), *Papers in Structural and Transformational Grammar*, (Dordrecht: Reidel) pp. 712–64 (originally in *Language*, 27 (1951) pp. 288–333).
Heath, S. (1977), 'Language, Literature, Materialism', *Sub-Stance*, 17, pp. 67–74.
Hegel, G. W. F. (1971), *Philosophy of Mind*, translated by W. Wallace (Oxford: Clarendon Press).
—— (1977), *Phenomenology of Spirit*, translated by A. V. Miller (Oxford: Clarendon Press).
Henry, P. (1977), *Le Mauvais outil. Langue, sujet et discours* (Paris: Klincksieck).
Höppe, W. (1982), *Karl Marx–Friedrich Engels: Sprache und gesellschaftlicher Gesamtkomplex. Das Verhältnis von Sprache zu Basis und Überbau nach den Sprachtheoremen in den Werken von Marx und Engels* (Bonn: Bouvier).
Houdebine, J.-L. (1977), *Langage et marxisme* (Paris: Klincksieck).
Ivanov, V. V. *et al.* (1977), *Michail Bachtin. Semiotica, teoria della letteratura e marxismo*, a cura di A. Ponzio (Bari: Dedalo libri).
Jendreiek, H. (1975), *Hegel und Jacob Grimm* (Berlin: Schmidt).
Kacnel'son, S. D. (1934), 'Voprosy jazykoznanija v 'Nemeckoj ideologii' Marksa i Engel'sa', in N. Ja. Marr and A. G. Prigozhin (eds), *K. Marks i problemy istorii dokapitalisticheskikh formacii* (Moskva-Leningrad: OGIZ) pp. 695–767.

Klaus, G. (1969), *Die Macht des Wortes. Ein erkenntnistheoretisch-pragmatisches Traktat* (Berlin: VEB Deutscher Verlag der Wissenschaften).
Kolb, H. (1970), 'Karl Marx und Jacob Grimm', *Archiv für das Studium der neueren Sprachen*, 206, pp. 96–114.
Kress, G. and Hodge, R. (1979), *Language as Ideology* (London: Routledge & Kegan Paul).
Kristeva, J. (1969), Σημειωτική. *Recherches pour une sémanalyse*, Paris: Seuil (partly translated in *Desire in Language: a Semiotic Approach to Literature and Art*, L. S. Roudiez (ed.) (Oxford: Blackwell, [1980])).
—— (1974), *La Révolution du langage poétique* (Paris: Seuil).
Labov, W. (1972), *Sociolinguistic Patterns* (Philadelphia: University of Pennsylvania Press).
Lacan, J. (1966), *Écrits*, Paris: Seuil (partial translation by A. Sheridan, *Écrits. A Selection* (London: Tavistock Publications, 1977)).
Laclau, E. (1981), 'La Politique comme construction de l'impensable', in B. Conein *et al.* (eds), *Matérialités discursives*, Presses Universitaires de Lille, pp. 65–74.
Laurat, L. (1951), *Staline, la linguistique et l'impérialisme* (Paris: Les Iles d'or).
Lavers, A. (1982), *Roland Barthes: Structuralism and After* (London: Methuen).
Lenin, V. I. (1947), *Materialism and Empirio-Criticism* (Moscow: Foreign Languages Publishing House).
—— (1958–65), *Polnoe sobranie sochinenij*, 5th ed. (Moskva: Gosudarstvennoe izdatel'stvo politicheskoj literatury).
Lénine, V. (1973), *Cahiers philosophiques* (Paris: Éditions sociales).
Lepschy, G. (1967), 'Nota sullo strutturalismo e sulla linguistica sovietica recente', *Studi e saggi linguistici*, 7, pp. 1–22 (also in Lepschy, G. (1981), *Mutamenti di prospettiva nella linguistica* (Bologna: il Mulino) pp. 89–105).
—— (1977), Review of Polivanov (1974), *Linguistics*, 195, pp. 67–70.
Lévi-Strauss, Cl. (1966), *Tristes tropiques* (Paris: UGE).
Lo Piparo, F. (1979), *Lingua intellettuali egemonia in Gramsci* (Bari: Laterza).
Lotman, Ju. M. and Uspenskij, B. A. (eds) (1973), *Ricerche semiotiche. Nuove tendenze delle scienze umane nell'URSS* (Torino: Einaudi).
Lucid, D. P. (ed.) (1977), *Soviet Semiotics: an Anthology* (Baltimore: The Johns Hopkins University Press).
Luporini, C. (1974), 'Marxismo e scienze umane', in *Dialettica e materialismo storico* (Roma: Editori Riuniti) pp. 362–72 (originally in *Il contemporaneo*, 12, pp. 1, 3–5, a supplement to *Rinascita*, 25 December 1965).
MacCabe, C. (1979), 'On Discourse', *Economy and Society*, 8, pp. 279–307 (also in MacCabe, C. (ed.) (1981), *The Talking Cure* (London: Macmillan) pp. 188–217).
Marcellesi, J.-B. and Gardin, B. (1974), *Introduction à la sociolinguistique. La linguistique sociale* (Paris: Larousse).
Marcellesi, J.-B. (1977) (ed.), *Langage et classes sociales. Le marrisme*, *Langages*, 46.
Marr, N. Ja. (1933–7), *Izbrannye raboty* (Leningrad: GAIMK).
Marx, K. (1973), *Grundrisse. Foundations of the Critique of Political Economy*, translated by M. Nicolaus (London: Allen Lane in association with *New Left Review*).
—— (1974), *Grundrisse der Kritik der politischen Ökonomie* (Berlin: Dietz).
Marx, K. and Engels, F. (1956–68), *Werke* (Berlin: Dietz).

—— (1974), Über Sprache, Stil und Übersetzung (Berlin: Dietz).
—— (1975 foll.), Collected Works (London: Lawrence & Wishart).
Meillet, A. (1928), Esquisse d'une histoire de la langue latine (Paris: Hachette).
Mercer, C. (1979), 'Gramsci and Grammar', in F. Barker *et al.* (eds), *1936: the Sociology of Literature*, vol. 1: *The Politics of Modernism*. Proceedings of the Essex Conference on the Sociology of Literature, July 1978, University of Essex, pp. 72–88.
Modica, M. (1974), 'Linguistica e marxismo', *Critica marxista*, 12:5, pp. 143–52.
Mounin, G. (1972), *La Linguistique du XXe siècle* (Paris: PUF).
Murra, J. V. *et al.* (eds) (1951), *The Soviet Linguistic Controversy* (New York. King's Crown Press).
Noiré, L. (1877), *Der Ursprung der Sprache* (Mainz: Zabern).
Norris, C. (1982), *Deconstruction: Theory and Practice* (London: Methuen).
Orwell, G. (1949), *Nineteen Eighty-Four* (London: Secker & Warburg).
Pêcheux, M. (1975), *Les Vérités de La Palice. Linguistique, sémantique, philosophie*, Paris: Maspero (in English: *Language, Semantics and Ideology. Stating the Obvious* (London: Macmillan, 1982)).
Polivanov, E. (1931), *Za marksistskoe jazykoznanie. Sbornik populjarnykh lingvisticheskikh statej* (Moskva: Federacija).
—— (1974), *Selected Works. Articles on General Linguistics* (The Hague: Mouton).
Ponzio, A. (1970), *Linguaggio e relazioni sociali* (Bari: Adriatica).
—— (1973), *Produzione linguistica e ideologia sociale. Per una teoria marxista del linguaggio e della comunicazione* (Bari: De Donato).
—— (1980), *Michail Bachtin. Alle origini della semiotica sovietica* (Bari: Dedalo libri).
Prevignano, C. (ed.) (1979), *La semiotica nei paesi slavi. Programmi, problemi, analisi* (Milano: Feltrinelli).
Ramat, P. (1975), 'Friedrich Engels tra antropologia e linguistica', in *Teoria e storia degli studi linguistici*. Atti del settimo convegno internazionale di studi (SLI, 8/II) (Roma: Bulzoni) pp. 347–59.
—— (1981), 'Il problema della traduzione in Marx ed Engels, in *Logos Semantikos. Studia Coseriu*, vol. 1, (Madrid and Berlin: Gredos & de Gruyter) pp. 237–43.
—— (1983), 'Grammatica storica' and 'Lingua-Linguaggio', in F. Papi (ed.), *Dizionario Marx Engels* (Bologna: Zanichelli) pp. 185–90, 223–7.
Robin, R. (1973), *Histoire et linguistique*, (Paris: Colin).
Rosiello, L. (1970), 'Problemi linguistici negli scritti di Gramsci', in P. Rossi (ed.), *Gramsci e la cultura contemporanea* (Roma: Editori Riuniti and Istituto Gramsci) pp. 347–67.
—— (1974), *Linguistica e marxismo. Interventi e polemiche* (Roma: Editori Riuniti).
—— (1983), 'Linguistica e marxismo nel pensiero di Antonio Gramsci', *Historiographia Linguistica*, 9, pp. 431–52.
Rossi-Landi, F. (1968), *Il linguaggio come lavoro e come mercato* (Milano: Bompiani).
—— (1979), *Semiotica e ideologia* (Milano: Bompiani).
Ryan, M. (1982), *Marxism and Deconstruction: a Critical Articulation* (Baltimore: The Johns Hopkins University Press).
Salamini, L. (1981), 'Gramsci and Marxist Sociology of Language', *International Journal of the Sociology of Language*, 32, pp. 27–44.
Sanga, G. (1977), 'Il dialetto. Appunti di linguistica materialista', *Rivista italiana di dialettologia*, 1, pp. 13–44.

Saussure, F. de (1972), *Cours de linguistique générale*, Paris: Payot (English translation by W. Baskin, *Course in General Linguistics* (London: P. Owen, 1960); revised edition (Glasgow: Fontana/Collins, 1974); new translation by R. Harris, *Course in General Linguistics* (London: Duckworth, 1983)).
Schaff, A. (1962), *Introduction to Semantics* (Oxford: Pergamon Press).
—— (1969), 'Sulla necessità di una linguistica marxista', in *Filosofia del linguaggio* (Roma: Editori Riuniti) pp. 9–28 (originally published in Polish in 1960).
Schweppenhäuser, H. (1983), 'Nome/Logos/Espressione. Elementi della teoria benjaminiana della lingua', in L. Belloi and L. Lotti (eds), *Walter Benjamin. Tempo storia linguaggio* (Roma: Editori Riuniti) pp. 49–64.
Shaumjan, S. K. (1961), 'Filosofskie idei V. I. Lenina i razvitie sovremennogo jazykoznanija', in ANSSSR, Institut Slavjanovedenija, *Kratkie soobshchenija*, 31, pp. 69–76.
—— (1971), *Filosofskie voprosy teoreticheskoj lingvistiki* (Moskva: Nauka).
Shklovskij, V. (1966), *Zhili-byli* (Moskva: Sovetskij Pisatel').
Silverman, D. and Torode, B. (1980), *The Material Word: Some Theories of Language and Its Limits* (London: Routledge & Kegan Paul).
Simon, J. (1966), *Das Problem der Sprache bei Hegel* (Stuttgart: Kohlhammer).
Stalin, I. (1950), *Marksizm i voprosy jazykoznanija* (Moskva: Gosudarstvennoe izdatel'stvo politicheskoj literatury).
—— (1952), *Il marxismo e la linguistica*. Traduzione di P. Togliatti (Roma: Edizioni Rinascita).
—— (1968), *Il marxismo e la linguistica*. Prefazione di G. Devoto (Milano: Feltrinelli).
Stubbs, M. (1983), *Discourse Analysis: the Sociolinguistic Analysis of Natural Language* (Oxford: Blackwell).
Szemerényi, O. (1982), *Richtungen der modernen Sprachwissenschaft. II. Die fünfziger Jahre (1950–1960)* (Heidelberg: Winter).
Tagliavini, C. (1951), 'La linguistica nell'Unione Sovietica', in *Scienza e cultura nell'URSS* (Roma: Associazione Italia-URSS) pp. 222–76.
Thomas, L. L. (1957), *The Linguistic Theories of N. Ja. Marr* (Berkeley and Los Angeles: University of California Publications in Linguistics, 14).
Timpanaro, S. (1963), 'A proposito del parallelismo tra lingua e diritto', *Belfagor*, 18, pp. 1–14.
—— (1975), *Sul materialismo*. Seconda edizione riveduta e ampliata, Pisa: Nistri-Lischi) (in English *On Materialism* (London: New Left Books, 1975)).
Vincenzi, G. C. (1978), 'Sul pensiero linguistico di Marx ed Engels: note per una lettura sistematica', *Rivista italiana di dialettologia*, 2, pp. 297–306.
Voloshinov, V. N. (1929), *Marksizm i filosofija jazyka* (Leningrad: Priboj).
—— (1973), *Marxism and the Philosophy of Language* (New York: Seminar Press).
—— (Michail Bachtin) (1980), *Il linguaggio come pratica sociale*. Introduzione di A. Ponzio (Bari: Dedalo libri).
Wilden, A. (1972), *System and Structure. Essays in Communication and Exchange* (London: Tavistock Publications).
Woods, R. (1977), 'Discourse Analysis: the Work of Michel Pêcheux', *Ideology and Consciousness*, 2, pp. 57–79.
Zhirmunskij, V. M. (1969), 'Marksizm i social'naja lingvistika', in A. V. Desnickaja *et al.* (eds), *Voprosy social'noj lingvistiki* (Leningrad: Nauka) pp. 5–25.

9 Literary Theory*

ZYGMUNT G. BARAŃSKI

9.1 INTRODUCTION

Soon after his arrest and imprisonment, Gramsci requested a copy of Dante's *Divine Comedy* and proceeded to write a series of scholarly notes on the poem (Gramsci, 1975, pp. 221–38). Earlier Marx too had revealed a great admiration and an intelligent knowledge of the poem, using parts of it to bolster his more specifically economic and historical arguments (for example, Marx, 1976, p. 198). And it should be immediately noted that Dante is not somehow anomalous in the intellectual biographies of these two great thinkers. A recourse to literature and a sustained interest in its status and function within society underpin a not insignificant section of both their *oeuvres* (for Marx, see Arvon, 1973; Lifshitz, 1973; Prawer, 1978; for Gramsci, see Stipčević, 1968; Sapegno, 1969; Thibaudeau, 1976). And Marx frequently commented on the enjoyment he derived from art. Nor are Marx and Gramsci unique amongst major Marxist thinkers as regards their interest in aesthetic concerns.

The discussion and utilisation of literature obviously confirm from yet another direction the all-embracing ambitions of Marxism as a theory of history and society. However, Marxism's interest in literature and the resultant development of its own brand of literary studies have had some peculiar, if not actually distorting effects for both sides of this relationship. From the perspective of literary theory in general, the only real measure of

---

* I should like to thank Maggie Barański, Mike Caesar, Verina Jones, Giulio Lepschy, John Short and Chris Wagstaff for their comments on an earlier draft of this chapter. I am also extremely grateful to David Forgács for allowing me to see the typescript of his and Geoffrey Nowell-Smith's edition of Gramsci's cultural writings.

Marxist discussions of literature is the extent to which they enrich and further understanding, both synchronically and diachronically, of this concept. This is a perspective, however, which Marxism's political and historical concerns have not always considered of prime importance. And yet the weakness of any method, of any analysis, regardless of its ideological origins, is the extent to which it obfuscates and conceals the object under consideration.

I shall develop this survey of Marxist contributions on literature from a historical perspective and by focusing on particular writers. I feel that this is the most adequate way, in the limits set, to give some idea, firstly, of the developments, shifts, relationships of the works in this area and, secondly, of some of the broader pressures which conditioned certain approaches and conclusions. To have concentrated on certain 'key' themes would have meant not only to distort the positions of particular thinkers, whose writings inevitably would have to be presented in a fragmented form, and even to omit important insights which might not fit into these *a priori* categories, but also to alter the flow of the work done by Marxists on literature (examples of surveys of Marxist literary theory by dominant themes are Eagleton, 1976b; Williams, 1977), The writers chosen for discussion are firstly, those older ones who have been deemed worthy of notice by many scholars, both Marxist and non-Marxist, in the course of the years. These can be basically divided into two groups: those Marxists who have made some still influential contribution to literary theory as a whole, for example, Lukács, Brecht, Benjamin (Benjamin's ideas, in fact, have only become properly appreciated since the 1960s with the recovery of his work by Adorno), and those Marxists, for example, Lenin, Trotsky, Marx and Engels themselves, whose principal contributions to Marxism have been elsewhere, but whose comments on literature, on account of their 'classic' status within this tradition, have served as compulsory reference points for scholars intent on fashioning a Marxist model of literature. Secondly, I shall discuss the work done during the last twenty to thirty years under the influence of and assimilating French discoveries in what can loosely be termed 'structuralism'; discoveries whose connections with and effects on the mainstream of Marxist thought and method are deeply problematic.

9.2 KARL MARX AND FREDERICK ENGELS

That Marx had a sound knowledge of contemporary aesthetic discussions and that he wished to contribute to this debate is now unquestionable (see especially Prawer, 1978, for an excellent analysis of this and related questions). In this he was consistent with a significant trend in the German classical philosophical tradition – his principal source in this area – in which aesthetic considerations were granted a position of some prominence. However, Marx (and similarly Engels) was never a systematic writer on these questions. His ideas are scattered throughout his writings, and often have a secondary status in relation to the general drift of specific arguments. Similarly Marx's contributions on art are not uniform during the whole span of his work, even though they are generally consistent with each other (Prawer, 1978, p. 401).

My survey does not have the space to deal with these shifts in emphasis, but will try less ambitiously to summarise and synthesise, by drawing on a wide range of interventions, what appear to be the nodal points of his aesthetic thought. In fact, Marx and Engels manage to touch on an enormous range of aesthetic topics (see, for example, Marx and Engels, 1974; 1976; Solomon, 1979). I shall underline here only their most significant and influential positions on (a) the nature and development of aesthetic sensibility, and linked to these alienation and disalienation, and the status of the artist; (b) the place of art in society, and hence the base-superstructure model; (c) ideology and consciousness; (d) realism and the 'typical'.

9.2.1 Aesthetic Sensibility

Under this general heading two distinct, albeit connected strands of Marx's thought are to be discerned. On the one hand, the potentially creative and aesthetic element in all work, and, on the other hand, the production of works of art.

Human beings, according to Marx, are the only species which produces even when there is no need. They toil for other than simply utilitarian ends (the assuagement of hunger, cold, etc.). And it is at the point at which the utilitarian ('crude need') is left behind to become 'human need' that all forms of human labour transcend the selfishly personal and take on a universalising dimension (Marx, *Economic and Philosophic Manuscripts of 1844*, in Marx and Engels, 1975 foll., vol. 3, pp. 301-2). Such work satisfies fundamental human, intellectual, ethical and emotional needs which are continually developing in tandem with changes in work activity; and the results of such labour can be enjoyed by other human beings who participate in this socially evolving aesthetic sensibility. This general human characteristic is not immutable or independent — Marx is not arguing here for the existence of certain 'natural' instincts in women and men, as certain of his commentators wish to suggest, but is consistent with his materialist framework: 'he [man] acts upon external nature and changes it, and in this way he simultaneously changes his own nature' (Marx, 1976, p. 283). The possibilities for the expression of human values in and through work are, however, regulated and modified in time by changes in the relations of production and consumption and in the general conditions of existence into which labour activity is inserted (see Short, ch. 7).

More specifically, in the past, what might be called works of art (poetry, painting, sculpture, etc.), Marx argued, had been more intimately involved with, had been closer to other forms of labour, emerging as they all did from a single, undivided social movement. Thus, while works of art offered a more quintessentially and aesthetically heightened record of the general conditions of their coming into being, they were nevertheless accessible to a broadbased audience. However, under capitalism and in fact progressively since ancient Greece, this tie has been cut (just as the 'human' enjoyable aspects of work have been eroded), resulting in 'the exclusive concentration of artistic talent in particular individuals, and its suppression in the broad mass' (Marx and Engels, *The German Ideology*, in Marx and Engels, 1975 foll., vol. 5, p. 394), a situation which is most manifest in the capitalist division of labour. It would only be in a communist society that 'there are no painters but only people who engage in painting among other activities' (Marx and Engels, *The German Ideology*, in Marx and Engels, 1975 foll., vol. 5, p. 394), and that work would take on again an aesthetic measure. The utopian and ahistorical bias of their scheme and solution is unmistakable; however, their comments on the commercialisation of art and on the monotony of much work are more acute. Under capitalism art objects are primarily consumed as commodities by an élite and the artist is separated from the mass of his/her fellows. In fact, this labour is often appropriated by the capitalist for his/her own gain, so that, as is hinted in the major economic texts, artistic activity is subsumed into production in general (for recent work in this area, see Lumley and O'Shaughnessey, ch. 10). However, this position is tempered by the insistence, which is far from clearly formulated, that certain 'great' artists are able to transcend this state of affairs (see Laing, 1978, pp. 11–12).

Such social decay had not always been the case – ancient Greece was the shining example of a properly 'human' form of social organisation. For Marx and Engels, the reason why the artistic, in both senses of the term, had reached its highest achievements at this period was because it had coincided with a period of relatively harmonious social existence. However, this championing of Greek art raised an unavoidable contradiction, which Marx, to his credit, did not attempt to ignore in a passage which has since become one of the cornerstones of recent discussions of his aesthetic thought:

> But the difficulty lies not in understanding that the Greek arts and epic are bound up with certain forms of social development. The difficulty is that they still afford us artistic pleasure and that in a certain respect they count as a norm and as an unattainable model.
> A man cannot become a child again, or he becomes childish. But does he not find joy in the child's naivete, and must he himself not strive to reproduce its truth at a higher stage? Does not the true character of each epoch come alive in the nature of its children? Why should not the historic childhood of humanity, its most beautiful unfolding, as a stage never to return, exercise an eternal charm? (Marx, 1973, p. 111)

Despite attempts to defend Marx's solution or to present it as original (Raphael, 1933, pp. 158–9, 163–7; Morawski, 1974, pp. 36–7; Eagleton, 1976b, pp. 11–12; Macherey, 1977b, pp. 44–5), the vagueness and the conservatism of his answer, even by contemporary standards, is apparent: principally, his insistence on art as synthesising the totality of a society (compare Hegel), and the suggestion that art expresses perennial human values, a position which begins to undermine his own rejection of 'natural' human attributes. Admittedly, Marx notes in passing to

234   *Cultural Theory*

Lassalle in 1861 that 17th-century French dramatists had necessarily misunderstood and misused classical theories of the three unities, when they appropriated these at a later historical moment (Marx and Engels, 1974, p. 98). However, normally Marx reveals a scant awareness of the fact that the reception of art, like artistic creation, must necessarily also be determined historically and is not eternally static.

9.2.2 Base-Superstructure

The general meaning of this model has been cogently analysed elsewhere in this volume (Urry, ch. 5). It needs to be stressed, however, as Engels did in several important letters in the early 1890s, aimed at countering the encroachment of a rigid economism into Marxist theory, that both Marx and he perceived a significant degree of mutual interaction between and within these two levels, although arguing that the economic would always have the final controlling power:

> Political, juridical, philosophical, religious, literary, artistic, etc., development [superstructure] is based on economic development [base]. But all these [superstructural] manifestations react upon one another and also upon the economic base. It is not that the economic situation [base] is *cause, solely active*, while everything else [superstructure] is only passive effect. There is, rather, interaction on the basis of economic necessity, which *ultimately* always asserts itself. (Engels to W. Borgius, Jan. 25, 1894, in Marx and Engels, 1976, p. 58)

In particular, one finds the repeated suggestion that art is somehow more independent than other superstructural manifestations: for example, the discussion of the unequal development between material progress and artistic achievement (Marx, 1973, pp. 104–11), and, by extension, the suggestion that art can actively function as an agent of social change. However, the implicit reductionism and rigidity of this two-storey system, despite Engels' efforts to present it as flexible, have not only led to serious reservations concerning the usefulness of this division for the study of cultural phenomena, but also to its abandonment by Marxists in favour of more elastic structural models, better equipped to accommodate the complexities of literature (see Hall, 1977; Williams, 1977, pp. 75–89; and see below for the work done on the specificity of literary practice within the social formation since Althusser's interventions). The bias of this model can also explain the reason for possibly the most notable omission within Marx and Engels' study of art, namely, the lack of an investigation of the constitution of the form of individual works and categories of art. Their analyses instead tend to concentrate on the content of art as knowledge or reflection of reality and on 'sociological' surveys of artists and their creations.

9.2.3 Ideology/Consciousness (For a general discussion of these concepts, see Urry, ch. 5.)

The point at which literature's relative autonomy, its political and didactic efficacy, and a first movement towards an analysis of its specificity do begin to come together in the work of Marx and Engels, is in their highlighting of the unintentional gap which may appear between an author's ideology and intentions and the substance of his/her literary work, and of the ideological contradictions which may exist within the structure of a single text. This critical and aesthetic enterprise comes closest to recent theories on the decentred and unstable properties of texts (see below According to Marx and Engels such dislocations may occur on account of the contradictions of material life and on account of the alienated conditions of art and artists. This is the first, if rather vague effort to explain those textual ambiguities which have taxed most subsequent Marxist students of literature, and which might be seen as a symptom of the literary. For both Marx and Engels the supreme example of this kind of 'contradictory' writer is Balzac. Despite his conservative and royalist ideology – and Marx and Engels always insist on the importance of the class ideology of a writer as a primary factor in organising his/her work's viewpoints – Balzac is often able, on account of his artistic genius, to transcend his class limitations (his ideology) in order to give a true picture of the actual conditions of existence. Such artistic integrity is not always apparent. Engels comments on how Goethe was 'capable of sacrificing his spasmodically eruptive and truer aesthetic instinct to a petty-bourgeois fear of all major contemporary historical movements' (Engels, 'German Socialism in

Verse and Prose', in Marx and Engels, 1975 foll., vol. 6, p. 259). However, lesser authors, despite intentions to the contrary, are unable to transcend their class origins (see the critique of Sue's *The Mysteries of Paris*, Marx and Engels, *The Holy Family*, in Marx and Engels, 1975 foll., vol. 4), or are unable to perceive fully the general conditions of existence (the correspondence with Lassalle on his *Franz von Sickingen*, Marx and Engels, 1956, pp. 138–43), or even end up by expressing a retrogressive ideology (the 'shopkeepers' and their 'literary representatives' of *The Eighteenth Brumaire*, Marx and Engels, 1975 foll., vol. 11). It is not surprising that in the light of such conclusions both Marx and Engels shy away from prescribing a specific poetics for communist authors to follow, or even from encouraging writers to compose propagandist literature. They see the short-term political advantages of such writing, but at the same time stress its negative and artificial qualities; its lack of subtlety, its sacrifice of aesthetic considerations for political ones, which renders it unattractive for the majority of readers.

9.2.4 Realism

Much of the discussion on the political value of literature, whether of a Balzacian or a propagandist kind, crystallises around the concept of realism and the closely related idea of 'typicality'. These concepts have proved to be the most troublesome and turbulent part of (Marx and) Engels' bequest to Marxist literary studies.

It is clear that, after a brief youthful infatuation with sentimental writing whose leanings were towards the evocation of ideal worlds, Marx for the rest of his life preferred literature which maintained connections with and depicted external reality. It is not surprising therefore that both he and Engels should wish to stress the contacts between the insights offered by such literature and their own analyses of the conditions of existence. However, the crucial question is whether by 'realism' Engels intended to designate a particular school of 19th-century literature or else a much broader and more flexible concept (the term does not appear in any of Marx's writings, see Morawski, 1974, p. 30; this has led to some recent unconvincing attempts to separate Marx and Engels' literary views to the detriment of the latter, Demetz, 1967; and see Morawski's refutation, 1974). An answer to this question is important in the light of subsequent developments in Marxist ideas on literature (in particular, socialist realism, Lukács, the early Macherey and the still-raging modernism-realism disputes).

In his letter of 1885 to Minna Kautsky and in that of 1888 to Margaret Harkness (Marx and Engels, 1974, pp. 113–17), Engels discusses the relationship between 'realism' and the 'typical': 'Realism . . . implies, besides truth of detail, the truthful reproduction of typical characters under typical circumstances' (p. 115); and in the earlier letter he praises the fact that in Minna Kautsky's novel 'each person is a type, but at the same time a distinct personality' (pp. 113–14). 'Typical' here seems to denote persons and events which, on the one hand, have specific functions within the narrative economy of the novel, but, which, on the other hand, also evoke general and universal pictures of private and social behaviour. Furthermore, realism and history are brought together by Engels to stress the relationship between art and life. However, these effects should not be achieved by means of an overt propagandist perspective: 'the tendency [political bias] must spring forth from the situation and action itself, without explicit attention called to it' (p. 114). And although in the second letter, Engels discusses Balzac's achievements as a 'realist', the principal drift of his arguments is away from associating 'realism' with a particular school, author or even technique, and instead is to present this more vaguely as a quality of successful literature.

Marx and Engels' contributions to aesthetic and literary thought are not negligible. On the one hand, their work is firmly embedded in contemporary discussions and delimited by contemporary aesthetic values and preferences, and is not devoid of inconsistencies and imprecisions. On the other hand, their comments do represent a serious and, at times, original effort to transcend their idealist sources and to come to terms with aesthetic phenomena in the light of their analyses of the general conditions of existence. However, their theories also point to possibly the major limitation of all explicitly Marxist work done on intellectual activity. While offering important and precise insights on the mechanisms of economic organisation, the nature of the connections between these and the reasons for human 'creativity' have been much less clearly defined. The actual operation of the base-superstructure model is far from clear; and although Marx and Engels did try to discuss both specific and general exemplifications of its functioning, their solutions are unsatisfactory (for example, oversimplified and utopian views of human progress, the reduction of differences between authors to the different historical moments of their respective artistic activities). Art is not so much looked at for itself, but generally in terms of a controlling other; and this remained the prevailing direction of Marxist literary studies until the beginning of the 1960s.

9.3 DEVELOPMENTS IN RUSSIA

Despite Engels' warnings against too rigid an application of his and Marx's categories, the history of Marxist interventions on literature, from the 1880s until Lenin's occasional contributions (1967) and until the rich intellectual ferment of the years immediately before and after the October Revolution, is characterised by an excessively oversimplifying economism (see especially Plekhanov, 1953). Lenin's most notable pieces are on Tolstoy and on the relationship between the artist and the party.

Between 1908 and 1911, influenced by contemporary debates (Morawski, 1965, pp. 7–9), Lenin wrote six articles on Tolstoy (five of these may be found in Lenin, 1967, pp. 30–5, 52–68, the sixth in Lenin, 1960–70, vol. 16, pp. 368–73). He points out that the author's greatness lay in his ability in his writings to go beyond his personal and class ideologies, and to depict the ideological bewilderment of the Russian peasantry. As with Marx and Engels, it is again honesty of vision which distinguishes the writer of genius and integrity, even though in Lenin the emphasis on the contradiction between text and author is less obvious, and instead the totality, the breadth of Tolstoy's vision as representative of the peasant masses is underscored. Again, how this is achieved is not explained, but is vindicated by romantically extolling the power of individual genius and greatness, which appears to float above history. Tolstoy, however, is criticised for adopting the ideology of a historically backward class, since true knowledge could only be achieved by participating in the proletariat's vision. (Lenin's work on Tolstoy has been particularly influential on Lukács (1972, pp. 126-8) and Macherey (1978a, pp. 105-35)).

The more practical and functional approach to literature which this position implies, is already clear in 1905 in Lenin's 'On Party Organisation and Party Literature' (1967, pp. 22-7), in which, despite recent attempts to soften his positions (Morawski, 1965, pp. 17-23; Eagleton, 1976b, pp. 40-1), it is difficult to disguise the restrictions which he feels must be imposed on artists for the benefit of political action: an emphasis which runs counter to Marx and Engels' conclusions on the desirability of artistic freedom.

It is exaggerated, however, to see in this occasional piece, written long before the Soviet seizure of power, either the origins of socialist realism or the deathknell of independent artistic activity in post-Revolutionary Russia. It was not until 1934, in a climate of increasing and widespread repression, that Zhdanov introduced (at the Union of Socialist Writers' Congress) the doctrine of socialist realism:

> It means, in the first place, that you must know life to be able to depict it truthfully in artistic creations, to depict it neither 'scholastically' nor lifelessly, nor simply as 'objective reality', but rather as reality in its revolutionary development. The truthfulness and historical exactitude of the artistic image must be linked with the task of ideological transformation, of the education of the working people in the spirit of socialism. (Zhdanov, 1950, p. 15; and also see Gorky *et al.*, 1977)

And although a specific style was not advocated by Zhdanov, in practice melodramatic and idealising effects combined with a 19th-century kind of realism quickly became the norm. The need to conform to officially approved notions of art, inevitably led to the persecution of artists who either did not observe such standards or who presented subjects and opinions disapproved of by the regime (on socialist realism and Soviet artistic policy and practice, see Kraiski, 1967; Strada, 1976). The victims of this political and aesthetic dogmatism have been many, to list names would be invidious. And unfortunately the idea that a properly 'socialist' art is possible, does exist and is desirable is still evoked and practised by governments in Eastern Europe and the USSR.

Prior to Zhdanovite repression, and especially in the early

1920s, Russian literary life had been marked by a rich pluralism. The most influential positions were those developed by the Formalists, who were working on the peripheries of Marxism, but benefiting from the intellectual charge generated by this (see Erlich, 1955; Matejka and Pomorska, 1971; and for not unsympathetic Marxist surveys, see Jameson, 1972; Bennett, 1979), and whose ideas in recent years have provided literary theory with an important stimulus in its pursuit of more formal approaches to literature. To a lesser extent Trotsky's writings on a broad range of cultural matters are also noteworthy (1960; and see Slaughter, 1980, pp. 86–113). He was particularly interested in the relationships between pre- and post-Revolutionary art and the values inherent in art. He also supported a high degree of freedom both within artistic practice and in art's relation to the economic base.

However, the most original and stimulating work to be written during the post-Revolutionary period and, surprisingly, during the Stalinist oppression did not begin to come properly to light on account of its unorthodoxy until the 1960s. Julia Kristeva's recovery of Mikhail Bakhtin for Marxist scholarship and for literary theory in general has been of signal importance (Kristeva, 1969).

Bakhtin's advances in linguistics have been noted elsewhere (Lepschy, ch. 8). Especially significant for his studies of literature are his views on language as dialogue and on the ideological nature of linguistic signs. The latter both detaches ideology from its traditional Marxist location in human consciousness, and places language at the heart of social interaction. Bakthin is the first thinker employing a Marxist framework to shift the emphasis from the content of a work of art to its formal properties. He stresses that the social significance of a literary text lies in its linguistic components and that through the connections established between these, the nature of specific historical conjunctures can be discerned. According to Bakhtin, literary texts – his analyses concentrate on prose, and novels in particular – are made up of a variety of discourses. Different relationships pertain between these utterances at different historical moments. For example, at moments of transition or crisis conflicts appear between the different discourses, while harmony is apparent in periods of stability. In his book on Dostoevskij, which came out in 1929 (1973), Bakhtin characterises the novelist's work as 'polyphonic' in opposition to Tolstoy's 'monologic' novels. In

Dostoevskij, the various discourses are not subjugated to the author's dictatorial voice – as is the case with Tolstoy – but are allowed to exist independently and to declare opposing views. These discrete voices are not primarily distinguished by their stylistic properties, but emerge as distinct, thanks to the positions they take up in relation to the authorial voice. Bakhtin's 1940 study of Rabelais (1968), develops the idea of a textual plurality of discourses by the introduction of the concept of 'carnival'. Thus, *Gargantua and Pantagruel* challenges and parodies in a multiplicity of voices the contemporary official monotonal languages (especially that of the Church) via the examples offered by the free-wheeling linguistic techniques of the carnival and of popular festivals. Bakhtin's approach, therefore, both highlights the peculiarity of literature as a linguistic fact and grants it a place within the fabric of society. Literature and language cease to occupy positions of subordination for a Marxist.

9.4 GERMANY AND THE REALISM-MODERNISM DEBATE

Among the principal victims of increasing Soviet repression of art were various avant-garde movements. The sustained attacks on these since the 1920s by figures close to the centre of power resulted in their progressive disappearance. However, experimental literature continued to be composed outside the USSR and to fascinate Marxists, not all of whom were prepared to accept every directive coming from Moscow. And it is the controversies between the groupings on the two sides of the realism–modernism divide which represent the most significant advance in Marxist aesthetics since the founding contributions of Marx and Engels. It is a debate which still challenges and captivates Marxists today. The basic reasons for this seem to be not only questions of what should or should not be perceived as the literary forms closest to and most useful for Marxist political action, but also, and more specifically, they point to differing conceptions of Marxism. This quarrel inevitably subsumes literature into politics; yet, almost paradoxically, it is also the stimulus for much more sophisticated discussions of literature within Marxism.

Germany was the centre for this debate in the 1920s and 1930s, and, after the Nazi takeover in 1933, German or German-influenced *émigrés* in the USSR, Western Europe and the USA. It was inevitable that with the increasing restrictions on Russian cultural activities, in which only one side of the argument (the realist one) could be tolerated, antagonistic positions within Marxism could only flourish elsewhere. Germany was ideally placed to act as host for this debate not only on account of a longstanding indigenous debate between naturalism and expressionism since before World War I, and a vital avant-garde movement in the 1920s in which Marxists, fascinated by the politically radical possibilities of artistic experimentation, actively participated, but also on account of a well-established and intelligent communist tradition there.

9.4.1 György Lukács

Lukács was a Hungarian by birth. However, his intellectual formation, particularly on aesthetic matters, was German. He maintained close and generally amicable connections with communist orthodoxy at least until the early 1950s, living in the Soviet Union and Eastern European countries from the 1930s until his death in 1971. On account of this, his work and political activity have been not surprisingly the subject of much controversy. At least since Brecht's unpublished strictures of 1938 (1977), he has been condemned as an apologist for socialist realism, as a bourgeois humanist who never really abandoned the idealism of his youth (neo-Kantianism, Hegel, mysticism), and whose views remained becalmed in an atrophying 19th-century realism hostile to artistic change. While not denying these criticisms, less partisan analyses of his career have been attempted in recent years, which have highlighted the degree of intellectual and even political independence Lukács was able to maintain within Stalinism and during the 1950s. These studies have also correctly stressed the coherence and breadth of much of his aesthetic thought and his fidelity to Marx and Engels. His was the first sustained effort within Marxism to show the relationships between historical movement and literary change. Furthermore, in the work of Lucien Goldmann (see below), and to a lesser extent in that of Raymond Williams (1979, pp. 220–22, 349–50; for a fuller discussion of Williams immensely rich *oeuvre* and its position within contemporary debates, see Lumley and O'Shaughnessey, ch. 10) and of Fredric Jameson (see below), Lukács has found a sympathetic hearing and an application of several of his ideas. Lukács perceived his task as a Marxist critic to be that of examining 'the interaction between economic and social development, and the outlook and artistic form to which they give rise' (1981, p. 11). However, rather than embarking on a detailed examination of the formal organisation of literary texts – at most he pointed out very general patterns into which narrative could fall – Lukács concentrated on genres. Amongst these he almost exclusively emphasised the novel as historically the dominant literary form since the Enlightenment, and hence closest to the movements of history out of which it had emerged. He concentrated his vision further by the introduction of the concept of 'realism' into his aesthetic; and although, in theory, 'realism' as an epistemological tool is granted considerable range (1972, p. 6) and is even associated with historical materialism (1972, p. 11), in practice it is perceived as an attribute only in the novels of a few pre-1848 Western European authors (Scott, Balzac), in Tolstoy, and in Thomas Mann in the 20th-century (1963; 1964). These works share a fundamental property, the organising presence of the 'typical':

> The central category and criterion of realist literature is the type, a peculiar synthesis which organically binds together the general and the particular both in characters and situations . . . in it all the humanly and socially essential determinants are present on their highest level of development . . . rendering concrete the peaks and limits of men and epochs. (1972, p. 6)

And it is this theory's strongly Hegelian bias towards 'totality', and its oversimplification of the relationship between reality and text, whereby the truth of the former is transparently given by the latter, that is most alien and irritating both to Althusserian Marxism and to post-structuralist theories with their championing of contradiction, production, and the connotative instability of texts. Literary works, for Lukács, 'reflect' (see Eagleton, 1976b, pp. 48–54; Williams, 1983, pp. 196–9 for brief surveys of this term in the Marxist tradition) historical situations, i.e. reveal the underlying movements of history; and even though this is an attribute of all literature, the 'realist' novel is the only one which does not give a partial or a distorted picture of the world. It offers full knowledge and an aesthetic appreciation of history. However, the reasons for this are not clarified, except by a recourse again to the relationship between history and art.

According to Lukács, before the defeats of 1848 (see, 1981, pp. 202–300), the 19th-century bourgeoisie was a progressive class whose consciousness was close to the mechanisms of history and to the development of the novel, which thus became its particular preserve. This permitted its most advanced representatives to depict honestly, even if unintentionally, the total movements of their epoch by transcending in their writings their personal ideological viewpoints. Their artistic prowess sublimated the positive insights of their class as a whole into the art of their novels, so that a correspondence was established between these and historical reality. As a result, a writer's private prejudices were left behind. For example, Scott not only achieves this by the 'typicality' of his creations, but also by the structure of his novels, whereby the hero is placed between two conflicting forces, so that both sides are clearly brought into focus. After 1848 the bourgeoisie, increasingly alienated from the people, began to decline and lose its contacts with history (to be eventually replaced by the historically triumphant proletariat). And its progress into false consciousness was mirrored by the degeneration of its literary forms. Bourgeois art eliminates from its vision capitalism's contradictions: from the microscopic analyses of everyday life of the Naturalists with their loss of the 'totalising' perspective, to the experimentation of the Modernists with their lapse into irrationalism, bourgeois art can no longer offer a full knowledge of the world. However, as a Marxist, or rather Lukácsian study can show, their formal choices do point obliquely to that very decadence of capitalism which their art is trying to conceal. It is the proletariat which henceforth is the custodian of 'realism'. Therefore, only those writers who share or adopt a proletarian consciousness can again link their artistic form with the movements of history, and thus hope to create 'great' ('realist') art (1981, pp. 314–39). It is important to note here that Lukács does not extol 'socialist realism', but presents it as a defective form of realism typical of a transitional revolutionary phase, a step towards the creation of a truly 'realist' socialist art. Whatever the sincerity or ability of a writer, it is history which in

Literary Theory 245

the end controls his/her art: 'it is very difficult for the writer to free himself from the currents and fluctuations of his time' (1981, p. 305); and the 'measure for . . . content and form is to be found in . . . reality itself' (1981, p. 403). Lukács does not accord any independence to the development of literary form and technique, nor grant these any power to control their own progress and meaning: a significant reduction in that 'autonomy' of art suggested by Marx and Engels.

9.4.2 Bertolt Brecht

During 1938, Brecht wrote four articles in which he defended artistic experimentation and freedom for art, and in which he criticised Lukács' aesthetic prescriptions (1977). His critique involves not only an acute pinpointing of some of the weaknesses in Lukács' method, but it also offers fundamental clues to his own critical and aesthetic preferences and to the independence of his views during the Marxist conformism of the 1930s. Brecht underlines in Lukács' theory (a) the anachronism of elevating 19th-century authors as artistic models for 20th-century ones and of utilising 19th-century techniques to discuss 20th-century problems; (b) the restrictiveness of concentrating on the novel as the literary form *par excellence*; (c) the restrictiveness of his 'attempt to solve problems of literary creation . . . in purely literary terms' (1977, p. 73), thus ignoring completely questions of reception (different readers at different conjunctures will apprehend a text or texts differently, so that there can be no eternal guarantor of a text's 'realism'). All these three criticisms show how, despite Lukács' insistence on the centrality of history in his thought, his theories, in fact, are marked by an astonishing lack of historical perspective. Most crucially, Brecht rejects the idea that 'realism' is merely an aesthetic category, but claims it more especially for politics and philosophy. Furthermore, he sees it as potentially inherent in any literary form and technique.

Brecht clearly defines this realism and transforms it into a tool of great flexibility:

> *Realist* means: laying bare society's causal network / showing up the dominant viewpoint as the viewpoint of the dominators / writing from the standpoint of the class which has

prepared the broadest solutions for the most pressing problems afflicting human society/emphasizing the dynamics of development/concrete and so as to encourage abstraction. (1964, p. 109)

And Brecht's art was geared to achieving precisely such effects. Around 1935 Brecht nearly summarised his literary aims and their differences in relation to traditional drama: 'Briefly the aristotelian play is essentially static, its task is to show the world as it is. The learning play is essentially dynamic; its task is to show the world as it changes (and also how it may be changed)' (1964, p. 79). His 'epic theatre' portrayed human beings 'as "the sum of all social circumstances"' and gave 'a comprehensive picture of the world'. 'The new school of play-writing must systematically see to it that its form includes "experiment". It must be free to use connections on every side' (1964, p. 46). Brecht himself blended together in his productions techniques from Chinese theatre, film, written commentaries, etc. These 'alienating' effects 'were directed to playing in such a way that the audience was hindered from simply identifying itself with the characters in the play' (1964, p. 93) and instead was shown 'the historical aspect of a specific social condition' (1964, p. 98). Such devices would not only serve a specifically didactic end, but would also be a means of giving enjoyment to the spectator. Brecht constantly stressed that rather than incomprehensible or dull, his commitment and experimentation gave intellectual pleasure, because they gave a true knowledge of the world.

The conscious fragmentariness of his projects is the first major challenge to the hitherto idealist emphasis in Marxist aesthetics on harmony as the artistic norm. Conversely, his poetic also returns to Marx and Engels' support for artistic freedom. He never presents his solutions as the sole ones possible for the achievement of revolutionary goals – it is simply that they are particularly suited to him and seem to be suited to his time. His emphasis on the complex relationship between literary form, reception and specific historical conjunctures – a relationship which is constantly in flux, constantly in a state of production – is Brecht's most significant and influential contribution to this area of Marxist thought.

Since the 1960s, Brecht has triumphed over Lukács, and Marxists have contributed significantly to avant-garde art, have defended its revolutionary potential, and have undertaken detailed analyses of the formal properties of texts (see also Lumley and O'Shaughnessey, ch. 10). Yet the ideas that Marxism and realism are epistemologically linked or that Marxism is, in fact, a realism, have not disappeared in the West (for example, Jameson, 1977, pp. 211–13; Lovell, 1980; and see Urry, ch. 5). However, quoting Brecht, the supporters of these views deny that epistemological realism *per se* requires or inevitably begets 'realism' in art (for good introductions to this extremely complex concept, see Nochlin, 1971; Lovell, 1980). Conversely, and again in Brecht's wake, various efforts have been made to eliminate this concept and its related practices as too tainted by reaction to be useful for radical artistic practice (MacCabe, 1974; 1976; see also McArthur's critique of the first article (1975); much of the work of *Screen* in the 1970s and in particular the 1974 special issue on Brecht (on *Screen*, see McDonnell and Robins, 1980). And yet, what has been minimised in the rush to condemn the use of realist techniques and perspectives is that Brecht is an uncomfortable mentor. At the end of his critique of Lukács, he notes that 'in each individual case the picture given of life must be compared not with another picture, but with the actual life portrayed' (1977, p. 85). Brecht attacks the conventions of realism and focuses on the gap between the text and the 'real' to which his 'pictures' point, but he does not attack the existence of a knowable external reality which can be artistically appropriated; while it is precisely the denial of such a reality which unites theorists of discourse (see below 'Language, Discourse, Subjectivity'; and also Coward and Ellis, 1977; Belsey, 1980). Furthermore, also implicit in many pro-Brechtian positions is the belief in his moral superiority in relation to Lukács – a Brecht untainted by Stalin – an oversimplification which ignores his didacticism and his progressive *rapprochement* and reconciliation with Stalinism in the immediate post-war years.

9.4.3 Walter Benjamin

Brecht's revolutionary artistic praxis with its emphasis on the 'productive', rather than the 'reflective' aspects of art was closely supported by Benjamin (1973c). Brecht's theatre 'shakes the social validity of theatre-as-entertainment by robbing it of its functions within the capitalist state' (1973c, p. 9). This strategy to reveal the nature of art and its use-value in capitalism is the keystone of Benjamin's work in the mid- and late 1930s. In 'Edward Fuchs, Collector and Historian' (1979, pp. 349–86), he warns against the reification and fetishisation of art, and in particular the way in which 'value' is ascribed to specific authors and epochs. Value and reception, he reminds, are ideologically and historically conditioned. Materialists therefore must be flexible in their definitions of art and not concentrate solely on 'high art' (1979, pp. 326, 360–7). In his essay, 'The Work of Art in the Age of Mechanical Reproduction' (1973b, pp. 219–53), he points to the revolutionary potential of film and of the mechanical reproduction of art objects: 'They brush aside a number of outmoded concepts, such as creativity and genius, eternal value and mystery' (1973b, p. 220). By increasing the accessibility and altering the relations of artistic consumption, these developments destroy the traditional 'aura' (1973b, p. 223) with which art has been surrounded, thus heightening the possibility of revolutionary knowledge. Although Benjamin's faith in technology is naive, it is based on the clear awareness that if this is left in the hands of capitalism, it will be used as an instrument of repression and exploitation (1973b, p. 234).

In 1934, Benjamin, in his lecture, 'The Author as Producer' (1973c, pp. 85–103), joined Brecht in a plea for artistic freedom; however, it is a freedom which entails responsibility: the refashioning of the means of artistic production and not only of the ideological directions of a work. Since 'by mentioning technique I have named the concept which makes literary products accessible to immediate social, and therefore materialist, analysis' (1973c, p. 87). A conclusion of great modernity.

Despite such statements, the extent of Benjamin's commitment to such materialist positions is problematic. Eagleton excellently shows (1981) that Benjamin's thought is extensively indebted to idealist philosophy; and it is difficult to agree with Julian Robert's argument, which tries to downgrade the importance of this (1982). For example, as well as his attacks on the idea of the 'great' author, Benjamin wrote a series of excellent essays praising the genius of canonical figures, for example, Baudelaire (1973a), Kafka (1973b, pp. 111–40), Proust (1973b, pp. 203–217). And although these do incorporate Marxist terminology, it is hard not to agree with Adorno's critique (1977b) that there is little that is materialist in either his methods or his discussions. Marxist concepts and historical analysis are pushed into the background, while the real substance of his investigations is controlled by the hermeneutics of his youth. Benjamin's rich eclecticism points to and influences that overt pluralism which has been the chief characteristic of post-war Western Marxism, and which has made it increasingly difficult to speak of a specifically Marxist literary theory.

9.4.4 Theodor Adorno

Adorno's writings on literature are fragmentary. They straddle both the pre- and post- World War II periods of his work and are on the margins not only of his philosophical and sociological work, but also of his much fuller analyses of other cultural phenomena (for example, music; and see Adorno, 1977a). However, as his literary comments are primarily critiques of Lukács and Brecht, and as he was closely involved with Walter Benjamin, he constitutes an integral part of this rich pre-war German intellectual community, which was attempting to discover the links between art and historical reality.

Adorno basically criticises both Lukács' and Brecht's prescriptions for a political literature on account of their narrowness and dogmatism and for their inability to appreciate properly the fundamental status of literary form. In Lukács' case, Adorno's attack is aimed against the former's oversimplified notion of 'realism' (in particular, his diminution of the distance between art and reality) and his inability to appreciate the stylistic effort inherent in every work of literature. In Brecht's case, it is not so much his theoretical writings to which Adorno objects, but his plays, with their oversimplification of social reality, their didacticism and their excessive formalism. For Adorno, style, not content, is the means by which each author expresses his/her attitude towards the world, and is, therefore, an inevitable mark of subjectivity. However, and Adorno's explanation of how this process functions is far from clear, it is the resistance which a style exhibits to presenting either subjectivity or objectivity as absolute (Kafka and Brecht, respectively), which is the means of measuring its 'truth content'; namely, the dynamic relationship between subject and object which can only be reached by texts which do not try to conceal their basic illusion-making directions, but which try to alter or rework these. Adorno's critique of both Lukács and Brecht is well-made and acute, although his counter-proposal is vague. It crystallises around European Modernism; but it does not pinpoint and clarify either what constitutes (politically) efficacious art or literature's relation to external reality.

9.5 ANTONIO GRAMSCI

Gramsci remains outside the prevailing modernism–realism conflicts of the 1920s and 1930s (see also Lepschy, ch. 8). His personal isolation is not only affected by his imprisonment, but also and more specifically, firstly, by the general isolation of Italy during this period and, secondly and linked to this, by the fact that most of his interventions on literature are primarily counters to prevailing views in Italian aesthetics and literary criticism.

Naturally these contributions – literature for Gramsci was always a peripheral interest and rarely treated *per se* – are closely tied to his Marxism, and to his more general analysis of the functioning of ideology in class societies: the struggles for hegemonic control and the intellectual's role in these (see Lumley and O'Shaughnessey, ch. 10). In his more specifically literary writings, Gramsci highlights the socio-political aspects of the text and focuses on the author as member of the intelligentsia. In his programme for cultural renewal, which was intimately tied to his analysis of the negativity of the main trends of Italian intellectual history, he saw the duty of the committed writer as that of creating works which, having their roots in popular and national culture and not exclusively in the academies, would appeal to the people, thus ensuring a genuinely radical literary culture. Although he does not offer precise guidelines, this was to be achieved by giving form to a particular historical moment in a manner which was both realistic and personal. He stresses, however, that realism and mimesis are not necessarily synonymous, but that realism is closely tied to an individual author's attitude to a historical moment. Furthermore, he rejects the view that the beauty of a work of art is achieved by its political or moral content, rather than by its formal properties. He thus arrives independently at positions which are close to those of both Brecht and Benjamin. For Gramsci, analysis of the literary must proceed along two paths: a recognition of the aesthetic effects of art and an investigation of its political implications, although it is on the latter that his vision principally rests.

In recent years in the United Kingdom, his ideas have been appropriated by scholars working in cultural studies, especially in investigations which have concentrated on resistance to dominant ideologies, the prime concern of the Althusserians (see Hall *et al*, 1980; Lumley and O'Shaughnessey, ch. 10).

9.6 POST-WAR DEVELOPMENTS IN FRANCE AND FRENCH INFLUENCES

9.6.1 Lucien Goldmann

What has most distinguished the developments in post-war Western Marxism from the views of its pre-war supporters, has been an increasing willingness to acknowledge limitations in historical materialism and to measure it against and borrow from other intellectual traditions and discoveries. Thus, one of the principal characteristics of post-war Western Marxist theories of literature, following in the wake of structuralism, has been the progressive substitution of the notion of the 'text' for that of the 'author'. And it is in Goldmann's work that a bridge between these positions may be found.

Goldmann begins by following Lukács. And the Hegelian impetus of his method with its emphasis on 'totality' is unmistakable: 'Knowledge proceeds ... from ... a continual oscillation between the whole and its parts' (1969, p. 86). As regards literature this demands a movement 'not only from the text to the individual, but from the individual to the social group of which he forms part' (1964, p. 11); and this is achieved via a correlation, a 'homology' between the structure of a literary work (and here Goldmann, unlike his mentor, does analyse more than just the novel) and the 'mental structure' of a social group. Structure, in his acceptation, refers not so much to formal organisation, but to the organisation of ideas and concepts. These are not the property of any single individual but are the expression of a transindividual subject, the 'world vision' of a particular social group (1964, p. 17). And this 'vision' is encapsulated by 'great' literature. Thus, 'the general climate of thought and feeling . . . can also provide an historical explanation as to why a particular work came to be written in its present form' (1964, p. 98). In *The Hidden God* (1964), Goldmann shows how the basic common structure of Racine's and Pascal's writings, what he calls their 'tragic vision', whereby the individual is pulled by conflicting demands which he is prevented from fulfilling by the world, is intimately linked to 'the expression which Jansenism gave to the social, economic and political situation of the *noblesse de robe* in 17th-century France' (1964, p. 99). Literary works are therefore not initially creations of an individual, but of the 'transindividual'; although it is the author's talent which guarantees the extent of their coherency, of their 'objective' meaning, often unintentionally achieved and distinct from their intentional, 'subjective' meaning.

Much of this re-echoes standard Marxist positions. However, this should not obscure the original emphases of Goldmann's work. Rather than propagating the Lukácsian 'reflectionist' view, he is much more intent on fashioning a sociology of literature. He wishes to establish both the relations between a social group and its artistic activity, and for whom such social processes function. Finally, returning to my opening contention, what is the evidence for Goldmann's transitional status? The pluralism which is at the basis of his thought, together with his unorthodox relationship with Marxism is typical of much recent work (see Glucksmann, 1969; Mayrl, 1977; Evans, 1981). Although he distinguished his particular brand of structuralism from that of the better-known linguistically based structuralists, and insisted on the centrality of the human subject in his method (1967, p. 149), his highlighting of group consciousness and his increasing use of psychoanalysis and linguistics do weaken the traditional bonds between creator and creation.

9.6.2 Louis Althusser

During the same period as Goldmann was developing his ideas, two important French Marxists, Althusser and Macherey, were becoming increasingly and more directly influenced by the revolution brought into French intellectual life by structuralism (on structuralism and its developments, see Culler, 1975; 1983; Coward and Ellis, 1977; Hawkes, 1977; Belsey, 1980; Norris, 1982; Leitch, 1983).

Althusser's direct contribution to the study of literature has been scant. None of his suggestions are potentially as interesting for literary studies as his concept of 'symptomatic reading', which he developed as a general epistemological tool (see Urry, ch. 5). However, his general analysis of the structure of the social formation and his 1970 essay on ideological state apparatuses and on the construction of subjectivity in/by ideology (1971, pp. 121–73) have been of fundamental importance for all those theories which have tried to study literature as a specific practice (on Althusser and Althusserianism in contemporary Marxism, see Urry, ch. 5; Lumley and O'Shaughnessey, ch. 10).

The thrust of Althusser's analysis is towards an investigation of the relationship between art and ideology. He unequivocally states: '*I do not rank real art among the ideologies*, art does have a quite particular relationship with ideology' (1971, p. 203; orig. publ. 1966). Equally it has 'a certain special relationship with knowledge' (1971, p. 204). On the one hand, 'real' or 'authentic' art (the precise nature of these attributes is not discussed) can reveal the functioning of ideology: it 'makes us "perceive" ... in some sense from *the inside*, by an *internal distance*, the very ideology in which they are held' (1971, p. 204). On the other hand, art cannot supersede knowledge, because it cannot grant a scientific access to the mechanisms of ideology, but merely a perception of an allusion to these. Althusser proceeds to discuss this effect in equally vague terms, suggesting that this is achieved via formal manipulations. Nor do his analyses of the theatre of Bertolazzi – a minor 19th-century Italian dramatist – (1982, pp. 129–51; orig. publ. 1962) or of the paintings of Cremonini – an Italian modern artist – (1971, pp. 209–20; orig. publ. 1966) offer much further clarification. However, while most of his discussion of art is banal, superficial and mystificatory, the overall bent of his argument is interesting and important within the Marxist tradition. By positing art as distinct from both ideological and scientific practice, Althusser is asserting its specificity in relation to other cultural and ideological forms. Literature is similarly granted its own position within the social formation, and is no longer, as it had been since

Marx's time (with the exception of the forgotten Bakhtin), merely a second-order 'reflection' of or commentary on reality. Althusser is unable in his attempt to establish a 'knowledge for art' (1971, p. 206) to go beyond a schematic foregrounding of a tension between ideology, 'real' art and science in the production of literary texts; however, he does support the need to distinguish between and correlate at the formal level and in their effects different signifying practices, paying lipservice at least to the premises of formalist approaches. It is in the work of his close collaborator, Macherey, that these positions are most cogently developed within a still recognisable Marxist framework.

9.6.3 Pierre Macherey

Macherey's methodological preface of 1966 to his *A Theory of Literary Production* (1978a) is an attempt to theorise Althusser's 'knowledge of art', or, more precisely, a knowledge of 'the act of the writer' (1978a, p. 12) which could be applied to all texts and which would revolve around formal considerations. Macherey argues that it is necessary to explain how texts are produced and to formulate the laws of this production. 'To know the conditions of a work is to define the real process of its constitution, to show how it is composed from a real diversity of elements which give it substance' (1978a, p. 49). The specific combination of these elements guarantees the separateness of literature from other forms of expression. Macherey does not deny the role of the author in this production; but it is a limited role determined by history, and especially by the history of literary forms and conventions. This 'means that they [forms, etc] cannot be defined exclusively by their immediate function in a specific work' (1978a, p. 42), but more appropriately in relation to their previous usages. At the same time, literary production is further conditioned by all the other elements which come together to constitute the historical conjuncture of which it is a part. Analysis

> reveals the work in so far as it entertains a specific but undisguised ... relation with history. We must show, through the study of an effort of expression, how it is possible

to render visible the conditions of this effort – conditions of which it has no awareness ... it is only aware of the conditions which it adopts or utilizes. We could account for this latent knowledge ... *by recourse to the unconscious of the work*. (1978a, p. 92)

This appeal to psychoanalysis is the most interesting dimension of Macherey's theory. It attempts to blend Freud's theory of repression and his method of interpreting patients' statements while under analysis to elicit what was being unconsciously repressed, with Althusser's ideas on ideology and with structuralist insights on the functioning of literary codes.

A writer 'works on' language; and the peculiarity of this labour is that it makes a text which, rather than a coherent object, as is normally assumed, is, in fact, a decentred, contradictory one, which has escaped its maker's power. It is also 'parodistic': 'Mingling the real uses of language in an endless confrontation, it concludes by *revealing* their truth' (1978a, p. 59). As in Althusser's work, literature ('fiction') can unmask ideology ('illusion': a system of illusory social attitudes) on account of their difference and, since it refashions ideology in the process of its production, 'the finished literary work (since nothing can be added to it) reveals the gaps in ideology' (1978a, p. 60), as 'it [the work] is not *created* by an intention; it is produced under determinate conditions' (1978a, p. 78). By placing ideology in a new context, it can show what this cannot normally admit. These 'gaps' which remain silent, i.e. never explicitly addressed or addressing in the text, reveal to the theoretically informed reader the inability of ideology to create coherence, but merely its illusion; and Macherey interestingly points out the ideological contradictions within Balzac's and Verne's texts (1978a). For example, Verne's effort in *The Mysterious Island* is to idealise imperialism as an innocent and beneficial harnessing of nature by science – a typical ideological perspective of the French bourgeoisie of the time. He does this by opposing his narrative to the Crusoe model. However, his ideological and narrative intentions are actually undermined by the progress of his story. It develops by showing that the castaways, rather than conquering nature by their intellectual and technological abilities in a pre-social environment, in fact rely, like Crusoe depending on his wreck, on a pre-existing power (Nemo's interventions). The Crusoe structure returns to challenge and ultimately undermine Verne's project, and the ensuing 'gap' between authorial intention and actual narrative development reveals the historical relations between capitalism and colonialism which the ideology intended to conceal.

In a series of recent articles and in a climate more critical towards structuralism, Macherey has subjected this earlier work to a significant auto-critique (1977a; 1977b; 1978b). He acknowledges its excessive 'formalism': the specificity of literature posited too squarely on its formal aspects and in the production of these in individual works. Under pressure from Althusser's essay on ideological state apparatuses and the work of R. Balibar (1974; see also Balibar and Laporte, 1974) on the French education system, Macherey begins to underline the reproductive processes, i.e. the modes of consumption which surround and categorise all writing and every communicative system. He challenges the belief in the eternal qualities of literature, and argues instead that 'works of art are processes not objects . . . which [= processes] are continually susceptible to "reproduction" ' (1977b, p. 45). Literature is not fixed, literary canons are continually being ideologically constituted:

> Literature *is a practical, material process of transformation which means* that in particular historical periods, literature exists in different forms. . . . Literature with a capital 'L' does not exist; there is the 'literary', literature or literary phenomena within social reality and this is what must be studied and understood. (1977a, p. 3)

This is a method which tries both to resolve the question of the relationship between art and reality and to underline the decentredness of texts. Thus, as Renée Balibar had argued, in 19th-century France 'literature reproduces and reinforces the conflictual process of linguistic practices started in the school' (1977b, p. 51), since literature asserts the primacy of bourgeois language over all others. Such analyses, according to Macherey, would take Marxist studies of literature beyond bourgeois aesthetics and would establish their independence, particularly as any 'aesthetic effect is also inevitably an effect of domination' (1978b, p. 12). Macherey's latest theories are stimulating, and they represent the first serious effort within

Marxism to analyse the historical formation of literary canons. Previously, Marxist literary theory had generally accepted uncritically (Benjamin is an exception) established value-judgements on what was to be considered 'good' or 'bad' literature. This is not to say, as some on the left might wish to suggest, that in essence no or few differences exist between Dante's *Divine Comedy* and an anonymous collection of limericks, but to recognise the historical and ideological pressures which condition the divisions into different categories of literature, whose edges, and at times whose centres, are constantly altering (belonging to a similar tradition as Macherey's are studies which concentrate on so-called 'popular', 'low' literature and on its audience; see Lumley and O'Shaughnessey, ch. 10). However, the extreme reductiveness of Macherey's positions is also apparent; for example, no distinctions are made between different forms of the literary, different classes of readers, texts written at different epochs, the varying pleasures given by different texts, i.e. the reasons and ways in which art can give enjoyment (see Bennett, 1979, for a defence of the later Macherey; a concise survey of different textual pleasures (intellectual, erotic, social) may be found in Lovell, 1980, pp. 94–5; and see also *Formations*, 1983).

9.6.4 Language, Discourse, Subjectivity

In *A Theory of Literary Production*, Macherey takes the structuralists and, in particular, Barthes to task for the unscientific and unhistorical qualities of their work – their concentration on the text's meaning as intrinsically, rather than socially constituted (1978a, pp. 136–56). However, despite this critique, there are striking similarities between Macherey's and Barthes' methods; for example, the emphasis on the text's self-production via the medium of the author or the utilisation of psychoanalytic insights. Such ambiguity is characteristic of the most significant structuralist thinkers in contemporary France (in addition to the ones so far mentioned, Lacan, Kristeva, the *Tel quel* group, Foucault, Derrida are the most important), which thus makes it difficult to establish with precision the points at which individual positions begin or end, and which of their ideas can or cannot be seen as compatible with Marxism (for surveys of how these tensions have been continued when transplanted into the British Marxist tradition, together with intelligent critiques of the relative strengths and weaknesses of these theories, see Johnson, 1979; Hall *et al*. 1980).

The most obvious reason why the collaboration between linguistics, structuralism, semiology and psychoanalysis has occurred and has achieved, since around the beginning of the 1960s, such a dominant status in contemporary literary studies, is that individually and in alliance these disciplines have managed very important interpretative advances. Although Marxism has offered to this already rich cross-fertilisation a knowledge of ideology and society, albeit essentially in Althusserian terms, and, to a lesser extent, of history and of processes of production, it has borrowed much more than it has contributed. From these disciplines have come sophisticated insights in areas which have become increasingly central for the study of literature, and yet in which traditional Marxist literary theory had found itself discomforted and unable to offer satisfactory explanations: for example, literary form, the specificity of the literary, the relationship between text and author, text and reader, questions of gender. It might, in fact, be fairer to say that, as regards the formal effects of literary texts, Marxism has not often considered these an area relevant to its concerns. Literature had been analysed less for its particularity, but rather for the ways in which it could offer a knowledge of external reality in keeping with the Marxist view of how this was structured. The manipulation of language was regarded as of secondary importance, and not as the very stuff of the literary, the essential nature of which was instead the ways in which it 'reflected', primarily via its contents, its connections with the economic base.

These disciplines and their methods have also called into question the institution of interpretation, highlighting the aprioristic theoretical and ideological assumptions which necessarily underlie all acts of reading, even where these are not acknowledged (Eagleton, 1983, has moved from these positions to discuss the ideological premises and historical pressures which structure different literary criticisms), and the extent to which an author 'controls' the meanings of his/her text. In fact, these advances with their questioning of the differences between categories of texts hitherto considered as discrete (for example, cinematic, literary, photographic, etc), have had a much greater resonance on Marxist studies of cultural phenomena in general (see Lumley and O'Shaughnessey, ch. 10), rather than on literary theory where, I feel, notable and interesting contributions have been few.

In Chapter 8, Giulio Lepschy discusses with great clarity the bases in language of these most recent trends. Their fundamental dependence on adaptations of Freudian psychoanalysis for their theories on the construction of subjectivity and on Saussurean linguistics for the division of the sign into signifier and signified (see also Coward and Ellis, 1977; Belsey, 1980). He also briefly mentioned the idealist and occasionally irrationalist and mystical elements within these disciplines, elements which are so difficult to reconcile with the premises of Marxism. At the same time, it is evident that, for the reasons sketched above, theorists of literature who are trying both to go beyond Macherey's positions and to maintain links with or work within the Marxist tradition have found it impossible not to acknowledge structuralist suggestions, although they have been drawn primarily, as might be expected, to the work of those French intellectuals contributing to structuralism who either declare themselves to be Marxists (Althusser, Macherey, Pêcheux; for the last of these see Lepschy, ch. 8) or who allow some room for history in their analyses (the early semiotic writings of Barthes possibly as far as S/Z of 1970, Lacan, Foucault and Kristeva).

At the centre of the most recent Marxist, or perhaps I should say neo-/post-Althusserian positions on literature, is found the concept of 'discourse' (see also Lepschy, ch. 8). This theory argues that language-use is separated into distinct discourses, each founded on a set of common assumptions and within each of which ideology is inscribed not as something occurring independently, but as an integral part of language, thus minimising the amount of control which any individual language-user has over the medium. Existence is experienced via the interplay of discourses (the connections with Althusser's Ideological State Apparatuses and his more general ideas on the production of knowledge in thought (see Urry, ch. 5) are clear), since each discourse offers up distinct subject-positions; and it is the inter-relationship between discourses which is the place of ideology's specific action.

This model has offered the possibility for theorists whose work still claims links with Marxism to develop the language–ideology–text matrix in a manner which is different from Macherey's, in whose early work these elements are more conventionally, in Marxist terms, seen as separate, yet inter-related, and not as fused. The notion of the 'classic realist text', which emerged primarily with reference to the predominant narrative structuring of commercial cinema, has been particularly influential and has been discussed in the light of earlier Marxist discussions of realism (for the 'classic realist text', see MacCabe 1974 and 1976; for evaluations of this formulation and its status within Marxism, see Lovell, 1980, pp. 84–7 and Collins and Porter, 1981, pp. 97–102). This concept is a development of Brecht's ideas on realism, together with insights drawn from Engels, Lenin and Althusser, and it is presented as characteristic of most narrative organisation under industrial capitalism. The major strategies of the 'classic realist text' are that it presents itself as an unproblematic and coherent picture of reality. It conceals both external contradiction, the world as known and knowable, and its own textual contradictoriness, its construction out of linguistically-based narrative codes. It achieves this, regardless of what the intentions of an individual author might be, by a series of ideological manoeuvres inherent in its narrative structure, whereby the primacy of a single 'realistic' discourse is asserted, which conceals and downgrades the text's other discourses. (The similarities between these conclusions and Bakhtin's discussion of the 'monologic' are striking, especially as MacCabe does not seem to have utilised the Russian's work in his articles.) The 'classic realist text' presents the 'realistic' as its single possible meaning, thus banishing contradiction from its vision; and this is accepted passively by the reader who is ideologically constructed by this operation, i.e. he/she accepts as unproblematic the position offered to him/her by the narrative strategies supporting this discourse. Language is accepted as transparent and not as ideological, and so Saussure's insistence on the conventionality of signs is repressed. The duty of criticism, therefore, is to display the ideological operation such narrative undertakes on capitalism's behalf, and to help develop narrative forms which challenge this view of literature (see also Lumley and O'Shaughnessey, ch. 10). This has led to a renewed championing of avant-garde texts which both reveal their construction and which rejoice in an indeterminacy of meaning and in contradiction, thus demanding an interpretative effort on the part of the reader. These processes both unmask the text's apparent connections with the real, since the main focus is now the text itself, and reveal its ideological functionings (for other analyses employing the notion of 'discourse', see, for example, MacCabe, 1979; Easthope, 1983; and see also Heath, 1977, on the need to place language at the centre of any Marxist analysis of literature).

The most significant weakness of discourse analysis for a stricter Marxist viewpoint is that this method is always on the verge of perceiving the whole of social reality simply as a manifestation of the discursive, an inversion which runs counter to the basic tenets of Marxism and which also abandons Althusser's ideas on the structure of the social formation. Eagleton underlines this point: 'Materialism must insist on the irreducibility of the real to discourse' (1981, p. 51); particularly as even the most careful proponents of this theory do minimise the importance of economic relations and of historical specificity: the foundation-stones of Marxism. They tend to see language and ideology as somehow autonomous and the real sites of struggle: limitations which do restrict the analyses of concrete situations and make it difficult to put forward alternative theories of subjectivity (for Marxist critiques of this tradition, see, for example, Barrett *et al.* 1979; Clarke *et al.* 1980; Hall *et al.* 1980; Lovell, 1980; Eagleton, 1981; Anderson, 1983). More sober and critical assimilations into the tradition of Marxist literary theory of the linguistic–psychoanalytic–Althusserian alliance have been undertaken by Frederic Jameson, with particular reference to psychoanalysis (1981), and by Terry Eagleton, who combines his reading of Althusser and Macherey with ideas on literature as production (1976a; but see also 1981). Both, as well as trying to develop their own brand of Marxist literary theory, have also turned their energies to substantial concrete analyses of texts and authors (Jameson, 1972; 1979; Eagleton, 1975; 1982) – a welcome counter to the contemporary obsession with grandiloquent and all-encompassing theorising. Their work, while acknowledging the importance of structuralism and post-structuralism, acts as a restraining force on the wilder exegetical excesses of these traditions by grounding its research firmly in history. In the late to mid-1960s, Galvano Della Volpe had also attempted to investigate the specificity of poetic language through its relationship to historical reality. Although he also makes use of Saussure, like the structuralists, the emphasis of his work is not so much on the signifier, but on the polysemous semantic values of poetic language (see 1978).

9.7 CONCLUSION

Two common and related assumptions support classical Marxist attitudes to literature: firstly, that Marxism can offer an adequate explanation for and definition of literature; and secondly, that literature is subordinate to and indelibly marked by extraliterary factors, namely, history and specific social formations. However, both these positions are deeply problematic, and, I feel, ultimately untenable. Literature is an infinitely rich – and I have chosen my words with care – concept; and it is one which is impossible to define with precision. Different epochs have had different opinions as to what might or might not be included within this category (an area in which Marxism could have had much to contribute, but has in fact on the whole remained strangely silent). At the same time, when subjected to analysis, literary texts can satisfy the methodological presuppositions of a whole range of discrete and often antagonistic approaches. Thus any attempt to imprison them within a single interpretation, a single method, within a single, self-confidently totalising viewpoint, (and by extension within a single creative practice) is doomed at best to failure or at worst to encourage intellectual repression and dishonesty. Furthermore, there is the possible danger that historicist readings, within which Marxism must necessarily be included, because of their emphasis on external forces and tensions, can downgrade or ignore the formal–semiotic properties of texts. And this is precisely what happened in Marxism. In recent years these limitations inherent in Marxist approaches to literature have been confronted by writers working within this tradition. However, this has only generated new problems. Although it is convincingly pointed out that certain earlier Marxists (specifically Brecht and Benjamin) had begun to broaden the perspectives of Marxist views of literature, the main thrust for change has not come from within this tradition. The stimulus has been given by psychoanalysis, formalism, (post-) structuralism, feminism – positions which had previously either been ignored or attacked by most Marxists. This is a significant shift, which has left the tradition in considerable confusion and without clearly discernible reference points. It has become increasingly impossible to assess whether many of those theorists of literature who interest themselves in questions of literary form and who accept the relative autonomy of literature within socio-economic organisation do, in fact, belong to a Marxist tradition of literary studies, or whether they are rather scholars working on literature in other methods, who are also sympathetic to left-wing politics and who allow Marxism's more general conclusions some space in their work.

What has happened in Marxist literary theory is not unusual. Like every other attempt to define literature and its practices (most relevantly for my present discussion, the arguments over the politically most efficacious literary forms and, hence, critical methods), Marxist literary theory has stumbled on the complexities and uncertainties of its supposed object of study. It has achieved most in those areas in which the method has always been strongest (economics, history, ideology; and Marxist analyses of the relationship between art and ideology have been undoubtedly the most sophisticated so far made by any branch of literary theory); areas, which play important roles in the creation, consumption and study of literature, but which are still only a few of its many aspects, and possibly among its more peripheral ones.

GUIDE TO FURTHER READING

For introductions to Marxist views on aesthetics in general and literature in particular, see Arvon (1973); Eagleton (1976b); Williams (1977); Laing (1978). A useful bibliography is Bullock and Peck (1980). The best collections of Marx and Engels' writings on art are 1974 and 1976. Prawer (1978) is an excellent survey of Marx's views and uses of literature. Lukács' most representative Marxist texts are 1972 and 1981. Brecht's major theoretical articles have been well edited and translated by John Willett (1964). Benjamin's rich and stimulating writings are at present scattered in several volumes (1973a; 1973b; 1973c; 1979). Adorno's main aesthetic writings are shortly to be published in a single volume by Routledge. A good collection of Gramsci's cultural writings is also due to be published (forthcoming). Goldmann's most interesting work is 1964. General surveys of structuralism are Culler (1975; 1983); Coward and Ellis (1977); Hawkes (1977); Belsey (1980); Norris (1982); Easthope (1983).

REFERENCES

Adorno, T. (1977a), *Ästhetische Theorie* (Frankfurt am Main: Suhrkamp).
—— (1977b), 'Letters to Walter Benjamin', in *Aesthetics and Politics* (London: New Left Books) pp. 110–33.
Althusser, L. (1971), *Lenin and Philosophy* (London: New Left Books).
—— (1982), *For Marx* (London: Verso).
Anderson, P. (1983), *In the Tracks of Historical Materialism* (London: Verso).
Arvon, H. (1973), *Marxist Esthetics* (Ithaca and London: Cornell University Press).
Bakhtin, M. (1968), *Rabelais and his World* (Cambridge, Mass.: MIT Press).
—— (1973), *Problems of Dostoevsky's Poetics*, Ardis.
Balibar, R. (1974), *Les Français fictifs: Le rapport des styles littéraires au français national* (Paris: Hachette).
Balibar, R. and Laporte, D. (1974), *Le Français national* (Paris: Hachette).
Barrett, M. et al. (1979), 'Representation and Cultural Production', in M. Barrett et al. (eds), *Ideology and Cultural Production* (London: Croom Helm) pp. 9–24.
Belsey, C. (1980), *Critical Practice* (London: Methuen).
Benjamin, W. (1973a), *Charles Baudelaire: a Lyric Poet of the Era of High Capitalism* (London: New Left Books).
—— (1973b), *Illuminations*, Fontana/Collins.
—— (1973c), *Understanding Brecht* (London: New Left Books).
—— (1979), *One-Way Street* (London: New Left Books).
Bennett, T. (1979), *Formalism and Marxism* (London: Methuen).
Brecht, B. (1964), *Brecht on Theatre*, edited and translated by J. Willett (London: Methuen).
—— (1977), 'Against Georg Lukács', in *Aesthetics and Politics* (London: New Left Books) pp. 68–85.
Bullock, C. and Peck, D. (1980), *Guide to Marxist Literary Criticism* (Brighton: Harvester).
Clarke, S. et al. (1980), *One-Dimensional Marxism: Althusser and the Politics of Culture* (London and New York: Allison & Busby).
Collins, R. and Porter, V. (1981), *WDR and the Arbeiterfilm: Fassbinder, Ziewer and Others* (London: British Film Institute).
Coward, R. and Ellis, J. (1977), *Language and Materialism* (London: Routledge & Kegan Paul).
Culler, J. (1975), *Structuralist Poetics* (London: Routledge & Kegan Paul).
—— (1983), *On Deconstruction* (London: Routledge & Kegan Paul).
Della Volpe, G. (1978), *Critique of Taste* (London: New Left Books).
Demetz, P. (1967), *Marx, Engels and the Poets*, 2nd edn (Chicago University Press).
Eagleton, T. (1975), *Myths of Power: a Marxist Study of the Brontës* (London: Macmillan).
—— (1976a), *Criticism and Ideology* (London: New Left Books).

—— (1976b), *Marxism and Literary Criticism* (London: Methuen).
—— (1981), *Walter Benjamin or Towards a Revolutionary Criticism* (London: New Left Books).
—— (1982), *The Rape of Clarissa: Writing, Sexuality and Class Struggle in Samuel Richardson* (Oxford: Blackwell).
—— (1983), *Literary Theory* (Oxford: Blackwell).
Easthope, A. (1983), *Poetry as Discourse* (London: Methuen).
Erlich, V. (1955), *Russian Formalism* (The Hague: Mouton).
Evans, M. (1981), *Lucien Goldmann* (Brighton: Harvester).
Formations (1983), 'Formations of Pleasure'.
Glucksmann, M. (1969), 'Lucien Goldmann: Humanist or Marxist', *New Left Review*, 56, pp. 49–62.
Goldmann, L. (1964), *The Hidden God* (London: Routledge & Kegan Paul).
—— (1967), 'Ideology and Writing', *TLS*, 28 September, pp. 903–5.
—— (1969), *The Human Sciences and Philosophy* (London: Jonathan Cape).
Gorky, M. *et al.* (1977), *Soviet Writers' Congress 1934: the Debate on Socialist Realism and Modernism in the Soviet Union* (London: Lawrence & Wishart).
Gramsci, A. (1975), *Marxismo e letteratura*, G. Manacorda (ed.) (Rome: Editori Riuniti).
—— (forthcoming), *Selections from the Cultural Writings*, D. Forgács and G. Nowell-Smith (eds) (London: Lawrence & Wishart).
Hall, S. (1977), 'Rethinking the "Base-Superstructure" Metaphor', in J. Bloomfield (ed.), *Papers on Class, Hegemony and Party* (London: Lawrence & Wishart) pp. 43–72.
Hall, S. *et al.* (1980), *Culture, Media, Language* (London: Hutchinson).
Hawkes, T. (1977), *Structuralism and Semiotics* (London: Methuen).
Heath, S. (1977), 'Language, Literature, Materialism', *Sub-Stance*, 17, pp. 67–74.
Jameson, F. (1972), *The Prison-House of Language* (Princeton University Press).
—— (1977), 'Reflections in Conclusion', in *Aesthetics and Politics* (London: New Left Books) pp. 196–213.
—— (1979), *Fables of Aggression: Wyndham Lewis, the Modernist as Fascist* (Berkeley-Los Angeles-London: University of California Press).
—— (1981), *The Political Unconscious* (London: Methuen).
Johnson, R. (1979), 'Histories of Culture/Theories of Ideology: Notes on an Impasse', in M. Barrett *et al.* (eds), *Ideology and Cultural Production* (London: Croom Helm) pp. 49–77.
Kraiski, G. (ed.) (1967), *Rivoluzione e letteratura. Il dibattito al 1° Congresso degli Scrittori Sovietici* (Bari: Laterza).
Laing, D. (1978), *The Marxist Theory of Art* (Hassocks: Harvester).
Leitch, V. B. (1983), *Deconstructive Criticism* (London: Hutchinson).
Lenin, I. V. (1960–70), *Collected Works*, 45 vols, (London: Lawrence & Wishart).
—— (1967), *On Literature and Art* (Moscow: Progress).
Lifshitz, M. (1973), *The Philosophy of Art of Karl Marx* (London: Pluto Press).
Lovell, T. (1980), *Pictures of Reality: Aesthetics, Politics, Pleasure* (London: British Film Institute).
Lukács, G. (1963), *The Meaning of Contemporary Realism* (London: Merlin).
—— (1964), *Essays on Thomas Mann* (London: Merlin).
—— (1972), *Studies in European Realism* (London: Merlin).

—— (1981), *The Historical Novel* (Harmondsworth: Penguin).
MacCabe, C. (1974), 'Realism and the Cinema: Notes on Some Brechtian Theses', *Screen*, 15, ii, pp. 7–27.
—— (1976), 'Principles of Realism and Pleasure', *Screen*, 17, iii, pp. 7–27.
—— (1979), *James Joyce and the Revolution of the Word* (London: Macmillan).
McArthur, C. (1975/76), 'Days of Hope', *Screen*, 16, iv, pp. 139–44.
McDonnell, K. and Robins, K. (1980), 'Marxist Cultural Theory: the Althusserian Smokescreen', in Clarke *et al.*, pp. 157–231.
Macherey, P. (1977a), 'An Interview with Pierre Macherey', *Red Letters*, 5, pp. 3–9.
—— (1977b), 'Problems of Reflection', in *Literature, Society and the Sociology of Literature*, University of Essex, pp. 41–54.
—— (1978a), *A Theory of Literary Production* (London: Routledge & Kegan Paul).
Macherey, P. and Balibar, E. (1978b), 'Literature as an Ideological Form', *Oxford Literary Review*, 3, i, pp. 4–12.
Marx, K. (1973), *Grundrisse* (Harmondsworth: Penguin).
—— (1976), *Capital*, vol. 1 (Harmondsworth: Penguin).
Marx, K. and Engels, F. (1956), *Selected Correspondence* (Moscow: Foreign Languages Publishing House).
—— (1974), *On Literature and Art*, L. Baxandall and S. Morawski (eds) (New York: International General).
—— (1975 foll.), *Collected Works* (London: Lawrence & Wishart).
—— (1976), *On Literature and Art* (Moscow: Progress).
Matejka, L. and Pomorska, K. (1971), *Readings in Russian Poetics* (Cambridge, Mass.: MIT Press).
Mayrl, W. W. (1977), 'Introduction', in L. Goldmann, *Cultural Creation in Modern Society* (Oxford: Blackwell) pp. 1–27.
Morawski, S. (1965), 'Lenin as a Literary Theorist', *Science and Society*, 29, pp. 2–25.
—— (1974), 'Introduction', in Marx and Engels (1974), pp. 3–47.
Nochlin, L. (1971), *Realism* (Harmondsworth: Penguin).
Norris, C. (1982), *Deconstruction: Theory and Practice* (London: Methuen).
Plekhanov, G. V. (1953), *Art and Social Life* (London: Lawrence & Wishart).
Prawer, S. S. (1978), *Karl Marx and World Literature* (Oxford University Press).
Raphael, M. (1933), *Proudhon, Marx, Picasso* (Paris: Éd. Excelsior).
Roberts, J. (1982), *Walter Benjamin* (London: Macmillan).
Sapegno, N. (1969), 'Gramsci e i problemi della letteratura', in P. Rossi (ed.), *Gramsci e la cultura contemporanea*, vol. 1 (Rome: Editori Riuniti – Istituto Gramsci) pp. 265–77.
Screen (1974), 15, ii (special issue on Brecht).
Slaughter, C. (1980), *Marxism, Ideology and Literature* (London: Macmillan).
Solomon, M. (ed.) (1979), *Marxism and Art: Essays Classic and Contemporary* (Brighton: Harvester).
Stipčević, N. (1968), *Gramsci e i problemi letterari* (Milan: Mursia).
Strada, V. (ed.) (1976), *Problemi di teoria del romanzo* (Turin: Einaudi).
Thibaudeau, J. (1976), 'Preliminary Notes on the Prison Writings of Gramsci: The Place of Literature in Marxian Theory', *Praxis*, 3, pp. 3–29.
Trotsky, L. (1960), *Literature and Revolution* (Ann Arbor: University of Michigan Press).

Williams, R. (1977), *Marxism and Literature* (Oxford University Press).
—— (1979), *Politics and Letters* (London: New Left Books).
—— (1983), *Writing in Society* (London: Verso).
Zhdanov, A. A. (1950), *On Literature, Music and Philosophy* (London: Lawrence & Wishart).

10 Media and Cultural Studies

BOB LUMLEY AND MICHAEL O'SHAUGHNESSEY

10.1 INTRODUCTION

Today it is not surprising that there should be degree and other courses in media, film, television and cultural studies. Yet behind these developments lies an ongoing history of conflicts over what can legitimately be called 'culture'. The setting up within the educational system of courses on media and cultural studies marks the recognition that it is not just Fine Art or Literature that constitute the 'cultural' in society. Left-wing intellectuals and Marxist ideas have played an important role in achieving this change in attitude. The contributions coming from these have not only entailed a positive assessment of the possibilities of the television age, but have also developed a radical politics. The campaign to broaden definitions of culture to include 'ways of life' has often been linked to struggles for a more democratic and egalitarian society. From this point of view, the problem has not been to make Culture more accessible to the people (in the manner of Mathew Arnold or Lord Reith), but to redefine 'culture' in order to valorise and explain areas of experience and meaning previously discounted within educational, broadcasting and other institutions (Williams, 1971, pp. 9–15; Mulhern, 1980). As will be shown, this led to important debates on the meaning of the term 'popular culture'.

These battles over the definition of 'culture' were, not surprisingly, waged mainly within the educational institutions. To use Pierre Bourdieu's terms, what has been at issue has been the constitution of a new and distinct 'intellectual field', and the fight for mastery within it (Bourdieu, 1971). Media and Cultural Studies have had to differentiate themselves from Sociology and English Literary Studies, although many of their exponents have come precisely from an initial training in these disciplines. At the same time, different theories have been championed and assessed in so far as they have succeeded in freeing the field from the shackles of other disciplines and in creating an independent, 'interdisciplinary' approach to questions of cultural analysis. Since the 1970s, Marxist approaches have gained a notable ascendancy in the field to the point that major debates have tended to occur primarily 'within' Marxism (Curran et al., 1982, pp. 11–29).

Nicholas Garnham and Raymond Williams write that different Marxist analyses developed in two successive stages:

> The first saw the rise out of literary studies of a culturalist Marxism in opposition to both the subjectivism of Leavisite literary criticism and to that empirical, ahistorical sociology of mass-communication whose intellectual roots lay in American sociology. The early development of the Birmingham Centre for Contemporary Cultural Studies marks that development. The second stage saw the development (and here the work of *Screen* is exemplary) under the influence first of Althusser and then of Lacan of a theoreticist Marxism which directed considerations of the problem of ideology away from economic and class determinants, seen as vulgarly economistic or sociologistic, and towards the text as the privileged site for a relatively autonomous signifying practice. (Garnham and Williams, 1980, pp. 209–10)

They add that a third approach can be identified which 'reasserts from within an older Marxist tradition the need to restress the social efficacy and explanatory power of economic and class determinations' (p. 210).

Our aim in writing this essay is to outline the key features and concepts of the competing approaches mentioned above. We could have done this by mapping the development of the field historically, but we decided that it would be more useful to focus on recent debates, especially as Chapter 9 on 'Literary Theory' covers the historical evolution of Marxist analyses of cultural forms. While it will be necessary to refer back to historical debates, these cannot simply be reiterated. Contemporary studies deal with phenomena such as television and the popular press which did not exist or were in their infancy in the early years of this century.

While this work, like Marxist studies in other areas, has been carried out within educational institutions (Anderson, 1976, pp. 92–3), it is important to put it in a wider political and social context. Preoccupations with questions of 'ideology' relate to the 'intellectual field' and to the position of an emergent group of intellectuals within it. Yet these concerns should, in turn, be connected to the growth of the mass communications industries and the presence of media representations in people's lives. This development was first systematically faced both in the pre- and the post-war periods by the Frankfurt School, which propounded the pessimistic 'mass society' thesis, according to which the consciousness of subordinate groups was increasingly moulded and manipulated by commercial corporations and governments (Marcuse, 1973; Adorno and Horkheimer, 1977). But in the late 1960s and 1970s awareness among Marxists of the need to understand the mass media gave rise to more optimistic analyses inspired by the ideas of Brecht and Benjamin (see Barański, ch. 9). These approaches put the emphasis on the contradictions within the capitalist system of production and consumption of cultural goods (Berger, 1972; Enzensberger, 1972; Ellis, 1977, pp. 2–12).

The new focus on the contradictory nature of the media resulted in important ways from the activities of protest movements. In Britain, for example, trade unionists denounced press reporting of strikes, the women's movement denounced the 'sexist' connotations of advertising images, and campaigns were launched against racism in the media. It was participants in and sympathisers of these movements who were responsible for studies which demonstrated the class, gender and racial 'bias' of media representations (see Glasgow Media Group, 1976; 1980; Women's Studies Group, 1978; National Association for Multiracial Education, 1981). But it is important to note that this work sought not only to reveal the mechanisms whereby forms of cultural domination were reproduced, but to open up inner contradictions (for example, in relation to broadcasters' claims to be 'impartial'), and to produce alternative representations.

The role of Marxist approaches in the resurgence of critical work was primarily to underline the determinacy of class relations in the cultural field. Unlike developments, say, in the United States, accounts of the representation of gays or women in the British context have usually related them to class. However, critiques developed by feminists, for example, have tended to explore areas which Marxists have traditionally ignored. They have re-evaluated ideologies of femininity previously dismissed by Marxist writers, and have shown that conceptions of masculinity deeply structure cultural forms (Winship, 1978; Cook, 1982). Feminist work, as will be seen, has particularly influenced the development of textual analysis and of audience research.

The capacity of Marxists to respond positively to the challenges of social movements has undoubtedly enriched their analyses of cultural phenomena. At the same time, they have faced the dilemmas and recurrent tensions between their aspiration to gain legitimacy for their ideas within the framework of the educational institutions and their commitment to a political project of subverting the structures which they see as guarantors of cultural inequalities. In the analyses which follow, we concentrate on the theoretical dimensions of some of the main debates on the media and on cultural forms – debates whose protagonists are largely engaged in academic studies and whose forums are specialist reviews – a situation rather different from that in which Brecht was operating. But we will try also to show the implications of such theoretical positions for the political/cultural activities of practising film-makers and others working in the media. While the validity of different approaches needs to be judged on their explanatory value, they should for Marxists also be measured in terms of their practical implementation and political effects.

10.2 FOUR AREAS OF DEBATE

We have chosen to look at four areas of debate which represent nodal points in the recent evolution of Marxist analyses of media and cultural forms. We begin with the discussion of economic determination, because this has been a traditional hallmark of Marxist analysis (see Barański, ch. 9). This will serve also to illustrate the polarisation between approaches grounded in sociology, and those having a structuralist orientation. Secondly, we examine how the latter developed modernist, text-based studies, which were ultimately literary–critical in emphasis, in the attempt to establish a 'deconstructive' cultural practice. Thirdly, we look at how the 'discovery' of the audience marked a break with determinist accounts, whether these were founded on economic or textual analysis. And, fourthly, we take debates on popular culture as a way of seeing the effects of such analyses on Marxist constructions of a cultural politics.

10.3 THE POLITICAL ECONOMY DEBATE

The issue of who controls and owns media organisations has been central to Marxist concerns ever since Marx himself wrote his famous passage in *The German Ideology*. This has been a point of reference for all subsequent debates about economic determinations, and is worth, therefore, quoting at length:

> The class which has the means of material production at its disposal has control at the same time over the means of mental production, so that thereby, generally speaking, the ideas of those who lack the means of mental production are subject to it. In so far, therefore, as they rule as a class and determine the extent and compass of an epoch, it is self-evident that they regulate the production and distribution of the ideas of their age; thus, their ideas are the ruling ideas of the epoch. (Marx, 1970, p. 64)

This formulation has frequently been used mechanically and polemically to underwrite 'conspiracy theories' and economistic accounts, rather than as a starting-point for empirical and theoretical inquiry. Thus, when Graham Murdock and Peter Golding relaunched discussion of the political economy of mass communications, arguing that 'economic determinacy' was the corner-stone of Marxist analysis, they claimed to have avoided such reductionist short-cuts and shortcomings. But not everyone agreed.

Reacting against what they saw as the prevailing tendency among Marxists working on the media to ignore or bracket off economic determinations, Golding and Murdock have insisted that 'the mass media are first and foremost industrial and commercial organisations which produce commodities' (Golding and Murdock, 1979, p. 210). They argue that the key to understanding contemporary cultural formations lies in analysing monopoly capitalist structures of ownership and control. These are not identical. Ownership, they claim, entails a power over the strategic allocation of resources that circumscribes room for manoeuvre at the operative level of control. This means that cultural producers have only a limited autonomy, and that it is possible, without summoning up the interfering figure of the press baron, to show how constraints are structural and operate at a general level to bring cultural production into conformity with economic interests (Golding and Murdock, 1977; Murdock, 1982). Golding and Murdock stress also that 'economic determinations' can be seen most clearly when they operate at a macro-level, promoting tendencies towards uniformity, standardisation, and consensus-values in overall output (Murdock and Golding, 1973).

However, these proponents of political economy are careful to note that analyses need to take account of the specific nature of production activities in order to go beyond generalities and crude instrumentalism. But they write that, while production studies provide evidence for the specificity and 'relative autonomy' of professional practices and ideologies, conceptions of news values or journalistic independence, for example, are not fundamentally at odds with the dominant forces in society. Likewise disputes between 'creative' personnel and media organisations tend to be localised and within frames of reference which do not call in question the underlining structures of resource allocation (Golding and Elliot, 1976; Murdock, 1980a; 1980b). This is why Golding and Murdock maintain that it is imperative to understand the workings of economic determinations (seen at various times as the profit-motive, or as mass production, or as monopoly ownership), which are said to 'penetrate and frame the forms of particular productions'. Yet this traditionally based Marxist approach to cultural analysis has been hotly disputed by other Marxists.

Where supporters of the political economy approach have concentrated on general explanations, their critics have tended to start with specific texts. They ask how economic determination can explain how meanings are created and how cultural forms develop. John Hill writes that Golding and Murdock's model leaves a gap between economic production and media forms, which is only overcome for them through a dissolution of media specificity (the particular organisation of matters of expression) and consequent reduction of the media to transcriptions of socio-political ideologies originated elsewhere. At most they account for the repetition and exclusion of particular forms once constituted not for their dominance within the media nor for their particular operations. (Hill, 1979, p. 114)

This gap between analyses of the political economy of the media and textual analyses (see next section) which emerged in the mid-1970s was in fact more like an abyss. Production studies did not examine the programmes themselves (Elliot, 1972; Alvarado and Buscombe, 1978), while elsewhere programmes were dissected without reference to how and under what conditions they were produced. This division of labour has tended to underpin differences between a 'sociological' Marxism with roots in the Frankfurt tradition, and a structuralist, Althusserian Marxism which has used the concepts of 'relative autonomy' and the 'ideological level' to explore the internal dynamics of 'signifying practices', without attempting to relate them to economic structures (see also Urry, ch. 5; Barański, ch. 9). These approaches have also led to different political priorities, depending on whether the emphasis has been put on questions of ownership, or on the transformation of representational practices (Garnham, 1979; Connell, 1983).

The conflicts within Marxism over how to understand economic determinations are far from resolved. However, there has perhaps been recently a greater readiness to acknowledge that the 'gap' between approaches which focus on the political economy and those which concentrate on cultural forms cannot be bridged from one side only. There is a recognition that a more complex model is needed which takes account of institutional, legal and political pressures, and which analyses the gender and racial, as well as the class nature of the divisions of labour and exercise of power within the industry (ACTT, 1975; Gardner, 1981; Ellis, 1982b). Moreover, interest has grown also in the development of an historical approach in the place of the ahistorical and schematic periodisations offered by Golding and Murdock (see Hill, 1979).

Recent developments within the mass communications industries, such as technological advances, and the decision to install cable-television under private ownership and control, have nevertheless brought home the importance of analysing economic determinations (Golding and Murdock, 1983). However, it is perhaps the work of Pierre Bourdieu which has provoked the most interest in developing concepts which overcome the 'gap' between analyses of culture and of socio-economic processes. By combining concepts worked up from the writings of Weber, as well as Marx, and drawing on the French anthropological tradition inspired by Durkheim, Bourdieu seeks to relate cultural manifestations to class relations, while recognising their specificity. For example, he constructs a general model whereby 'symbolic goods' have 'economies' in which transactions take place in order to accumulate 'symbolic capital' or prestige, while insisting that these operations also contain forms of economic rationality. He illustrates his argument, in one instance, by comparing the working of a large commercial and of a small avant-garde publishing house (Bourdieu, 1980a). Bourdieu's commitment to empirical research, as well as his theoretical sophistication, have been greeted enthusiastically in the UK, though his contribution is only slowly being evaluated as his work becomes available in translation (Nice, 1978; Garnham and Williams, 1980).

10.4 TEXTUAL ANALYSIS

This area of communication studies, as distinct from the determinist model, is concerned with the processes of represenation in the media. It has concentrated on textual analysis, looking at the ways texts are constructed, working out *what* they mean by analysing *how* they mean, using a mixture of semiotic, structuralist and literary critical approaches (see Hawkes, 1977; Nichols, 1981; see also Lepschy, ch. 8; Barański, ch. 9). Marxist approaches in this field seek primarily to reveal the ideological make-up of texts. Furthermore they try to discover alternative radical textual strategies in opposition to dominant forms. Unlike most literary studies this work has focused on popular texts – cinema, TV, the press and so on – and has asked how texts which are ideologically reactionary successfully win the support of an audience made up predominantly of subordinate social groups.

Early studies examined how a wide range of cultural activities, from wrestling to news photos, served to construct and confirm certain commonsense ways of seeing the world, creating and perpetuating ideologies and cultural myths (see Barthes, 1973; Hall, 1973b). The 'ideological work' of texts was understood by identifying how texts represented social problems and contradictions in such a way that they would 'mask', 'fragment' or impose on these an 'imaginary unity or coherence', and so not showing the basic class antagonisms of society (Hall, 1977, pp. 336–7).

Building on this, a body of work developed a polemical line against mainstream popular media. This work, which is classified as structuralist and/or formalist, drew on several sources: Modernism, Russian Formalism, the ideas of Brecht, structural linguistics and the work of Louis Althusser. The basis of this position was the belief that particular textual forms will guarantee that readers will unconsciously accept a certain view of the world, that the reader will be 'fixed' in position by the text, and that therefore form determines meaning (for accounts of this, see Althusser, 1971, pp. 160–70; Jameson, 1972; Harvey, 1978, pp. 45–82; Bennett, 1979).

The ways in which the reader could be positioned or 'fixed' by the text were shown primarily through a critical examination of the dominant forms of cinema, exemplified by the Hollywood system, and of television, and their use of *narrative* and *realist* forms. The argument is that the dominant form of narrative in the cinema and TV constructs a particular way of seeing the world: its concern with enigmas and suspense focuses audience attention on the *process* of narrative resolution rather than on subject matter; it demands and provides endings which appear to offer clear-cut solutions and closures to the problems it has represented, so that it presents a 'closed' view of the world; interest is usually centred on individual protagonists rather than groups, and motivation is understood in psychological rather than social terms (see Drummond, 1979, pp. 9–16; Neale, 1980, pp. 19–30; Ellis, 1982a, pp. 62–77, 145–60). In addition to these, the structure of a narrative always offers a particular point of view from which events are seen, and a particular time sequence and order in which they are shown. These are not 'innocent' or 'natural' positions from which to see the events: they are chosen to present a specific viewpoint, but unless the reader is made conscious of this process of narrative construction it will appear that this is simply the truth of events, since the process of narration will itself remain hidden. In representing women such narrative structures have tended to show them as objects of sexual spectacle, or as objects of sexual mystery and danger whose threat is removed through the resolution of the narrative. Other narrative roles assigned to women are as passive protagonists who suffer rather than act, or simply as secondary characters (see Mulvey, 1975; Kaplan, 1978).

The effects on an audience of this kind of narrative are to produce an identification and emotional involvement with the characters, which will lead to a cathartic release at the narrative's closure and will encourage passive acceptance of the narrative's world view, discouraging critical distance and reflection on the events represented (see Brecht's distinctions between 'Epic and Narrative Theatre' in Willett, 1973, pp. 40–53). Finally it should be noted that the dominant position of narrative forms within the institutions of cinema and TV is such as to marginalise any non-narrative or alternative forms, because audiences will not consider these acceptable viewing material.

As regards 'realism' (see Barański, ch. 9), cinema and TV have been criticised for adopting aesthetic techniques which purport to show the world *as it is*, offering us a 'window on the world'. These techniques are said to concentrate on reproducing surface reality, masking its contradictory deep structures, and to hide the processes of construction involved in producing any film or TV programme. Realism has been used as a narrative form by radical and socialist practitioners, but these too have been criticised because, although they are critical of the realities they depict, they present knowledge of reality as unproblematic and do not formally present the possibilities or processes of changing the world. They also offer an unproblematic 'truth' about the world. This is the central problem with realism: that it puts forward an interpretation which it regards as the truth, neither questioning the processes of representation nor placing readers in a position from which they have to work to make sense of a text.

The relevance of this work for Marxists is that mainstream cinema and TV are seen as two of the sites through which 'dominant ideology' is represented and achieves its effects (see Althusser, 1971, pp. 127–89; see also Urry, ch. 5). Narrative and realist forms are ideological, and their 'naturalness' and apparent neutrality are ways of masking the fact that they construct a particular view of the world.

As a challenge to this dominant system, Marxist and avant-garde critics and practitioners have attempted to produce radical alternative forms which would try to put the spectator in a different relation to the text. This work was 'deconstructive', in that it drew attention to its own means of production, subverted narrative forms and adopted anti-realist techniques, such as the use of Brechtian alienation techniques (see Wollen, 1982, pp. 79–92; see also Barański, ch. 9). These strategies were developed particularly by feminists who sought to establish a 'feminine aesthetic' and ways of representing women which would challenge the dominant spectator-text relationship through new narrative forms (see Mulvey, 1979; Kuhn, 1982). They also recognised the need to provide new 'pleasures' for the spectator.

While considerable work was done in the 1970s on uncovering the ideological workings of texts, little attention was paid to the pleasures which these could engender. The move towards developing progressive textual strategies had resulted in the production of many films which audiences found difficult and unpleasurable, and which ignored or denied the pleasures still found in reactionary film and TV texts. As a result, Brecht's stress on providing 'pleasurable learning' was invoked, and more recently there have been attempts to theorise the workings of pleasure. Psychoanalysis, and the work of Freud in particular, have been used extensively in this area, but the significance of pleasure and its relation to ideology and popularity still needs much greater study (see Barthes, 1976, p. 14; Neale, 1980, pp. 30-55; Jameson, 1983).

Structuralist criticism was first applied to cinema. When it focused on television, it found a different object of study made up of different narrative patterns – the series, serial, soap opera, different genres – situation comedy, quiz shows, a range of 'factual' programmes, and all of these contained within a continuous broadcast flow. And it was in examining these forms that some of the most valuable critical work was done. In particular the work on the formal structures of 'factual' programmes – news, current affairs, documentaries, sports – has thoroughly debunked the myths of the objectivity, balance and impartiality of television, and has instead revealed the processes of construction and mediation at work in all programmes and the liberal, pluralist ideology which lies behind them. Further examination has revealed how through its scheduling and its mode of address to the audience, television constructs viewers as members of a domestic family (for examples of this work on TV, see Hall 1974b; Buscombe, 1975; Collins, 1976; Glasgow Media Group, 1976; Brunsdon and Morley, 1978; McArthur, 1978; Hood, 1980, pp. 7–28; Dyer, 1981).

However, while structuralist/formalist criticism reached its peak in the analysis of television, and led to a body of radical work in film and TV, in the last few years it has been heavily criticised by Marxists and feminists for a number of reasons. Firstly, the constitution of different audiences was not taken into account: a formalist position accepted too unproblematically that texts would fix or control audiences, not allowing spectators any autonomy in how they actually received and used the texts (see Section 10.5 below). In addition, the 'alternative' and 'deconstructive' films which were produced often demanded an intellectual approach which made them élitist and inaccessible to a popular audience. Secondly, the formalists became so concerned with examining the processes of representation *per se*, that they lost sight of producing any useful knowledge about the 'real' world. Harvey concludes: 'If there is a sense in which modernism offers the only way forward, there is also a sense in which it constitutes a dead end, a graveyard. Only those who pass through it can learn from it; the rest remain buried within it (1978, p. 82). Thirdly, formalism ignored history. In idealist fashion, it saw textual forms as the sole determinants of meaning and ignored the fact that different historical moments require different textual practices, that radical practitioners have to work within the limitations of institutions and audience reception, and that texts will actually have different meanings within different historical and cultural contexts (see Lovell, 1980, pp. 64–100; Bennett *et al.*, 1981). Finally, the attack on mainstream cinema and TV was too purist and élitist. It saw the mainstream system as unproblematically reproducing dominant ideology; recent work suggests that actually this is a 'leaky' system, that is, one in which it is possible to find some contradictory and radical elements (Dyer, 1979, pp. 2–4; 1981). The most recent textual criticism and practice has shifted from the earlier intention to provide ideologically correct analyses. It now aims to provide pleasurable experiences, which can win the support of large popular audiences, and aims to investigate the contradictory and complex ideological workings of any text.

10.5 AUDIENCES

Research into audiences and into how they respond to media messages is relatively underdeveloped. On the one hand, the media organisations have shown a remarkable lack of curiosity about this, except when it has been a question of quantifying data, while, on the other, there are several quite specific reasons why Marxists in particular have ignored the problem. Firstly, the 'political economy' approach has tended to assume, like the Frankfurt School, that the increasing 'standardisation' of the contents of newspapers or television programmes has induced cultural conformism (Murdock and Golding, 1973, pp. 227–32), or that the media's operations can be largely explained by their aim of 'selling audiences to advertisers' (Smythe, 1977). In fact, audience subjugation to the 'effects' of 'mass persuasion' advertising strategies has often been cited as evidence of its general passivity (Morley, 1980, pp. 1–6). Secondly, as has been seen in the preceding section, analyses that have focused on cultural forms have assumed an identity between the 'reader' inscribed in the text and the 'real reader'. Thus, approaches developed from within the seemingly opposed Frankfurt School and structuralist methodologies have converged in proposing analyses in which audiences are shown to be the victims of manipulation or structural positioning. They have suggested, in some instances, that the cinema or television institutions themselves isolate, privatise and colonise the audience (Sahin and Robinson, 1980; Ellis, 1982b). It should be noted, furthermore, that both approaches have ascribed great powers to the media, often without testing or exploring this assertion. In the process, they have astonishingly failed to reveal how it has happened that the analysts themselves have escaped subjection.

Within Marx's writings there are passages which can be said to have encouraged analyses in which consumption is treated as secondary and 'predetermined'. Moreover, Marx's insistence that production 'produces' consumption (Hall, 1974a, pp. 142–3), and his statement about the primacy of the ownership of the means of mental production in determining the predominance of ruling class ideas, have led Marxists to focus attention on production relations. However, work done since the early 70s at the Centre for Contemporary Cultural Studies (CCCS) at Birmingham University has represented an alternative approach to the problem. Above all, it has dealt with the conflicts and resistances inherent within the processes of cultural consumption (Hall, 1980a; 1980b). Using concepts derived from Gramsci, studies of youth subcultures and women's magazines, for example, have shown how subordinate groups appropriate consumer goods in a way that resist or negotiate dominant values in society (Hall and Jefferson, 1977; McRobbie, 1977; Winship, 1978; see also the following section on 'popular culture'). This perspective has been interestingly applied to media analyses, to examine the mechanisms whereby the press and television 'imagine' their audiences and develop strategies to win them over by cultivating populist modes of address or surrogate forms of participation (Brunsdon and Morley, 1978; Hall *et al.*, 1978, pp. 53–138; Connell, 1979). Yet research on the 'real' audience has been slow in taking shape.

The problem of understanding media audiences was first addressed by Marxists wanting to get away from oversimplified models of 'determination'. Important landmarks in this development have been Stuart Hall's theoretical essays which, in the early 1970s, set out to integrate Eco's semiological approach (Eco, 1972) with Althusser's and Gramsci's conceptions of ideology (Hall, 1973a). Hall argues that researchers need to find out more about how audiences 'decode' media messages. This means seeing not only if they 'comprehend' these as intended by the 'encoders', but seeing also whether they decode in ways which accept, negotiate or oppose the meanings 'preferred' in the text by the producer. In this model, the audience becomes a 'subject' as well as an 'object' in the communicative chain, which in turn is analysed as a site of conflicts rather than as a transmission-belt for the dominant ideology. Work done at CCCS has stimulated discussion of theories of 'reading', and has given an impetus to empirical studies designed to test such hypotheses (Morley, 1980).

The main usefulness of the empirical research carried out by David Morley, as he himself has been the first to admit, has been in showing up the weaknesses of the 'encoding-decoding model' (Morley, 1981). It has been argued that, instead of overcoming the gap between sociologies of the 'real' and textual analyses, the model has reproduced the base-superstructure metaphor in disguise by analysing audiences largely in terms of socio-economic position (base) and the programmes in terms of signifying practices (superstructures) (see Wren-Lewis, 1983). Criticisms have also been made of the tendency of the model to exclude notions of pleasure, and therefore to be more applicable to analyses of responses to news/current affairs than to fictional texts. Recent attempts to study genres such as soap opera and melodrama in relation to the female audience have promised richer rewards to researchers.

Whereas Marxists involved in audience research have tended to look mainly at differential 'readings' in terms of class and class-related ideologies, with a special emphasis on industrial relations coverage, feminist approaches have analysed how 'readings' are 'gendered'. While a Marxist conception of domination/subordination has often been retained, it has been enlarged to understand how media messages privilege representations of men's activities and interests. Studies have shown that women audiences resist or refuse these programmes (Hobson, 1980). Furthermore, feminist work has examined ways in which women have 'used' rather than 'been used' by the media, and has suggested that soap operas, for example, need to be understood in relation to how feminine competences and skills are mobilised in the reading process (Brunsdon, 1981; Cook, 1983).

It is worth pausing for a moment to note that conceptions of 'mass culture' or of the 'classic realist text' (see Barański, ch. 9), which have had a prominent place in Marxist accounts, have shared an antagonistic attitude to popular forms such as soap operas and other 'opiates', like sport. When feminists have challenged these assumptions, in order to 'reappropriate' despised genres and to propose that they should become areas for cultural struggle, they have had an important role in challenging such cultural élitism. The re-evaluation of audience analysis, they have helped to stimulate, has contributed to the new approaches to popular culture which are the subject of the next section.

10.6 POPULAR CULTURE

The term 'popular culture', as Raymond Williams has noted, presents many difficulties; just as 'culture' is a shifting noun, so 'popular' is a shifting qualifier. The term has been used in a general way to designate activities which are 'well-liked'; it has also been used to refer to the culture produced *for* the people (bread-and-circuses), and also to speak of the culture produced *by* and *for* the people (Williams, 1976). Much of the debate between Marxists on the nature of popular culture has oscillated between these two poles, but there have also been important attempts to produce more adequate conceptualisations of the field.

The debate on popular culture in Britain has usually been traced back to the late 1950s and early 1960s, when certain key texts were published, notably Hoggart's *Uses of Literacy* (1969; orig. publ. in 1957), Williams's *The Long Revolution* (1971; orig. publ. in 1961), and Thompson's *The Making of the English Working Class* (1968; orig. publ. in 1963). While Hoggart's and Williams's books were not Marxist, they made a contribution which Marxists have tried subsequently to appropriate and refashion, rather than reject. They were important for the way they wrote about cultures as 'lived experiences', popular knowledges and ways of life rather than as texts or specifically intellectual activities. Hoggart in particular celebrated popular culture as an autonomous sphere or enclave which was separate from the dominant culture, and lamented the incursions of television and consumerism into people's lives. (If some of his analyses now seem dated, it is worth bearing in mind that Jeremy Seabrook has given them a new currency (Seabrook, 1978)). However, Hoggart and Williams's conceptions of popular culture were severely criticised by Thompson from a Marxist viewpoint.

While Thompson (see also Corner, ch. 4; Urry, ch. 5), in using the broader definition of culture, participated in the opposition to cultural élitists, he insisted that popular culture was not only produced by and for the people, but that it was the product of their struggles against the dominant order. He attacked approaches, such as those of Hoggart and Williams, which he saw as insufficiently historical and lacking in a conception of the determinant role of class conflict in shaping knowledge and ideas (Thompson, 1961). Although his work is often categorised as 'social history', it is significant that it has greatly influenced cultural studies debates (Hall, 1980b). However, with the rise of structuralist Marxism, his approach was in its turn criticised for ignoring the subordinate and conservative aspects of popular culture in the era of imperialism (Stedman Jones, 1977), and for perpetuating a form of analysis which separated out an area of culture as if it were autonomous (Johnson, 1978).

For Althusserian Marxists, the British 'culturalist' approach was guilty of 'historicism', by which was meant that it assumed culture to be the 'expression' of social classes and of conscious human agency (Johnson, 1979). By contrast, they proposed a model in which 'ideology' displaced the concept of 'culture', and in which subordinate groups were seen to be 'bearers' of ideological structures and 'subjects' held in the grip of the state ideological apparatuses (Althusser, 1971; Brohm, 1978). This formulation effectively abolished the notions of 'experience' and of the generation of culture 'from below', and arrived at a position similar to that of the Frankfurt School, for whom 'mass culture' was entirely the product of capitalism's need to exercise social control (Marcuse, 1973; Adorno and Horkheimer, 1977).

However, there were also some critical appropriations of structuralism which tried to redefine the category of popular culture in terms of its relations with the state and with the 'deep structures' of cultural formations. Readings of Gramsci's *Prison Notebooks* (1971) played a crucial part in bridging the gap between the 'culturalist' and 'structuralist' paradigms (Hall, 1982, pp. 69-74).

Gramsci provided a range of useful concepts, (Hall *et al.*, 1977), but perhaps the most valuable of these was the concept of 'hegemony', which enabled analyses to overcome the compartmentalisations or simple determinisms of existing approaches. Tony Bennett has written:

> To rethink the concept of popular culture in and through the concept of hegemony is to define it as a system of relations – between classes – which constitutes one of the primary sites upon which the ideological struggle for the construction of class alliances and the production of consent is conducted. . . . It brings into analytic focus not this or that enclave of the cultural field, but the transactions that take place between them. (Bennett, 1980, p. 26)

The concern for the relational nature of popular culture, which is found in a number of influential studies, owes much to Gramsci. This can be seen in work on subcultures (Hall and Jefferson, 1977), in historical work (Thompson, 1978), and in theorisations of culture (Williams, 1980). In addition, Gramsci's ideas have fuelled attacks on avantgardist cultural strategies, and stimulated re-evaluations of the contradictions and radical elements within popular forms (Dyer, 1981).

The Gramscian inspired rethinking of the term 'popular culture' has proved fruitful both for Marxist theories of culture and for empirical work. However, its very success in hegemonising the area of cultural and media studies has had some negative consequences. Firstly, it has established itself as an orthodoxy within certain institutions and courses, such as the Open University Popular Culture Course (U203), and has thereby acquired some of the self-perpetuating and exclusivist tendencies of all orthodoxies. Secondly, this version of Marxism has tended to reproduce a preoccupation with the class dimensions of popular culture, a perspective which has traditionally identified it with male sections of the working class, thereby placing women in the shadows (McRobbie, 1980). Thirdly, this approach has focused on the relationships between cultural practices and the state without paying sufficient attention to the economic and market relations involved in the making of popular culture (Golding and Murdock, 1979).

10.7 SOME CONCLUSIONS

The debates in media and cultural studies which we have summarised have not been concluded. Differences between Marxist approaches continue to give rise to discussions, but perhaps recently there has been less of a polarisation and less polemic than in the 1970s. This change has resulted primarily from the crisis of the structuralist method. Althusserian Marxists led the way in iconoclastic attacks on Marxisms which they regarded as 'sociological' and 'economistic' or as 'culturalist'. While their contributions usefully focused attention on the 'relative autonomy' of signifying practices and developed textual analyses, it was not until their hold was broken, that it became possible to open up inquiries into the subjectivities of the audience and the contradictory nature of popular cultural forms and into their historical variations.

In the struggle between different Marxist approaches for the establishment of an orthodoxy in the intellectual field, it has been the work associated with Stuart Hall and Raymond Williams (as well as works already cited, see 1968; 1973; 1974) which has prevailed in Britain. Their conceptions of determination, ideology, hegemony and class have gained considerable acceptance, and have informed the curricula and pedagogic practices of courses in numerous polytechnics and the Open University. From being outsiders engaged in a long 'war of position' with the academic establishment, they have managed to become powerful figures in the determination of educatonal policies and spokespersons on cultural matters consulted, among others, by the media. However, this success of Marxist approaches in establishing the new intellectual field has not been without its costs.

Success itself has involved a tendency towards institutionalisation. In achieving academic respectability, something has been lost of the radical edge which characterised an earlier period. This can perhaps be seen in the academic orientations of the Open University's Popular Culture Course which has gained a certain notoriety for the difficult terminology it uses. (In fact, awareness of this type of problem has given rise to some interesting pedagogical discussions among teachers (see Alvarado, 1981; Williamson, 1981/2)). But while such developments are, to some extent, inherent in the logic of the field, which requires the separation of learning from other social activities, it should be noted that these developments relate also to the fact that Marxist approaches in Britain have been largely confined to educational milieux.

Despite this situation, it is worth pausing for a moment to consider the practical consequences which have stemmed from some of the theoretical positions, by taking the examples of public policy and cultural production. Marxist approaches to policy have traditionally upheld the principle of state-control and ownership against free market ideas. Opposition to the establishment of ITV, and the current rallying to the defence of the BBC against the threat of cable TV characterise a commitment to statism (Connell, 1983; Garnham, 1983). It has been argued that only regulation guarantees the provision of 'cultural programmes', news and current affairs, and British as opposed to American products. Thus, through the backdoor, the old distinctions between 'Culture' and 'Mass Culture' have been reintroduced, and it has been felt necessary to protect the people from themselves and from the media industries. A strong current in Marxism has, in brief, renewed a long-standing attachment to High Culture (see Barański, ch. 9). This position has drastically reduced the capacity for making practical proposals in relation to changes in the media that are other than traditionalist and defensive.

Again, in the field of cultural production, this élitism has continued. Marxist projects have tended to shy away from popular forms. Thus in television the single play and the documentary have been the preferred vehicles for radical work. Concern with formal innovation, especially in film-making, has led to the cultivation of a 'film versus television' aesthetic, which has shared a High Art esteem for intellectual rather than emotional responses on the part of the audience (Bourdieu, 1980b).

Significant tendencies within Marxism (especially those espousing political economy or structuralist approaches) have thus maintained an attitude to popular culture reminiscent of that of the Frankfurt School. Their pessimism has grown with the advent of new technologies. However, other commentators, who have looked more to the Brechtian project of combining avant-garde and popular forms, have noted the new possibilities for oppositional practices. Peter Wollen, for example, has written that developments, especially in modern music, point to a breakdown in the old distinctions, so that 'popular culture can no longer be seen simply in terms of the old "Hollywood" mass-media model. It is a complex, multiple, fissile system' (Wollen, 1982, p. 213). It is this perspective on the conflictual nature of cultural processes which has produced the most illuminating Marxist work, and opened the way for Marxist approaches to study and learn from subcultural currents and critiques developed by feminist and other movements.

GUIDE TO FURTHER READING

It is worth noting, to begin with, that many texts are free or cheap, namely, television, advertising hoardings and the plethora of signs that surround us every day. To help you decipher them a good starting-point is Roland Barthes, 1973; on subcultures, see Hebdige, 1979. For general readers on the media, see Bennett, 1981 and Gurevitch *et al.* (1982). For more specialist but accessible writing on film and television, see the British Film Institute's catalogue of its own and other publications (look out for the 'monographs', 'dossiers' and 'teaching materials'). Currently available reviews which are worth consulting include: *Formations, Framework, Media, Culture and Society, Primetime, Screen*. The Open University Course Units are useful even if you do not follow the programmes; see especially the Popular Culture Course (U203) and the Changing Experience of Women Course (U221). For contemporary discussions of alternative media politics and projects, see the publications of the Comedia Publishing Group.

Useful Addresses: The British Film Institute, Education Department, 81, Dean Street, London W1V 6AA; Comedia Publications Group, 9 Poland Street, London W1V 3DG.

REFERENCES

ACTT (1975), *Patterns of Discrimination in the Film and Television Industries* (London: Association of Cinematograph, Television and Allied Technicians).
Adorno, T. W. and Horkheimer, M. (1977), 'The Culture Industry: Enlightenment as Mass Deception', in J. Curran, M. Gurevitch and J. Woollacott (eds), *Mass Communication and Society* (London: Edward Arnold) pp. 349–83.
Althusser, L. (1971), *Lenin and Philosophy* (London: New Left Books).
Alvarado, M. (1981), 'Television Studies and Pedogogy', *Screen Education*, 38, pp. 56–68.
Alvarado, M. and Buscombe, E. (1978), *Hazell: the Making of a TV Series* (London: Latimer New Division).
Anderson, P. (1976), *Considerations on Western Marxism* (London: New Left Books).
Barthes, R. (1973), *Mythologies* (London: Paladin).
—— (1976), *The Pleasure of the Text* (London: Johnathan Cape).
Bennett, T. (1979), *Formalism and Marxism* (London: Methuen).
—— (1980), 'Teaching Popular Culture', *Screen Education*, 34, pp. 17–31.
Bennett, T., Boyd-Bowman, S., Mercer, C. and Woollacott, J. (eds) (1981), *Popular Television and Film* (London: British Film Institute).
Berger, J. (1972), *Ways of Seeing* (Harmondsworth: Penguin).
Bourdieu, P. (1971), 'Intellectual Field and Creative Project', in M. F. D. Young (ed.), *Knowledge and Control* (London: Collier-Macmillan) pp. 161–88.
—— (1980a), 'The Aristocracy of Culture', *Media, Culture and Society*, 2, pp. 225–54.
—— (1980b), 'The Production of Belief – Contribution to an Economy of Symbolic Goods', *Media, Culture and Society*, 2, pp. 261–93.
Brohm, J.-M. (1978), *Sport: a Prison of Measured Time* (London: Inklinks).
Brunsdon, C. and Morley, D. (1978), *Everyday Television: Nationwide* (London: British Film Institute).

Brunsdon, C. (1981), '"Crossroads" – Notes on Soap Opera', *Screen*, 22, iv, pp. 32–8.
Buscombe, E. (ed.) (1975), *Football on Television* (London: British Film Institute).
Cardiff, D. (1980), 'The Serious and the Popular: Aspects of the Evolution of Style in the Radio Talk, 1928–1939', *Media, Culture and Society*, 2, pp. 29–47.
Cohen, S and Young, J. (eds) (1973), *The Manufacture of News* (London: Constable).
Collins, R. (1976), *Television News* (London: British Film Institute).
Connell, I. (1979), 'Television News and the Social Contract', *Screen*, 20, i, pp. 87–109.
—— (1983), 'Commercial Broadcasting and the British Left', *Screen*, 24, vi, pp. 70–80.
Cook, P. (1982), 'Masculinity in Crisis', *Screen* 23, iii/iv, pp. 39–46.
—— (1983), *Gainsborough–Melodrama* (London: British Film Institute).
Curran, J., Gurevitch, M. and Woollacott, J. (1982), 'The Study of the Media: Theoretical Approaches', in M. Gurevitch *et al.* (eds), *Culture, Society and the Media* (London: Methuen) pp. 11–30.
Drummond, P. (1979), 'Notions of Avant-Garde Cinema', in *Film as Film: Formal Experiment in Film 1910–1975* (London: Arts Council) pp. 9–16.
Dyer, R. (1979), *Stars* (London: British Film Institute).
Dyer, R. (ed.) (1981), *Coronation Street* (London: British Film Institute).
Eco, U. (1972), 'Towards a Semiotic Enquiry into the Television Message', *Working Papers in Cultural Studies*, 3, pp. 89–103.
Elliot, P. (1972), *The Making of a Television Series* (London: Constable).
Ellis, J. (ed.) (1977), *Cinema, Ideology, Politics* (London: Society for Education in Film and Television).
Ellis, J. (1982a), *Visible Fictions* (London: Routledge & Kegan Paul).
—— (1982b), 'Television, Video and Independant Cinema', in S. Blanchard and D. Morley (eds), *What's This Channel Four?* (London: Comedia) pp. 145–51.
Enzensberger, H. M. (1972), *Constituents of a Theory of the Media* (Harmondsworth: Penguin).
Gardner, C. (1981), 'Black Employment in the Media', *Multiracial Education*, 2, pp. 69–75.
Garnham, N. (1979), 'Contribution to a Political Economy of Mass Communication', *Media, Culture and Society*, 1, pp. 123–46.
—— (1983), 'Public Service versus the Market', *Screen*, 24, i, pp. 6–27.
Garnham, N. and Williams, R. (1980), 'Pierre Bourdieu and the Sociology of Culture: an Introduction', *Media, Culture and Society*, 2, pp. 209–23.
Glasgow Media Group (1976), *Bad News* (London: Routledge & Kegan Paul).
—— (1980), *More Bad News* (London: Routledge & Kegan Paul).
Golding, P. and Elliot, P. (1976), *Making the News* (University of Leicester: Centre for Mass Communication Research).
Golding, P. and Murdock, G. (1977), 'Capitalism, Communication, and Class Relations', in J. Curran *et al.* (eds), *Mass Communication and Society* (London: Edward Arnold) pp. 12–43.
—— (1979), 'Ideology and the Mass Media: the Question of Determination', in M. Barrett *et al.* (eds), *Ideology and Cultural Production* (London: Croom Helm) pp. 198–224.

—— (1983), 'Privatising Pleasure – the Communications Revolution', in *Marxism Today*, October, pp. 32–8.
Gramsci, A. (1971), *Selections from the Prison Notebooks* (London: Lawrence & Wishart).
Gurevitch, M. et al. (1982), *Culture, Society and the Media* (London: Methuen).
Hall, S. (1973a), 'Encoding and Decoding the Television Message', *Stencilled Paper 7* (Birmingham University: Centre for Contemporary Cultural Studies).
—— (1973b), 'The Determinations of News Photographs', in S. Cohen and J. Young (eds), *The Manufacture of News* (London: Constable) pp. 176–91.
—— (1974a), 'Marx's Notes on Method: a "Reading" of the "1857 Introduction"', *Working Papers in Cultural Studies*, 6, pp. 132–72.
—— (1974b), 'External Influences on Broadcasting', *Stencilled Paper 4* (University of Birmingham: Centre for Contemporary Cultural Studies).
—— (1974c), 'The Structured Communication of Events', *Stencilled Paper 5* (Birmingham University: Centre for Contemporary Cultural Studies).
—— (1977), 'Culture, the Media and the "Ideological Effect"', in J. Curran et al. (eds), *Mass Communication and Society* (London: Edward Arnold) pp. 315–48.
—— (1980a), 'Cultural Studies and the Centre: Some Problematics and Problems', in S. Hall et al. (eds), *Culture, Media, Language* (London: Hutchinson) pp. 15–48.
—— (1980b), 'Cultural Studies: Two Paradigms', *Media, Culture and Society*, 2, pp. 57–72.
—— (1982), 'The Rediscovery of "Ideology": Return of the Repressed in Media Studies', in M. Gurevitch et al.
Hall, S., Lumley, B. and Mclennan, G. (1977), 'Politics and Ideology: Gramsci', in Centre for Contemporary Cultural Studies, *On Ideology* (London: Hutchinson) pp. 45–77.
Hall, S. and Jefferson, T. (eds) (1977), *Resistance Through Rituals* (London: Hutchinson).
Hall, S., Critcher, C. and Clarke, J. et al. (1978), *Policing The Crisis* (London: Macmillan).
Harvey, S. (1978), *May '68 and Film Culture* (London: British Film Institute).
Hawkes, T. (1977), *Structuralism and Semiotics* (London: Methuen).
Hebdige, D. (1979), *Subculture: the Meaning of Style* (London: Methuen).
Hill, J. (1979), 'Ideology, Economy and the British Cinema', in M. Barrett et al. (eds), *Ideology and Cultural Production* (London: Croom Helm) pp. 112–33.
Hobson, D. (1980), 'Housewives and the Mass Media', in S. Hall et al. (eds), *Culture, Media, Language* (London: Hutchinson) pp. 105–17.
Hoggart, R. (1969), *The Uses of Literacy* (Harmondsworth: Penguin).
Hood, S. (1980), *On Television* (London: Pluto Press).
Jameson, F. (1972), *The Prison House of Language* (Princeton University Press).
—— (1983), '"Pleasure": a political issue', *Formation*, 1, pp. 1–14.
Johnson, R. (1978), 'Edward Thompson, Eugene Genovese and Socialist–Humanist History', *History Workshop Journal*, 6, pp. 79–81.
—— (1979), 'Culture and the Historians', in J. Clarke et al. (eds), *Working Class Culture* (London: Hutchinson) pp. 41–71.
Kaplan, A. (ed.) (1978), *Women in Film Noir* (London: British Film Institute).
Kuhn, A. (1982), *Women's Pictures* (London: Routledge & Kegan Paul).
Lovell, T. (1980), *Pictures of Reality* (London: British Film Institute).

MacCabe, C. (1974), 'Realism and the Cinema: Notes on some Brechtian Theses', *Screen*, 15, ii, pp. 7–27.
McArthur, C. (1978), *Television and History* (London: British Film Institute).
McRobbie, A. (1977), '*Jackie*: an Ideology of Adolescent Femininity', *Stencilled Paper 53* (Birmingham University: Centre for Contemporary Cultural Studies).
—— (1980b), 'Radical Drama, Radical Theatre', in *Media, Culture and Society*, 2, pp. 37–51.
Marcuse, H. (1973), *One-Dimensional Man* (London: Abacus).
Marx, K. (1970), *The German Ideology* (London: Lawrence & Wishart).
Morley, D. (1980), *The 'Nationwide' Audience* (London: British Film Institute).
—— (1981), 'The "Nationwide" Audience: a Postscript', *Screen Education*, 39, pp. 3–15.
Mulhern, F. (1980), 'Notes on Culture and Cultural Struggle', *Screen Education*, 34, pp. 31–7.
Murdock, G. (1980a), 'Authority and Organisation', in *Screen Education*, 35, pp. 19–34.
—— (1980b), 'Radical Drama, Radical Theatre', in *Media, Culture and Society*, 2, pp. 151–68.
—— (1982), 'Large Corporations and the Control of the Communications Industry', in M. Gurevitch et al. (eds), *Culture, Society and the Media* (London: Methuen) pp. 118–51.
Murdock, G. and Golding, P. (1973), 'For a Political Economy of Mass Communications', *Socialist Register*, pp. 205–35.
Neale, S. (1980), *Genre* (London: British Film Institute).
Mulvey, L. (1975), 'Visual Pleasure and Narrative Cinema', *Screen*, 16, iii, pp. 6–18.
—— (1979), 'Feminism, Film and the Avant-Garde', *Framework*, 10, pp. 3–10.
National Association for Multicultural Education, (1981), *Multiracial Education: Race and the Media Issue 2*.
Nice, R. (1978), 'Bourdieu: a "Vulgar Materialist" in the Sociology of Culture', *Screen Education*, 28, pp. 23–33.
Nichols, B. (1981), *Ideology and the Image* (Bloomington: Indiana University Press).
Rowbotham, S. (1973), *Hidden from History* (London: Pluto Press).
Sahin, H. and Robinson, J. (1980), 'Beyond the Realm of Necessity: Television and the Colonisation of Leisure', *Media, Culture and Society*, 3, pp. 85–95.
Seabrook, J. (1978), *What Went Wrong: Working People and the Ideals of the Labour Movement* (London: Gollancz).
Smythe, D. (1977), 'Communications: Blindspot of Western Marxism', in *Canadian Journal of Political and Social Theory*, 3.
Stedman-Jones, G. (1977), 'Class Expression and Social Control', *History Workshop Journal*, 4, pp. 163–71.
Thompson, E. P. (1961), 'Long Revolutions', in *New Left Review*, 9/10/11.
—— (1968), *The Making of the English Working Class* (London, Penguin).
—— (1978), 'Eighteenth-Century English Society: Class Struggle without Class', in *Social History*, 2, pp. 133–65.
Willett, J. (ed.) (1973), *Brecht on Theatre* (London: Methuen).
Williams, R. (1968), *Culture and Society, 1780–1950* (Harmondsworth: Penguin).

—— (1971), *The Long Revolution* (Harmondsworth: Penguin).
—— (1973), *Communications* (Harmondsworth: Penguin).
—— (1974), *Television: Technology and Cultural Form* (London: Fontana).
—— (1976), *Keywords* (London: Fontana).
—— (1980), *Problems in Materialism and Culture* (London: New Left Books).
Williamson, J. (1981/2), 'How Does Girl Number Twenty Understand Ideology?', *Screen Education*, 40, pp. 80–8.
Winship, J. (1978), 'A Woman's World: "Woman" – an Ideology of Femininity', in Women's Studies Group, *Women Take Issue* (London: Hutchinson) pp. 133–55.
—— (1981), 'Handling Sex', *Media, Culture and Society*, 3, pp. 25–41.
Wollen, P. (1982), *Readings and Writings — Semiotic Counter-Strategies* (London: Verso).
Women's Studies Group (1978), *Women Take Issue* (London: Hutchinson).
Wren-Lewis, J. (1983), 'The Encoding/Decoding Model: Criticisms and Redevelopments for Research on Decoding', *Media, Culture and Society*, 5, pp. 179–97.

Index

Aaronovitch, S., 13, 26
Abercrombie, N., 116, 120, 128, 130, 131, 132, 133
Accumulation of capital
  aided by state intervention, 142
  causing reduced rate of profit, 21
  contradictions, 12
  determined by profit for investment, 34
  determining organisation of labour process, 129
  disproportionality, 124–6
  function of state intervention, 156
  internationalisation, 130
  link with city construction, 182–3
  link with environmental degradation, 169–70
  primitive (or 'primary'), 43
  regional variations, 180
  regular swings, 19
  regulated by profit rate, 20
  role of space, 175–8
  social structure, 26
  wave characteristic, 176
ACTT, see Association of Cinematograph, Television and Allied Technicians
Adey, G., 122
Adorno, T., 121, 230, 248, 249–50, 270, 284
Aesthetic sensibility, 231–4
Agamben, G., 213
Agrarian question, 4, 58–86, 117
  classical Marxist position, 62–9
  contemporary positions, 69–81
  origin, 58
Agricultural production
  attempts to categorise, 78
  decline in 20th century, 69
  different from other industries, 58
  essential nature, 61
  household, 69–70, 74, 81
  inherent uncertainties, 61–2
  low market value, 70
  organisational differences, 61
  peasant, factors affecting, 75
  relations, 81
  tenant control, 79
  time-span, 62
Agriculture
  capitalist: development, 59, 62, 72 (production relations, 59, 60–1, 73–81; properties, 69–73)
  cycle of indebtedness, 76–7
  distribution of surplus value, 64–5
  East Africa, 78
  English conditions, 63
  food production, and population growth limits, 171–2
  'green revolution', 80
  India, 77, 78
  inherent uncertainties, 71
  investment problems, 71
  investible surpluses, 72–3
  need for more investigation, 82
  particularity of, 60–2
  pre-capitalist, factors shaping, 80 (relations, 79)
  separation from industrial production, 63
  simple commodity and peasant producers compared, 72
  social relations, categorisation, 77
  state intervention, 68, 81
  superiority of large scale, 66
Alavi, H., 179
Althusser, L., 81, 102, 103–4, 122–6, 205, 217, 218, 235, 252–4, 259, 269, 276, 277, 282, 284
  extreme positions untenable, 106
  on empiricism in scientific texts, 123
  Thompson's critique, 103–5, 125
Alvarado, M., 274, 286
Ambrose, P., 184
Amin, S., 175
Anderson, B., 179, 180, 187
Anderson, P., 1, 90, 101, 106, 107, 112, 118, 120, 128, 141, 213, 218, 261, 270
Ardrey, R., 168

Index

Art
  Benjamin's warning against fetishisation, 248
  expression of human values, 233
  link with labour cut under capitalism, 232-3
  Marxist contribution to avant-garde, 246-7
  mechanical reproduction, 248
  more independent than other superstructural elements, 234
  relationship with ideology, 253
Artisan, role in social development, 95
Artistic freedom, 248
Arvon, H., 229
Association of Cinematograph, Television and Allied Technicians, 274
Audience research, 280-2
Audiences
  cultural conformism, 280
  decoding media messages, 281
  response to media messages, 280
  subjugated to mass persuasion, 280
Avant-garde movements
  in literature, 260-1
  in media, 287
  Marxist contribution to art, 246-7
  Soviet attacks, 241
Avineri, S., 113, 115, 116

Babbage, C., 129
Bahro, R., 120, 170, 173, 174
Bakhtin, M., 212, 240, 254, 260
Bakhtin's Circle, 212
Balibar, E., 122, 221
Balibar, R., 219, 256
Balzac, H. de, 235, 237, 243, 255
Banaji, J., 66, 75, 76, 82
Bankruptcies, 13, 15
  as economic purge, 19
Banks
  failures, 16
  international dealings, 16
  see also Central banks; Financial system
Baran, P., 22, 183
Barrell, J., 170
Barrett, M., 6, 261
Barthes, R., 217, 257, 259, 276, 278
Bartoli, M. G., 214
Base, 116-17, 282
  base-superstructure model in literary theory, 234-5, 238
  determining language, 208
  language, 209, 214
  relationship with superstructure, Gramsci's contribution, 103
Bassett, K.A., 177, 182, 188
Baudelaire, C. P., 248
Bauer, O., 206
Baumol, W. J., 55
Bax, E. B., 95
Belsey, C., 247, 253, 259
Benjamin, W., 213, 230, 247-9, 249, 262, 270
Bennett, T., 240, 257, 276, 279, 284
Bentham, J., 113
Benton, T., 126, 127
Berger, J., 270
Bernstein, B., 221, 222
Bernstein, H., 76, 77, 82
Bertolazzi, C., 253
Best, M., 150
Beynon, H, 129
Bhaduri, A., 79, 82
Bhaskar, R., 126
Biological basis of social action, 168, 173
Birmingham University: Centre for Contemporary Cultural Studies, 269, 281
Blackburn, R., 129
Blaut, J. M., 175
Bleaney, M., 22
Bloch, J., 214
Bloomfield, L., 205
Bluestone, B., 149
Bodammer, Th., 201
Boddy, M., 162, 184
Böhm-Bawerk, E. von, 33
Bolelli, T., 214
Booms, effects, 19
Borbe, T., 208
Bortkiewicz, L. von, 47
Bourdieu, P., 268-9, 275, 287
Bourgeois ideology, 120
Bourgeoisie, progressive class in 19th century, 244
Braverman, H., 128, 129, 130
Brecht, B., 230, 245-7, 247, 262, 270, 271, 276, 277, 278
  Adorno's critique, 249
  on Lukács, 242, 245
Brohm, J.-M., 284
Brookfield, H. C., 175
Brown, G., 219
Brunsdon, C., 279, 281, 282
Buchanan, K., 175
Buci-Glucksmann, C., 119
Burawoy, M., 129, 130
Bureaucracy, 161

Index

Burgess, E. W., 168
Burnham, W., 158
Buscombe, E., 274, 279
Byres, T. J., 61, 79, 82
Byrne, D., 187

Cable television, 275
Calhoun, C., 125, 133
Callinicos, A., 218
Calvet, L.-J., 205, 206
Capital
   as social relationship, 26
   circuit: 13–15; types of crisis, 14
   expansion, conditions, 25
   global functions, 130, 143
   in opposition to wage labour, 115
   interests dictating state policy, 152
   organic composition, 123–4
   realisation of surplus value, 21–2
   restructuring: factors controlling, 25 (to remove imbalances, 26)
   sectoral segmentation, 149
   state policy involvement, 154
   symbolic, 275
   translation of money into, 41 (for investment, 34)
   see also Accumulation of capital
Capitalism
   analysis of finance-capitalism, 117–18
   appraisal of political life under, 141–2
   causing indirect social connections through commodities, 114
   coercive property relations, 31
   commodity fetishism, 119
   competition, 27
   conditions for purchasing labour power, 42
   crisis as inherent part, 26–7
   crisis in Britain, features, 14–15
   dominance of money relations, 32
   dynamics of production mode, 43
   export of capital, 118
   growth and crisis, 12
   history of, characteristics, 11
   implications of crisis, 27
   nature of capitalist state, 120
   phases of boom and slump, 17
   rationality and irrationality, 12
   social control through mass culture, 284
   ultimate collapse, 14
   see also Agriculture, capitalist
Cardechi, G., 130, 143
Carney, J., 175, 187
Carr, E. H., 102

Castells, M., 150, 156, 159, 180, 181, 182, 185, 187
Catalano, A., 177
Cawson, A., 157, 158
CCCS, see Birmingham University: Centre for Contemporary Cultural Studies
Central banks, intervention to prevent financial collapse, 15–16
Chagall, M., 212
Chattopadhyay, P., 78
Chayanov, A. V., 73, 81
Childe, V. G., 97
China, Marxist impact on peasant society, 4
Chomsky, N., 221–2
Cinema
   positioning of spectator, 276
   presenting dominant ideology, 277
   realism criticised, 277
   structuralist criticism, 278
City
   as investment outlet, 183
   concentration of workers, 182
   link with capital accumulation, 182–3
   links with community, 184–6
   Marxist views, 181–2
Clark, G., 175, 182, 186
Clarke, S., 261
Class(es)
   antagonisms, in evolution of society, 30
   as cultural phenomenon, 100
   balance of class forces model, 155–6
   bias in media presentations, 270
   competition between, 27
   contemporary analyses, 128
   contemporary categories, 143–4
   culture as expression, 284
   definitions, 30, 134
   definitions affected by race and gender studies, 6
   discussion by Thompson, 99–100
   divisions between, 142
   domination, and role of state, 152–60
   emerging from homogeneous peasantry, 76
   existence of 'fractions', 147
   ideologies, 133–4
   language, 206–7, 209, 218–20
   literature, 235–6, 238, 244, 251–2
   need for 'within-class' categories, 145
   need to respecify definitions, 145
   organised as collective actors, 132
   problematising, 131–5
   redefinition of concept, 100

296　Index

Class(es) – *continued*
  relations, in cultural field, 271
  relative powers, disproportionality, 24
  revolutionary tradition, 100
  social categories within, 148
  stratification within classes, 147
  structure, related to residential area, 184
  struggle over exploitation, 48
  theory of society, 116
Class conflict
  after class formation, 146
  'displaced', 147
  dominant in political scene, 142
  related to political conflict, 142–52
Cloward, R., 155, 162
Cobb, J., 150
Cockburn, C., 187
Cohen, G., 106, 113, 115, 116, 127–8
Cohen, M., 214
Colenutt, B., 184
Collins, R., 260, 279
Commodities
  agricultural production, 72
  capitalist fetishism, 119, 121
  commensurability, 38–9
  consumed by unproductive sector, 130
  exchange value, 38, 39, 45–6
  free exchange economy, 41
  in production, 114
  indirect connection between people, 114
  input values compared with prices of production, 46
  specialisation in production, 41
  use-value, 40
  wage bundle consumed by workers, 47
  see also Symbolic goods
Communications, between members of labour, 133
Communist Party Historians' Group, 98
Community, city links, 184–6
Community associations, 181
Competition
  between capitalists and between classes, 27, 44
  equalising rate of profit, 35
Connell, I., 274, 282, 286
Connolly, W., 95, 150
Constitutional history, 91
Consumption
  politics of, 181
  realising use-values, 42
Cook, P., 271, 282
Cooke, P., 180, 187, 188

Coward, R., 247, 253, 259
Cowen, M., 78
Cremonini, L., 253
Crime studies, 108
Crisis
  factors controlling frequency, 25
  form, 27, 13–20
  implications for capitalism, 27
  inherent in dynamic of capitalism, 26–7
  origin of term, 11
Crisis theory, 4, 11–29
  capital restructuring, 12
  discussions in writings of Marx, 11–12
  mechanisms, 20–6
  structure, 12
Croall, S., 173
Croce, B., 214
Crompton, R., 143, 146
Cuba, Marxist impact on peasant society, 4
Culler, J., 253
Cultural studies
  courses set up, 268
  Marxist analyses, 269
Culture, 6
  as expression of social classes, 284
  broadening definition, 268
  class relations, 271
  see also Popular culture
Curran, J., 269
Cutler, A., 33, 56, 126, 129

Dahl, R., 154
Dante Alighieri, 229, 257
Dear, M., 182, 186
Della Volpe, G., 261
Delphy, C., 125
Demand, disproportionality with supply, 24
Democratic dissent, 94
Depressions
  periods, 17
  preceded by financial collapse, 15
Derrida, J., 217, 257
Dickens, P., 155
Dickenson, J., 71
Discourse theory, 218–19, 259–60
  notion of 'subject', 219
Disraeli, B., 92
Dissent, democratic, 94
Distribution of social product, 33–4
  effects on valuation, 35
Djurfeldt, G., 70, 71, 74
Dobb, M., 48, 55
Dostaler, G , 55

Dostoevskij, F. M., 212, 240–1
Drummond, P., 276
Duhring, E. K., 204
Duncan, J., 189
Duncan, S., 159
Duncan, S. S., 187
Dunford, M., 176, 187
Dunleavy, P., 135, 150, 181
Durkheim, E., 92, 275
Dyer, R., 279

Eagleton, T., 230, 233, 239, 248, 258, 261
East Africa, agriculture, 78
Easthope, A., 261
Eco, U., 217, 282
Ecology
　causes of crisis, 170
　human, 168
Economic determinism, 89
　in media, 271, 272–5
　understanding workings of, 273
Economics
　categories, limitations of, 31
　Marxist legacy, 4
Economy
　collapse in West, 120
　determination/dominance debate, 124
Education, social implications, 120
Edwards, R., 129
Ehrenreich, J. and E., 131
Ehrlich, P. R. and A. H., 171
Elliott, P., 273
Ellis, J., 247, 253, 259, 270, 274, 276, 280
Elson, D., 55
Elster, J., 128, 132–3
Empiricism, in scientific texts, 123
Employment, patterns matching profitability and investment, 19
Engels, F., 58, 89, 112
　literary theory, 230, 231–8
　on language, 200–5
　social theory, 112–17
　view of city, 181–2
Ennew, J., 74
Entrepreneurship, 25
Environment
　context of social relations, 5
　degradation, link with capital accumulation, 169–70
　pressure groups, 181
Environmentalism
　development, 172
　Marxist positions, 173
　reaction of Marxist commentators, 172–3

Enzenberger, H. M., 270
Erckenbrecht, U., 204
Erlich, V., 240
Ethnic conflicts, 151
Ethnicity
　basis of working class division, 130, 134
　bias in media presentations, 270
Eurocurrency markets, 16
Evans, M., 252
Experience
　'lived' and 'perceived', 106
　relationship to social consciousness, 105

Factors of production, in price theory, 36
Fainstein, N. I. and S. S., 188
Family studies, 108
Farrington, B., 97
Feminist movement, 6, 262
　re-evaluation of ideologies of femininity, 271
　see also Women
Fetishism-based theory of society, 116
Fetishism of commodities, 119, 121
Feuerbach, L., 115
Finance-capitalism, analysis, 117–18
Financial collapse, 14, 15–17
　central bank intervention, 15–16
　international, current potential, 15
Financial system
　fragility, 15
　international, problems of regulation, 15–16
　periods of near-collapse, 16–17
　regulation, 15–16
　see also Banks
Fine, B., 13, 24, 49, 51
Foley, D. K., 51, 55
Forester, J., 188
Formigari, L., 206, 207
Forster, E. M., 220
Foster, J., 101
Foucault, M., 217, 218, 219, 257, 259
Fowler, R., 219
Fox-Genovese, E., 108
Frank, A. G., 175
Frankfurt School, 1, 121, 270, 274, 280, 284, 287
Frankish dialect, 203, 204
Franklin National Bank, failure, 16
Frazer, J. G., 97
Free exchange economy, 41
'Free rider' problem, 132, 133
French Communist Party, 122
French Revolution, 206
French structuralist school, 102, 103

Index

Freud, S., 93, 216, 218, 255, 259
Friedland, R., 188
Friedman, A., 129
Friedmann, G., 129
Friedmann, H., 72
Frisby, D., 122
Frobel, F., 130
Fudge, C., 162
Fundamentalist theory, 21

Gadet, F., 208
Galbraith, J., 154
Gardner, C., 274
Garnham, N., 269, 274, 275, 286
Garramon, C., 78
Gender, 6
  basis of working class division, 130, 134
  bias in media presentations, 270, 282
Geras, N., 113
German Social Democratic Party, debates on peasantry, 58, 66
Gerstein, I., 55
Giddens, A., 184, 190
Ginsburg, N., 129
Gladstone, W. E., 92
Glasgow Media Group, 270, 279
Glucksmann, M., 252
Glyn, A., 23
Godard, F., 180
Godwin, M., 187
Goethe, J. W. von, 235
Golding, P., 272–3, 275, 280, 285
Goldmann, L., 242, 251–2
Gordon, D. M., 26, 182
Gorky, M., 239
Gorz, A., 129, 173
Gough, I., 150, 156
Gramsci, A., 102–3, 119, 213–15, 250–1 281, 284–5
Green, J. R., 94
Green Party, 173
'Green revolution', 80
Greenberg, E., 153
Gregory, D., 174, 176, 190
Grimm, J., 203
Gubay, J., 143, 146

Habermas, J., 122, 133, 135, 150, 156, 157, 159, 213
Haeckel, E., 97
Hall, G., 170
Hall, S., 106, 134, 235, 251, 258, 261, 276, 279, 280, 281, 284, 285, 286
Halliday, M. A. K., 219
Harkness, M., 237

Harley, A. M., 168
Harloe, M., 182
Harré, R., 126
Harris, L., 13, 24
Harris, R., 68, 185
Harris, Z., 205, 218
Harrison, M., 74
Harriss, J., 78
Hartmann, H., 130
Harvey, D., 13, 165–7, 172, 174, 177, 181, 182, 184
Harvey, S., 276, 279
Hawkes, T., 253, 275
Heath, S., 261
Hegel, G. W. F., 201, 203, 207
Hegemony
  established by proletariat, 119
  Gramscian, 102–3, 214, 284
Heinrichs, J., 130
Held, D., 121, 122, 133
Herr, 91
Herstadt Bank, failure, 16
Heyderbrand, W., 141, 157, 161
High Culture, Marxist attachment, 287
Hilferding, R., 117–18
Hill, C., 95, 96, 98
Hill, J., 273–4, 274
Hill, S., 128
Hillel-Ruben, D., 126
Hilton, R., 98
Himmelweit, S. F., 49, 51, 55
Hindess, B., 103, 125, 126
Hirst, P., 103, 125, 126
Historical materialism, 89, 97, 113, 122
  Marx's definition, 106
  technological interpretation, 127–8
  Thompson's defence, 103
Historiography
  current place of Marxism, 107–9
  development, 89–90
  French structuralist school, 102–3
  'History Workshop' methodology, 101
  Marxist, 5: emergence, 98–101 (origins in Britain, 93–8)
  theoretical debate, 102–7
'History Workshop', 101
Hobsbawm, E. J., 98, 99, 135, 180
Hobson, D., 282
Hobson, J. A., 118
Hodge, R., 219
Hodgson, G., 48
Hodson, R., 149
Hoggart, R., 283
Holland, S., 175
Hood, S., 279

Horkheimer, M., 270, 284
Houdebine, J.-L., 204, 205, 221
Human behaviour, biological basis, 168
Human geography
  influence of Marxist theory, 165
  scope, 165
  work of David Harvey, 165–7
Hussain, A., 66, 68, 126
Hyden, G., 75
Hyndman, H. M., 95

Ideology, 39–40, 219, 235–6
  art's relationship with, 253
  bourgeois, 120
  class ideology of writers, 235
  class re-examined, 133–4
  'dominanant ideology', 277
  related to mass communication growth, 270
Illich, I., 173
Ilyenkov, E. V., 56
Imperialism, as monopoly stage of capitalism, 118
India, agriculture, 77, 78
Industry
  disinvestment in old areas, 176–7
  new classes within, 134
  restructuring during slump period, 18
Inner city problems, 174
Instrumentalism, 153–5
Internationalism, 206–7
Interpersonal relationships, 6
Investment
  determining capital accumulation, 34
  patterns matching employment and profitability, 19
  problems of regulation, 22
  protecting profits, 20
Israel, bank failures, 16
Italy, bank failures, 16

Jakobson, R., 207, 212
Jameson, F., 240, 243, 247, 261, 276, 278
Janvry, A. de, 78
Japhetic theory, 208
Jaurès, J., 91
Jay, M., 121
Jefferson, T., 281, 285
Jendreick, H., 203
Jesop, R., 120, 151–2, 157, 158
Johnson, R., 106, 125, 258, 284
Johnson, T., 131, 162
Johnston, R. J., 95, 186, 189
Jones, B., 130

Kafka, F., 248, 249
Kaplan, A., 277
Katznelson, I., 185
Kautsky, K., 58, 59, 66, 66–8, 70, 75, 91, 117, 118, 206
Kautsky, M., 237
Keat, R., 126, 127
Kindleberger, C. P., 15
Klingender, F. D., 130
Kolakowski, L., 117, 135
Kolb, H., 203
Kondratieff, N. D., 17
Kondratieff long waves, 14, 17
  peaks as bunched investments, 175
Kraiski, G., 239
Kress, G., 219
Kreye, O., 130
Kristeva, J., 218, 240, 257, 259
Kuhn, A., 278

Labour
  collective identity, 133
  deskilled by technology, 44, 129
  growth of aristocracy within, 128
  need for undistorted communications, 133
Labour power
  abstract, 51, 53; distinguished from 'useful', 40
  as productive capital, 13
  capital able to obtain precise requirements, 129
  coercion, 31
  compliance, 25
  consumption in production, 42
  distinguishing human characteristic, 113
  distribution struggle, 23
  effects of shortage, 23
  exploitation, 48, 143
  forced from peasant societies, 43
  from agriculture, 63
  in class definition, 30
  Marx's distinction from labour, 122
  measurement through commodity values, 40–1
  quantity employed, in price determination, 34
  rate of exploitation, 24
  reduced demand with falling profits, 20–21
  surplus, form analysis, 31
  value, defined, 43
  see also Wage labour; Workers

Labour time
  in determination of value, 36
  not corresponding to price, 52
Labov, W., 221, 222
Labriola, A., 91
Lacan, J., 218, 257, 259, 269
Laclau, E., 133, 217
Lafargue, P. 205–6
Laing, D., 233
Land
  nationalisation, 178
  nature of ownership, 177–8
Lane, D., 118
Language
  and nation, 206
  as cultural and spiritual force, 214
  Bakhtin's views, 240
  development, 202
  empirical study, 221
  importance to internationalism, 206–7
  individual, 202–3
  mathematical theory, 210–11
  mixing, 204
  use by authors, 255
  see also Linguistics
Laporte, D., 219, 256
Larrain, J., 116, 120
Larson, M., 162
Lash, S., 133
Lassalle, F., 234
Latin America, peasant societies, 78
Laurat, L., 210
Lebas, E., 175, 182
Legitimation function of state
  intervention, 156–7
Leitch, V. B., 253
Lender of last resort facilities, 16
Lenin, V. I., 59, 66, 75, 179, 230
  agrarian question, 68–9, 117
  contribution on literature, 238–9
  critique of work on differentiation, 73
  on bureaucracy, 161
  on export of capital, 118
  on language, 207
Lepschy, G., 211
Lévi-Strauss, C., 102, 205
Ley, D., 189
Liberal democracy, resilience, 141
Liberal tradition, 90
Liberalism
  British and European traditions
    compared, 91
  impact of World War I, 92
  positivism buttressed by, 191
Lifshitz, M., 229

Lindblom, C., 154
Linguistics, 5
  disparities in ability, 199
  importance to literary studies, 258
  positions of early Marxists, 205–7
  poverty of Marxist writings on, 220–1
  role of Gransci, 213–15
  Saussure's contribution, 216–17
  sign, signifier and signified, 216–17, 259
  Soviet structuralism, 210–11
  Stalin's intervention, 209–10, 221
  see also language
Lipietz, A., 51, 55, 180
Liquidations, 15
Literary criticism, in textual analysis of
  media communications, 275
Literary theory, 6
  base-superstructure model, 234–5, 238
  German, 241–50
  post-war French developments, 251–62
  realism, 236–8
  realism-modernism debate, 241–50
  relationship between historical
    movement and literary change,
    242
  Russian, 238–41
  substituting notion of 'text' for 'author',
    251
Literature, reflecting historical situations,
  243–4
Littlejohn, G., 74
Littler, C., 129, 130
Lo Piparo, F., 214
Long waves, 17–19
  characteristics, 17, 18
  growth phase, related to type of
    production organisation, 18
  slump, 14
  see also Kondratieff long waves
Lotman, Ju. M., 213
Lovatt, D., 182
Lovell, T., 247, 257, 260, 261, 279
Lowe, P., 173
Lukács, G., 119, 120, 230, 237, 239,
  242–5, 251
  Adorno's critique, 249
Luporini, C., 205
Luxembourg, R., 117

McArthur, C., 247, 279
MacCabe, C., 247, 260, 261
McDonnell, K., 247
McDowell, L., 190
Macherey, P., 122, 233, 237, 239, 252,
  254–7, 259, 260

McRobbie, A., 281, 285
Madden, E., 126
Maddison, A., 17
Mallet, S., 129
Malthus, T. R., 22, 168
Management structure, 129
 direct control of labour process, 129
 divisive effect on workforce, 130
 professional-managerial class, 131
 see also Scientific management
Mandel, E., 4, 135
Mann, M., 129
Mann, S., 71
Mann, T., 243
Marcuse, H., 121, 270, 284
Marcuse, P., 188
Market forces, 27
Markets
 availability, 25
 exchange of value-equivalents, 41
 external, 22
 failure, 13
 problems of overproduction, 117
Markusen, A., 188
Marr, N. J., 208
Marrism, 207-8
 Stalin's intervention, 209-10
Marx, K.
 agrarian question, 62-9
 analysis of ground rent, 59
 condition of English working class, 89
 criticism of Bentham, 113
 critique of political economy, 30-3
 critique of Ricardo's value theory, 36-8
 distinguishing between labour and labour power, 122
 literary theory, 230, 231-8
 no systematic treatment of crises, 11
 on control of media, 272
 on language, 200-5
 on poetry, 229
 opinion of peasant production potential, 65
 relationship to Ricardo's work, 32-3
 significance of writings, 112
 social theory themes, 112-17
 value theory, 38-45; Böhm-Bawerk's attack, 33
 views on city, 181-2
Marx, Laura, 205-6
Marxism
 academic methodology, 2
 and British working class tradition, 92
 basis in rationalism and freethinking, 96-7

 contemporary, defined, 3
 diversity of approaches, 1
 gaining attention from 1950s, 99
 grafted onto existing influences, 94
 hostility towards, 90 (from academics, 98)
 intellectual approach, 1
 radical changes in emphases, 108
Marxist writers, definition, 3
Mass communications
 growth, ideology related to, 270
 political economy debate, 272
 see also Cinema; Media; Media studies; Television
Mass production techniques, effect on space, 176
'Mass society' thesis, 270
Massey, D., 175, 176, 177
Matejka, L., 240
Mayrl, W. W., 252
Meadows, D. H., 171
Means of production
 and politics of consumption, 180-1
 in defining classes, 30
 money exchanged for, 13
 reduced demand with falling profits, 21
Mechanisation, effect on profits, 23-4
Media
 economic determination, 271, 272-5
 gender differences, 282
 influence of protest movements, 270
 messages decoded by audiences, 281
 ownership and control, 272 (by state, 286)
 policy approaches, 286
 regulation to guarantee cultural content, 286
 technological advances, 274-5
Media studies
 approaches confined to educational field, 286
 audience research, 280-2
 courses set up, 268
 struggle between Marxist approaches, 286
 textual analysis, 275-80
 see also Mass communications
Medvedev, P. N., 212
Meek, R. L., 48, 55
Meillet, A., 214, 215
Mepham, J., 113
Merseyside Socialist Research Group, 180
Methodism, evident in Marxist historians, 95
Michels, R., 92

302 *Index*

Miliband, R., 123, 124, 141, 142, 144–5, 151, 153, 154, 155, 161
Military expanditure, 22
Mingione, E., 182
Minns, R., 178
Mississippi Bubble, 15
Mitra, A., 81
Modernism, 241–50; media textual criticism based on, 276
Mohun, S., 49, 51, 55
Money
 dominance in capitalist society, 32
 expressing value of products of labour, 32
 in value theory, 39
 translation into capital, 41
Montgomery, D., 132
Morawski, S., 233, 236, 237, 238, 239
Morley, D., 279, 280, 281, 282
Morris, D., 168
Mosca, G., 92
Moscow Linguistic Circle, 207
Mouffe, C., 119
Mouzelis, N., 72
Mulhern, F., 268
Mulvey, L., 277, 278
Murdock, G., 272–3, 275, 280, 285

Nairn, T., 151, 161, 179, 187
Namier, L., 92
National Association for Multiracial Education, 270
Nationalism, 179–80
Nationalist movements, 187
Nature
 human production of, 169–71
 reproduction in cultural forms, 170
 society's relationship with, 167–74
Neale, S., 276, 278
Neo-Ricardian theory, 21
New Deal (1930s), 146
'New Right', 134
Newly industrialised countries
 adopting new technologies, 26
 investment related to cost of workforce, 176
 old industries re-established in, 18
 see also Third World
Nice, R., 275
Nichols, B., 275
Nicolaus, M., 130
Nochlin, L., 247
Noiré, L., 201
Nordlinger, E., 155
Norris, C., 253

North-South dialogue, 174
North Tyneside Community Development Project, 180
Novel, as dominant literary form, 243

O'Connor, J., 150, 156, 188
Offe, C., 133, 157, 159, 160
O'Hagan, T., 126
O'Keefe, P., 169
Ollman, B., 115
Olson, M., 132, 133
Open University, 286
 Popular Culture Course, 285, 286
Opojaz, *see* Society for the Study of Poetic Language (Opojaz)
Organisations, theory of, 162
Orwell, G., 219
Outhwaite, W., 126
Owen, R., 95

Pareto, V. F. D., 92, 93
Parkin, F., 148, 151
Parsons, H. L., 165
Pascal, B., 252
Pascal, R., 97
Patnaik, U., 74, 77
Pearce, R., 79
Pearn, M., 130
Peasant societies
 agricultural production, 72
 changes in landholding structure, 73–4
 classes emerging from, 76
 cycle of indebtedness, 76–7
 dispossession of means of subsistence, 43
 evolving capitalist agriculture, 68
 factors affecting agrarian production, 75
 impact of Marxism, 4
 independence lost, 95
 Latin America, 78
 precarious position in agriculture, 81
 production potential, 65
 revolutionary potential, 63, 65–6
 see also Agrarian question
Pêcheux, M., 218, 219–20, 259
Peet, R., 167, 175
Perrons, D., 176
Perry, D., 177
Petty bourgeousie, rising numbers, 130–1
Philology, comparative, 203
Physical coercion of labour, 31
Pickvance, C. G., 182
Pilling, G., 55
Piven, F., 155, 162

Planning
  problems in current slump, 18–19
  urban, 188
Pleasure, 257, 278, 282
Plebs League, 96
Plekhanov, G. V., 238
Plender, J., 178
Pluralism, 154
  in Russian literary life, 240
Political conflict
  class analysis, 144–52
  class-inclusive explanations, 145–7
  cross-class explanations, 149–52
  defining 'people' and 'officialdom', 151
  in city, 185
  related to class struggle, 145–52
  within-class explanations, 147–9
Political economy
  critique, 30–3
  critiques of Marx and Engels, 112–13
Political movements, local, 181
Political relations, analysis, 115
Political theory, life under advanced capitalism, 141–2
Polivanov, D., 211–12
Pollution, and technological development, 170
Pomorska, K., 240
Popular culture, 257, 283–5
  antagonisms to forms, 282
  complexity of system, 287
  debate, 268, 283
  rethinking of term, 285
  struggle against dominant order, 283
Population, limits to growth, 171–2
Porter, V., 260
Positivism
  impact on historical study, 90–1
  Marxism taking place of, 92
Poulantzas, N., 123, 124, 130, 133, 143, 147, 148, 159
Prague Linguistic Circle, 207
Prawer, S. S., 229
Price
  Adam Smith's determination, 34
  deviation from money values, 46
  expressing value of products of labour, 32
  not corresponding to labour time, 52
  of production, 46 (anti-Ricardian position, 50)
  related to rate of production, 35
  related to slump periods, 34
  Ricardian determination, 34
  theory, replacing value theory, 36
  see also Value theory

Problematic, Althusser's thesis, 122–3
Production
  capitalist mode, 113; changes, 117 (dynamics, 43)
  consumption of labour power, 42
  decreasing participation, 130
  defined by forms of labour, 31
  for profit not need, 20
  forces of, environmental position, 173
  human need, 231
  labour adding value to raw materials, 44
  material and social processes, 113
  organisation, related to growth phase of long waves, 18
  problems of overproduction, 117
  rate, determining price, 35
  relations of, distinguished from forces of, 127–8
  sectors, balance between, 25
  specialisation, 41
  surplus, 47 (sectoral, 60)
  theory of differing modes, 124
  see also Agricultural production; Factors of production; Means of production
Production relations
  among people, 114
  related to media, 281
Production studies of media programmes, 274
Productivity
  agricultural, increases, 69
  raised, effect on commodity values, 44
Professions
  managerial class, 131
  proletarianisation, 131
  role in policy making, 162
Profit
  as aim of production, 20
  effect of mechanisation, 23–4
  in circuit of capital, 13
  maximised by low wages, 22
  ploughed back, 22
  rate equalised by competition, 35
  rate reduced by accumulation, 21
  realisation of surplus value, 21
  regulating accumulation process, 20
  surplus value from agriculture, distribution of, 64–5
Profitability, patterns matching employment and investment, 19
Proletarian movement, 143
Proletarianisation, 130
  of the professions, 131

Property development, 184
Property relations, 31
Property sector, 184
Protest movements, influence on media, 270
Proust, M., 248
Przeworski, A., 132, 145
Psychoanalysis, 259
  importance to literary studies, 258
  in mass media, 278
Public expenditure, competing demands, 188
Putney debates, 96

Quaini, M., 165

Rabelais, F., 212, 241
Race, 6
  bias in media presentations, 270
  discrimination, in employment, 147
Racine, J., 252
Radicalism, 94
Raikes, P., 71
Ramat, P., 203
Rankin, W., 173
Raphael, M., 233
Raw materials
  supply, 25
  value added by labour, 44
Realism
  author's attitude to historical moment, 250
  'classic realist texts', 260
  in Gramsci, 250
  in mass communications, 277
  literary theory, 236–8 (relation with the 'typical', 237
  rejected by Brecht as aesthetic category, 245
  theoretical, 126–7
Realism-modernism debate, 241–50
Recessions
  capital restructuring, 22
  effects, 19
Regional problems, 174, 187
Reification, Lukács' analysis, 119
Rent
  absolute, 64, 177
  as transfer mechanism, 65
  concept in location studies, 177
  derivation of payments, 65
  determination by land fertility, 34
  differential and monopoly, 177
  differential rent I and II, 63–4

Marxian theory, 63
Ricardian theory, 63
Rentier class, and market maintenance, 22
Residents groups, 181
Resler, H., 147, 150
Resources, limits to growth, 171–2
Revolutionary change
  brought about by collapse of state, 132
  not purely a class concern, 131
Revolutionary consciousness, not evident in Western working classes, 128
Revolutionary party, vanguard role, 118
Revolutions, related to space, 179
Rhodes, E., 130
Ricardo, D., 54
  differential rent theory, 63
  relationship to Marx's work, 32–3
  value theory, 33–8 (Marx's critique, 36–8)
Roberts, J., 248
Robertson, A., 97
Robins, K., 247
Robinson, J., 280
Rogers, T., 94
Ronge, V., 160
Rosdolsky, R., 49, 55
Rosenthal, M., 170
Rosiello, L, 214, 221
Rowbotham, S., 95
Roweis, S., 188
Rowthorn, B., 13
Rubin, I. I., 49, 55, 113
Rudra, A., 77, 81
Ruskin College, 'History Workshop', 101
Russia, Tsarist, Marxist impact on peasant society, 4
Russian Formalists, 207, 240
  textual criticism based on, 276
Russian Revolution, Trotsky's analysis, 118–19

Sahin, H., 280
Samuel, R., 94, 95, 97, 98, 101
Sandbach, F., 165, 172
Sandberg, L. G., 25
Sapegno, N., 229
Saunders, P., 157, 158, 181, 182, 185, 187
Saussure, F. de, 213, 216, 260
Sawyers, L., 182
Sayer, A., 190
Sayer, D., 112, 126, 127
Schumpeter, J. A., 17
Schwarz, J., 55
Schweppenhauser, H., 213

Index

Science
  as metaphor of human achievement, 97
  theoretical realism debate, 126
Scientific management, degrees of deskilling associated with, 130
Scientific rationalism, 97
Scott, A. J., 182
Scott, Sir W., 243, 244
Screen, 247, 269
Seabrook, J., 283
Secessionist movements, 161
Semantics, 218
Semiology, 217
  importance to literary studies, 258
  in textual analysis of media communications, 275
Sempler, K., 173
Sennett, R., 150
Service industries, 134
Seton, F., 47, 55
Shanin, R., 179
Sharecropping, 79
Shaumjan, S. K., 210-11
Shklovskij, V., 211
Short, J. R., 177, 179, 181, 182, 185, 186
Sign, signifier and signified, 216-17, 259
Simmie, J. M., 182
Simon, J., 201
Simon, R. M., 180
Skocpol, T., 131
Slaughter, C., 240
Smith, Adam, 34
Smith, M. P., 182
Smith, N., 167
Smith, R. P., 13, 26
Smith, W., 169
Smythe, D., 280
Social action, biological basis, 168
Social behaviour
  influence of nature, criticisms, 168-9
  role of nature, 168
Social conflict
  in city, 185
  through disparities in linguistic ability, 199
Social consciousness, significance of experience, 105
Social democracy, from growth of labour aristocracy, 128
Social Democratic Federation, 92
Social Environment and Resources Association, 173
Social justice, 94
Social movements, urban, 185
Social product, distribution, 33-4
Social relations
  analysis, 115
  changes to overcome wage labour/capital opposition, 115
  historical variability, 113
  in agriculture, categorisation, 77
  varying over space, 178
Social structure, impact of state intervention, 150
Social theory, 5
  contemporary debates, 120-35
    (methodology, 121-8;
    problematising class, 131-5)
  labour process and social class, 128-31
  one-dimensional society, 121-2
  themes in Marx and Engels, 112-17
  work in western universities, 120
Socialist realism, 237, 239, 242, 244
Society
  analysis of social and political relations, 115
  British, hierarchical basis, 94
  evolution through class antagonisms, 30
  legal and political superstructure, 116
  relationship with nature, 167-74
  theories of, 5
  western, Gramsci's analysis, 119
Society for the Study of Poetic Language (Opojaz), 207
Solomon, M., 231
South Sea Bubble, 15
Space
  and accumulation of capital, 175-8
  and location, 174-81
  and social reproduction, 178-81
  effects of transport developments, 176
  state's relationship to, 186-7
Speech, articulate, 202
Spencer, H., 168
Sraffa, P., 47, 54
Stalin, J., 117, 221
  on language, 207, 209-10
Stark, D., 132
State
  accumulation and legitimation roles, 159-60
  bourgeois nature of personnel, 153
  central and local, relationship, 187-8
  collapse, as precondition for revolutioon, 132
  decentralisation of powers, 161
  illusory separation from business, 154
  notion of corporatism, 157
  organisation, 131, 160-2

State – *continued*
 ownership of media, 286
 policy: changed by social unrest, 162 (dictated by capitalist interests, 152; instrumentalist view, 153–5 involvement with capital, 154)
 policy-making, functional accounts, 156–60 (link with input politics analysis, 157–8; role of professions, 162)
 problems of relative autonomy, 159
 relationship with space, 186–7
State intervention, 25
 effect on class formation, 146
 effect on trade cycle downturns, 19
 functions, 156
 impact on social structure, 150
 in agriculture, 68, 81
 in liberal democracies, 142
 necessary and contingent features, distinguishing, 159
 partial social regulation of capitalism, 27
 see also Welfare state
Stedman Jones, G., 89, 92, 93, 101, 284
Steedman, I., 48, 55
Stipčević, N., 229
'Stop-go' policies, 19
Storper, M., 175
Strada, V., 239
Structuralism, 251–9, 261–2
 analysis of television and cinema, 278 (attacked by Marxists, 279)
 in textual analysis of media communications, 275
Stubbs, M., 219
Sue, E., 236
Superstructure, 116–17, 282
 base-superstructure model in literary theory, 234–5, 238
 'class-for-itself', 132
 language, 208, 209
 relationship with base, Gramsci's contribution, 103
 relative autonomy, 217
Supply, disproportionality with demand, 24
Sutcliffe, R., 23
Sweezy, P., 22, 183
Symbolic goods, 275

Tabb, W. K., 182
Tawney, R. H., 92
Taylor, G., 125
Technological determinism, 126–7

Technological development, 18, 25–6
 and increased pollution, 170
 cost-benefit, 25–6
 deskilling workers, 44, 129
 forming new working class, 129
 in agriculture, 69
 in long wave theory, 175
 in media industries, 274–5
Technology, critique of, 122
Tel quel group, 257
Television
 effect in positioning reader, 276
 presenting dominant ideology, 277
 realism criticised, 277
 structuralist criticism, 278
Territorialism, 168, 181
Textual analysis
 effect in positioning reader, 276
 of media presentations, 275–80
 success of reactionary texts, 275
Theoretical realism, 126–7
Thibaudeau, J., 229
Third World, 179
 debt problems, 16
 Marxist impact on peasant society, 4
 see also Newly industrialised countries
Thomas, L. L., 208
Thompson, E. P., 95, 99–100, 102, 103, 124–5, 155, 283, 285
 criticisms of, 105–6
 critique of Althusser, 103–4
Thompson, G., 118, 178
Thompson, J. B., 122, 133
Thrift, N. J., 190
Timpanaro, S., 218
Tolstoy, L., 238, 243
Trade cycle downturn, 14, 19–20
 in 19th century, 19
 role of state intervention, 19
Transformation problem, 45, 55
Transport, effect of improvements on space, 176
Tribe, K., 66, 68
Trotsky, L., 230
 analysis of Russian Revolution, 118–19
 writings on cultural matters, 240
Trubeckoj, N., 207
Tullock, G., 155
Turner, B., 128
Tylor, E. B., 97

Under-consumptionist theory, 21
Unemployment, 13
 capitalist advantage, 19
 distribution struggle, 23

Index

Union of Socialist Geographers, 167
United Kingdom, fringe bank collapse, 16
Urban planning, 188
Urbanisation, 182
  specific agents, 184
Urry, J., 116, 120, 126, 127, 130, 131, 132, 133, 135, 174, 178
Uspenskij, B. A., 213

'Value added' concept, 44
Value theory, 4, 30–57
  anti-Ricardian positions, 49–53, 54
  commentaries, 55–6
  commodities' value in exchange, 38
  concept of surplus value, 122
  conflicting calculations, 52
  labour theory, 143
  Marxian, 38–45, 53, 54–5
  Marxian and Ricardian compared, 48
  money in, 39
  post-Ricardian positions, 47–9, 54
  replaced by price theory, 36
  Ricardian, 33–8, 47–9, 53 (Marx's critique, 36–8)
  transformation problem, 45, 55
  uses, 53–4
  see also Price
Vergopoulos, K., 69–70, 72, 74
Verne, J., 255
Vietnam, Marxist impact on peasant society, 4
Voloshinov, V. N., 212
Vroey, M. de, 49

Wage labour
  in opposition to capital, 115
  intermediate classes, 143–4
  see also Labour power
Wages, reduced to maximise profits, 22
Walby, S., 130
Walker, P., 131
Walker, R., 170, 175, 183
Wall Street Crash, 15
Warboys, M., 173
Warde, A., 125
Watkins, A. J., 177
Weber, M., 92, 93, 275
Weeks, J., 49
Welfare state, 128, 160
  redistribution within classes, 150
  tensions with accumulation process, 157
  see also State intervention

West Germany, Green Party, 173
Westergaard, J., 147, 150
White, J., 101
Wiener, M. J., 170–1
Willett, J., 277
Williams, M., 50
Williams, R., 170, 230, 235, 242, 268, 269, 275, 283, 285, 286
Williamson, J., 286
Winship, J., 271, 281
Winstanley, G., 96
Wollen, P., 278, 287
Women
  as 'readers', 282
  attempts at 'feminine aesthetic', 278
  exclusion from history, 101
  magazines, 281
  new middle class in labour force, 134
  representation, 271, 276–8
  role in society, 108
  see also Feminist movement
Women's Studies Group, 270
Wood, S., 129
Work, alienating character, 120
Workers
  concentration in cities, 182
  consuming wage bundle of commodities, 47
  deskilled by technology, 44
  failure to think politically, 142
  unproductive, 130
  see also Labour power
Working class
  British, tradition, 92
  changes in Marxist emphases, 108
  definitions, 143
  divisions, 130 (greater than in dominant class, 144)
  effect of political and industrial organisation, 23
  emergence of 'dual consciousness', 129
  historical role, theories of, 89
  in England, work of Marx and Engels, 89
  little evidence of revolutionary consciousness, 128
  manual, decline in importance, 129
  redefined as 'class-for-itself', 152
  role of revolutionary party, 118
  struggle affected by behaviour of other classes, 146
  transformation to 'class-for-themselves', 115–16
World War I, impact on liberalism, 92

Wren-Lewis, J., 282
Wright, E. O., 13, 131, 143, 144, 146

Yaffe, D., 50, 55

Youth subcultures, 281
Yule, G., 219

Zhdanov, A. A., 239

GPSR Compliance
The European Union's (EU) General Product Safety Regulation (GPSR) is a set of rules that requires consumer products to be safe and our obligations to ensure this.

If you have any concerns about our products, you can contact us on

ProductSafety@springernature.com

In case Publisher is established outside the EU, the EU authorized representative is:

Springer Nature Customer Service Center GmbH
Europaplatz 3
69115 Heidelberg, Germany

www.ingramcontent.com/pod-product-compliance
Lightning Source LLC
Chambersburg PA
CBHW031518100426
42873CB00013B/125